Web of Italian Intrigue

A Legacy of St. Johnsville Immigrants

Cora Lee Palma

Includes biographical references.

Cover design by Cora Lee Palma and John Vincent Palozzi.

Cover Photo: Giuseppe Sindici and Edvige Cacciotti, grandparents of author,
Rosina Maria Sindici, mother of author.

ISBN-13:
978-1725974722

ISBN-10:
172597472X

Published by
Scarlette Rose Press
clpalma35@gmail.com
Printed in
United States of America

Other books by the author:
A Touch of Venus – Wedding Planning with the Bridal Zodiac;
Bella Italia; St. Simons Island and other Spiritual Sojourns

Alphabetical Listing La Famiglia

ARDUINI	142	MASSARI	57
BARCA	210	MASTRACCO	102
BATTISTI	95	MONTONI	177
BATTISTI, JAMES J.	137	NAPOLEONE	254
BATTISTI, PETER C.	132	NARDACCI	30
BOVINO	234	PALITTI	83
CACCIOTTI	118	PALMA	33
CAMPIONE	72	PALOMBI	244
CAPECE	235	PALOMBO	186
CAPONERA	250	PAPA	262
CAPRARA	253	PATREI	100
CARELLI	275	PEDRO	158
CASTELLUCCI	277	PERFETTA	279
CASTRUCCI	113	PERUZZI	190
COCHI	91	PIETRANDREA	144
COCO	150	PIETROCINI	87
COLORITO	105	PISTILLI	52
CORSO	145	POLIDORI	271
CROCE	119	PONZI	128
DeANGELIS	111	POTENZIANI	31
DENOFRIO	269	RISCICA	108
FIACCO	54	ROMANO	122
FIOGGIA	281	SACKETT	202
FONTANA	97	SALVAGNI	162
FRANCISCO	60	SANGUINE	166
GIARUSSO	130	SCACCIA	82
GIAQUINTO	266	SINDICI	11
GIOVAMPIETRO	202	SPINELLI	169
GUARNACCI	259	STAGLIANO	257
IACOBUCCI / PERUZI	77	TERRANOVA	40
IACOBUCCI / SCHIRO	85	TERRICOLA	206
LAURORA	124	TOLFA	195
LOCCIA	180	TRIUMPHO	225
MACCI	202	VALLECORSO	80
MANCINI	171	VECCIARELLI	177
MAROCCO	216	ZUCCARO	221
MASI	152		

Web of Italian Intrigue
A Legacy of St. Johnsville Immigrants

The threads of this Web I weave
into Italian tree I now conceive
A massive trunk which I retrieve
reaches its roots out to the sea

With special recognition of my maternal immigrant Italian grandparents, Guiseppe Sindici and Edvige Cacciotti, I dedicate *Web of Italian Intrigue ~ A Legacy of St. Johnsville Immigrants* to all those who overcame the tedious, harsh journey from their homeland in Italy, faced the discrimination and challenges of a new country, and discovered their "pot of gold" with a new and fruitful life in America.

My focus is on those strong willed Italian immigrants who settled in my hometown of St. Johnsville, New York in the early part of the 20th century to raise their families, and contributed their menial skills and in-born knowledge to the growing community.

I've allowed our immigrant ancestors to speak and share their special memories through my research and writings of this extensive memoir. I literally had the feeling of living with each family as I dug into the roots of their lives, confirming their personal data and allowing them to tell their stories through me. If only the walls could talk! Due to the sensitivity, and with respect for the descendants, I choose not to reveal some of my findings.

This legacy is written from what I have discovered in my research through Ancestry.com, Ellis Island, Census Records, Find-A-Grave, local newspapers, descendant family input and personal recollections. Discrepancies may occur due to the lack of original documents and language barriers, which is common with genealogical research.

The *Italians of St. Johnsville* formed what I call a *Web of Italian Intrigue*. They shared a special bond, knotted together through blood, marriage and other familial relationships. It is amazing that so many of these St. Johnsville Italian families are intertwined, many into the fourth generations. You will find some repetition of the stories, but it's important that they are tied into each other.

Although I know you will go directly to your own family, I suggest you read this cover-to-cover. You will discover many little tid-bits of history of Italy, the village of St. Johnsville and its immigrant residents. Who knows, you may even find your name mentioned.

Families are grouped together as they are linked to each other in the Web. Refer to the Table of Contents to find a particular *La Famiglia*, listed alphabetically.

It shall be left to family descendents to determine any relationship with other *La Famiglia*.

GRAZIE!

To all those family members who have worked with me to verify
and add more interesting information to this extensive memoir.

I would especially like to thank Lena Barca Terricola for sharing her keen memories of many of these families; Sharon Fuller for sharing her extensive research of St. Johnsville businesses; Mat Rapacz who served as my historian, clarifying events and dates; my cheerleader Joyce Peruzzi Politt, always available to do on-site research in the village and cemetery; and la *mia bellisima figlia* Lisa Palma Clemons for assisting with technical difficulties.

I am most grateful to my talented Sicilian friend, John Vincent Palozzi for processing the photos and assisting me in bringing this manuscript to life through his expertise of book publishing and printing.

With John's artistic assistance, my vision for the attractive Cover came to fruition.

Featured in the front cover frame are my handsome *Nonno* Giuseppe Sindici,
my *bella Nonna* Edvige Cacciotti
and my adorable *Madre* Rosina Maria Sindici Perry.

Cora Lee Palma

Passage to a New Life

They came in Ships! Magnificent Steam Ocean Liners of elegance and comfort, designed for wealthy travelers going to and from Europe via the Atlantic Ocean. Much like the Cruise Ships we enjoy today, but not as large and elegant. However, today we are able to fly to Italy and other areas before boarding elegant Cruise Ships, which can take us to various ports to explore our roots. We are treated with the utmost of service - unlike our immigrant ancestors.

They came in Steerage! Poor Italian immigrants - searching for America, the land of hope and promise. The voyage took an average of twelve days ~ their passage to a new life.

The following excerpt is quoted from the publication, *"The Story of Italian Immigration, Passage to Liberty and the Rebirth of America"* by authors, A. Kenneth Ciongoli and Jay Parini, who describe the conditions much better than I am able. I highly recommend the book.

"Most Italian immigrants were booked in steerage, crowded into the noisy, smoky area near the ship's steering mechanism. The stench wobbled with these ships, a briny outhouse stink. The bed-slots were narrow, double-decked shelf spaces; the mattresses were lumpy, straw-filled sacks. Food was served merely as fuel – rotten, smelly, vile scraps that Italians would not feed to their animals. Ships were overcrowded. There was no place to wash or groom.

Finally, Lady Liberty raised her torch in welcome and cleansed the air. Many would be turned back to the sea, due to diseases, to again endure the unthinkable. Poor, but proud-hearted people were stripped of their clothing, poked in the most private places, hooked under the eyes to check for trachoma (a common eye disease), and asked terse questions in an incomprehensible tongue."

It surely was worth the suffering. Those who first made the voyage sent for other family members and friends, or returned themselves to their homeland, bringing family back with them to the land of promise. Some made the trip many times, coming to America only to work and earn money where jobs were available. They were referred to as "Birds of Passage".

Many of the early Italian immigrants included teenaged men and women as young as 13 years of age traveling alone. The men usually claimed their trade as "farmers" on the ship's manifests; the women as housewives, even though not married. Many of them made the journey alone or accompanied by an older friend. And there were those who came as infants with a parent, usually the mother. It was rare that a whole family traveled together.

Most spoke no English, had very limited elementary school educations and were claimed as "illiterate" due to not speaking the English language. They had an instinct to save and manage their minimal wages. With great pride they raised talented future generations of lawyers, businessmen, engineers, musicians and natural born athletes.

During the major Italian immigration influx of the early 1900s, 4,600,000 Italians came to America ~ the mysterious land. Among them were the numerous *Italians of St. Johnsville.* They bravely journeyed from their native birthplaces in Italy to discover the quaint village of St. Johnsville, situated in the peaceful Mohawk Valley area of New York State.

Including Sicily, most came from Southern Italy - Supino, Maenza, Baranello, Patrica, and Torrice, all within a couple of hours of each other. With the majority arriving from Supino, I often wonder who was left? Maenza boasted second place.

Italy was the only country that shared so many immigrants to America, especially during the late 1800s into the 1920s. 1913 was a record high year. Poverty and overpopulations in their native land were the major factors, along with farming soil becoming so bad, making it difficult to grow crops. The eruption threats of Mount Etna and Mount Vesuvius only added to the problems. Most immigrant families were poor agricultural laborers.

It remains a mystery how the original emigrants discovered this peaceful little known village of St. Johnsville along the Mohawk River/Barge Canal, which adjoined the New York Central Railroad system. It's noted that Joseph (Zaccheo) Sackett, who arrived in 1907, was given the responsibility of overseeing the railroad workers. As he was one of the few who could speak the English language, he was sent by the Immigration Department to oversee the construction of the New York Central Railroad in this area. Sackett encouraged many of the men from his hometown to relocate. I have discovered many of the Italian men also worked in the textile industry, which was booming at the time in the small village, before employment on the railroad.

But, the question remains – what brought these Italians to the area? Of course, once some had become established, they sent word - sometimes money - back to their homeland, encouraging friends and family to join them. Other than becoming a bride or hoping for a better life, what caused single young ladies to leave their homes and family, and endure the demeaning rigors of the passage to come to St. Johnsville?

With an in-depth-page-by-page review of the 1920 Federal Census for St. Johnsville, I have determined there were at least 66 Italian families – with a total of over 300 Italians, including children – residing in the village by that moment in time. Many were boarders who married within the Italian community and in a short time had families of their own, thus, expanding the influx of Italians to St. Johnsville.

It was noted that many familiar names were missing from the 1920 Census. Without doing another extensive search of the 1925 New York State and 1930 Federal Censuses, I would venture to say that by the 1930 Census, the Italian population of the village of St. Johnsville had increased to over 100 families and possibly over 400 residents, including children, a significant figure considering the total village population averaged 2,000 residents. This decade surely peaked the number of Italian immigrants discovering the quaint village of St. Johnsville, New York.

Like the mighty oak tree, these immigrants were strong and determined. Firmly planting their new roots into the fertile soil of the Mohawk Valley, they contributed extraordinary inborn work skills to the commerce of the area even with their lack of proper education. Not kindly accepted, the branches of the sturdy Italian oak stood firm, reaching out to welcome others as they immigrated to the wonderful land of opportunities in search of a better life. They overcame hostility and prejudice.

By 1925 the *Italians of St. Johnsville* were well settled into this mysterious land. Living through the recession of World War I, and the Great Depression of the 1930s, they made up the greater portion of the population as St. Johnsville's economy expanded.

The majority was able to purchase homes, many taking in boarders to supplement their income, even when renting. Not only did the men work daily, some of the women worked in the various knitting mills that were in operation at the time - Allter's Union Knitting Company, Reaney's Royal Gem and Lion Knitting Company, along with the Engelhardt Piano Factory and Cozzolino's St. Johnsville Dress Corporation. Little Falls Felt Shoe took over the Engelhardt factory after its demise. Many of the women did piece work at home until their children were grown enough to leave them at home. St. Johnsville boasted a big manufacturing community in the early 1900s.

The building and maintaining of the New York Central Railroad provided continuous work for many of the Italian men for numerous years. This was a huge calling card to entice families back in Italy to come to the St. Johnsville area for employment. Tragically, it was also responsible for the loss of some of its dedicated employee's lives. I know of at least five Italian railroad workers who lost their lives - Kain Fontana, John Pedro, Gino Polidori, John Ponzi and Anthony Vicciarelli.

Enterprising Italians were able to invest in their own businesses. Grocery stores, produce stands, bakeries, barbershops, cigar stores, mercantile, and, of course, restaurants and bars appeared all over the Italian sections on the south side of the village.

In 1918, at the time of World War I, the firm of C and L Terranova conducted a meeting of what seemed to be an Italian businessmen's association. In attendance was James Pietrocini, storekeeper, with Andrea Barca, baker, as vice-chairman of the group. Their purpose was to create a plan for the conservation of depleting food supplies. Brothers Carmine and Luciano Terranova were the very first Italian businessmen in St. Johnsville, followed by Andrea Barca of Barca's Bakery.

From 1919 to 1929 the Italians in St. Johnsville held large celebrations honoring St. Anthony of Padua.
St. Anthony is noted as the "finder of lost things."

Italians were an industrious and frugal community of people. Many raised large families and kept them fed with the fresh produce they harvested with pride from their bountiful summer gardens. They canned for winter's Sunday sauces and other simple meals they thrived on.

St. Johnsville grew and grew into its own little Italian *comune*. Census records show that Italians rarely ventured into residing in streets north of Main. With most living near the railroad tracks, they settled mainly into areas south of Main Street throughout the village. Roth, Hough, South Division, East and West Liberty, Mechanic, Ann, Spring and New Streets housed most of the Italian population, with Sanders Street, which paralleled the railroad, most known as the "Italian section" with its saturation of Italian immigrants.

Italians began arriving in St. Johnsville before 1882 when there were some who lived along the West Shore Railroad. Records show they had gone on strike in 1882. I found no Italians listed in the 1890 or 1900 Census. It is my belief they weren't counted, as they weren't permanent residents. An April 1882 news article states, *"the cider mill opposite village, which was headquarters for Italians, gave way under pressure of 125 persons. No one was hurt. The beams were decayed. With no place to go to protect them from the weather, they crossed over into the village and secured the blacksmith shop of John Saltsman for $8.00 per night."*

1905 Census records show a total of 87 Italians with the Joseph Triumpho family, who lived at 21 Sanders Street, and James Carelli family, who lived on Ann Street, being part of this group.

1910 shows 137 immigrants with eight children being born in the village for a total of 145 Italian residents, although the majority were boarders at the time. This includes an area on the Albany Turnpike called Good Roads Camp, which housed 40 immigrants, who apparently worked to build and repair "good roads". I didn't see any familiar names, so I assume they moved on to other employment. I wonder if they were instrumental in building the Turnpike (Route 167) from Route 5 out of St. Johnsville to its connection with Route 10 and other country roads further out on the way to Amsterdam?

Once again, Sanders Street aka "Italian Quarters", as noted on the 1910 Census, comes into the picture. In five years time there are 62 residents, including seven children born here and 39 boarders crowding into two separate homes - 16 in one, 23 in another.

Spring and Bridge Streets also housed many Italians, a total of 26, which included 18 boarders. In 1910, there was a total of 90 Italians living in village homes.

Many of the very first immigrants rented rooms, particularly at 21 Sanders Street. Once settled into their own homes, the majority continued their residence until the date of their passing, with second and even fourth generations still residing there to this day. Some moved to Troy and Rensselaer in search of better employment.

Although they suffered a great deal of discrimination, the Italians of St. Johnsville persevered, eventually gaining the respect they truly deserved, as they proved to be a huge asset to the growth and economy of the little village of St. Johnsville, New York.

Thus, unfolds the ancestral legacy of the *Italians of St. Johnsville.*

~ *La Famiglia SINDICI* ~

~ GIUSEPPE SINDICI et EDVIGA CACCIOTTI ~

Giuseppe Sindici and Edviga Cacciotti were very special *Italians of St. Johnsville.* They were my maternal grandparents. Call me prejudiced, but I believe they were the best ever. Both of them came from horrible conditions in their home villages of Italy, overcame the harshness of their long ocean journey to America and arrived in St. Johnsville, where they discovered a much better life.

My grandparents arrived in the United States via Ellis Island during the early nineteen hundreds, both settling in St. Johnsville. They were from little hill towns in Italy - Nonna from Maenza and Grampa from Torrice near Napoli, both near Rome and each other.

I know very little of my Grampa and Nonna's journey to this country. The extensive research I've done on Ancestry.com, the Ellis Island site and the U.S. Census has clarified for me the journey they never spoke of.

Cousin Dan Matis shared that his father, Daniel Matis told him our grandparents met while working at Allter's Union Knitting Mill, upper North Division Street, St. Johnsville. I had always heard it was an arranged marriage. Being from different villages in Italy, this is questionable. The only other answer is that her sister, Marcianna, and brother-in-law, Giuseppe Narducci, who had come to St. Johnsville earlier, may have had something to do with the matchmaking.

Edvige Cacciotti and Giuseppe Sindici were married on February 20, 1914 at St. Patrick's Roman Catholic Church, St. Johnsville NY. (The front cover photo shows them in their wedding attire with their first daughter, Rosina in her baptismal outfit.) Carmine Terranova and his wife, Mary Napoleone attended them. Carmine was an uncle to my mother-in-law, Carmela Terranova Palma. Four beautiful daughters were the result of this union - Rosina Maria, Stella Adelina, Assunda and Viola.

In 1954 the Sindici's celebrated forty years of marriage with a party in their home, hosted by their four daughters and Nonna's niece, Yolanda Narducci Potenziani, daughter of Marcianna and Giuseppe Narducci.

In my possession is their treasured actual *Certificato di Matrimonio*, all in Italian, even though Rev. Arthur A. Cunningham married them in St. Patrick's Roman Catholic Church in St. Johnsville.

It states as follows:

Con Questo si Certifica rhe
Guiseppe Sindici, figlio di Francisco et Rosaria Staccomore, native di Torrice Provincia di Roma,
e Edwegia Cacciotti, filia di Francesco and Stella Valle, native di Maenza, Provincia di Roma,
Furono congiunti in Santo Matrimonio secondo il Rito della Santa Chiesa Cattolica
Apostolica Romana, e secondo le leggi civili delo Stato di N.Y.
Nel giorno 20 del mese di Feb. dell' anno 1914.
Nella chiesa suddelta dal Rev. John L. Morissey,
I testimoni furono: Carmine and Mary Terranova
In fede di cio – Il Parroco
Rev. Arthur A. Cunningham

I also inherited and cherish their rather large, charming wedding photograph, framed in old-fashioned oval style gold gilding with a curved glass, which has graced a wall in my home since 1973. They were a handsome couple. My cousin, Dan's daughter, Dina Matis Brundage looks very much like Nonna and has the matching frame containing a beautiful photo of just Nonna.

An Italian gold necklace with a locket that Nonna was wearing in the photograph was handed down to my Mom, Rose. I now have just the chain as Mom claimed she had lost the locket. While going through my Mom's old photos, I discovered a photo of what I recognized as Nonna's parents. Checking closer, I found her mother wearing the same necklace with a locket, so I'm assuming she gave it to Nonna as a memento when she left to come to America. Recently, my brother, Richard's wife, Connie told me that she has the locket, which is actually a brooch. Mom had given it to her to be handed down to their daughter, Alexandra Rose. I've often wondered what was in the locket, as it contains no photos. I'm thinking there may have been photos of my great-grandparents Cacciotti.

Although my grandparents had left their homeland in Italy, many of their Sundays were spent with immediate family and other Italian friends. This was their social life, which was very important to them.

My grandparents never had a car, so they relied mostly on my parents, especially my Mom, to take them out of town to visit friends. I remember visiting a family in Rome NY. I believe the couple were godparents of my mother and aunts. I don't recall any children for me to play with, just sitting quietly in my pretty little dress, while the adults visited. I was taught that children were "seen and not heard."

Grampa worked on the New York Central Railroad much of his life, laying track and tarred railroad ties - an extremely dirty job. Thus, his nickname became "Blackie". Being from Southern Italy, he was darker complected. I just can't visualize the women washing these soot and tar filled clothes.

Nonna, of course, was a housewife and mother for her first married years, later laboring in the local slipper factory, the Little Falls Felt Shoe Company on Hough Street, to help support the family's needs. She also did some piecework at home.

With the bankruptcy of Engelhardt Peerless Player Piano factory, open from late 1890 to 1915,
Little Falls Felt Shoe Company purchased the factory and opened in 1919.

Nonna and Grampa lived across from the shoe factory and railroad tracks at 4 Roth Street, a dead-end cul-de-sac off Hough Street, in a cluster of four homes, theirs being rather dominant at the end of the street and viewed first as one entered the gravelly street. The whole front of the gray-shingled two storied home had an enclosed porch, which served as the main sitting room.

With childhood overnight stays, we always begged to sleep in the upstairs front bedroom with Nonna on the lumpy featherbed so we could hear the whistles and feel the rumblings of the trains whizzing by. Poor Grampa got sent to another bedroom.

Breakfast was always a special treat for me. Nonna would beat an egg, adding warm milk with a little sugar, which she called "pla-pla", and also prepare hand-sliced Barca's Italian bread, toasted in the oven with a butter spread. Italians do not eat the type of breakfasts as here in America, usually espresso or cappuccino with a sweet biscuit or dry bread with homemade jam. When I traveled in Italy that's all that was offered; it was always sufficient.

Behind Nonna and Grampa Sindici's home was a large grapevine, where Nonna would hang her wash to dry and Grampa would harvest the abundant crop for his famous red wine. As children, we loved to play under the shade of these luscious vines and use our imaginations for many wonderful fantasies. My grandparents also entertained their friends here at times. The neighboring Italian men would play Bocce, a traditional popular Italian game similar to bowling.

My brother, Joe, tells that Grampa Sindici had his own little bootleg distillery in the damp cellar, where he brewed wine from the lush abundant crop of grapes from his backyard vines. I do not know whether he actually distributed or sold any of his homemade brews. He did come from a long line of Sindici wine makers in Ceccano, Italy.

However, from what I was told, the youngest daughter, Viola, did earn a rather prosperous wage from his labors. She would receive a quarter from a neighbor lady, Theresa Olivieri Sanguine aka Tedesina every time she secretly filled her glass jar with the homebrew. She thought herself quite the young business lady – until my grandparents discovered her little business venture. Aunt Vi claims she caught Tedesina helping herself to the brew, but I always heard the other version.

My grandparents also had a small fruit orchard of plum, apple, pear and cherry trees. Each of the four sisters had their own cherry tree, which they would harvest. Nonna would can and make jelly out of the fruits. I'm sure they all helped with the process.

12

Both of my grandparents were very ethnic in their lifestyle and habits. Grampa spoke English rather fluently. Nonna never truly learned the English language and spoke to me mostly in Italian. Though not understanding each word exactly, I did know what she was saying. How I had yearned to learn that beautiful romantic language even back then. But, we children weren't taught, as my Mom and her sisters would speak Italian whenever they didn't want us to know what they were talking about.

EDVIGA ANNITA MARIA CACCIOTTI was born in Maenza, Latina, Lazio in Southern Italy, on September 25, 1889 at 5:30am, daughter of Francesco Cacciotti, a 36-year-old farmer, and Stella Valle at their home – via del Tocco 15. My great-grandmother, Stella walked down the cobblestones to the *comune* office to record the birth with the City Registrar. I acquired this information on my trip to Maenza in June 2013. At that time, they only put the father's information on birth records, so I'm not certain of Stella's age or exact last name. Valle is on my grandparents' marriage certificate. Many times, if there was a midwife, she did the recording. As I recall, my Nonna never really knew her true age or date of birth. My Maenza visit confirmed the correct date and time.

There was no record of her parent's marriage because they were married in the church, not in the courthouse, which made it official. Strange? I've always thought it to be tradition that Catholics be married in the church to have the union recognized. Italy has different requirements. I have since discovered that many of the Italian couples had two ceremonies performed due to this rule.

At age 22, Edvige Cacciotti left her Maenza homeland and family and arrived in the United States on July 19, 1913, coming directly to St. Johnsville from Naples, Italy, via Ellis Island. I was fortunate to find her listed on the *Napoli* ship manifest as passenger #22 having $30.00 in her pocket, an identifying scar on her face, and sponsored by her brother Guiseppe of Box 88, St. Johnsville. She had no brothers. I think she had listed her brother-in-law Guiseppe Narducci as her sponsor, but they left in-law off. I have discovered that the manifest information isn't always accurate, sometimes misinterpreted by the clerk who is filling out the manifest from the point of departure. (It is noted that no names are changed at Ellis Island.)

According to the Napoli manifest there were 881 passengers on the ship. There were eighteen passengers accompanying her from Maenza, eleven coming to St. Johnsville.

My grandmother's cousin, Desiderio Coco, his father, Luigi, a brother-in-law of Giuseppe Narducci; Caterina Coco (don't know the relationship), and Gino Polidori were among those coming to live in Box 88. Sure must have been a very tight squeeze in that box. I found this address used numerous times by the incoming Italians. This makes me wonder just how closely they monitored the departing or arriving passengers at that time.

Also on the Napoli ship were Filomena Baccari, who married Antonio Fontana and Antonio's sister, Rosa Fontana, who married Biaggio Mastracco. Others listed on the passenger manifest were Quintilina Olivieri, Sinisio Petrei, Lorenzo Cipriani, and Giuseppe Petronzi. I haven't been able to find anything about the last four passengers.

Like so many new arrivals, some of this group boarded at 21 Sanders Street until they found further living accommodations. There was also another boarding house at 31 Mechanic Street, owned by Cesare and Maria Grazie Guarnacci, now the home of Domenick and Barbara Stagliano. I think my Grampa Sindici boarded there until the marriage.

From bits and pieces of information I've gathered, I believe 21 Sanders Street was a duplex, whose mailing address was obviously Box 88. According to Mat Rapacz, it housed a grocery store in the downstairs area with four bedrooms upstairs, probably on each side. In this era, homeowners took in boarders, giving them one or more rooms per family, probably all sharing the same downstairs kitchen. Built in 1900, this has been the Pedro home for many years. You will find a complete article about 21 Sanders Street with *La Famiglia Pedro* story.

This was also Edvige Cacciotti's first home. However, checking the June 1915 NYS Census thoroughly, I could find no record of my grandparents living in St. Johnsville nor anywhere. Since they were married in St. Johnsville in February 1914 and my Mom was born in May of 1915, there should be a record. Giuseppe Sindici's World War I registration form does verify that they lived at 21 Sanders Street in June 1917, with two children, and the Lion Manufacturing Company employing him.

As shown in the 1920 Census, they were renting a home at 44 Hough Street with two daughters, Rose and Lena. Desiderio Coco, Guiseppe Narducci and Pasquale Montoni were boarders.

By the time the 1925 Census was taken, my grandparents owned and resided in the 4 Roth Street home in the dead-end street off Hough. By this time Assunda "Susie" and Viola had joined the family. Also living with them were their best friends, Pasquale Montoni and Elena Vecciarelli with their daughter, Ella and son, Nello. There was a close friendship between the Sindici's and Montoni's. The Montoni's came from the same towns as Nonna and Grampa – Elena from Maenza, Patsy from Torrice. Patsy was my Baptismal Godfather.

Nonna was strong in her Roman Catholic religious beliefs, attending church regularly and practicing its strict traditions. She had wonderful values with a heart of gold. She always had money hidden in her apron pocket to give her grandchildren – when Grampa wasn't around. Guess that carried over from her voyage across the Atlantic with $30 in her pocket, a great deal of money that had been raised by her family and neighbors in Maenza. Although she lived frugally, she was generous with her hard earned money, which I think she saved doing piecework at home.

Cooking in the poor Southern Italy style of simple meals, Nonna prepared pasta dishes like spaghetti and meat balls and homemade chicken soup with her own hand cut noodles. On occasion, she would splurge and make Braciole, a thin-sliced roll of beef she stuffed with hard-boiled eggs. Most of the time she cooked frugally from the reaping of Grampa's bountiful garden. They canned tomatoes for sauce, and other fruits and vegetables kept for winter use in the damp cellar. I vividly recall the delicious pears in the glass canning jars.

Most family holidays would feature her finely cut homemade noodles or gnocchi, made from ricer-squeezed boiled potatoes, with flour and eggs added for consistency. She would knead the soft gnocchi dough and roll out long lengths, cutting them into bite size pieces. I had the important job of pressing my thumb into each piece. This made them easier to absorb her delicious fresh basil-spiced red sauce that she simmered for hours. There was a definite knack with the consistency of these – and pressing the thumb just right, I might add.

Nonna had an amazing talent for crocheting meticulous doilies, table covers and colorful lace edgings on handkerchieves out of fine thread. She taught me the skill at an early age, which I used into my adult years. Sadly, I don't have any of her beautiful handiwork. I've only found similar items in antique shops. This has become a lost art, except in Italy.

Italy is the main producer and center of the world's lace trade with the Island of Burano near Venice, Italy, famous for its delicate hand crocheted lace creations. The older ladies sit there for hours nimbly working their fingers with the fine threads to produce their fabulous products for sale, somewhat like a spider's web. I had the great pleasure of observing them when I visited the island on a Venice tour. Burano can only be reached by boat.

During World War II, Nonna would send care packages to her family still residing in Italy. She would bundle up clothing and other personal items, wrap them in old cotton bed sheets, stitched by hand with strong heavy rope twine and lug them to the Post Office.

Edvige Sindici's obituary says she had two sisters who still lived in Italy – Marcianna and Antonia. Marcianna, wife of Giuseppe Narducci, was Yolanda "Viola" Narducci Potenziani's mother. She had come to America before Nonna, but returned to Italy where she lived out her life. I've often regretted that I didn't spend some quality time with Grandma's niece, Yolanda to hear the many stories she could tell about the family.

From my recent trip to Nonna's hometown, I came to realize how poor her family actually was. Most of the male residents of Maenza were farmers at that time. The current residents don't seem to live much better. Many of the households still have two to three generations living together in sparse apartments.

Through Grampa's employment with the New York Central Railroad, the family had access to free passes to travel by train. Many were the times Nonna would take us across the railroad tracks at the end of South Division Street, walking the short distance to the railroad station, situated along the Mohawk River, for a trip to Little Falls. As I recall, children traveled for free and also received a lollipop from the conductor.

I now understand why Nonna treasured the newer furniture in her simple home. Used only on holidays, the formal living room sofa and chairs were always covered with the traditional Italian plastic protectors. One of the bedrooms had a lovely set of new Art Deco furnishings, which they purchased in later years, after their daughters were all married. C. Curtis Lull Furniture and Funeral Home on Bridge Street provided the selections of furniture available for purchase to most Italians.

My beautiful Nonna was stricken with uterine cancer shortly after my wedding and after two years of horrific suffering, passed away in the comfort of her home on June 6, 1957, at the age of 67, the day after my wedding anniversary and almost two months after the birth of her first great-grandchild, my son, Rodney John Palma.

Nonna, like so many other Italians, had her "superstitious" beliefs. I would visit with her most Saturday nights while pregnant with Rodney. One night we were watching Ernie Kovacs and his monkey band, which I found hilarious. She told me to turn it off, as it would mark my baby. Well, lo and behold, I did give birth to a rather hairy individual with tons of curly hair and sideburns. Italians also believed if you craved something, you should eat it or the baby would have a birthmark in that particular shape. One of my cousins had a lobster shape on her leg due to her mother's craving. Not to mention the *"malocchio"* – evil eye, one of the most ancient Italian superstitions, which can be warded off with the famous *cornicello* horn pendant.

Edvige Cacciotti Sindici was waked at home in her formal living room, where she had spent the remaining days of her life and taken her last breaths on the living room couch she had meticulously cared for – minus the plastic. People were waked in the comfort of the family home back then, especially the Italians. It was an Italian custom to never leave the body alone. Grampa sat up for two nights with his beloved "Dolly" of 43 years.

It was so unfair that my kind, beautiful Nonna had to live her final days suffering such a horrible disease. She had lived her first 22 years in poverty and endured the many challenges of the long voyage to America. Strong and determined, she always served as a shining example for me. My most cherished inheritance!

GUISEPPE "Joseph" SINDICI was born in Torrice, Italy on November 22, 1894, son of Francesco Sindici and Rosaria Staccamore. He arrived in the United States coming to St. Johnsville NY from Naples on May 8, 1911, at 16 years of age, aboard the *Duce Degli Abruzzi*. He was listed as Guiseppe Snidaci, sponsored by his uncle Fiacco. I haven't discovered who his uncle might be, but he always referred to his friend, John Fiacco, as his cousin.

John Fiacco had a cousin, Angelo, in Troy NY, who would take time to visit with Grampa, whenever he came to St. Johnsville to visit. It's my understanding that Angelo was a good friend of Grampa's from Italy. Angelo also had a relationship with the Romilda Terricola family through his wife.

When first coming to America, Grampa worked on the East Creek Dam. A bus would pick him up on Monday mornings. He would stay in a barracks at the site all week, returning to St. Johnsville Saturday nights. He also had employment at Allter's Union Knitting Mill, where he met his beautiful wife, Edvige.

Giuseppe "Joe" worked most of his life as a laborer for the New York Central Railroad. In January 1944, Guiseppe was elected to serve on the Grievance Committee of Local 854 NYC System Division Brotherhood - Maintenance of Way Employees Union.

On April 19, 1940, one of the worst disasters in the Mohawk Valley involved the tragic derailment on the Gulf Curve of the NYC Railroad system near Little Falls NY, killing 30 people and injuring 100. Joe Sindici and many other railroad workers were dispatched to the scene, where they worked 60 hours with minimal breaks, clearing the cluttered tracks of debris.

Known most of his life as Joe, Giuseppe Sindici died on Saturday, August 11, 1973 at the age of 78 from complications of esophageal surgery, which determined he had cancer. He had smoked for many years, but did live a long life. It was especially sad that he died on his daughter, Susie's birthday.

In searching Ellis Island records for Grampa, I found Francesco Sindici, a 47-year-old widower from Torrice, arriving in the United States on March 15, 1906 aboard the *Nord America* leaving from Naples, Italy. His brother-in-law, a Fiacco from NYC, sponsored him. I don't know for sure if this was Grampa's father. Many immigrants went back and forth, coming here to work, then returning home for a while. It's interesting that the Fiacco name has appeared again.

I've spoken with Nicki Sindici, Grampa's niece who lives in Montreal, Canada. She has done considerable research on the Sindici family, her father, Sante Sindici, being Grampa's half-brother. From the information Nicki and I have discovered in our extensive research, Grampa's father, Francesco Sindici was born around 1870 in Ceccano, Italy. It seems he was born out of wedlock, given up for adoption and raised in an orphanage by nuns. Francesco's last name could be his biological father's, his adoptive parents, or the name given to him by a priest? The practice in Italy was to keep the family surname for inheritance purposes. I'm sure he never received an inheritance.

After being among the missing for several years, around 1915, Francesco suddenly appeared in the neighboring town of Torrice, where he met and married a local young lady, Anna Fiacco, 20 years younger. Born July 9, 1891 to Vincenzo Fiacco and Maria Trasolini, she had inherited her father's house and land.

Anna and Francesco became the parents of Sante, born 1919 and Marieta, born 1923. They would be Grampa's half-siblings.

Francesco Sindici disappeared again around 1924. There is no paper trail of him after that, not even Italian cemetery records. He seems to have abandoned all three of his children. Town folklore tells that he was quite the mysterious scoundrel, who had defamed the prominent Sindici name of Ceccano, site of the famous Castel Sindici.

I met Grampa's brother, Sante Sindici when he came to St. Johnsville for Grampa's funeral from Montreal, Quebec, Canada. I can still see him sitting in the lounge chair in my living room after the funeral. Some of the Sindici family later motored to Canada to visit Sante and his family.

Grampa first met his siblings in Italy when he returned during the 1940s, then again in the United States in the 1950s, while Sante lived in Connecticut before later settling in Montreal, Canada.

I don't know what happened to Francesco's first wife, Grampa's mother, Rosaria Staccamore. I'm thinking she may have died before Grampa left Italy. It is frustrating to me that I have hit two "brick walls" with my research on both of my Italian grandparents. But I shall persevere!

In March 1960, Grampa accompanied Philip Francisco of Francisco's Market on a trip to Supino, Italy. Supino is not far from Torrice. They arrived home on April 21, 1960. I have no information of why he made this trip, except to revisit his native land and reunite with some relatives still residing there. I do have some unidentified photos of him with what could be family members.

An article and large photo in the *Gloversville Morning Herald* on Fultonhistory.com shows Grampa was involved with the Young Men's Republican Club of St. Johnsville. In August 1935, the GOP Clambake and Field Days was held at the New Pyramid Dance Pavilion in West St. Johnsville, also featuring a band concert and dancing. Grampa was on the Tables Committee. My father-in-law, John Palma was listed on the Refreshments Committee. Grampa always had a framed photo of the event hanging in the front parlor, showing him seated right up front with his white apron and a big smile on his handsome face.

Joe Sindici was noted for his vast vegetable garden, which he had for decades, mostly to supplement the family's simple Italian menus. Summertime meals consisted of vegetables out of the garden. My favorite was the leafy lettuce that sprouted like weeds every summer. This was a nightly staple. A light sprinkling of oil and vinegar transformed it into a tasty *Insalada*. They didn't have the huge selection of salad dressings as we do today. In the fall he would reap the harvest. Excess tomatoes were canned for Nonna's wonderful spaghetti sauce.

Grampa was a great cook. He made awesome fried zucchini flowers. Grampa also loved his Italian music. After attending the early Mass every Sunday morning, he would listen to a Utica radio station that played his favorites. In the summer he would take his portable radio to the garden. Perhaps the musical chords from his native Italy were accountable for his succulent garden?

During World War II, when Victory Gardens were encouraged, Grampa not only worked his own home garden, but developed a garden in a large area on my parents' property at 10 South Division Street, extending it into the Robert Failing land next door. He always shared his bounty. My cousin Pauline and I planted red poppies that enhanced the whole neighborhood for years with their seedlings.

After his retirement from the New York Central Railroad, Grampa would spend the better part of his day working the soil from sun-up to sundown, gathering the fruits of his labor for his family and neighbor friends. Whenever anyone stopped to visit, they would be taken on tour of his ever-expanding garden, leaving stocked up with his precious bounty. By the time he passed away, his meticulous garden had taken over most of the back yards from Roth Street to the Zimmerman Creek at the end of Hough Street. He compensated his neighbors with bags of fresh veggies.

Perhaps he felt a strong connection to the end of Hough Street, having lived there in his early years of marriage, before purchasing the home at 4 Roth Street. Perhaps he felt the need to share the fruits of his labor. Sadly, the acreage that my Grampa so lovingly tended every summer has been devastated by the Felt Shoe Company, now a barren blacktopped empty parking lot with no reminder of his great love for the rich soils of the earth.

My cousin, Tim Matis, son of Lena Sindici and Daniel Matis, Sr., shared with me some of his wonderful memories about our Grampa Sindici. Tim purchased the Sindici home after Grampa passed away. He tells about *"the sense of Grampa's presence in the home that was pretty much intact as when our grandparents lived there."* He noticed, *"as he sorted through the belongings left, how frugal and conserving he was. Nothing went to waste. He understood "recycle and reuse" before that idea became a popular saying in the environmental movement."*

Tim mentioned how our *"Grampa was known for his impressive garden."* Another interesting observation Tim made was *"his landscaping ability, how there seemed to be a sequence to the blooming of the flowering plants and bushes that lasted throughout the growing season. There would always be something coming into bloom as one of the other flowers wilted away."* I was always fascinated by the pink bleeding hearts that adorned the front of the home, perhaps signifying the ever-present familial love inside?

Tim also reiterated, *"I think Grampa had a keen interest in nature, and enjoyed his time outdoors. I can only imagine the hours he spent in his garden and among the beautiful flowers he planted after spending many long, hard hours working for the railroad. I also recall him coming up to the farm to help out and I heard stories of all the hard work he did helping my parents make improvements that were needed to make this place livable for their family. We all remember Grampa as a hard working and humble man. Grampa may have been small in height, but he will always be a giant in my mind."*

I couldn't have expressed this more eloquently.

ROSINA MARIA SINDICI, aka Rose, my mother, arrived on Tuesday, May 4, 1915, the eldest of four sisters born to Giuseppe Sindici and Edvige Cacciotti at 21 Sanders Street.

Regrettably, I don't know anything about my Mom's early life other than what I've discovered through my extensive newspaper research. If she and her sisters ever talked about their youth, I don't recall. I do know she was a strong woman physically, spiritually and in her values. She exuded a charm that drew a great deal of attention.

Graduating in June 1934, she was quite active throughout her high school years at St. Johnsville High. I have a lovely portrait of Mom wearing a beautiful tea length pink dress of layered chiffon, carrying the traditional red roses arm bouquet. She always portrayed the fashionista.

Shortly after graduation, her engagement to my Dad was announced. They had attended a Commercial Club banquet together in 1932 and been partners in a 3-legged race. I must interject this little "tidbit" from an article in one of the St. Johnsville High School newsletters. I discovered that before dating my Mom, my Dad, Floyd Perry and Olga Sackett Tolfa were an item. Dad was scheduled to graduate in 1933, but had to give up his education due to the dire need to assist his family with expenses during the Depression years after the loss of his mother.

Mom and her sister, Lena's future husband, Daniel Matis were in the same class. She gave a speech in November 1933, "Our School Spirit." Mom was in the Commercial Club, played on a softball team and the 10th grade basketball team. I'm sure she was a good athlete, being a good bowler in later years.

In September of 1932, Rose was part of the cast of over 150 who performed in "The College Flapper." She, Dad's sister, Helen Perry and Catherine Mentis were in the chorus. She was also part of the cast for the musical comedy, "Heads Up", held at the Masonic Temple, where many of the productions were held during those years. Mom and Aunt Lena were part of the "Sorority Girls" segment. Dad was a "Fraternity Boy", his brothers Bill and Bob Perry were also in the play.

In later years, both Mom and Dad were active in the Little Theater Group, formed by Dad's brother, William "Bill" Perry, who wrote and directed most of the plays. Mom and Dad hosted the group's Christmas parties at their home.

Since my mother got married right after graduation and never did anything further with her high school education, her sisters were not allowed to graduate. That is so sad. She continually devoted her enormous energies to working with others in so many pursuits her entire life.

The *Enterprise & News* announced that *a popular young couple, Rose Marie Sindici, daughter of Joseph and Edvige Sindici, and Floyd Benjamin Perry, Jr., son of Floyd Benjamin Perry, Sr. and the late Cora Lee Hanlon, were married on November 3, 1934 in a small evening ceremony at the St. Patrick's parish home on Center Street in St. Johnsville with Rev. Arthur Cunningham officiating.* Mom's sister, Lena, and her future husband, Daniel Matis, stood up with them. Thinking for years that Dad's brother, Robert Perry, was the best man, I discovered in my research it was Uncle Dan. They made their first home on Cross Street at a home owned by Charles McCrone, where I was born.

Lou Gehrig won the Triple Crown in baseball on the day my parents were wed.
Ironically, my Mom died from Lou Gehrig's disease.

Lena Sindici and Daniel Matis were married a week later on November 10, 1934 in the St. James Catholic Church parish hall in Fort Plain with Rose and Floyd Perry as witnesses. Later in the month, wearing my Dad's only suit, Robert Perry and Anne Root were also married. They could have had a triple ceremony.

On December 7, 1934, a wedding shower for Mom was held at Sadie Palombi's American Grill on New Street with five hostesses, all friends of hers. My Dad's sister, Helen, also hosted a shower at the Perry family home on Ann Street. Shortly after my birth, Mom entertained thirty-two ladies at a bridal shower for Mrs. Sam (Mary Wolinski) Fredericks on December 2, 1934 on Cross Street.

1934 was the turning point of the Great Depression, when President Franklin Delano Roosevelt
instituted his programs to aid the country's recovery.

Always a hard worker, Mom usually handled two jobs at the same time. In the early days of her marriage, she worked at the upper mill of the Palatine Dyeing Company, while we were living on Kingsbury Avenue and then 59 North Division Street. The 1940 Census shows her occupation as a "tacker" earning $390 a year for 42 hours a week, 26 weeks. Who could live on that amount for one week now?

In 1942 we had moved from the North Division Street apartment to 10 South Division Street on the corner of West Liberty. This is where my brothers and I grew up.

I have discovered that the Antonio Campione family owned and lived in the home until 1939 after selling their farm in Mindenville to Dominick and Minnie Perry. My parents purchased the home from Kenneth and Mary Klock, being deeded over on September 2, 1947.

I also discovered that in 1909 a Daniel Fisk had a laundry business at the site until 1917.

After my Dad's return from World War II, my parents became the proprietors of Perry's Luncheonette for 10 years. It was first located at 23 East Main Street near Washington Street for five years, then at 1 West Main Street at the corner of Bridge.

I also worked there from the age of 12, along with my Evening Times paper route. My Dad paid me a salary of $2.00 per week and it went a long way. Brother Joe and I would relieve our parents during the dinner hour to go home and rest before returning until the 10 o'clock closing. Perry's Luncheonette was most noted for its homemade ice cream and the spicy Turpin Mexican Hots. Mrs. George Snell made the delicious pies for dessert.

Mom also took a job as the hemmer at Corso Dress Company in St. Johnsville, working in addition to the long hours she spent with the family business. After the close of the luncheonette, she worked as a waitress at Capece's Restaurant, St. Johnsville, and Elm Tree Hall in Fort Plain, continuing with her hemmer's position.

In her retirement years, she was the coordinator of the "Meals on Wheels" program for St. Johnsville seniors. When it came to work, she could "run rings around anyone," including any man. I recall a story Mom told of hitting a disruptive inebriated male customer at Capece's over the head with a pizza pan and telling him to get out. He later apologized, and always showed her utmost respect.

My Mom was always available to participate in school fund raising activities, often playing chauffeur when she would drive my friends and me to dances at Sherman's Dance Hall in Caroga Lake. My Dad and she were always mentors to other young people of the village. Both of them were actively involved in community affairs, usually serving as an officer of any organization. They were the epitome of the phrase, "It Takes A Village!"

Growing up in a Roman Catholic Italian family, Mom was very devout in her beliefs and raised her three children in the concepts of the church. As an active member of the Altar Rosary Society, she gave much of her energy to chairing St. Patrick's Church ham dinners every March, overseeing either the kitchen or dining room activity. She was an active member of the St. Johnsville Business Girls and Senior Saints and a regular traveler with Dort Tours and Cora Lee Tours. In 1942 she was a member of a Home Nursing Class, which was a preparation for World War II events.

Floyd Benjamin Perry, Jr. son of Floyd Benjamin Perry, Sr. and Cora Lee Hanlon, was born December 13, 1913 in German Flatts (Herkimer) NY. The family moved to St. Johnsville within the year after his birth and resided at 45 North Division Street. My Dad's parents seemed to have moved around a lot, especially in St. Johnsville. They were renting the Capt. Isaac Smith home next to the Margaret Reaney Library, when Joseph Reaney purchased the home and had it torn down to make room for the park that has taken its place.

Dad was employed at Ottman's grocery and soda fountain when my parents married. Then he also worked at the Palatine Dyeing Company upper mill as a Dyer, with serving part time as a police patrolman in St. Johnsville. By the time he was drafted into WWII, he was working at the Beech-Nut Packing Company, his last place of employment before his retirement.

Through my research I found an article in the Tuesday, January 25, 1944 edition of the Amsterdam Recorder. It states that 385 up-county men from the townships of Canajoharie, Palatine Bridge, Minden and St. Johnsville had been added to the Inductees Pool. Two of those mentioned were Floyd Perry and Daniel Matis, both inducted into the US Navy on the same day. In February 1944, just before their deferment to the Sampson Naval Base, the Auxiliary Police Association gave a farewell dinner for Dad, his brother Bob and Uncle Dan on their enlistment in the US Navy.

In March of 1944, while stationed at Sampson, Dad was in a conversation with a Fort Plain sailor regarding a two-year fugitive search conducted by authorities for an Indian named George Youngs from the St. Johnsville area. The other sailor knew the name and gave Dad some pertinent information, which he in turn related to the St. Johnsville Police, aiding in the capture of Youngs.

I thought this would be of interest to my male readers: I discovered Muster information in my Dad's military papers about his eighteen-month stint in the Navy. On February 18, 1944, he enlisted and was sent to the US Naval Training Station at Sampson, NY near Seneca Lake, where recruits trained for 90 days. He received a stipend of $50.00 per month and was issued $119.19 worth of clothing, a pea jacket being the most expensive. His personal clothing was sent home.

After the 90 day training, he became a Seaman 2nd Class. He was discharged on December 11, 1945 as Seaman 1st Class, 2 days before his 32nd birthday. He had served on the USS RENO – CL96 Aircraft Carrier in Okinawa and was in the Philippines at the end of the war. A search on Wikipedia of the ship shows that it departed San Francisco on April 14, 1944 and was the first to make contact with Japanese planes on May 19-20, 1944. Dad joined the crew on March 31, 1945, when they were deployed to Okinawa. He served as the ship's cook.

My father never spoke about his tour of duty during World War II. He brought back souvenirs, some I still have. I believe he viewed horrific incidents and experiences that brought him back as a different man emotionally.

With his honorable discharge, Floyd returned to his job at the Beech-Nut. Shortly after this, Dad and Mom opened Perry's Luncheonette at 37 East Main Street on January 3, 1947, later moving to the 1 West Main location on January 15, 1952 until October 1956. While owning the luncheonette, he worked part-time at two other jobs, a used car salesman for a firm in the building on East Main at the end of Averill Street and as a Life Insurance agent for John Hancock. I still have the policy he sold me over sixty years ago.

After closing the restaurant, Dad was employed first by Smith's Market, St. Johnsville, then returned to Baker-Beechnut of Canajoharie, where he had worked between his Naval service and restaurant gig. He worked there until his forced retirement in 1973, due to a leg injury in the performance of his job. He passed away before he was compensated; Mom received the judgment years later.

Dad was active in politics as a Democrat. He ran for Town Justice-4 years in 1939 and Town Clerk in 1961. In 1967 he was Chairman of the St. Johnsville Democratic Committee. He held several offices with the Beech-Nut Employees Association. He was also a member of the King Hendrick Tribe of Red Men in Oppenheim in 1939 and the M.J. Edwards American Legion Post, installed as Adjutant in 1971.

Floyd aka "Friday" was actively involved with sports his whole life. In high school football he was noted as a "hard hitting full back" and "fleet footed". He could outrun anyone. This reminds me of a story my brother Joe told me. The four Perry brothers - Bill, Bob, Floyd and Joe - all played football on the same team at one time. In the very first radio broadcasted game out of Johnstown the announcer was going crazy with "which Perry made the play?" Uncle Bob and my Dad were the best players of the four, both excelling in football. They were of Irish origin, but they had many Italian friends, most of whom also excelled in the game of football and baseball.

My father always encouraged my two brothers and me to perform to our fullest capabilities. He was always involved in youth sporting programs. Along with several other businessmen, he was responsible for the development and promotion of the St. Johnsville Little League Field and its youthful baseball players and the American Legion Baseball teams.

In April of 1967, Floyd Perry was the recipient of the Individual Civic Award honoring his continual promotion of youth athletic activities, including his participation in organizing the Little League and management of American Legion baseball. At the same event, Carlo Polidori was the recipient of the new Police Award.

Floyd Benjamin Perry, Jr.'s life came to an early demise on Christmas Eve, December 24, 1975, around 1:30 in the afternoon at age 62, like his father before him, stricken with a heart attack at the same age. Numerous donations in his memory were given to the St. Johnsville Youth Center in commemoration of his many achievements with the youth of the village.

After my Dad's sudden death my mother, Rose, went on with her life, renewing her friendship with an old childhood friend, Columbus "Russ" Fiorini from Amsterdam. In my family research I discovered that Russ, as a little boy, and his parents had lived in the 4 Roth Street house where my mom grew up, just before my grandparents bought it from his DeAngelis grandparents. I believe Russ was born there. You will find more information regarding 4 Roth Street in La Familia DeAngelis. You'll recognize many of the residents who had lived there before the Sindici's.

Almost every Saturday night, no matter what the weather, Mom and her good friends, Perina Fontana DiCamillo and Mary Jones, would get all dolled up in their best dresses and high heels and drive to Amsterdam to dance and listen to the saxophone sounds of Russ Fiorini and his fellow musicians. Russ played the meanest sax and was totally dedicated to his music, playing right up until the night of his passing, when he returned home to his apartment, sat in a cozy chair and went to sleep forever.

On these Saturday evenings as the eleven o'clock news came on, the newscaster would say "It's eleven o'clock. Do you know where your children are?" And I would reply, "Yes, but I'm not sure where my mother is." She was quite the swinger with her love for music and dance, but would refuse to dance with any man shorter than her.

While sorting through all my inherited photos, I found photos of Mom with Aunt Lena Sindici Matis, Mary Jones and Perina Fontana Di Camillo taken on their trip to Hawaii in the late 1970s. Mom and Perina are dressed in hula skirts. One of them shows Mom up on stage with a group of other ladies, some in floral Hawaiian muumuus, and Don Ho, Hawaii's most famous entertainer at the Polynesian Palace in Waikiki. He seems to be presenting Mom with a bottle of champagne. She most likely won the "Queen of the Evening" prize.

Mom was very creative. I remember that she made a lovely bedspread with matching curtains for my bedroom at 59 N. Division Street. She crocheted, and knitted Afghans and made beautiful ceramics. In her later years, she designed many macramé items, including the beautiful kissing balls that hung at her granddaughter, Lisa's wedding reception.

My mother was one of my biggest supporters of any endeavors I was involved with. When I owned the Red Palette Bridal Center, she donated numerous hours to help me succeed. She was always reliable, as with anything else she was involved with. She was helpful with my wedding catering business. She loved modeling the mother's dresses in my Fashion Shows.

Like so many of the ladies, Bingo was a passion with Mom. She was in her glory while living in Florida, with games available most any day or night. Armed with her array of little good luck charms to surround her numerous cards, she would head out for the evening.

Tragically, this beautiful woman of great strength and dignity was stricken with ALS in her early 70s and was forced to finally retire back in the village of her childhood at the newly built St. Johnsville Nursing Home, where she was selected as the "Queen of Valentine's Day."

Rosina Maria Sindici passed away in the pre-dawn hours of July 15, 1990. She was gifted with a strong magnetic personality, accompanied by a beautiful friendly smile and proudly boasting a legacy of having accumulated numerous friends during her lifetime.

STELLA ADELINA SANTINA SINDICI was born May 19, 1917, two years after her sister, Rosina, also at the 21 Sanders Street residence, later living at 4 Roth Street until her marriage. Her December 12, 1917 Baptismal certificate states her godparents were Virginio and Rosa Vincenzo from Rome NY.

Most of the Italian youth living on Roth and Hough Streets were playmates and became good friends with those their own age. This seemed to be the case with Lena and Rose Peruzzi, who lived just around the corner on Hough Street. In September 1933, when they were teenagers of 16 years, both were apparently unhappy at home and devised a plan to explore their curiosity of the world outside St. Johnsville. Early one Sunday morning they left their homes, most likely crossed the railroad tracks, and boarded the local train to Albany. They quickly found jobs as waitresses and a place to room. They even changed their names, disguised as sisters. Their families reported them missing to the local police. However, Lena decided to send a postcard to her boyfriend, Daniel Matis, addressing it with their return address. Receiving the card the following Monday, Dan immediately shared the information with the distraught parents. Lena's sister, Rose and Rose's brother, Domenick Peruzzi accompanied St. Johnsville Police Officer William MacMahon to Albany to locate the girls and bring them home. I've been told - after some considerable convincing by their siblings.

It seems Aunt Lena was also very athletic in her school years. I found an article regarding her playing on the girl's ninth grade basketball team, defeating the eighth grade team. I'm sure she developed many more muscles during her many years on the farm. I recall her playing the violin in her early life.

On November 10, 1934, Lena Sindici and Daniel Matis were married at the St. James Parish in Fort Plain with her sister Rose and brother-in-law, Floyd Perry, as attendants. They had four children - Pauline, Daniel Jr, Sharon and Timothy. Aunt Lena was my Baptismal Godmother.

Due to the impending snowfall at the time of the birth of Pauline in January, my Dad drove up to the farm they were leasing to bring Aunt Lena into town. My Dad always told the story of later trudging through knee-deep snow after the big snowstorm that isolated the farm to inform Uncle Dan of Pauline's birth. Lena's sister, Viola, being only eleven and not aware of birthing, told of being so upset that they were hurting her sister. Aunt Lena had a yearning for gnocchi, which Nonna and her sisters prepared for her, while she awaited birth. Pregnant Italian women always ate whatever they craved for fear of birth-marking their baby.

Always a hard worker, Lena's life wasn't easy as a struggling farmer's wife. Living for a few months on his brother Paul's farm, they moved to the Fox "tenant farm" in the "boonies" off old Route 167, located past the Matis family farm where her husband, Dan grew up. They were paid $30.00 monthly with free board for working the farm. I have a memory of staying at the Fox farmhouse with Pauline, but I couldn't tell you where it was located. It seems we all slept in one large bedroom, which I recall as very dark. The house was sparsely furnished. Pauline and I always played in the vacant upstairs.

Aunt Lena was a fantastic cook and baker. Being very frugal, as she always had to be, she could take an onion or green pepper, stretching it out for several meals. But, she was very generous in sharing whatever she had. She obviously inherited her father's green thumb and grew her own vegetables and beautiful flowers.

Lena and Dan moved a lot in the first years of their marriage before finally settling into the farm on Kringsbush Road in the town of Ephratah. Dan had worked at the Cherry Burrell plant in Little Falls before and after his service in the US Navy.

Uncle Dan had enlisted on February 18, 1944 in the same group as his brother-in-law, Floyd Perry. They received their training at Sampson Naval Base and S1C Daniel Matis was sent to Piney Point MD for the duration of his service. Aunt Lena would take the train occasionally to visit him for a weekend.

It is safe to say that farming was in Dan Matis' bloodline. His parents, John Matis and Mary Peruben, and two brothers, Paul and George, were all full-time dairymen. It wasn't long before Dan found the opportunity to purchase his own farm site from Howard Robinson in 1950 at the price of $10,000.

After Aunt Lena and Uncle Dan bought the farm on Kringsbush Road, we would gather many Sundays in the winter, skating on the little ice rink she made. Christmas time we would traipse through the surrounding woods to select a freshly cut tree. Many times family members would just drop in unannounced. She would always have a fresh baked cake, pie or cookies waiting to serve with coffee. Their youngest son, Tim, later inherited and now operates the dairy farm.

Creativity was prevalent in the genes of the Sindici-Cacciotti family. Aunt Lena helped me design and make my own paper dolls. She arranged creative floral arrangements.

She was always there when anyone was in need. When my brother, Joe Perry opened the Summit Inn, outside of Little Falls across from the Shumaker Mountain ski tow, Aunt Lena helped in the kitchen, while Mom waited table. Her son, Dan and his wife, Maxine took over the Kyser Hotel on Main Street for several years, and where did you find Aunt Lena – in the kitchen, helping Maxine with the cooking. Mom waited table. It always seemed to be a family affair when someone was in business or planning an event.

In her later years, Aunt Lena socialized more. She and Uncle Dan would go out dancing and also spent some time with Mom in Florida. After Uncle Dan passed away, she and Aunt Sue made a few trips to Florida to spend quality time with their sister, Rose. She was also a regular passenger on my motorcoach tours, going to Salem MA and Nashville TN, Uncle Dan's dream trip.

Children were always special to Aunt Lena. Her grandchildren and great-grandchildren were her life. One of her great-grandchildren, Dina Matis Brundage's daughter, shares her name - Adelina.

It's interesting to note that there are several variations of the name Daniel in this family - Daniel Sr., Daniel Jr., Dana, Dina, Diane, Danielle, Dane and Ann, the latter six names being grandchildren. I guess you could include Adelina. Unscramble it and remove one A. Interesting!!

Lena Sindici Matis passed away while residing in the St. Johnsville Nursing Home on February 23 in the winter of 2005 at the age of 87 from dementia.

Daniel Matis, Sr. was born in Little Falls on March 12, 1915, son of John Matis and Maria Poruben of Czechoslovakia. Tragically, his life was taken as he was bound for the Johnstown Library to participate in his book club on the evening of May 12, 1987. Due to the bright evening sun, a truck coming from the other lane crossed over and hit Dan headon. He was an avid reader and loved to debate and share his knowledge of politics. He was designated the best athlete of the Class of 1934.

ASSUNDA M. SINDICI aka Susie was born August 11, 1920 at the Hough Street home, which her parents were renting.

In 1934, the Central Mohawk Valley Council awarded Susie her Girl Scout badge and she played right guard on the 7th grade girl's basketball team. In her later years, while employed by the Cozzolino St. Johnsville Dress Company, she modeled some of their fashions.

On Saturday, June 15, 1940, Susie Sindici and Guido Corso, son of Guy Corso and Mary Iacobucci, were married in St. Patrick's Catholic Church, followed by a reception for close relatives and friends at the home of her parents at 4 Roth Street. My grandparents certainly didn't have the means for a large reception. Her friend, Mary Papa nee Stankewich and Dante Corso, Guido's oldest brother, were maid-of-honor and best man.

Sue purchased her own wedding gown with money she had saved through the years. She went to work at age fifteen earning $5.00 a week for 40 hours. She told me the story of leaving the iron on after ironing her veil and going off to church. Luckily, there wasn't a fire. I have photos of her wedding day with my cousin Pauline, my brother Joe and me, taken in front of the house at 4 Roth Street, all dressed in white for the occasion.

Sue and Guido's honeymoon was spent at the Lenz camp on Caroga Lake. Since they had no car, a friend and neighbor, Fred Sanguine, drove them. Guido worked as a plumber for Lenz Hardware, St. Johnsville at the time.

Upon their return, the couple lived upstairs in the Sanguine home right next door to my grandparents. They paid $9.00 per month for rent, which included their heat. Pauline and I loved to spend time visiting her, as she would let us try on her pretty clothes and jewelry.

When S1C Guido Corso was called to serve in the U.S. Navy on October 16, 1943, he was sent to North Ireland. Aunt Sue moved into our family home at 10 South Division Street to live with her two sisters, Rose and Lena and children. We had three women and five children residing there during World War II. Their son, Peter was born at Little Falls Hospital in November, shortly after Guido's deployment.

After returning from the war, Guido worked for his brother Dario at Corso's Men's Clothing and Dry Cleaning. The business sat between the Palmer Grill and Francisco's Grocery on West Main.

The Corso's later purchased a 2-family home on North Division Street, living upstairs while her sister Lena's family lived down. After Aunt Lena's family moved out, they moved downstairs and put in a new kitchen. The upstairs apartment may have been the first home of Susie's friend, Fedora Fiacco and James Richard before they purchased their home on West Main Street. In the 1960s Aunt Sue's niece, Pauline Matis Smith and her family lived upstairs before the move to Florida with Pauline's husband, Mel's job transfer through his employment with General Electric.

Susie's employment throughout her life was always with dress manufacturing. After raising her son, she became employed with her father-in-law Guy Corso, who established Corso Dress Company. It first shared space with Palatine Dye Company on New Street, before purchasing the small wooden building by Zimmerman Creek at the end of Smith Street. Local ladies, including many Italians, were hired as seamstresses, doing mostly what was called piecework. There were about 68 employees at one time at the height of the fashion business.

Upon the death of his father, Guido and Susie took over the operations of the dress business. They both were very proficient in the assembling of garments, knowing all the little tricks of the sewing trade. I attribute my sewing skills to their sharing these with me.

With Guido's early death Sue continued with the business until dress manufacturing in the U.S. became a dying trade, being sent out of the country to cheaper laborers. She then retired and decided to enjoy a social life.

Other than their son, Peter and his family, Corso Dress was pretty much Sue and Guido's whole life. Many were the evenings that they worked until six, bringing hand work home to ready for the lady employees the next day. They produced high-end quality dresses for the New York City markets, but were paid minimal amounts for their efforts. When I worked for them, doing their bookkeeping and payroll, I was shocked to see the amount received for a garment, compared to the high retail price it brought. Sue's sister, Rose, my mom was their primary hemmer until the closing.

With the death of Guido's father, they moved to the 18 Bridge Street family home, where both resided until their passing. Guido's sister, Gloria Corso Laraway and her family had lived in the downstairs apartment until building their new home on Rockefeller Drive.

A smoker most of his life, lung cancer ended Guido's life. He died at the young age of 59 on August 29, 1979. He was born October 6, 1920. In his younger years, everyone thought Guido looked like Clark Gable, the handsome movie star who played Rhett Butler in *Gone With The Wind*. You can read more about Guido Corso in *La Familia Corso*.

For years, Susie always prepared her own pizza dough, ready for Sunday morning's treat of *pizza fritta* for anyone who stopped by after church. Aunt Sue's were light and crispy. Her grandson, Kevin Corso, has carried on her tradition. The true name is *Zeppole*, originating in Napoli, Italy. They were also popular in Rome and called St. Joseph's Day cakes. The pizza dough was stretched out into round flat or rolled cigar shapes similar to fritters, then simmered lightly in olive oil, usually sprinkled with powdered sugar. They are also delicious, with sprinkled salt or rolled in regular sugar. Some prefer dipping them in sauce.

After Guido's passing, Aunt Sue became a couple with Bernie Mancini, whose wife had also passed away. Probably the most fun time of her life, for almost 25 years they attended many social affairs, dances and traveled. Bernie's passing left another huge void in Aunt Sue's life and heart.

On October 8, 2011, after spending a wonderful day with lunch and reminiscing of the past with her sister, Viola, and nieces, Pauline and me, Susie experienced a fall that evening while getting out of her chair. She broke her hip, which aggravated some other health issues and caused her residency in the St. Johnsville Nursing Home like her sisters, Rose and Lena, before her.

On Sunday morning, January 22, 2012, after attending Mass on the TV in her hospital room, Assunda Sindici closed her eyes and quietly went to visit her sisters, Rosie and Lena, who were there to greet her with open arms, along with her loving parents, her husband, Guido and companion, Bernie. The week before she passed, she told about wanting to be with her sisters, Rosie and Lena and how she had been talking with them. She was 91.

VIOLA R. SINDICI was the youngest daughter of Guiseppe and Edvige Sindici, being born May 30, 1923, just before her parents purchased the 4 Roth Street home. Only twelve years older than me, she was always more like my older sister and good friend. Everyone always thought I looked like her.

Wearing her sister, Susie's wedding gown, Viola R. Sindici married Torquato Joseph Perry, son of Francesco Perri and Rosina Barberio from Herkimer, on Sunday, April 12, 1942. Serving as attendants were Torquato's siblings, Dolores and Forino Perry. They had pretty much the same type wedding and reception as Aunt Sue. They later left for an auto tour of New York City.

Being the youngest, she claimed she always got the hand-me-downs from her sisters. From the photos I have, she inherited some very stylish dresses. All the Sindici girls were fashion plates.

Viola was able to join her husband, Joe for a while in Gulfport, Mississippi, San Antonio and Galveston, Texas, while he was in the US Air Force during World War II. Three of the Sindici sons-in-law were in the Navy, Uncle Joe in the Air Force.

Being of Italian descent, Torquato Joseph Perry was only related to my Dad, Floyd Perry as a brother-in-law. His family's Italian name of Perri was Americanized. Actually, there are three Joseph Perry's in my family - this uncle, my brother and Dad's brother. Confusing at times!

They both loved children, but were never blessed with them. They loved when their nieces and nephews on both sides of their families came to visit and sometimes stay for the weekend. Pauline and I spent many fun weekend overnights with Aunt Vi and Uncle Joe, when they lived next door to his parents on Washington Street, Herkimer.

Vi and Joe met at the Pyramid Roller Skating Rink, which was just outside St. Johnsville on Route 5 West, heading toward Little Falls. In the winter they would also meet for ice-skating at Gilbert Hough's rink on South Division Street. One night, Aunt Vi spied her mother hiding behind a tree watching her. She asked her friend, Rita Papa, to pretend she was with Uncle Joe.

Following in her three sister's footsteps, Viola was awarded a Perfect Attendance certificate for the years 1933 and 1934. Carlo Polidori was in her class. She was on the Junior High honor roll in March 1938. I don't think she was athletic like her sisters.

While in high school, she and Nonna attended the World's Fair in New York City with a group of other Italians from St. Johnsville. I have a photo of part of the group showing them with Mildred and Philip Terricola, Velina and Flora Macci, Harry and Dora Palombi, Anna and Richard Mancini, Rose Colorito and Jimmy Battisti. Lena Cochi, Delia and Jim Pietrocini also attended. I'm thinking they went by chartered bus.

Torquato lived in Herkimer, Viola in St. Johnsville. He often told the story of his frightening experience traveling back home one night after a date, via the old Route 5 past Beardslee Manor, noted for numerous ghostly apparitions and scary hauntings.

As a young man just leaving his sweetheart, his head was still in the clouds from spending the evening with her. All of a sudden, there appeared a man in a long coat carrying a lantern, who crossed in front of his vehicle, then disappeared. Thinking he had hit the man, although he felt no thump, he stopped the car, got out and looked all around, even under the car. Remembering the tales he had heard about this area, he jumped back into his car and took off like "a bat out of hell", scared to death. Mind you, he wasn't someone who believed in anything that wasn't tangible.

Vi worked for a short while as a sales clerk in the Munger's Department Store in Herkimer. Mostly, she was more like a Suzy Homemaker, a Domestic Goddess, always at Uncle Joe's beck and call with his meals and a cup of coffee for his afternoon break from his custom furniture business in his expansive basement workshop. She was rather an old-fashioned type wife and a wonderful hostess. She always fussed over her lovely ranch style home that Uncle Joe built for her in 1957 in East Herkimer. Except for the last five years of Viola's confinement to a Herkimer nursing home, they both lived there for the rest of their lives.

Torquato "Joe" was considered a wood craftsman; he didn't like being called a carpenter. He fashioned all the cherry cabinets in their kitchen and bath, also a bookcase divider and fireplace mantel in the spacious living room. He designed and constructed most of the wood furniture in their home, hand rubbing each piece with TLC. It was difficult to find a flaw in any of his work. He had quite a lucrative business of cabinet making and restoring furniture, working at his trade almost to the time of his death. His artistry was most evident in my St. Johnsville home.

Until they went out of business, Joe worked part-time for Rush Furniture Store in Herkimer, doing all the touch-ups on the furniture that came in, following up with any problems after delivery to customer's homes. Dominic Stagliano worked as a salesman with him.

Torquato "Joe" Perry was born Thursday, April 29, 1920 and passed away Saturday, April 6, 2002 at the age of 81, just short of his 82nd birthday, in the arms of his beloved wife. Six days later he and Aunt Vi would have celebrated their 60th wedding anniversary on April 12.

Ironically, as fate would have it with the four sisters, Viola also resided in the Mohawk Valley Health Care Center in Herkimer NY, the victim of a massive stroke, which she suffered the Monday after her sister, Susie broke her hip. She passed away 5½ years later on July 18, 2017.

Maenza, Italy

Located about 43 miles southeast of Rome, Maenza is a quaint *comune* (municipality) in the *Province* (county) of *Latina* in the Italian region (state) of *Lazio*. It borders Supino and Roccagorga, plus many other *comunes*.

The current Mayor is Francesco Mastracci, whom I personally met on my stopover. He was most welcoming and helpful in my quest to find information about my grandmother, Edvige Cacciotti. The Mastracco's from St. Johnsville came from Maenza. I don't know if they are related.

Like so many of the Old Italian towns, Maenza is also home to Baronel Castle that dates back to the 9th century. It became a watchtower in the 12th - 13th centuries, and was enlarged in the 16th century.

There are 239 Cacciotti families in the Lazio region. More than any other regions combined. Altogether, there are approximately 404 Cacciotti families in all of Italy.

The 1920 Federal Census boasts New York State as having the largest number of immigrants from Maenza. St. Johnsville NY may be able to make the claim they acquired most of them.

Torrice, Italy

Torrice is a *comune* of approximately 4800 residents in the Province of Frosinone in the Lazio region southeast of Rome.

Ceccano, Italy

The *comune* of Ceccano is near Torrice. It boasts a current population of approximately 24,000. During World War II the Church of *Santa Maria a Flume* was destroyed by enemy airstrikes. Ceccano has a vast amount of history as stated in the following article.

Ceccano is the site of *Castel' Sindici* and original home of the regal Sindici family.

Castel' Sindici di Ceccano

The *comune* of Ceccano, Frosinone, Lazio Provence, Italy is the home of *Castel' Sindici*, a huge part of my Grandfather Guiseppe "Joseph" Sindici's heritage. From my extensive research, it seems he may have come from an aristocratic family, which boasts many famous Sindici's.

Castel' Sindici, located just a short walk from the village of Ceccano, is entered through a large iron gate, which leads through a path of meticulous landscaping. In 1928 the estate was declared a "National Artistic Area of Interest". It served as a command post during World War II.

Descendants of the Sindici family inhabited it until the 1990s, when the municipality of Ceccano took it over. It is currently undergoing extensive renovations.

When visiting in June 2013, I was not able to get up close due to the gates being chained. I did, however, enjoy the welcoming gestures of some elderly gentlemen conversing in front of a building in Old Towne Ceccano, who were most helpful in my quest. The square in the town was getting ready for some type of celebration.

Designed by Giuseppe Sacconi, affluent wine maker and Knight Stanislaus Sindici constructed the castle for storage of wines he produced. Sindici's were famous for their wines into the 1930s. The castle dates back to the late 1800's. My Grampa Giuseppe Sindici was noted in his neighborhood for his home brewed wine made from the fruits of his vines.

Ceccano has a large population of Sindici's. The ancient name is considered aristocratic, possibly originating in north Italy in the 10th century. They were officials who collected documents and officiated over townspeople, like a mayor. The Sindici name means "mayor". There are currently only 31 Sindici (Sindico) families in Italy, most likely residing in Ceccano.

The castle became the residence of the Sindici family and housed numerous prominent Italian figures. Some of the many famous artists are Oreste Sindici, famous musician who composed the Colombian national anthem; Poet and Cavalier Augusto B. Sindici, (1836-1921), believed to be Stanislaus's cousin, published a Memoir; Augusto's artist wife, Francesca, noted painter of horses and cavalries, and their daughter, Magda Stuart Sindici, author of *Via Lucis, 1898*.

Magda Stuart Sindici was a close friend of James McNeil Whistler, who was commissioned to paint her portrait by her husband, but never completed it. It is rumored he fell in love with her while going through the portrait painting process. He served as best man at her marriage to William Henry Heinemann, publisher of her novel, on February 22, 1899 at 12 Noon in St. Antonio's Church, Anzio, Italy. This was followed by a reception at Villa Sindici.

There is another famous medieval castle still standing in Ceccano – *Castello dei Conti*, which overlooks the Sacco River valley. Although I didn't take the time to visit this castle, we did drive past the grounds in our effort to locate *Castel' Sindici*.

Searching My Roots

In June 2013, I journeyed to Italy on a quest to discover my *Famiglia Italiana* roots. Unfortunately, I didn't plan the trip properly and was only able to spend an 8-hour day with my search. The one and a half hour drive to and from my hotel in Rome cut the time considerably. This side trip was included with an Art/Prayer Retreat I was attending in the hills of Tuscany. In hindsight, I should have concentrated on my quest and not done the retreat. But then, I wouldn't have had the inspiration to write my new novelette, *Desiree*.

Most of my daywas spent in Maenza, searching the archives for information of my beloved Nonna, Edvige (Cacciotti) Sindici, and visiting her homestead. I came away with such mixed feelings about my amazing discoveries.

My bilingual guide/driver, Daniele Melaragno, whom I hired for the day from *DriverInRome*, took me first to Maenza City Hall, where Mayor Francesco Mastracci welcomed us. (He may be related to the St. Johnsville Mastrocco's, as they also came from Maenza.) The building was clearly well over 100 years old, not modern at all in structure or organization. Only a small sign on the outside front wall signified the office. In fact, we entered through the wrong door, going into an area of cluttered books and papers we had to climb over.

The gracious Italian-speaking clerk patiently searched the registry of heavy, tattered, century-old bound books. Just as the young woman was ready to give up, she found a whole paragraph about my grandmother and her birth, as registered by her mother. The information she gave me clarified many questions our family always had concerning my Nonna Sindici. Even she was never certain of her actual birthday or age. I wish I had asked more questions about the whole family, but felt I was interfering with their lunch hour.

After the clerk was finished, a woman showed at the door and advised she would take us to Nonna's birthplace. We literally chased her up a steep incline of cobblestoned steps, my guide, Daniele, in the middle with me lagging behind. Most everywhere I went in Italy the streets and sidewalks were paved with difficult to maneuver cobblestones.

We were not able to drive the car up there. The residents living in this particular area probably don't have cars. Nothing is handicap accessible. And, you certainly don't find many heavy or obese people, even though breads and pastas are staple in their diets. I think it's the daily exercise they get maneuvering the steps and stones and going to market daily.

As we arrived at the haphazardly arranged apartment complex, which I can only describe as being somewhat of a cul-de-sac, I saw attached 2-story apartment buildings of concrete and stone, all well over 100 or more years old. Two to three generations live together. Their lifestyle today isn't much better than that of a century ago.

Upon seeing two ladies in their housedresses and aprons hanging out their wide-open windows, conversing with each other across the way, a movie I once saw came to mind. It was like, "Hey, Guiseppina, did you hear about Rosina?" The whole scenario took me back in time. Of course, they were curious about us as strangers.

Daniele told them whom we were searching while I headed down into a little alleyway which divided a smaller building from the rest of the complex. Our lady escort took me right up to the door of *via dei Tocco 15*.

Words cannot describe the overwhelming feeling I experienced when I actually touched the door and house number of the home where my Nonna was born and lived for 22 years until coming to America. I never found out if the house was currently occupied. I'm assuming not, as I'm certain the neighborhood watch would have insisted they take me to meet the present tenants. They may have been at work.

The door to the home was in a dark alleyway, likened to a tunnel with a light at the other end. I saw a young woman come up from that opening carrying some packages, so I assume there was something of significance on the other side. I didn't venture down the cobbled slope to check it out for fear of falling.

There were no windows on the front of the home. I'm assuming there were some on the back end, which overlooked the valley. I'm thinking this was the basement of the apartment in the front of the building. It was sad to see where my Nonna had been born and lived until her journey to America.

After taking several photos, I came back out of the tunnel and was greeted by a middle-aged woman, dressed in mourning black dress and apron with a huge smile on her face. Introducing herself as Luigia Crudetti, she came over and gave me a big hug with kisses all over my face.

She told me she was a niece of Desiderio Coco. Her mother was his sister, Pasqualina Coco; her father was Ugo Crudetti. For years Desiderio had sent her family care packages - with one dollar for each - at Christmas, Easter and some other Italian holiday. They hadn't heard from Desiderio in 50 years. He had passed away in 1985.

In December of the year 2013, I sent them a package with some old family photos, a letter I translated into Italian and 3 one-dollar bills with Santa's face, which I had purchased at a local Publix Market. I've never heard back from them. I do hope I didn't insult them. They were such a sweet family.

Luigia asked me to wait while she went to her home to find some photos. Shortly after, she appeared again and invited us to come up to her apartment to meet her daughter and grandson. Her husband had passed away about a year and a half ago, thus the black mourning attire.

We climbed dark, steep, narrow concrete steps with no railings. The apartment was very small, looked like only four rooms. They watched a small TV sitting at the kitchen table in the cramped dining area past the sparse kitchen.

There was a blanket covering the kitchen fireplace, which was most likely used for heat and cooking in the winter. The curtained dining room French doors opened to a small iron balcony overlooking a magnificent valley.

Luigia's daughter graciously offered us a cool drink and some cookies. During my time in Italy, I discovered they don't serve drinks with ice, a habit I am accustomed to. She and her mannerly son sat at the kitchen table conversing with us through my guide, while Luigia continued to search for photos. I was remiss in not asking their names. I do have their address and phone number.

Finally, Luigia came out with two photos – one a family group photo with her as a child, her mother, father and grandmother (Desiderio's mother). There was also another photo of Desiderio's sister, Agnese, all of which I photographed for my files.

Giovanna Cacciotti was Luigia's other grandmother. This would make her a relative of my grandmother, Edvige Cacciotti Sindici. We finally determined that we were distant cousins. Her daughter also observed that we have similar eyes, both being hazel. Luigia was glowing with the revelation that we were related and asked me to come visit again.

I was disappointed that I wasn't able to spend more time discovering stories about Nonna and her relatives, especially those who may still be living in Maenza. Lena Terricola told me that she met some of Nonna's nieces when she and Cus vacationed there, visiting his relatives. They reminded her of my Aunt Vi, about same age. They most likely would not be living now.

There are numerous Maenza residents who came to America. Eighteen of them on the same ship with my Nonna, with thirteen settling in St. Johnsville.

Our next stop, before leaving Maenza, was at *Bar-Caffe della Plaza*, a short slide down the hill and just below where the limo was parked. A distant cousin of Tracy Montoni – Giovanni Vecciarelli owns this little café. He was about 50 years old. A Bar-Café is a small restaurant that serves alcohol, cold sparkly drinks and coffees – namely espresso and cappuccino, along with sandwiches, pastries and frozen gelato.

We caught up with Giovanni as he was closing for the customary "Siesta Hour." In Italy it is the custom to close for an hour – or more - to give employees a lunch break. He was also very excited to meet me, especially being from St. Johnsville. He had visited here many times, staying with Andy and Teresa Fontana Susi.

Through my extensive research, I later discovered Teresa is related to him through her mother. I told him I would put him in touch with Tony Susi, whom I contacted upon arrival home.

Unfortunately, Giovanni didn't speak English either, so it was difficult for me to communicate with him, as well. I was able to thank him for the tasty cappuccino and biscotti, as we ventured out on my further quest with my Famiglia Italiana.

Maybe you are searching among the branches for what only appears in the roots." ~ *Rumi*

~ *La Famiglia NARDUCCI* ~

~ GIUSEPPE NARDUCCI et MARCIANNA CACCIOTTI ~

GIUSEPPE NARDUCCI immigrated to America from Maenza at 21 years of age on February 26, 1904, first landing in New Bethel PA, before coming to St. Johnsville. Born Christmas Eve, December 24, 1882 in Maenza, Italy, he was the son of Antonio Narducci and Genaeffa Cochie (Cochi?). I am not certain if there may be a relationship with sisters, Ersilia Nardacci Castrucci and Olympia Nardacci DeAngelis or Carlo Cochi? They were also from Maenza.

Arriving from Maenza on March 18, 1913, Marcianna Cacciotti was married almost two weeks later on March 30, 1913 to Giuseppe aka Joseph Narducci. She was the daughter of Francesco Cacciotti and Stella Valle and sister to my grandmother, Edvige Cacciotti Sindici.

The couple was united in marriage at St. Patrick's Church, attended by Prosper J. Napoleone and his wife, Victoria Terranova. Their first child, Yolanda was born on New Year's Eve, December 31, 1913 in St. Johnsville. They also had two sons, Antonio and Arminio. Judging by the records I have located, I'm assuming the two sons were also born in St. Johnsville, but later returned to Italy with their parents, where they remained.

The wedding took place before my grandmother, Edvige was able to arrive on July 19, 1913. On the passenger manifest it is stated that she is going to live with her brother, Giuseppe. I questioned this for quite a while, as that was her soon to be husband's name, whom she hadn't yet met. Now it makes sense that it should have read "brother-in-law". She also resided at 21 Sanders Street when first arriving, where Giuseppe and her sister, Marcianna, were living.

When Giuseppe registered for World War I in 1919 at 36 years old, the couple was still living at 21 Sanders Street; he was working at Allter's Knitting Mill aka Union Knitting Mill. His wife was living with him. Marcianna may have returned to their hometown of Maenza with the three children sometime between then and before the June 1920 Census. I do know that she had gone back to Maenza. Their daughter, Yolanda went back and forth to Maenza several times in her young adult years before finally settling down in St. Johnsville.

The June 1920 Census shows only Giuseppe Narducci living with my grandparents, the Sindici's, at 44 Hough Street. He applied for a passport on September 8, 1920 to go back to Italy to visit his mother and bring back his wife and three children. I don't believe he ever came back.

I discovered the publication of a subpoena, dated February 2, 1926, originating from the desk of the President of the United States. It was posted in the Fort Plain Standard with a request for him to appear concerning his Naturalization Papers. As I understand the item, his papers were being revoked. Perhaps, because he never returned to the United States?

MARCIANNA CACCIOTTI was born about 1887. She was an older sister of Edvige, who was the youngest of three. I have no exact records of Marcianna's birth or death. The oldest sister, Antonia, had remained in Maenza, most likely married there.

~ ALESSANDRO POTENZIANI et YOLANDA NARDUCCI ~

ALESSANDRO "Alec" POTENZIANI came to St. Johnsville via Buffalo NY, where he located after immigrating on October 27, 1920. Also traveling with Alec was a cousin, Francesco Potenziani and Elenterio Caponera aka Larry Mastromoro. Alec and Francesco were meeting an uncle Damiano Cesare. I also found Giovanni Potenziani, who could be Alec's father on the same ship.

Alec was the son of Giovanni Potenziani and Anunziata Porta of Terentino, Italy. It was a few years before he settled in St. Johnsville. He may have been one of the immigrants that went wherever there was employment, as many others did.

A 1925 NYS Census I found states that Alessandro Potenziani lives in Lawyersville near Cobleskill, and shows his employment as working on a State Road. All of the information listed seems to confirm this is Alec. Also listed in this Census was a Giovanni Potenziani, age 44, who could be Alec's father. In checking further with Giovanni, I found he had immigrated to Buffalo NY in 1920, the same day as Alec. All of these details fit the story. It does seem that Giovanni returned to Italy and came back in April 1924. I don't find that his wife ever came.

Coming to St. Johnsville, Alessandro Potenziani met Yolanda "Viola" Narducci, who was living with the Peter Mastracco family on Lion Avenue at the time. Engaged on September 30, 1935, they were married on Sunday, October 20, 1935 at St. Patrick's Catholic Church. Attendants were Perina Nobile, Utica, a sister of Viola Nobile Peruzzi, serving as maid of honor; Gilda Caponera as a bridesmaid, Victor Caponera, best man and Oscar Cochi as an usher. A reception was held at the home of Mr. and Mrs. Philip Caponera on Ann Street. After returning from a western trip for their honeymoon, they resided on East Main Street.

Alec and Viola had a son, John Joseph and daughter, Mary Ann. The 1940 Census shows them living on Hough Street, perhaps with the Pasquale Montoni family? They later purchased a home at 10 East Liberty Street, where they resided most of their lives.

Alessandro Potenziani was born October 4, 1904 in Ferentino, Italy. After a long illness, he passed away at Little Falls Hospital in March of 1986 after being stricken at home. He was a maintenance worker for New York Central Railroad for 35 years, serving as secretary of the Railroad Union for two years. He had two brothers and two sisters in Italy.

YOLANDA "Viola" NARDUCCI was born New Year's Eve, December 31, 1913 in St. Johnsville. She passed away March 29, 2004 at the age of 91 in Coupeville WA, where she had moved to be closer to her son, John and his family.

In her formative years, Viola was shuttled around quite often. Born in America, her parents took her back to Italy for a few years. I don't know when she came here permanently, but I do know she went back and forth several times before her marriage. She lived for a while with her aunt, Edvige Sindici, who treated her like her four daughters. She was boarding with the Peter Mastracco family before her marriage.

Viola was quite the "fashionista" before she married. I have a copy of her beautiful colorized wedding portrait. She loved nice clothes and often borrowed her cousins' Rose and Lena Sindici's stylish fashions. After her marriage, she took on the role of the typical Italian housewife, donning housedresses, aprons, tied up black shoes and house slippers. When asked by her daughter-in-law, Annette, why she stopped dressing so well, she replied, "I already had a husband."

A very religious and generous woman, she was always there to donate and volunteer where needed. Viola was very active with the local Cerebral Palsy Association, from which her daughter, Mary Ann received benefits. She never worked outside the home due to the responsibility of Mary Ann's care.

JOHN JOSEPH POTENZIANI was another young Italian man who dedicated his life to his country. Following his graduation from St. Johnsville High School in June 1954, he enlisted in the US Navy in October 1954. Receiving his basic training at Bainbridge MD, he was sent to McGuire Air Force Base, where he served on a military transport for two years. For two more years, he was stationed at Guantanamo Bay, Cuba, during the

Cuban Missile Crisis. He became an A-6 Instructor-Trainer, retiring from the Navy on August 31, 1979 after 25 years of active service.

John received the Good Conduct Medal and US Navy Expeditionary Medal. Not one to be idle, John began a second career at Grumman Aircraft, headquartered in Bethpage NY as a Tech Representative, retiring 18 years later.

On May 24, 1974, John Potenziani married Annette David. They had a son, Alessandro, plus five other children from their previous marriages. John, Jr., Michael and Kevin were sons with Marjorie Difenderfer. Jenene and Charlene were daughters from Annette's first marriage.

John was a cousin to the members of the Cacciotti-Sindici family. As cousins and best friends, he and my brother, Joe Perry, shared many adventures. He was a member of the St. Johnsville High School basketball team.

John Joseph Potenziani was born November 10, 1936 in St. Johnsville. He passed away on November 6, 2013, just four days short of his 77th birthday in Coupeville WA.

MARY ANN POTENZIANI was named after her grandmother, Marcianna Narducci, born sometime in the mid-to-late 40s.

Sadly, Mary Ann had a birth defect and required a lot of care from her mother. A van would pick her up at her home to attend special classes and in her adult years she would be transported to Liberty Enterprises to work. She felt so important going to work every day. Mary Ann was a member of the Cerebral Palsy community.

Mary Ann Potenziani was in her 40s when she passed away in 1988, not too long after her father's death. She missed him dearly and would always remember him in conversations. She enjoyed visiting with everyone.

~ *La Famiglia PALMA* ~

~ GIOVANNI PALMA et CARMELA TERRANOVA ~

In 1910, at the young age of 15, Giovanni Palma ventured out on his own, searching for a better life than what he was living in Patrica, Italy. I do not find the passenger manifest to confirm the date of arrival or where he was headed.

Patrica, Italy is an ancient hilltop "*comune*" of about 8400 residents, located 43 miles from Rome. It borders Supino and Ceccano. The largest influx of Patrica immigrants went to Aliquippa PA to work in the steel mills.

GIOVANNI "John" PALMA was born September 6, 1896 in Patrica, the son of Salvano Palma and Josephine Baloni. He had a brother, Eduardo "Fred" from Schenectady, and two sisters, Iola Palma Buffalini, with another still in Italy.

The 1915 Census shows John Palma and Frank Colorito, both age 18, living at a boarding house in Governeur, St. Lawrence NY with many other young men. They were working on a State Road, employed by Bugard Company, Waddington NY. He is still residing there in 1917, as per his World War I registration document.

By 1920, John had come to St. Johnsville and resided at 29 Ann Street as a boarder with the Tony Fonda family, working at one of the St. Johnsville Knitting Mills.

On January 20, 1921, John's brother, Eduardo "Fred", age 16, came to join him. I have been told that John had sponsored and found work for his brother, Fred in Pennsylvania. Fred eventually settled in Schenectady, where he married, raised his two children, Shirley Josephine and Fred, Jr. and died at the age of 80. I never knew his wife as she died at an early age.

On December 19, 1927, Giovanni Palma and Carmela Terranova, daughter of Giuseppe Terranova and Michelina Terranova, were joined in marriage at St. Patrick's Roman Catholic Church. Attending the couple were Carmela's brother, Benjamin Terranova, as best man with their cousin, Angelina Doganieri as maid of honor. Marie Francisco, daughter of Christina Terranova and niece of Carmela and Ben, was the flower girl. In June of 1955, the Palma's became my mother and father-in-law with my marriage to their son, John.

Angelina Doganieri was the daughter of Costantino Doganieri and Emanuella Terranova. Emanuella was the sister of Carmela's mother, Michelina Terranova.

1930 finds the Palma's living with Carmela's sister, Christina Terranova Francisco's family at 7 West Main Street. I am thinking this is the second floor apartment in the building that housed Caponera's Liquor Store. John is employed as a highway worker and they have their first child, Josephine.

In January 1931, Giovanni Palma was naturalized at the Fonda Court House along with Antonio Mancini.

Records show that the Palma's first opened a restaurant in 1931. I have been told the business began as a Cigar Store, but have no confirmation.

On June 14, 1933, John and Carmela were granted a liquor license to operate as Palmer's Grill at 17 West Main Street, which they operated for over 40 years. The sign makers "Americanized" the name and it wasn't worth the bother to correct it. The living quarters were on the second level of the brick 3-story building. Their son, my husband, John has now joined the family in 1932. He would always tell the story of his mother holding him on her hip, while she stirred whiskey in the family bathtub.

On June 22, 1933 the Palma's purchased the block, then owned by a Raymond Walrath, for $2900. It seems a Francis Wittenback had owned it at one time. An old 1928 advertisement notes that the *Venice Restaurant* was located at 17 West Main. I'm not able to find further information about this restaurant.

John never drank. When a patron offered to buy him one, he would have a glass of ginger ale. A soft-spoken, gentle man of few words, he was well liked.

When televisions first made their debut, Palmer's Grill had the distinction of having the first set in the village. People would walk up to the front windows, peering in to watch this new attraction. It drew new customers inside, who wanted to keep up with the intriguing everyday "soaps".

The Palma's survived the Great Depression and continued to service their daily customers, as they stopped by for a quick happy hour after a hard day of physical work. Carmela lived in the kitchen preparing home-cooked foods and her famous hamburgers made with ground chuck, fried in her "spider" (frying pan), always spilling out between fresh white slices of Wonder Bread. They catered many affairs and business meetings at the restaurant.

John joined the active Young Men's Republican Club of St. Johnsville. In August 1935, they held a Clambake and Field Days at the new Pyramid Dance Pavilion in West St. Johnsville, which also featured a band concert and dancing. John was listed on the Refreshments Committee. My grandfather, Giuseppe Sindici, was on the Tables Committee. In 1938 they hosted another affair at Klock's Park, now H.C. Smith Benefit Club. There were at least 10 noted Italians who were members of this political group.

Living most of his adult life, seven days a week, behind the shiny mahogany bar of his restaurant, John had few pleasures. During the spring baseball season he would walk down to the Soldiers and Sailors Baseball Park to watch his namesake, John, Jr. pitch. When we installed a concrete driveway at our North Division Street home, he walked up to observe, sharing his expertise from his early job's training.

I specifically recall one beautiful Sunday when we all attended his niece, Shirley Josephine Palma's wedding in Schenectady. It was most likely the first - and definitely the last - outing my in-laws had taken together since the wedding of their son, John and me. While Carmela was anxious to get back to the business, John was enjoying being with his brother and sister and their families. He even asked me to dance with him.

On January 30, 1952, the downstairs bar business and upstairs dwelling suffered what could have been a disastrous fire. It seems there was a careless cigarette dropped and unnoticed, which smoldered until it burst into flames in the middle of the night. It was a blessing that the St. Johnsville Volunteer Fire Department had recently purchased a ladder truck; this became its trial run. After an extensive cleanup, the family was able to return to the structure and the business reopened.

On April 17, 1953, the day after John Jr's birthday, his father presented him with his own business, Palma's Esso Station. It was formally opened on November 19, 1953. The land it was situated on had been owned by Biaggio Pistilli, a cousin of Carmela's, with John Sr. as the executor of Pistilli's estate. It was put up for sale. With no bids, he acquired the property after paying off the remaining mortgage. The Pistilli building was torn down, and replaced with the construction of a 2-bay garage, front office and gasoline pumps.

At the age of 66, on March 6, 1963, Giovanni Palma passed away in the ambulance on the way to Little Falls Hospital, in the arms of his namesake, John, stricken with his second heart attack.

Carmela continued to operate the business with the aid of their son, John, along with her sister and brother-in-law, Virginia Terranova and John Brandow. After six years she retired, moved in with her daughter, Josephine, and sold the business and building to Robert and Grace Snell in 1969.

CARMELA TERRANOVA was a child from a very large family of 10 siblings. She was born in Canajoharie NY on September 14, 1904, the daughter of Michelina Terranova and Giuseppe Terranova. A Terranova married a Terranova. It's unusual, but not uncommon that couples have the same surname. They are not always cousins. Terranova is quite a common name in Italy. Carmela's mother, Michelina, was a sister of Carmine Terranova, who was a well-known, respected businessman in St. Johnsville in the early 1900s.
You will read more about Carmine in a separate article.

Since there will be three complete stories featuring the entire Terranova family, I will only recognize Carmela in this article. She was very close to her family, especially her two sisters, Christina and Virginia, who lived just a short walk away from her - like a triangle.

Carmela was in her element in her simple, typical Italian kitchen, greeting anyone who entered her space with, "Did you eat?" An archetypal Italian woman, with food being her main concern, she dressed daily in cotton frocks, full aprons and laced up black shoes. She was noted for her homemade orange cakes, pasta noodles and huge hamburgers, as mentioned above.

On occasion, she would prepare stuffed artichokes, which I considered rather gross, as I sat there watching her son, John aka "Buttsy" tenderly break off the leaves in his quest to reach the heart. Our children, Rodney and Lisa also loved them. It was only in later years that I ventured into tasting them in a dip and then trying the hearts, which have now become a favored delicacy of mine. One time, I attempted to make them for Buttsy not knowing the recipe but guessing at the ingredients and method of preparation. The best compliment he ever gave me, "These taste just like my mother's."

A little interesting history of artichokes and the Terranova's: *The artichoke is a thistle flower, native to Southern Italy, more likely Sicily. Ciro Terranova was a New York City gangster and member of the Morello crime family. He would smuggle artichokes in from Sicily, holding them hostage for ransom. He threatened Italian shopkeepers to purchase them only from him.* I don't know if there is a connection with him and my Terranova family?

Carmela's favorite way of relaxing on summer evenings was sitting outside in front of the business, listening to the New York Yankees game on her portable radio, while visiting with passersby. It's interesting that her Yankees would be the winners of a game with the Boston Red Sox on the very day she gave birth to her son, John. Wonder if that was the reason the Yankees were her favorite? During the winter, when John played basketball, she would attend the home games, cheering him on, rosary beads in hand. I inherited a large scrapbook filled with discolored crumbling newspaper articles that Carmela collected and pasted, referencing her son, John and his baseball and basketball accomplishments. It's at least 70 years old and a treasured family heirloom.

When Carmela's brother, Orlando, came back to St. Johnsville in the early 1970s, she moved into his apartment over Walrath's Pharmacy. She would cook and clean for him. On January 14, 1976, Carmela was stricken with a heart attack at the apartment and died at Little Falls Hospital.

JOSEPHINE ANN PALMA was born New Year's Eve, December 31, 1929 in St. Johnsville.

On June 4, 1950, Josephine "Josie" Palma married Philip "Phil" Terricola, son of Mildred Giovampietro and Graziano Terricola. Before purchasing their Center Street home, next to the St. Patrick's parish home, they lived for two years with her parents in the apartment over the Palmer Grill. They were living there at the time of the fire. They had two daughters - Phyllis and Linda.

Graduating together from St. Johnsville High, Josie and Phil were high school sweethearts and selected as king and queen of their senior prom. Josie was Valedictorian of the class of 1947 and a member of the cheerleading squad. After attending Mildred Elley Secretarial School, she became employed with Waner's in Fort Plain. The village of St. Johnsville employed Josephine for several years. In 1961 she was appointed Clerk Treasurer and later served as Mayor.

Philip Terricola's story can be found with his family *La Famiglia Giovampietro ~ Terricola.*

JOHN JOSEPH PALMA, Jr. aka "Buttsy" dedicated most of his life to the village and township of St. Johnsville. He served for almost 30 years as Superintendent of the Department of Public Works and the Village Water Treatment Plant. Always working side by side with his men, he was noted for being the one "down in the hole." One time, he almost succumbed to Freon gas while there. His men had to pull him out and revive him.

As the village supervisor, he was also on call 24/7. The village experienced a disastrous chlorine spill the Saturday evening before the June 1977 high school graduation, causing the upper part of the residential areas to be evacuated as the gases drifted down into the village. John was called to check out the situation and the fire department was brought in. Although they were equipped with hasmat suits, both he and fireman Gary Swartz were taken to the hospital with chlorine burns to the skin as a result of their efforts to contain the leakage. John suffered from this the remainder of his life.

After his retirement, John Palma served as clerk of the works on several village projects. It took many years for the village to recognize his dedication. In August of 2000, on the suggestion of board member Frederick Lee, the new bridge on William Street, with the Zimmerman Creek flowing underneath, was named the "John 'Buttsy' Palma Bridge."

For 12 years John was elected to the position of Town Justice, serving on the Town Board, as well. John acted as officiate of numerous marriages over those years, most of them being performed with a musical background in the comfort of our home, where I served champagne to celebrate the unions. It is my belief he performed more unions than all of the St. Johnsville churches combined during those 12 years.

I always told him that he was named after the village. "Workaholic" was his middle name. He gave his all to whatever project he was working on, many times working into the late hours of darkness.

While filling the Village and Town positions, he also oversaw the operation, development and maintenance of Serenity Mobile Home Park on the outskirts of St. Johnsville on Route 5 West, where he developed 13 spacious lots, nestled among the shade of the trees.

In the summer of 1971 we purchased the land and concrete block building that had been built many years previous by Fred Giarusso, from Floyd Snell. After a major renovation, I first utilized the building as an Arts and Crafts consignment shop. It later evolved into my one-stop bridal shop, The Red Palette Bridal Center for 15 years. Sadly, a few years ago, the entire building was consumed by fire and is no longer. Memories lost but not forgotten!

At high noon, Sunday June 5, 1955, John Joseph Palma, Jr. and Cora Lee Perry, daughter of Floyd Perry, Jr. and Rose Sindici, were married at Saint Patrick's Roman Catholic Church with Reverend Walter Burns officiating. In attendance were my cousin, Pauline Matis, maid of honor, and my cousin, M. Lee Perry, and close friend, Audrey Stock as bridesmaids. Our long time friend, Sam Papa, was best man, with my brother, Joseph Perry and friend, Alexander "Sandy" LaStarza as ushers. My little brother, Richard was ring bearer, with John's niece, Phyllis Terricola as flower girl. After a year of planning, my dream of Cinderella marrying her Prince Charming came to fruition. We had two children - Rodney John and Lisa Marie.

Our wedding was a large typical Italian affair of close friends and family in attendance. They came from as far as New York City to attend a catered home-cooked dinner at the Community House, prepared and served by the ladies of the Grace Church. It was followed by an Italian "football" reception at Klock's Park aka Benefit Club. Everyone pitched in to decorate the hall, tend bar, serve sandwiches, and pass the fabulous Italian "Zuppa Inglese" rum-filled wedding cake and assorted Italian cookie trays. And, of course, an Italian wedding was not complete without *confetti* - sugarcoated almond favors wrapped in netting and tied with ribbons.

A Wedding Tradition ~ 5 Sugared Almonds for each guest to eat / to remind us that life is both bitter and sweet
5 wishes for the new Husband and Wife / Health, Wealth, Happiness, Family and a Long Life.

My bridal gown was a duplicate of the pink ball gown worn by Leslie Caron in the movie, *The Glass Slipper*. Always one to be different, I had decided I'd like it in pink as in the movie with my attendants in white with rose and pink trim on the gowns I had designed for them. After leaving the bridal shop in Utica, I began to think about how my poor Nonna would react. Out of respect for her feelings, I returned to the shop and changed my order to white. I did leave the tiny pink silk rosebud trims, but later was told they caused a stir among some of the guests.

Although we lived near each other, John and I first met at a birthday party when I was only 13 years old; he was 16. We danced. He was a beautiful dancer, much in demand by all the girls. This was the beginning of our many years of swinging and swaying to the wonderful music of the 40s and 50s.

We also lived for two years with John's parents in the apartment over the grill until a month before the birth of our son, Rodney. For 2½ years we rented an apartment at 119 West Main Street next door to the Maymo Peruzzi family. Before the birth of our daughter, Lisa, we moved to the turn-of-the-century brick home at 30 North Division Street, where we lived for 46 years until John's passing in 2001.

Due to the demands of his parent's business, John did not experience the luxury of family time and holiday celebrations. Christmas was usually celebrated at the home of one of his mother's two sisters, usually at Virginia's, who lived nearby. The family didn't gather all around the kitchen table for meals, as was common with most Italian families.

"Buttsy" was most likely the leader of the famous Mechanic Street gang in the early 1940s, consisting of his close friends - mostly Italians - James Capece, Janet Castellucci, Tom Croce, Delores Colorito, and a couple others who weren't Italian.

Graduating in 1950, John was voted the most popular boy, best dressed, best dancer and best athlete in his class. He was awarded Best Boy School Citizen at graduation. Serving as president of his class for four years, he was selected king of his Senior prom with Margaret Capece, his girlfriend at the time, serving as queen. Marge and I became the best of friends before our marriage and remain so to this day. Close friends, James Capece and Janet Castellucci were second runner-ups.

After graduation, Buttsy went to Morrisville College near Oneonta for a short while, then to Oswego State College. However, the devastating fire in the restaurant brought him home to help with the cleanup, thus ending his collegiate studies. While at Oswego, he was active in college activities and a starting player on the basketball team.

On April 17, 1953, the day after his 21st birthday, John's father gifted him with his own business, Palma's Esso Station. Working daily from 7am to 10pm, he delivered exceptional service to his customers from the date of the opening on November 19, 1953 to the date he sold the business in 1966 to Donald Hoffman, who had been employed by him. Many years later the property was sold to Cumberland Farms.

Before his employment by the village, he worked a construction job, which took him away from home during the week. He had several other job opportunities through the years, which he declined because they were in another town, sometimes requiring us to move there. St. Johnsville was his comfort zone.

A stellar athlete, he excelled in basketball and baseball as a pitcher, with bowling and golf in his later years being his sport of choice. He played baseball on Sundays with the traveling town team for several years and bowled in a traveling classic league, where it was required to maintain at least a 200 average. I recall that he bowled the perfect 300. The game of golf came along after his retirement.

Always active in community affairs, John and I were instrumental with assisting his niece, Linda Terricola in the organization of the St. Johnsville Youth Center. We both served on the Advisory Board from its inception for several years, John as president.

As a trumpet player, John was a member of the high school band and the St. Johnsville Band under the direction of James Pietrocini in the late 1940s. He was a Volunteer Fireman. John served on the Recycling Commissions of the Village of St. Johnsville and Montgomery County, and as a member of the county organization of Town Justices.

Italian creativity and craftsmanship was quite evident in John's DNA, as he meticulously designed birdhouses that looked like actual buildings, one a replica of St. Patrick's Church. He also sculpted various creations from logs with his chain saw. He could magically bring a piece of furniture back to life with his delicate refinishing touch. He was very adept working with both wood and concrete. His list of accomplishments goes on and on, too lengthy to include in this article.

John Joseph Palma, Jr. was born April 16, 1932 in St. Johnsville. He passed away on May 14, 2001 after a five-week stay at Little Falls Hospital, a victim of colon cancer. He now resides in the serenity of Prospect View Cemetery, overlooking the village he so loved and tended.

PALMA ~ Since 1161

This surname is known for its deep sense of responsibility to the point where just hearing the name Palma has inspired both respect and trust. This family never left a task undone and even went above and beyond the call of duty with their sense of responsibility to their community.

Carmela Terranova et Giovanni Palma Wedding

Bride Carmela Terranova; Flower Girl Marie Francisco; Groom Giovanni Palma
Best Man Benjamin Terranova; Maid-of-Honor Angelina Doganieri

Giovanni Terranova
Aka Red Cap Wilson - Lightweight Boxer

Carmine Terranova

Prospero Napoleone

~ *La Famiglia TERRANOVA* ~

~ GIUSEPPE TERRANOVA ~ VIRGINIA PISTILLI ~

Giuseppe Terranova and Virginia Pistilli of the *comune* of Baranello, Italy, were the parents of six children - Angeline, Michelina, Emmanuela, Carmine, Vittoria and Luciano. All of the Terranova siblings were born in Baranello and later came to America. Four of them lived in St. Johnsville at various times. The other two lived their lives in Fort Plain and Canajoharie.

VIRGINIA PISTILLI, age 56, born in 1852 in Mirabel, arrived on February 11, 1907 with the two youngest children, Vittoria, age 15, and Luciano, age 13, enroute to Canajoharie to meet her oldest son, Carmine Terranova. I am assuming her husband, Giuseppe, had died. I find no records of him except that he was born in 1824.

On June 23, 1916, Virginia Pistilli Terranova passed away at the age of 64 from heart failure at the 38 Bridge Street home of her son, Carmine, with whom she had always resided.

ANGELINE TERRANOVA, the oldest child, was born September 10, 1877. She died October 18, 1925 in the Amsterdam Hospital, Amsterdam NY at the young age of 48.

Angeline Terranova married Peter Palm from Canajoharie. They had eleven children - Joseph, Carmela (Ianniello), Virginia (Ianniello), John, Anthony, Ralph, Angelo, Louis, Lucius, Michael and Victor, who died at three days old on May 15, 1918. Tragically, Michael also died in 1928 at age 12, when he ran out in front of a car and suffered a deadly skull fracture.

Peter Palm was from Abruzzo, born about 1876 and died in 1940. He arrived in 1896. He was a well-known grocer in Canajoharie, first residing in Jones Alley, then later his permanent address at 17 Mohawk Street. He took over the produce business of his brother-in-law, Giuseppi Terranova, when he became ill and moved to St. Johnsville.

Angelina and Peter's daughter, Virginia Palm married Ernesto Ianniello on April 10, 1926 with their siblings, Carmela Palm and Joseph Ianniello as witnesses. The couple's daughter, Rose Marie Ianniello married Rudolf Salvagni, son of Paolo Salvagni and Adelgesia Pasquale on August 29, 1951. They also had a son, Angelo.

Although I also have complete details of the other Palm children, it will not appear here as my focus is on St. Johnsville immigrants.

MICHELINA TERRANOVA was born February of 1878 in Baranello, Italy. On March 28, 1899, at age 24, she traveled to America with their two oldest sons - Raphael, age 6, and Giovanni, age 4, reuniting with her husband, Giuseppe Terranova in Canajoharie, where he had established a produce business.

Michelina and Giuseppe had nine more children – all born in Canajoharie – Christina, Carmela, Nicholas, Orlando, Benjamin, Virginia and three that had died at birth – twins, Brasso & Anthony and also another Anthony.

You can read more about Michelina and family in *La Famiglia Guiseppe Terranova et Michelina Terranova*.

EMMANUELA TERRANOVA was born in 1885 and died in December 1928 in Fort Plain. In 1905 Emmanuela Terranova married Costantino Doganieri of Fort Plain, originally from Spinete, Italy. The couple had six children - John, Angelina, Donato, Nicola, Anthony and Joseph.

The Doganieri family lived on State Street, Fort Plain, and were noted as being in the "scrap" business most of their lives. Their daughter, Angelina, was the maid-of-honor in the wedding of her cousin, Carmela Terranova and John Palma.

CARMINE TERRANOVA had come to America alone on March 30, 1903 at the young age of 14. The ship's manifest claimed he was a shoemaker and for some reason he was "tagged". Perhaps due to traveling alone at his young age he had to wear a tag of some sort? The old manifests did not give as much detail as the later ones, which stated who they were traveling to see, where and the sponsor.

In 1905 he was a boarder at a home in Jones Alley, Canajoharie working at the sack factory. A noted St. Johnsville resident and businessman with an extensive resume, Carmine Terranova is featured in his story, *La Famiglia Carmine Terranova et Mary Magdeleine Napoleone*.

VITTORIA TERRANOVA aka Victoria was born in 1892. First arriving in Canajoharie in 1907, she soon moved with her brothers and lived out her short life in St. Johnsville. She was very close to her brother, Carmine and always in a partnership. Victoria and Carmine's names are noted on several marriage licenses. The *Enterprise & News* once called them the "best looking couple in St. Johnsville."

On September 17, 1908, at the age of 18, the priest of St. Patrick's Catholic Church married Victoria Terranova and Prospero Napoleone. Prospero, 21, was the son of Louis Napoleone and Mary DelBene of New Jersey. Prospero was the brother of Carmine's wife, Mary Napoleone. The couple had four children - Louis Donald, Victor, Mary and Pauline. Sadly, Victoria and Prosper both lived short, tragic lives. You can read more about this couple in *La Famiglia Prospero J. Napoleone et Vittoria M. Terranova*.

LUCIANO TERRANOVA aka Louis was the youngest sibling, born November 17, 1894. He died on October 22, 1959 in New York City.

Louis worked and lived most of his life in St. Johnsville, always in a partnership with his brother, Carmine. He later moved to New York City, where he continued the partnership until their businesses went bankrupt. He later operated a Fish Market in the city.

Luciano Terranova married Josephine Montana from New York City. They had one daughter - Virginia Rose. You will read more of him in the Carmine Terranova article.

The Terranova's were a tightly knit family, as were so many of the Italians.

~ GIUSEPPE ANTHONY TERRANOVA et MICHELINA TERRANOVA ~

Arriving August 14, 1895 from Baranello, the passenger manifest shows Giuseppe Anthony Terranova aka Joseph first going to Pittsburgh PA before settling in Canajoharie, where he conducted his produce business on Main Street. His wife, Michelina Terranova followed almost four years later on March 28, 1899, bringing their two oldest sons, Raphael and Giovanni.

I find no records of Giuseppe between his arrival and 1905. However, Michelina's arrival confirms him living in Canajoharie by early 1899. They do not show up in the 1900 Census, but I found them later in the 1905 Census living in Jones Alley, Canajoharie. In 1912 Giuseppe and Michelina moved into a building on Main Street owned by Mary L. Probst in Canajoharie, where Giuseppe conducted his produce business and shoeshine service.

In March of 1916, they suffered a slight loss to the business and building due to a fire. The Waller & Eackler Meat Market was next door. Giuseppe conducted his business until 1919, when he became ill and moved his family to St. Johnsville. He sold the business to Peter Palm, whose wife, Angelina Terranova was the sister of Michelina.

By the time of their relocation to St. Johnsville, the couple had nine more children, all born in Canajoharie - Orlando, Christina, Carmela, Nicholas, twins Brasso and Anthony, Benjamin and Virginia. Brasso and Anthony may have died at birth, as I don't find them in the 1910 Census; there was also another Anthony, who apparently also died at birth. They are included in a family tree I possess, that was researched by a Terranova family member several years ago. It is my belief that the two twins who died were brothers of Benjamin making triplets.

One summer day in August 1915, Giuseppe was treating his family to a Sunday outing in his horse drawn wagon. Coming down the Randall hill, the harness broke causing the horse to be crowded against the wagon. The horse immediately responded, kicking furiously, causing a compound fracture to Giuseppe's leg and severe injuries to the fingers of two of the children.

GIUSEPPE ANTHONY TERRANOVA was born in Baranello in 1870, the son of Filippa Terranova and Angela Palmeri. He died suddenly on October 22, 1919 at the age of 48, in a rented home on Sanders Street, St. Johnsville, where the family had moved when he became ill. He was taken to the SS Peter and Paul Cemetery, Canajoharie, for burial. Besides his wife and eight children, two brothers, a sister in New York City and another sister in Buffalo survived him. I do not have their names.

For many years his grandson, my husband, John Palma and I would take care of his gravesite for Memorial Day. Since recently discovering that he died in St. Johnsville, I find it strange that he was not buried in St. Johnsville. Perhaps the three babies that died were also buried in Canajoharie?

After his death, Michelina moved to a home at 22 Monroe Street with the four children who were still living at home. Her daughter, Christina worked for her uncle, Carmine Terranova as a bookkeeper, supplementing their income. From information I have discovered in a news article, it seems her son, Orlando may have purchased the home for his sister, Christina when she had married.

Biaggio Pistilli, a nephew, was boarding with the family. Also listed was Michelina's grandson, Joseph Terranova, son of Raphael Terranova and Elizabeth Theresa Chest. Michelina was raising Joseph due to the untimely death of Elizabeth. The younger grandson, Carmine, was living with Elizabeth's parents in Canajoharie.

MICHELINA TERRANOVA was also born in Baranello in February 1876, where she and Giuseppe were married. She was the daughter of Giuseppe Terranova and Virginia Pistilli.

Michelina had five siblings - her three sisters, Emanuela, who married Costantino Doganieri from Fort Plain; Angeline, who married Peter Palm from Canajoharie; Vittoria, who married Prospero Napoleone and her two brothers, Carmine and Luciano.

On September 18, 1918, Michelina and her children were living with her brother, Carmine and family at 36 Bridge Street.

The 1925 Census shows the family living at 14 East Main Street. Raphael, Giovanni and Christina have married and left the nest. Orlando, Nicholas and Benjamin all work as truckers, Carmela works as a packer at Beech-Nut and Virginia is a sales lady for her sister, Christina's grocery store. In later years, 14 East Main Street was the location of the American Legion Post.

On January 23, 1926, after a two-year illness, Michelina passed away at 14 East Main Street, the home of her daughter, Christina Terranova Francisco. She is buried in Prospect View Cemetery, not with her husband in Canajoharie. Her large tombstone is quite visible, located in Section B of the cemetery, which is commonly referred to as the "Italian section." I am assuming that her brother, Carmine, may have assisted with the purchase, as I'm certain her children had very little means.

At this time, Christina conducted a produce stand with her husband, Philip Francisco at the 14 East Main Street location. They now had their first two children - Joseph and Marie.

RAPHAEL "Ralph" TERRANOVA was the oldest child of the eleven siblings. He was born on February 11, 1892 in Baranello and emigrated with his mother and brother, Giovanni in 1899, first making his home in Canajoharie. After a quite lucrative business life, he died in July 1972 in San Antonio TX.

Around 1910-1911, the Beech-Nut Packing Company of Canajoharie formed varsity and junior varsity basketball teams. Ralph was a member of the junior varsity, which was honored to be the Mohawk Valley champions that year. There is a photo of the winning team in the Courier-Standard's "Down Memory Lane" in an issue between 1957-1959.

On June 1, 1911 Raphael Terranova, age 18, married Elizabeth Theresa Chest, age 17, daughter of Carmine Dicei aka Frank Chest and Rosa "Minnie" DiStefano of Canajoharie. Witnesses to the union were both sets of parents, and Ralph's aunt and uncle, Victoria Terranova and Prospero Napoleone. The reception was held at the IOOF building at 10 Bridge Street, St. Johnsville, with the couple spending their honeymoon in a room overhead. They were the parents of two sons - Joseph and Carmine. The 1915 Census shows the family of four living at 27 Mohawk Street, Canajoharie.

Elizabeth Chest died at Little Falls Hospital from pneumonia after having abdominal surgery. She was born in 1894 in Canajoharie. With her death on February 9, 1916 at the age of 22, the two sons were cared for, separately, by the two sets of grandparents. It seems Ralph Terranova abandoned his two sons to further his own ambitions.

In 1915-1916 Ralph was well known in the Central New York area as an All-Star Boxing promoter. He set up bouts in Amsterdam, Albany and locally at the Wagner Opera Hall in Canajoharie and the St. Johnsville Opera House, which hosted such events. He teamed up with his brother, Giovanni aka Red Cap Wilson, for several years as his boxing manager, most likely getting him involved in the sport that was quite popular in that era. I believe Joseph Capece was also among those who participated in the various bouts.

Ralph Terranova became well known as a Contractor and Developer of home sites. His introduction to the construction business commenced as Superintendent of East Creek construction.

In 1938, his dream of a huge residential development came to fruition with the development of *The Terranova's*, a community of 2100 upscale homes in East Hempstead, NY. The homes were built of brick with all the modern amenities of that period. They sold between $4400 and $5500. The Brooklyn Eagle newspaper features him overlooking the project along with a photo of some of the already built homes. At the same time, he was working on a $4-million dollar project in Roslyn Hill NY. He was known as an outstanding residential developer.

Ralph had the distinction of being one of ten contractors to build the 1939-1940 NYS World's Fair in New York City. My grandmother, Edvige Sindici, and Aunt Viola, attended the fair with a group of other Italians from St. Johnsville.

When World War II came along shortly after the World's Fair, Ralph joined the Navy, serving as a Major with the See Bee's in Alaska. The See Bee's were a Construction Battalion formed of skilled construction workers to assist in building naval bases. You can "google" an interesting article about them. He also worked on the construction of the new Alaskan Highway.

By 1952, Ralph had retired from construction development and was the owner-operator of a restaurant-nightclub, The Anchor Room in Quantico, MD. During this time he returned to St. Johnsville for a surprise visit with his dying sister, Christina, and other family members, whom he hadn't seen or been in touch with for almost 20 years.

Sometime during those 20 years, he remarried and had two more sons - Marine Sgt. Ralph, Jr. and Paul. It seems he moved around the country quite often, not keeping in touch with local family members. He was the only sibling in this family that I never met, but I probably now know more about him than any of the other family members ever did.

Joseph Ralph Terranova was the oldest son of Ralph Terranova and Elizabeth Chest, born April 24, 1912 in Canajoharie. After his mother's passing, he was sent to live with his paternal grandmother, Michelina in St. Johnsville. With his grandmother's illness and death, Joe later reunited with his brother, Carmine, who had been cared for by the Chest grandparents in Canajoharie. Joe lived out his life in Canajoharie.

In October 1933, Joseph Terranova married Evelyn Mary Mosher of Sharon Springs. They were the parents of three children - Joel D., Ronald J. and Carol Sue.

On March 21, 1944 Joe enlisted as a private in the US Army in World War II, stationed at Fort Dix. Upon his discharge, he became the proprietor of Joe's Tavern in Canajoharie for 48 years. In March 1969, the tavern suffered fire damages.

Many will recall Joe as the custodian of St. Johnsville High School. Upon his retirement from this job, he was commended with a plaque, extolling his appreciated services. Joe and Evelyn traveled with me on several of my bus trips. As I recall, they especially enjoyed going to Atlantic City.

Carmine Terranova, the second son of Ralph and Elizabeth, was born November 18, 1913 in Canajoharie. He passed away in Gloversville in January 1986.

On January 21, 1938, Carmine married Constance Moyer, daughter of Mr. and Mrs. Fred Moyer, Canajoharie. The couple moved to Gloversville, where they lived out their lives. They were the parents of a daughter, Judith Anna, born March 15, 1940. I don't have any further information regarding Carmine.

GIOVANNI "John" TERRANOVA was also born in Baranello on December 1, 1895, coming to America with his mother, Michelina, and brother, Ralphael, on July 12, 1908. Due to his father, Giuseppe's recent immigration to America in August 1895, the midwife recorded Giovanni's birth. From what I learned this was usually either the father or midwife's responsibility.

Known as "Young Wilson" at the start of his boxing career, John was later known as "Red Cap Wilson" when he became a noted lightweight boxer. His name was derived from the scarlet headgear he wore in the ring for good luck. He began his career on January 1, 1912, until retiring from the sport around 1925. John Terranova was one of the top lightweight contenders of his time.

On July 15, 1915 he fought 10 rounds with Tommy Honch, who was the Champion Lightweight of Connecticut, at the Amsterdam Opera House. If you "google" his name, you can view John's photo with his entire boxing history and statistics. The February 21, 1917 edition of the Canajoharie Courier has a lengthy article extolling his talents and accomplishments in the world of boxing. They also portray him as good looking with a likeable nature, soft-spoken and musically talented. He was the only Italian in the Miller stable of boxers.

October 5, 1917 to January 1918, John served in World War I as a Private in the Army. At the time of his registration, he was living and working for his uncle Carmine at 36 Bridge Street.

August 24, 1918 was the wedding date for Giovanni Terranova and Maria Rozzo, daughter of Felix Rozzo and Nunziatta Massucci of Manhattan. With the marriage, John settled in Manhattan. When not boxing, he worked part-time in his brother-in-law's fish market. The couple resided in an apartment over the business for the remainder of their lives. They had four children - Michelina, John Jr., Anna and Felicia. John's uncle, Carmine Terranova and family drove to New York City from St. Johnsville in his Roadster to attend the wedding.

Sadly, as is told by family members, the many blows he suffered during his boxing career affected his cognitive abilities. He would often be found wandering the streets of Manhattan, sometimes sleeping on a park bench, sometimes found lying in the street, beaten. At age 60, missing for days, he succumbed to his sufferings doing exactly that on February 6, 1966. I attended his funeral in New York City, along with other upstate family members.

Maria Rozzo was born in Campagno, Italy on July 9, 1898 and died in August 1990 at 92 years of age. I knew Aunt Mary and most of the family well, as they spent many summers visiting her husband, John's St. Johnsville relatives. They first stayed with Christina Francisco and later with cousin, Josephine Palma Terricola.

CHRISTINA MICHELINA TERRANOVA was one of the most well known members of this family, as she and her husband, Philip Francisco, were the original proprietors of Francisco's Market. You can read the complete story of the business and much more about Christina in the article, *La Famiglia Mastrofrancesco aka Francisco*.

On October 24, 1920, "in one of the prettiest weddings of the time", as expressed in the news write-up of the event, Christina Terranova was joined in marriage to Filippo Mastrofrancesco. Thus, they began their long business partnership. They had three children - Joseph Proctor, Marie and Michelina, named after her maternal grandmother.

Christina was the first-born sibling in Canajoharie on August 11, 1902. She pretty much became the matriarch of the Terranova family after her parents' death. With the family's move to St. Johnsville, she became employed as a bookkeeper and sales clerk in her uncle Carmine's produce business. Christina later set up several little businesses of her own, before finally purchasing the market building, apartments and large Colonial home adjoining at 27 West Main. She lived out her life in this beautiful home, plagued by her struggle with cancer, which took her life in March 1952, shortly after the emotional family reunion with her brother, Ralph.

CARMELA TERRANOVA was born in Canajoharie on September 14, 1904. On January 14, 1976 she was stricken with a heart attack in the apartment of her brother, Orlando, where she resided, and died at Little Falls Hospital with her children at her side.

Carmela was most at home in her sparse traditional Italian kitchen, where she prepared food, not only for her family, but also the customers who frequented the bar that she and her husband, John Palma, owned - Palmer Grill in St. Johnsville.

She was very close to her family, especially her two sisters, Christina and Virginia, who lived just a short walk away from her - like a triangle. You can read more of Carmela's story in *La Famiglia Palma ~ Terranova*.

NICHOLAS "Nick" TERRANOVA was born in Canajoharie on June 25, 1906. He passed away in March 1983 in Brooklyn, where he lived his life after his marriage.

In January 1924, during his early adult years of age 17, while returning home from work with 20 other men, he was involved in what could have been a life threatening accident near the Bert Klock farm in East Creek. The truck he and a gang of men were riding in overturned after colliding with a larger truck. He was pinned under the truck and later confined to the hospital with a dislocated shoulder. I assume they were working on the construction of the East Creek Dam, where Nick's brother, Ralph, was superintendent. Giuseppe Sindici, my grandfather, also worked there at the time.

Nicholas Terranova married Frances Olivia Herrman and had two daughters - Barbara and Gloria. I have no information of where they met and married. Frances was born in Maryland. When their first daughter, Barbara was born in July 1928, they were living in St. Johnsville at 37 Bridge Street. I'm assuming Gloria was also born here. By 1935 they had moved to Brooklyn, where "Nick" and "Olie" passed away.

ORLANDO "Al" TERRANOVA was born February 11, 1900. He passed away in New York City in April 1985. Orlando remained a bachelor his entire life. He never owned a home, always boarding with others or renting an apartment in New York City. He may have moved to the city along with his brother, Nick. They were very close.

He did move back to St. Johnsville twice after his retirement, once residing in the Peter Barca downstairs apartment on West Main Street, later on Main Street over Lewis Yuchniewicz' TV business until his sister, Carmela died and he moved back to the city. I still have the cutlery set he gave his nephew, John and me as a wedding gift.

BENJAMIN TERRANOVA was born March 15, 1908. He died in August 1985 in Gloversville, where he resided with his wife, Grace, and children.

Like his brother, Giovanni "Red Cap Wilson", Benjamin Terranova aka "Tornado Ben", also became involved in the fete of boxing as a lightweight. Both were small men, short and weighing less than 130 pounds.

Boxing was a popular sport in St. Johnsville in the 1920s - early 1930s. Many bouts were held in the Opera House on Center Street. On August 8, 1928, Tornado Ben and his friend, George Matis, participated in a boxing bout in Little Falls. Ben didn't stay with the sport his entire life as his brother, John did. For some reason, he was suspended from boxing on December 24, 1928.

When Barca's Bakery switched from a horse drawn wagon to a truck for delivering their pizza, home baked Italian bread and other goodies to the local stores, they employed Ben as their driver.

On September 28, 1930 Benjamin Terranova married Grace Miles from Dolgeville at a ceremony held at St. Joseph's Church there. The attendants were Ben's nephew, Joseph Ralph Terranova, of Canajoharie, as best man, and his sister Virginia Terranova, as maid of honor. A wedding dinner was served at the home of the bride's parents before the ceremony, with a reception at the home of Ben's sister, Christina. They had five children - Benjamin, Jr., who died at 4½ months, Donna, Philip, Joseph, and Benjamin.

In 1940 the family was living in Gloversville, with Ben working at a Tannery, where he was employed most of his life. Ben loved to dance, especially jitterbug. Dancing was definitely in the Terranova genes.

BRASSO & ANTHONY TERRANOVA, it seems, were twin boys born in 1908, apparently dying at birth. I'm not able to verify this, except from a Family Tree that I acquired, researched by a Terranova family member. I have determined that the twins, Brasso and Anthony, may have been triplets with Benjamin. Given the dates of their births, it verifies for me. There is no other explanation for the three births in less than a year.

VIRGINIA TERRANOVA was the youngest living sibling. She was born May 10, 1911 in Canajoharie and passed away August 20, 1969 in Little Falls Hospital, another family victim of cancer, which kept her confined to her bed for many months.

Virginia married John Proctor Brandow, who lived in a little home on Mechanic Street, almost in the backyard of her two sisters. The home had been in the Brandow family for many years, John being born there. John had two sons, Proctor John and Bernard. His first wife died giving birth to Bernard. Virginia raised the two boys along with their daughter, Mary Lou.

After her marriage, she never worked outside the home, except to assist her sisters in their businesses, when needed. She would also babysit Carmela's grandchildren, two of which were my children. Carmela's children, Josephine and John, spent most of their holidays with Virginia's family.

ANTHONY TERRANOVA, born in 1912 would have been the youngest child. He died at birth.

To clarify: Michelina Terranova and her children were related to the Doganieri family of Fort Plain and the Palm family of Canajoharie. Brothers, Joseph Terranova, who lived in Canajoharie and Carmine Terranova, who settled in Gloversville were her grandsons. Giuseppe Terranova was personally related to the grandsons only. The other families would have been in-laws.

~ CARMINE TERRANOVA et MARY MAGDELEINE NAPOLEONE ~

From what I have confirmed through my research, and as stated in an old newspaper article, Carmine Terranova was the first Italian immigrant to open a business in St. Johnsville – at 18 years of age. He was a well-respected St. Johnsville citizen and businessman and aided other Italian immigrants in their quest for a better life. He has quite an extensive resume and life story. He was considered a "progressive patriot."

Carmine was a handsome Italian gentleman. A news article I read mentioned that he and his sister, Victoria, were "the handsomest couple in the village."

CARMINE M. TERRANOVA was born in Baranello, Italy on July 15, 1888 to parents Giuseppe Terranova and Virginia Pistilli. He had five siblings – four sisters, Michelina, Emanuela, Vittoria, Angelina, and a brother, Luciano. They were a very close-knit family. Carmine was the uncle of Carmela Terranova Palma and her siblings, their mother being his sister, Michelina.

At the age of 14, Carmine Terranova journeyed to America, alone, on March 30, 1903, from the port of Napoli on board the ship Sardegna, sponsored by a brother-in-law, Vito Palma of Canajoharie. I haven't found out who Vito might be. His name has popped up several times in my research. He seems to be an uncle to my mother-in-law, Carmela Terranova who married John Palma. I don't believe Vito and John Palma are related, as they came from different comunes in Italy.

The ship's manifest claimed Carmine was a shoemaker. For some reason he was "tagged", perhaps due to traveling alone at his young age he had to wear a tag of some sort? The old manifests did not give as much detail as the later ones, which stated who they were traveling to see and where they were bound.

The 1905 Census for Jones Alley, Canajoharie, shows Carmine Terranova was living here as a boarder, working at the sack factory. His sister, Michelina was already living on the same street with her husband and children. Also noted in this Census were Carmine's sister, Emanuella and her husband, Costantino Doganieri, and Tomase Terranova, 18 years, who claimed Vito Palma was his brother-in-law, all living in Jones Alley.

I don't know why, but by 1909, Carmine Terranova had moved to New Jersey, where he married Mary Magdeleine Napoleone. They had three children - Joseph, Virginia and Prosper, all later born in St. Johnsville. Mary was the sister of Prospero Napoleone.

MARY MAGDELEINE NAPOLEONE was born in New York City on July 16, 1895, the daughter of Louis Napoleone and Mary DelBene. She died April 11, 1978 in Los Angeles CA, where her daughter, Virginia, was residing.

I don't believe Mary participated a great deal in her husband's business ventures, staying at home with their three children and later her brother, Prosper's four orphans.

JOSEPH ALFRED TERRANOVA was born January 3, 1911. He died September 6, 1990 in Broward FL. He was married to Mabel Pearl Smith, daughter of Clinton Smith and Minnie Roof of Van Hornesville. They had two children - Joan and James.

VIRGINIA TERRANOVA was born June 14, 1912. She was twice married. Her first husband was Phillip Mascari, her second, Joseph Wilson. She passed away September 11, 1996 in Los Angeles CA.

PROSPER TERRANOVA, who Americanized his last name to Terry, was born February 24, 1916. Attending St. Johnsville Schools, he worked at Remington Arms in Ilion until his World War II enlistment in the Army Air Corps in January of 1942, serving as a Transport Pilot.

While enroute from India to Burma, his plane was shot down. The transports carried supplies from India to China on the Burma Road. On July 12, 1944 he was considered missing-in-action. He had been commissioned as a Captain just two weeks previous. The plane and remains of the entire crew were later recovered and buried together in the Honolulu, Hawaii National Memorial Cemetery of the Pacific. Declared dead on May 23, 1944, he was posthumously awarded the Distinguished Flying T, Air Medal, the awards being presented to his mother, Maria Napoleone Terranova.

Following is a timeline of Carmine Terranova's productive and enterprising life of 49½ years.

While living in Canajoharie, Carmine opened a produce business in St. Johnsville. His sister, Michelina's husband, Giuseppe Terranova, had arrived in 1901, and set up his own business on Main Street, Canajoharie.

In 1903 he helped his cousin, Biaggio Pistilli, open a Shoe Repair business in the Limber block of St. Johnsville, now Midtown Estates, which Pistilli conducted until 1911, before opening his own fruit and vegetable business on East Main Street, where the Esso Staion and Cumberland Farms were located. You can read more about Pistilli in *La Famiglia Pistilli et Fiacco*.

In 1906, at age 18, Carmine and brother, Luciano, began their fruit and vegetable wholesale and retail business in Markell Mansion on the corner of West Main and Center Streets, which later became the 1st National Bank, then Central National Bank. According to his obituary, it was the first Italian grocery store in St. Johnsville.

Carmine's mother, Virginia Pistilli, and two of his siblings, Luciano and Vittoria arrived in February 1907 and lived at 11 Mohawk Street, Canajoharie, where it shows Carmine lived at the time. This information is confirmed through a copy of the ship's manifest. Apparently, he resided in Canajoharie, though doing business in St. Johnsville. This is where it becomes rather confusing!

In July 1909 Carmine disposed of his grocery store in Markell Hall to Antonio Mancini with intentions of moving to New York City to enter into business. I don't find any further records of Antonio Mancini being in the grocery business.

In 1910, Carmine was living in North Bergen, NJ where he opened a grocery store. Then he obviously moved back to St. Johnsville with his wife.

In late September 1910, he purchased the building at 36-38 Bridge Street at the price of $4000, from Timothy Dineen, St. Johnsville Postmaster at the time, who used it as a blacksmith shop. This was close to the railroad bridge, next door to the famous Dempsey Hotel on the corner of Bridge and East Liberty. In later years, 36-38 Bridge Street was known as John Francisco's Bridge Street Grill and home.

1914 – Carmine and his brother-in-law, Prosper Napoleon, of the Democratic commission were sworn in as Notaries.

February 20, 1914, Carmine and his wife, Mary, were the attendants at the wedding of my grandparents, Guiseppe Sindici and Edvige Cacciotti, in the St. Patrick's Roman Catholic Church's newly built parish home.

1915 NYS Census - Carmine and family are living at 36 Bridge Street.

May 31, 1915: His sister, Victoria's husband, Prosper Napoleone, age 27, was killed at his business, the Napoleon Café at 20 East Main Street. Prosper was also an influential member of the Italian community and Democratic Party.

1916 – Peter Palm bought the Terranova business in Shaper block, corner of Church and Mohawk, Canajoharie. This was most likely Michelina and Giuseppe's business. Giuseppe had become quite ill and the family moved to St. Johnsville, where he died three years later.

June 16, 1916, Carmine's sister, Victoria Terranova Napoleone opened a Dry Goods Store at 36 Bridge Street.

In November of 1916 Carmine leased the old First National Bank building on Main Street for storage purposes. The building was later demolished.

September 3, 1917, Victoria, age 24, died of a broken heart. It was said she never recovered from the shock of her beloved husband, Prosper's death.

1917 Phone Listing shows an address of 28 Bridge Street for Carmine. He was one of the first few businesses and residents who had phone service. I believe the address is incorrect, should be 38. World War I records of June 5, 1917 show that Carmine lives at 38 Bridge Street and he had become a naturalized citizen in 1911.

Further research shows that in March 1918, Carmine was collecting rent as the administrator of the P.J. Napoleone Estate. This continued until January 1924, when Carmine apparently sold the property. I did find a foreclosure sale advertised in the *Enterprise & News* for August 14, 1929.

On August 24, 1918, while Carmine and members of his family were on their way home from New York City, where they attended the wedding of his nephew, John "Red Cap Wilson" Terranova to Mary Rozzo, a fire engulfed the three buildings he owned at 36-38 Bridge Street – the C&L Terranova Grocery and his sister Marietta's Dry Goods store. Their residence adjoined both. The barking of their small dog aroused the occupants who were there at the time. The firemen efficiently kept the flames from The Dempsey, a large hotel just a few feet to the north and also the residence of Mrs. Kate Wilson to the south. The family temporarily located to Sanders Street.

To add to the tragic events, while driving home that evening from the wedding in his Roadster, the family came upon an accident blocking the road in Palatine Bridge, which in turn caused a fatal accident, when two Canadian ladies rear-ended Carmine's Roadster, which had slowed down. The Canadians went off the road near the railroad tracks. Tragically, both ladies were killed.

On September 25, 1918 it was advertised the C&L Terranova Company was opening a new store on Sanders Street, opposite the New York Central Terminal. A new brick building was in the process of being built for the grocery and dry goods stores on Bridge Street.

In April 1919, C&L Terranova returned to the Markell Hall building, now the First National Bank, and opened a retail store in the west wing on the first floor, with Wholesale business storage on the second floor. The company imported olive oil and other Italian specialties, distributing them throughout the Mohawk Valley. Pure Olive Oil importation from Italy had been halted due to World War I.

In May 1919 C&L Terranova were appointed as Money Order agents for the American Express Company all over the world.

By January 21, 1920, C&L Terranova were remodeling the Bridge Street property and would occupy a portion as its residence, using the previous store as offices and warehouses for their wholesale business.

The June 1920 Census shows Carmine's family living at 8 Mechanic Street with his brother Luciano, the four adopted children of his sister Victoria, and mother-in-law, Mary Napoleon. They had temporarily moved there from Sanders Street after a fire had destroyed their Bridge Street home and business. By October 1920 they were back in the newly renovated home and business at 36-38 Bridge. His sister, Michelina and children now lived with him.

I believe Luciano Terranova later moved from St. Johnsville to New York City, where he supervised the importing of olive oil and Italian products for the St. Johnsville business.

August 1920: Prosper and Victoria Napoleone's son, Victor, age 9, while riding his bicycle, was abducted by James F. Kelley, a transient, from the home of Carmine on Mechanic Street. The boy was found with Kelley, who had come off a railroad car. Carmine was a stepparent to the four Napoleon children.

1920-1922: Carmine was authorized to sell Steamship tickets. One of his customers was Giuseppe Narducci, a naturalized American citizen, who returned to Italy to get his family. Narducci was Yolanda "Viola" Potenziani's father.

In 1922 Carmine worked with Joseph Reaney and Patrick Ryan on the St. Johnsville War Chest Association. The proceeds were used for the purchase of the Soldiers and Sailors Memorial Park. I don't find where he ever received any credit for his efforts in this cause.

May 1922: Carmine was the Commander of Sons of Italy and member of the Italian Pershing Club, of which Luigi Vallecorsa, brother-in-law of Natalino Iacobucci, was commander.

Records for 1921-1924 list C&L Terranova as owners of the 36-38 Bridge Street property.

September 1922: Carmine and Luciano aka C&L Terranova Company's three land parcels went on the auction block after filing bankruptcy on August 8, 1922. (Parcel #1: 36-38 Bridge St. next to Kate Wilson. Parcel #2: land on north side of Hough. Parcel #3: land on south side of Sanders by NYCRR, next to James Triumpho.)

April 4, 1923 - 1925: Carmine opened a new store on Bridge Street, the Market Basket. He featured produce from local farms.

By 1924, Carmine and family had moved to Brooklyn, where he lived out his short life.

1924 records show that Paul Salvagni is living with his mother, Maria Benedetti Salvagni, and working out of his barbershop at the 36 Bridge Street address, before returning to Italy to bring his family to St. Johnsville.

March of 1926 records report of another fire at the Terranova's grocery store. It claims Christina Francisco, the niece, who was also manager of the store, owned the building

From 1926 to 1928, Carmine's wife, Marietta Napoleane is listed as the owner of the property.

On November 20, 1927 the 2-story Bridge Street building was sold under foreclosure.

The St. Johnsville tax rolls from 1929 to 1934 show a Rocco Perretta from Utica listed as the owner. Perretta had been a retail grocer in 1910 and became a private banker in September 1918. My theory is that the Terranova brothers met him through their respective grocery businesses and the Terranova's later borrowed money from Perretta, which they were unable to repay. Thus, the bankruptcy proceedings and the purchase by Perretta during the foreclosure proceedings.

The 1930 Census records show Carmine and his family living in Brooklyn, where his occupation is that of a Traveler in the Auto Industry.

1935 tax rolls show John Mastrofancisco (Francisco) as the owner of 36-38 Bridge Street.

A 1931 *Enterprise & News* article refers to the Terranova's: *"Markell Mansion, with its colonial front and towering elm tree sheltering it, was pride of the village at one time. Somewhat run down, it was in process of transformation. Dr. Furbeck had occupied it with the west wing occupants of the Terranova brothers, among earliest to operate Italian grocery store. It was considered a prominent business among commercial enterprises in the whole Mohawk Valley, where their trade extended. The brothers conducted an extensive Olive Oil and Italian imports trade."*

Carmine Terranova's enterprising lifetime came to an early demise at age 49 on January 22, 1938 in Brooklyn NY, six months short of his 50th birthday. For most of his life as an active member in St. Johnsville community affairs, he was significantly instrumental in the village's economical development, and was the stimulus for many other Italian immigrants.

Christine Terranova Francisco acquired her business skills while working as the bookkeeper for her uncles' Carmine and Luciano. In future years, she partnered with her husband, Philip Francisco.

~ PROSPERO J. NAPOLEONE et VITTORIA M. TERRANOVA ~

PROSPERO J. NAPOLEONE was born in New Jersey on November 27, 1887, the son of Louis Napoleone and Mary Del Bene. He was the brother of Mary J. Napoleone, wife of Carmine Terranova.

On September 17, 1908, St. Patrick's Roman Catholic Church in St. Johnsville was the setting of what was then called "a pretty wedding" - the contracting parties being Prosper Napoleane, age 21, a resident of New Jersey, and his beautiful bride Victoria Terranova, age 18, of the village of St. Johnsville. She was the daughter of Giuseppe Terranova and Virginia Pistilli and sister of Carmine Terranova. Prosper's sister, Mary Napoleone Terranova, also Carmine's wife, and Costantino Doganiere, Fort Plain, uncle of Victoria, served as witnesses to the union.

The couple initially settled in North Bergen, New Jersey, where Prosper was employed with his father as a bartender. The wedding write up I found claimed he was a thriving young businessman of New York City. I had also heard that he had been a police officer at one time, not in St. Johnsville; perhaps in New Jersey? I am unable to find any documentation of his employment.

The 1910 Census shows Prosper, Victoria and their infant son, Louis, living with his parents, Louis and Mary Napoleone at 110 Boulevard in North Bergen NJ. Louis owns a saloon and Prosper is the bartender. Living next door at 108 Boulevard is Carmine and Mary Terranova with his mother Virginia. Carmine is listed as a Grocer.

Shortly after the 1910 Census, the couple moved to St. Johnsville with their son, Louis Donald, and Prosper's parents, Louis Napoleone and Mary Del Bene. They had three more children - Victor, Mary and Pauline, all born in St. Johnsville.

On June 6, 1911 Prosper and Victoria served as attendants for the wedding of Victoria's nephew, Ralph Terranova and his wife, Elizabeth Chest in Canajoharie.

With the move to St. Johnsville, Prosper became a noted influential member of the Italian community and Democratic Party, also serving as a Notary. In January 1914, he was appointed the agent to sell "Pride of Knickerbocker Bonded Whiskey."

Prosper established the Napoleon Café, an Italian style bar and poolroom with his father, Louis Napoleone, serving as a bartender at 20 East Main Street. He also conducted a fine restaurant in the upstairs area, the Roma Café, where they served Italian and French cuisine.

As far back as I am able to research, Prosper J. Napoleone was the owner of the 20 East Main Street building in St. Johnsville at the time. He had purchased the property on August 29, 1910 from Albert and Gelestia Duesler, who were administrators of the estate of Henry Whyland. Nine years later, on August 14, 1929 a Foreclosure Sale was held to settle Napoleone's estate.

Nine years after his marriage, Prosper Napoleone's funeral would be held at the same church of his wedding, and a local youth from a large Italian family would be found guilty of his murder.

I have heard and read conflicting accounts of the shooting that took place at Napoleon's Café on May 31, 1915. Due to the sensitivity of this tragic event, I will not address the whole incident, only the following details.

The final result of the confrontation that took place at Napoleon's Café was that Prosper J. Napoleone was shot in the abdomen, while trying to break up a fight. He died the following day, June 1, 1915, at the office of Dr. Charles Wagner, where he had been carried. Dr. Wagner conducted his medical practice in the brick octagonal building on the southeast corner of Kingsbury Avenue and Main Street, just a short distance from the Café. The unigue building still stands today, owned by Roy Thomson, architect.

Prospero J. Napoleone's funeral was cited as one of the largest ever held in the village. The procession was led by the St. Johnsville Home Guard brass band, which was followed by the Roma Italian Society of which Napoleone was the honored secretary. They proceeded from East Main Street down Bridge Street, through New Street, to Kingsbury Avenue, thence to East Main Street, passing the home of the deceased. The group continued on to Center Street to St. Patrick's Catholic Church. The numerous floral offerings testified to the high esteem in which Prospero Napoleone was held. Interment was in Prospect View Cemetery. A newspaper accounting expressed that he had a "remarkable capacity for leadership and his influence was always on the side of justice."

On the day of Prosper's funeral, Canajoharie firemen were called to a dwelling occupied by the families of Frank Chest and his son-in-law, Ralph Terranova in Canajoharie. All of the Terranova family, except an older woman, was attending the funeral of Prosper Napoleone. Ralph Terranova was the nephew of Prosper and his wife, Victoria Terranova. The Napoleones had been attendants in Ralph's wedding.

The 1915 Census shows that Victoria and her children are living at the 20 East Main Street location with her four young children and her in-laws, Louis and Maria Napoleone.

On July 17, 1915, letters of administration of the estate were granted to Prosper's wife, Victoria. It also seems his brother-in-law, Carmine Terranova, was involved with the handling of the estate for Victoria, who was the recipient of the contents.

On February 21, 1916, Napoleone's building that he had refurbished into an inviting bar, poolroom, fine restaurant and living quarters burned to the ground. Pieter Baptiste (Battisti) was the occupant at this time. It seems he may have been renting the bar and poolroom from Carmine Terrananova. It suffered a $6000 loss.

A year after her husband's death, Victoria Terranova Napoleone decided to open a Dry Goods Store to offer clothing, fabrics and other sundries not readily available in the Italian community. Her brother, Carmine, assisted her with her enterprise, which was opened on June 16, 1916 in the C&L Terranova building at 36-38 Bridge Street.

The following year, Victoria became quite ill and passed away in September 1917. It was said she died of a broken heart in her vain attempt to cope with her dear husband, Prosper's death.

VITTORIA M. TERRANOVA was born in 1892 in Baranello, Italy. She came to America on February 11, 1907 with her mother, Virginia Pistilli, and her brother, Luciano, to join another brother, Carmine Terranova.

After Victoria's passing, her brother, Carmine, and sister-in-law, Mary Napoleone Terranova adopted and raised her four children as their own.

In 1920 Carmine Terranova and his family, along with his brother Luciano, his sister Victoria's four children and his mother-in-law, Mary Del Bene Napoleone, now a widow, were living at 8 Mechanic Street due to repairs being made to the 36 Bridge Street property, which had been consumed by fire in August 1918. Victoria had passed away in September 1917, and her father-in-law, Louis Napoleone, had passed away sometime the same year. He was born in May 1860 in Italy.

By 1930 Mary Del Bene Napoleone was living in Brooklyn with Carmine and his family. She was born in November 1862, daughter of Donato Del Bene and Angela Ferrara. I have no date of death.

LOUIS DONALD NAPOLEONE was born December 5, 1909, in New Jersey. He died October 10, 1987 in Suffolk County.

VICTOR C. NAPOLEONE was born February 5, 1911 in St. Johnsville. He died August 13, 1993 in North Bellmore NY. He was married to Louise A. Allmer.

As a youth of nine, Victor was the victim of an attempted kidnapping. While riding his bicycle outside the home of the Carmine Terranova family on Sanders Street, where he was living, one James F. Kelley enticed him to follow him across the railroad tracks to the Barge Canal Terminal. Noting his disappearance, the police were immediately notified. In their search they discovered the young lad hidden in the bushes. Kelley had come off a freight train. He told officials he was from New York City and was looking for work with the New York Central Railroad. He insisted he only wanted to play cards with the boy.

MARY NAPOLEONE was born in St. Johnsville in 1913. She died August 1968 in Philadelphia, PA.

PAULINE MARIETTA NAPOLEONE was born January 16, 1914 in St. Johnsville. She died on July 29, 2001 in Pompano Beach, FL. I recall my mother-in-law, Carmela, speaking of her often. I believe she would visit Carmela when in the St. Johnsville area. They apparently had been very close in their younger years.

~ *La Famiglia BIAGGIO PISTILLI et MARIE FIACCO* ~

Many villagers knew Biaggio Pistilli as "Shoe-make". When arriving on September 18, 1913, with his emigration to America, Biaggio headed to his cousin, Carmine Terranova's home on Bridge Street. The passenger manifest states he is 30 years old, a shoemaker, married and his wife's name is Madalena. Since he later married Marie Fiacco in December 1920 in St. Johnsville, I am assuming he was married in Baronello and his wife may have passed away after he left Baranello.

Through the assistance of his cousin, Carmine, he set up a shoe repair business in the block that once housed Leon Limbers Candy and Soda Fountain, a popular place to stop after attending the movie theater. The property is now Midtown Estates.

A familiar figure, in later years Biaggio was noted for the large fruit and vegetable stand in front of the home he owned on East Main Street, on the property that later became Palma's Esso Service Station, most recently Cumberland Farms. It bordered the Antonio Marocco home and restaurant.

BIAGGIO PISTILLI was born Biase Francesco Pistilli on March 21, 1883 in Baranello, the son of Michele Pistilli and Maria Taburro. His father and Carmine's mother, Virginia Pistilli, were siblings.

The June 1920 Census shows him residing with his aunt, Michelina Terranova, at 22 Monroe Street and the owner of a shoe repair business.

MARIE FIACCO immigrated December 15, 1920 from Torrice. One month after her arrival, she married Biaggio at the age of 18. Justice of the Peace Martin Walrath married them on January 22, 1921. This is most unusual for Italians, as a priest usually marries them. Marie's brother, John Fiacco and Giuseppe Assalti were witnesses. This is also unusual with both being male. Marie was living on South Division Street. I wonder if her brother, John Fiacco prearranged the marriage?

Among others in the village, in March 1922, Biaggio was cited and pled guilty for dispensing liquid refreshments from his rear apartment. This was at the commencement of Prohibition and law enforcement was cracking down hard at that time.

By 1925 the couple was residing at 37B East Main Street with two children, Joseph, 4 years and Arduyne, two. He was proprietor of a fruit store. The 1928 St. Johnsville Directory shows Marie having a fruit and vegetable business at 4 West Main Street. Perhaps the business was in her name? The 1930 Census shows them at 32 East Main; he owns the home valued at $2800. There is no record of any living children.

In and out of the hospital, it seems Marie was sickly most of her life. Five of the six children she birthed were either still born or died really young. They were buried in Prospect View Cemetery. I don't find Joseph and Arduyne on the list of Pistilli burials. She also may have had more children.

In 1934, a baby was found at the village dumpsite. The police were notified. Knowing that a child had recently been born to the Pistilli's, they questioned Biaggio. He told them his child had died, but had been at their home in a shoebox for two weeks. They were immediately ordered to bury the baby. Apparently they had no funds for burial at the time, being burdened with hospital bills for Marie. The investigation of the discovery of the other baby continued.

On March 5, 1922, Marie birthed a healthy baby boy, Edwin Rocco, who lived a long life. On June 17, 1926, she had a little girl who, sadly, also died at birth.

In 1940, the couple is shown living at 33 East Main, this is an error, should be 32. Biaggio claimed he was a shoemaker again. His 1942 World War II registration form states he is unemployed.

"Shoe-make" had a pet crow, which he had tamed. The crow accompanied his son, Edwin, to work at Palatine Dye every day, returning home to entertain the neighbors. One day it was found dead on Bridge Street with its mate next to her, crying his eyes out. Was it murder or an accident?

Marie Fiacco was born in 1902 in Torrice. She died on May 8, 1941 at St. Mary's Hospital in Amsterdam. She was the daughter of Arcangelo John Fiacco and Luisa Steppi. Besides her brother, John, in St. Johnsville, she had another brother, Joseph, in Italy and a sister, Mary, in Binghamton.

Around 5:30 pm on October 17, 1950, Biaggio Pistilli was stricken and dropped to the ground in front of his fruit stand. Some of the men in the area brought him inside his home and ran for Dr. Adler, who pronounced him dead.

The story does not end there. On April 12, 1952 a public auction was held to sell the home and business. There remained an unpaid mortgage of $1,000. John Palma, Sr., my father-in-law, was the executor of the Pistilli estate. I'm assuming there were no bids, as he acquired the property. I don't know all of the details.

Contracting with the Standard Oil Company aka Esso, John Palma had a service station built, which he deeded to his son, John "Buttsy" Palma. Biaggio Pistilli and Carmela Palma were first cousins.

EDWIN ROCC0 PISTILLI was another exceptional Italian young man who went on to greater heights. I'm sure his parents would have been so proud of all his accomplishments. Many years of his life were dedicated to his country with his serving in the US Army.

A 1940 graduate of St. Johnsville High School, he was on the Honor Roll and awarded the Best School Citizen Award at graduation. This award always went to a graduating senior, both boy and girl. Edwin created the Thanksgiving cover artwork for the St. Johnsville High School Spectator of November 1936, which sold for five cents. He was also musically talented.

In September 1941, Edwin helped form the St. Johnsville Drum Corps, where he served as the manager and head drummer. Others in the corps were Carlo Polidori, Nicholas Carroll, Fred Lagerman, and Mario Iacobucci on drums; Joe Barca, Genero Croce, bass drums; Jack Mac Gregor, cymbals; and buglers, John Nirri, Joe Croce, Rich Mancini and James Howe. The new corps worked with the Defense Unit and American Legion. Take note that all but two of them were Italians.

Pfc. Edwin Rocco Pistilli enlisted in World War II on October 27, 1942 and was honorably discharged November 26, 1945, arriving back in the United States on Thanksgiving Day. He did quite a tour of duty, being stationed in Africa, Sicily, Sardonia, as well as 16 months in Italy. In his spare time he was able to play in an orchestra, most likely Army.

As an intelligence specialist, Pistilli was given the Good Conduct Medal, the Combat Infantry Badge, the Battalion Decoration for Meritorious Service and three Battle Stars for service with his 88th Division in Italy.

During the time Edwin was in service, Palatine Dye employees were feting my uncle, William Perry, at a going away party for his enlistment in the service. Edwin thoughtfully made arrangements to have a lovely bouquet of flowers presented to Uncle Bill's wife, Katherine.

Edwin returned home from service to join the St. Johnsville Band, directed by James Pietrocini in the summer of July 1946, when they performed their first concert of the season on the Methodist Church lawn. The *Enterprise & News* published a group photo of this band in the July 11, 1946 edition. All of the names of members are listed with 18 of the 25 members being Italians.

He later went on to attend the Jacksonville FL College of Music and was employed as a musician in Jacksonville.

Once again, he volunteered to protect his country. As a veteran of the Korean War on December 8, 1957, Corporal Edwin Pistilli was again honored for his service to his country. He was one of seven infantrymen decorated for outstanding performance of duty in a ceremonial review by the Headquarters Commandment Troops at Fort Jackson SC. He received the Bronze Star from Brigadier General Charles L. Dasher, Jr., assistant to the 8th Division Commander. He also served as a CID agent (Criminal Investigator) for the Department of Defense.

After 25 years, he retired as a security manager for *Fieldcrest Mills* and *Wackenhut*, along with being a licensed private investigator and security consultant. He worked with "Crimestoppers" and law enforcement.

Edwin Rocco Pistilli passed away at age 72 on November 8, 1994 in Eden NC after an extraordinary life of service to his country and enjoyment of his musical interests. His wife, Mildred Citty and three daughters - Marie, Tina and Patti survived him.

~ *La Famiglia FIACCO* ~

~ GIOVANNI FIACCO et MARY MASSARI ~

GIOVANNI "John" FIACCO arrived in America in 1913, and from records I've found, came directly to St. Johnsville. He worked most of his life with construction, which often took him away from home.

On January 14, 1917, John was working in a Paper Mill in Mechanicville. This was the date of his marriage to Mary Massari of St. Johnsville, who was working as a housekeeper, both living at the same address, where Mary may have joined him for their marriage. They were married by a Roman Catholic priest in Saratoga Springs with Sante Fiacco and Giuseppa DeSanctis as witnesses.

June 5, 1917 World War I registration records show John working on the West Shore Railroad, indicating they may have moved back to St. Johnsville after their marriage.

Sante Fiacco arrived in April 1905 to Mechanicville; his wife was Annunziato. I found him eventually living in Renssalaer, where I do know there were many other Fiacco families. I also discovered Enrico and Joseph, who were brothers of Sante, both arriving in Mechanicville in May 1920. Their parents were Luigi and Concetta Fiacco.

I know of an Angelo living in Renssalear, who was also a good friend of my grandfather, Giuseppe Sindici. Angelo would always visit him whenever he came to St. Johnsville. He was somehow related to the CJ Terricola family through his wife.

Many Fiacco's lived in the St. Johnsville and Albany area. The 1915 NYS census shows a Joseph Fiacco as a boarder with Carmine Peruzzi in Canajoharie. Umberto Fiacco lived in St. Johnsville, when he was inducted into the military during World War I on May 25, 1918. He was born in Torrice in January 1896. Immigrating on December 1920, Arcangelo Fiacco, age 17 arrived in Mechanicville from Torrice. His father was Pietro, brother Arduino. Surely, all of these Fiacco's were cousins?

My cousin, Dan Matis tells me that my grandfather Sindici referred to John as his cousin. My grandfather did state in his ship manifest that "cousin Fiacco" was sponsoring him. And, he also called John his cousin in conversations, but I have been unable to find any confirmation. I need to research this further. Many Italians considered their *amici* "friends" cousins. Ironically, Grampa's father, Francesco Sindici, remarried a very young woman from the same town of Torrice, whose name was Anna Fiacco.

John had a sister, Maria, who was married to Biaggio Pistilli. They lived on Main Street, where Biaggio conducted a fruit and vegetable stand, until the day he dropped dead in front of his business. You'll find more about this couple in *La Famiglia Pistilli*.

The 1920 Census shows John and Mary were living in St. Johnsville at 28 Sanders Street with their first two daughters - Fedora and Laura. Unless the house number is incorrect, they were boarding with the Rapacz family, who were still residing there? However, from information I have obtained from family, it was more likely Mechanic Street on the corner of Sanders. John and Mary were both working in a knitting mill. At the time, many of the Italians were employed at the Union Knitting Mill on upper North Division Street near Thumb Road or the Reaney Mill on New Street.

The 1925 NYS Census shows the family living at 31½ Mechanic Street, part of the Cesare Guarnacci home. Fedora was 7, Laura 6 and Marguerite "Peggy", 4 years old.

1930 found the family renting next door at 29 Mechanic Street and John had begun his career as a carpenter, working with road construction. By now they had daughter Elnora.

1938 finds John employed in Portland Me. In 1939 John was working on the construction of Post Office buildings and the new Federal building in Albany. They were renting the 12 West Liberty Street home, where the couple, and also, their daughter, Marguerite "Peggy" lived out their lives. They were able to purchase the home in 1944 from Hattie Fox Healey. I seem to remember Hattie living in the larger brick home next door, now Jubar's.

Giovanna "John" Fiacco, son of Giovanni Fiacco and Luigia Steppi, was born January 10, 1894 in Torrice. He passed away at home on October 1, 1972.

MARY MASSARI was the daughter of Anthony Massari and Angelina Sausto of Mindenville. She was the oldest and only child of the eight Massari siblings born in Balvano in 1899, before arriving in America with her mother in 1901. All of Mary's seven siblings were born in Minden - Lillian, Concetta (Helen), Emma, Clara, Agnes, Chester and Ernest.

I recall Mary as a sweet, quiet hard worker, raising her four daughters while John was away most of the time earning a living. By 1940, she was also working in a textile mill operating a machine. Though she had a rather difficult life, she always had a smile on her face.

Mary was a good friend of my grandmother, Edvige Sindici. Her three oldest daughters were great friends with my mother, Rose Sindici and her sisters, Lena and Susie.

During the time of World War II, my family lived down the street from the Fiacco's at the corner of South Division and West Liberty. While the men were away, some of the young Italian lady friends in the neighborhood would enjoy the camaraderie of a relaxing Friday evening. I've always had the fun memory of my cousin, Pauline Matis and I coming home one Saturday morning from babysitting across the street. I babysat Viola Iacobucci Dunton's daughter, Cheryl, while Pauline babysat the two Constantino children. We always stayed overnight. As we walked into the messy kitchen covered with the remnants of their party, I discovered some glasses half-filled with a pretty pink liquid. Being very curious, I tasted the tempting liquid. It was very good! We asked and were told it was sloe gin. We never did admit that we had done a taste test, as we realized it was surely forbidden fruit for us.

Mary Massari passed away December 1, 1985. She raised four beautiful daughters.

FEDORA FIACCO was born September 23, 2017 on Mechanic Street in St. Johnsville. Fedora passed away on November 20, 1975, after a courageous battle with cancer.

In 1941 Fedora, her sister, Peggy, and their friends, Alyce Peruzzi and Mildred George were involved in an accident near their home. They were passengers in an automobile driven by A.L. Palombo, when they were rear-ended by a truck that sent the vehicle skidding up over the curb and sidewalk on Union Street. They all received some minor injuries.

On Christmas Day, December 25, 1946, Fedora was married to Joseph C. Richard of Fitchburg MA, who had recently been honorably discharged from the military. She was attended by Alyce Peruzzi Johnson as maid of honor with her sister, Elnora, as bridesmaid. After a dinner at the Ideal Restaurant on Route 5 east of St. Johnsville, a wedding reception was held at the family home. The couple was the parents of two children - Carol and James.

Carol Richard was married to Richard Pedro, who has passed away. His story is related in *"La Famiglia Pedro"*. "Jamie" may still reside in the family home. He worked for Robert C. Failing Ford for many years.

Joseph C. "James" Richard was born February 21, 1919 in Fitchburg MA and passed away at the St. Johnsville Nursing Home on April 27, 2005. Always known as Jimmy, during his World War II enlistment in the army, there were so many GI "Joes" that the name Jimmy was more recognizable. His parents had named all the boys Joseph and all the girls Mary using middle names for recognition.

Jimmy worked at Univac, then Beech-Nut Life Savers until his retirement in 1981.

Fedora's aunt, Agnes Massari, had been married to Jimmy's brother, Ernest Richard. It seems she had met him through Fedora. I have no further information about Ernest.

LAURA FIACCO was born September 12, 1918. Records show the birth in Fort Plain. It is possible that John and Mary, along with Fedora, moved in with the Massari family in Mindenville for a short while. It was a common occurrence for young families to reside with the parents at one time or another, usually early in their marriage.

In high school, Laura was an honor roll recipient. She married Michael Bryn of Little Falls. They had a daughter, Michelle, while living in Collinsville, Hartford CN. She passed away on June 17, 2008. Michael M Bryn was born in Little Falls on November 27, 1916 and died on January 14, 2010 at the age of 93. They lived in Collinsville over 56 years.

MARGUERITE "Peggy" FIACCO was born in St. Johnsville on September 10, 1920. During the war, she married Pvt. Warren Putman from Nelliston at the St. Patrick's parish home on July 10, 1942, with James La Lone and Rose Carroll as witnesses. They were the parents of four children - Mary Lou, Jon, Lori and Michael.

Better known to all as Peggy, she was always a diligent worker, raising her four children mostly on her own. Living just a few houses up the street, I baby-sat Mary Lou and Jon as babies numerous times. I can still visualize Jon in the playpen. I spent a lot of time at the Fiacco home.

Peggy could be found working in the St. Johnsville School cafeteria for many years, with her weekend nights taken up by her kitchen service at Capece's Restaurant. Her family was very important to her with the tradition of Thursday night spaghetti dinners. Peggy was famous for her lemon drop cookies. She loved to crochet baby blankets and little booties for the new arrivals, not only in her family but also for others.

At 90 years of age, Peggy passed away at the St. Johnsville Nursing Home on April 26, 2011.

ELNORA FIACCO, the youngest of the four sisters, was born in Little Falls Hospital, August 6, 1928. After graduating with the St. Johnsville High School Class of 1946, she went on to attend Mildred Elley Business School in Albany, as did many of the young women graduates of that time. She was very popular in high school.

Elnora's first work experience was with the Margaret Reaney Memorial Library. Upon her move to Broadalbin with her marriage, she worked at the former Broadalbin Bank and then in Accounts Receivable of Amsterdam Print before retiring.

On June 26, 1948, she married Alexander Klymkow, a union that lasted for 67 years. They had six children. Like her sister, Peggy, she carried on the tradition of a family pasta day every Sunday at "Granny's".

Elnora Fiacco was known as a sweet, kind lady. She passed away October 1, 2015 at her home on the 43rd anniversary of her father, John's death.

Elnora had a special flair for fashion. When I was a teenager, my mother purchased some of her lovely outfits for me that she was selling. I especially recall a brown gabardine skirt with a rust colored vest.

~ *La Famiglia MASSARI* ~

~ ANTONIO MASSARI et ANGELINE SAUSTO ~

Antonio "Tony" Massari was one of the first Italian immigrants to arrive in St. Johnsville in 1898. His wife, Angeline "Angela" Sausto came over in 1901 with their first and only child born in Italy, Mary. Antonio and Angeline had been married in 1895 in their hometown, Balvano.

After Angela's arrival they immediately settled in and lived the remainder of their lives in the River Road home in Mindenville, with the Capece family as their neighbors for many years. The Massari daughters became very good friends with the Masi girls, who also lived nearby.

In 1905, Antonio and Angeline were naturalized in Fonda and became American citizens.

By 1910 the couple had three more children - Lillian, Concetta (Helen) and Emma. Tony worked odd jobs. To supplement Antonio's income, they took in boarders - James Petron, Angelo Petron, Tony Rock, Joe Coppesol and Donnie Cobe. I'm not familiar with any of these names. They may have been railroad or highway workers, who moved from one site to the next.

The 1920 Census shows three more children joining their growing family - Clara, Agnes and Chester. This census is not entirely correct as it shows all but Agnes and Chester being born in Italy with the rest of family immigrating together. Although Census records can be very useful when researching, sometimes the Census taker didn't understand the foreign language or just wrote down anything to complete the procedure.

By 1925 Tony was working for New York Central. They had another son, Ernest, and lived near the Dominick Capece family. 1930 shows they were able to purchase the home they had been living in since their arrival. Their three oldest daughters had married and left the family nest.

ANTONIO "Tony" MASSARI was born on February 7, 1872 in Balvano. I find no records of his birth parents. He died on February 23, 1960, at the Canajoharie Nursing Home, two weeks after celebrating his 88th birthday.

ANGELINE "Angela" SAUSTO was the daughter of Pasquale and Theresa Sausto. She was also born in Balvano on April 8, 1876. Angeline died at the home of her daughter, Clara Massari Luft, on November 9, 1954 at 78 years. She had been in ill health for some time.

MARY MASSARI was the oldest daughter of Anthony Massari and Angelina Sausto of Mindenville. She was the only child of the large Massari family of eight siblings, born in Balvano in 1899. Mary was brought to America with her mother in 1901. All of Mary's siblings were born in Minden.

On January 14, 1917, Mary Massari married John Fiacco in Mechanicville. She passed away December 1, 1985. You will read more about Mary and John in *"La Famiglia Fiacco"*.

TERESA MASSARI was the first-born child in America. She was born in St. Johnsville on June 8, 1903 and died in 1908 at the age of five. She was buried in St. Mary's Cemetery, Amsterdam.

LILLIAN E. MASSARI was born on February 22, 1905 at the family home on the River Road in Minden.

On Christmas Eve, December 24, 1923, Lillian and Michael Edward Giarrusso, son of Victorio Giarrusso and Philomena Aldi of Little Falls, applied for a marriage license. The wedding took place January 6, 1924, with Father Cunningham officiating and William Lucas and the groom's sister, Stella Giarrusso, serving as witnesses.

The couple lived most of their married life in Little Falls, where their two sons - Harold and George were born. Tragically, Harold was killed when colliding with a car while riding his motor scooter in Caroga Lake on August 8, 1946 at the age of 21. I believe he was a veteran, as I found his name in a Montgomery County list of deceased veterans who were buried in Prospect View Cemetery. He may have returned from service recently.

Michael Giarrusso was born January 11, 1900 in Canajoharie and died October 19, 1986. Michael worked as a security guard at Remington Arms during World War II and later at the H.P. Snyder Bicycle Manufacturing Co. He also had a lot of siblings, one being Fred Giarrusso, Sr. who lived in St. Johnsville for several years.

In 1958 I found that Lillian was living at 42 North Division Street in St. Johnsville.

Lillian moved to Arizona in 1991 to be with her son George. She passed away in November 28, 1995 in St. Joseph's Hospital, Phoenix AZ.

George Giarrusso served as best man for his cousin Fred Giarrusso's marriage to Joan Lenig.

CONCETTA "Helen" M. MASSARI was born January 3, 1907 in Minden and died September 7, 2000 in Delmar.

On June 28, 1927, she and Anthony N. DeAngelis filled out a marriage application to be wed at St. Patrick's Church. It doesn't state exact date of marriage. They both resided in St. Johnsville. Attending the couple were James Sanguine, next-door Roth Street neighbor of Anthony, and Emma Massaro, sister of Helen. Rose Fiacco served as flower girl, most likely one of her sister, Mary's daughters? This could be a misprint in wedding article, as Mary had no daughters with this name. I know of no other Fiacco's in St. Johnsville.

The couple had three children - Dorothy, Richard and Donald. Dorothy DeAngelis Dharni recently passed away on June 5, 2017 in Raleigh NC. She was Valedictorian of the Canajoharie Class of 1947. Richard was a graduate of St. Lawrence University. Donald David graduated from Albany Law School. All of the siblings were excellent students and went on to have professional careers.

A Prudential Insurance Agent most of his life, in 1930 and 1935 Anthony's family was living in Schenectady. They moved to Nelliston by 1940; Anthony continued his insurance practice in Canajoharie, where their three children attended school. While a young man, Anthony had been the proprietor of a grocery store.

Anthony was born in Maenza, Italy, June 6, 1901, the son of Lewis DeAngelis and Olympia Nardacci; and the brother of Rose DeAngelis Colorito. He died June 7, 1980 at the Albany Medical Center, one day after his 79th birthday.

You will find more information about the DeAngelis family in *La Famiglai DeAngelis*.

EMMA MAGDALENA MASSARI was born February 12, 1909. She passed away December 6, 1997 with burial in the Fort Plain Cemetery next to her husband.

On April 22, 1930, Emma Magdalena Massari and George Henry Beck of Fort Plain were married in St. Patrick's Church. Emma's sister, Clara, served as maid of honor, Edward DeLuis of Little Falls as best man. They had three daughters - Gloria Jane, Marlene Ann and Myrna; also an infant who died at birth in 1935.

Although the news article of their marriage states they would reside in Fort Plain, I found them living in Minden in 1935 and 1940. (Note: Minden is considered Fort Plain.) I know they later moved back to the village of Fort Plain, where the girls attended the Fort Plain schools. Gloria was Salutatorian of the Class of 1948. It seems only Myrna had married.

Emma was a member of the St. Johnsville Senior Saints and loved to travel together with her sister, Agnes, on my motorcoach day trips. They were very close and watched out for each other.

George Henry Beck was born June 17, 1908 in Fort Plain; he passed away October 22, 1975 in Little Falls Hospital.

CLARA W. MASSARI was born January 26, 1912 in Minden, where she attended the Mindenville Country School. She died October 28, 2011 at the St. Johnsville Nursing Home.

On May 9, 1936, Clara W. Massari was joined in holy wedlock with Raymond Leland Luft of Minden. Clara's brother Chester Massari and her cousin, Fedora Fiacco Richard served as attendants. They had three children - Janet, Ronald and James.

Clara was a member of the Altar Rosary Society and life member of the Fort Plain American Legion Post Auxiliary. She had worked at the P&K Dress Shop in Little Falls for many years.

Raymond Leland Luft was born April 17, 1915. As the clock struck midnight, he passed away at 90 years of age, on what would have been the couple's 70th wedding anniversary, May 9, 2005. It was a very difficult day for Clara. As the day progressed, endless bouquets of flowers were delivered wishing them a Happy 70th Anniversary.

AGNES R. MASSARI lived most of her adult life in the village of St. Johnsville, near her sister, Mary Fiacco. She was born August 9, 1911 in Minden.

In March of 1936, Agnes was released from the Ray Brook Sanitarium at Saranac Lake in the Adirondack Mountains, where she apparently had been treated for Tuberculosis, which was quite prevalent at the time.

Agnes R. Massari was married twice, the first time on April 8, 1938, to Carlton Boslet of Nelliston, where she lived the first few years of her marriage. They had a son, Charles. It's rather confusing to determine any information on his family, as there were so many with the names Carlton and Charles.

After the passing of Boslet, Agnes married Ernest J. Richard, the brother of Joseph "James" Richard, her cousin, Fedora Fiacco's husband. They had a son, David.

A very pretty woman in her early years, Agnes Massari passed away at 95 years on the day after Christmas, December 26, 2015 and is buried in Prospect View Cemetery. She was the last surviving child of Antonio and Angeline Massari.

CHESTER ANTONIO MASSARI aka Chet was the first son born to the Massari's. Born April 4, 1917 at the family homestead in Mindenville, he passed away at Ellis Hospital, Schenectady on June 2, 2011.

On August 5, 1939, Chester Massari and Ida DiGiorgio were united in marriage in Schenectady. The 1940 Census shows Chet and Ida living at 30 East Liberty Street after their marriage, near his sister, Mary Fiacco. The couple lived most of their married lives in the South St. Johnsville area.

They had two sons - Chester, Jr. and David, who both graduated with honors from Fort Plain High School. Chester, Jr. attended Renssalear Polytechnic Institute in Troy and went on to active duty as a 2nd Lieutenant with the U.S. Air Force for three to five years.

Chet was drafted in the Army during World War II. Upon his discharge he worked for Remington Arms in Ilion for 35 years, retiring in 1978.

Chet was quite the craftsman, building his home on State Highway 5S near St. Johnsville. He loved gardening, hunting and fishing. Chet was also a gourmet cook and wine connoisseur.

Ida T. DiGiorgio was born on February 26, 1919, daughter of Ralph and Rosena DiGiorgio, in Schenectady and passed away at St. Elizabeth Hospital, Utica on February 1, 2000. She worked for 20 years with Nelson Laundry, retiring in 1978.

ERNEST J. MASSARI was the youngest of the eight siblings. He dedicated most of his early adulthood in service to his country. After graduating from St. Johnsville High School in 1938, he attended Fort Monroe Preparatory School, Newport News VA, where he received an appointment to the West Point Military Academy in 1942. I believe he was the first St. Johnsville Italian resident appointed to West Point, which was quite an achievement.

On May 24, 1945, Ernest graduated from West Point and was inducted into the Army for overseas service from December 1945 to January 1946. He served as a 1st Lieutenant in the 17th Infantry Regiment with duty in the Far East Command. Ernest was awarded the American Campaign Medal, the Asiatic Pacific Campaign Medal and the World War II Victory Medal.

Upon his honorable discharge, Ernest was employed at Wall Street in New York City until his retirement in November 1984. Ernest J. Massari was born February 16, 1920. He died at the age of 94 on January 16, 2015 at the Folts Home, Herkimer. I find no record of a marriage or children.

~ *La Famiglia MASTROFRANCESCO aka FRANCISCO* ~

While searching for information with the Francisco family, I discovered an interesting historical article in the St. Johnsville *Enterprise & News* that took up at least two full pages on two different dates – July 13, 1937 and August 2, 1938. The title was *"Franciscos in America"*, focusing mostly on the family in the Mohawk Valley and New York State. It was difficult to read the fine print on my laptop, but would be a great history lesson for the Francisco's to search out. The Reaney Library would most likely have this available in their files or you can find it on fultonhistory.com. Although we all know this name as Italian, it actually originated in France.

In the early 1900s, there were three Mastrofrancesco, aka Francisco families who located and conducted businesses in St. Johnsville. All came from Supino, Italy. Mastrofrancesco was Americanized and shortened to Francisco.

We're all familiar with these businesses - the landmark Francisco's Market on Main Street, the popular Bridge Street Bar and Grill aka "the bucket of blood", and longtime well-known barber Richard Francisco.

As you will discover in your reading, two of these Francisco families have numerous ties to other immigrant Italians of St. Johnsville - Filippo, the grocer and John, the bar owner.

~ FILIPPO MASTROFRANCESCO et CHRISTINA TERRANOVA ~

FILIPPO "Philip" MASTROFRANCESCO aka FRANCISCO, familial brother of Giovanni, arrived in America in 1909 and came to St. Johnsville in 1910. He was born March 7, 1895 in Supino, the second son of Giuseppe Mastrofrancesco and Maria Demesi.

By 1915, he and his older brother, Giovanni, were listed with 19 residents of 12 Spring Street as boarders. Included in the list were Joseph Tolfa, his wife Loretta and son Larry; Rocco and Cataldo Zuccaro; the farmer Peter Battisti, his wife Anna and daughter Rosa; Peter's mother, Rosa Battisti and brother Angelo; Pietro Battisti, Egidio Battisti, Juilio Corji and Jimmy Colonna; also Sam Rose, his wife Almerina Caccioti and daughter, Teresa Mastracco. Philip Francisco was working at a knitting mill.

Philip's 1917 World War I application states he lived at 42 Bridge Street and worked on the railroad. 42 Bridge Street seems to have been the home of Mrs. Kate Wilson, who died in December 1929. She lived next door to 36-38 Bridge, occupied by the Carmine Terranova family and later John Francisco.

At various times Phil was employed with the Reaney Knitting Mill, Taylor's Mill, Little Falls Felt Shoe, New York Central Railroad for three years, and construction companies in different areas of the country.

October 24, 1920, Filippo Mastrofrancisco was united in marriage with Christina Terranova, age 18, daughter of Giuseppe Terranova and Michelina Terranova. The ceremony took place at St. Patrick's Church. Her cousin, Carmela Palm and her future husband, Giuseppe Ianniello of Canajoharie served as witnesses. The newspaper account states, "It was one of the prettiest weddings of the time."

I will leave you to read the following October 27, 1920 *Enterprise & News* article describing in vivid detail this special occasion, some of which seems to contradict my research of documents. However, it also indicates some new data I had not been aware of.

POPULAR BUSINESS WOMAN WEDDED
Miss Christina M. Terranova and Philip Francesco were married Sunday at St. Patrick's Church

"To acquire a husband and nice going business, all on the same day, are an uncommon circumstance, but that is exactly what happened to Miss Christina Michelina Terranova, who on Sunday became the bride of Philip Francesco and proprietor of an extensive retail grocery business on Main Street, which she so competently managed for two years. Miss Terranova has been engaged in business for the past six years and during that time steadily advanced from junior, as well as juvenile clerkship, up to general manager and new

owner. The transaction was completed just in time to make the business transfer assume proportions of a wedding gift, for in matters of devotion to business she was deserving of preferment.

The wedding of the young people was attractively arranged and every detail in keeping with the spirit of the occasion. Miss Terranova was married from the beauty of the new home of her uncle and aunt, Mr. and Mrs. Carmine Terranova with whom she has resided since living here. The bridal procession formed and made its way to St. Patrick's Church, where the ceremony was performed by Rev. John J. Finn, resident pastor. The supporting couple was Miss Carmela Palm, daughter of Peter Palm, president of the boys' band and Joseph Aielle, also of Canajoharie.

After the ceremony, the company formed and marched to Cleary Hall, Main Street, where the reception was held from 12 to 9. Here it was that the first surprise gift was tendered in the form of the Canajoharie Boys' Band, brought here by her uncle Peter Palm of Canajoharie, president and treasurer of the musical organization. The juvenile band contained no less than 10 cousins of the bride, under tutelage of Instructor Venitozzi, who mastered many different selections. It was surprising to know that six months ago these just ordinary boys had no dream of musical accomplishments. At the hall, music was furnished by the Mentis Orchestra, interspersed with selections from the Boys' Band. They opened with the singing and playing of "America."

Visualize the entire bridal party walking from the end of Bridge St. near the old bridge, west on Main and up Center Street to the church. Then, from the church back to East Main Street to the reception venue at Cleary Hall, being led by a musical band of young boys. Italians surely knew how to put on a performance of celebration.

"In the evening, Mr. and Mrs. Carmine Terranova, Mr. and Mrs. Ralph Terranova and Orlando Terranova accompanied the bride and groom to Utica, where a wedding supper was tendered the couple by Ralph and Orlando, the two brothers of the bride. The happy couple were then allowed liberty and immediately left on a honeymoon trip, which will be necessarily brief owing to business engagements at home. After next week they will be at home in a handsome residence on the corner of Washington and Monroe, recently purchased by Orlando Terranova of Detroit for special occupancy of his sister.

Mr. Francesco, the groom, is well known here as an industrious, promising young man and best wishes of this community are extended to this young couple for a happy and prosperous career."

The article also vividly described the bridal and attendant's gowns and floral bouquets. However, some of the details do not seem to be accurate. I'm thinking the reporter was referring to Christina's employment with her uncles' grocery business. News reporters love to embellish.

At the time of their marriage Phil was living at 21 Sanders Street and working as a mill hand. Christina was a merchant, working for her Uncle Carmine Terranova. The 1920 Census shows Christina already living at 21 Monroe with her mother and siblings. It seems her brother, Orlando had purchased the home for his mother and siblings. I believe this home to be the brick house on the right at the foot of the steps leading to the high school.

In 1925 Phil and Christina were living at 14 East Main Street, Cleary Hall aka Joe Cleary's Cigar and Pool Room, the site of their wedding reception. The building had been the site of the original 1st National Bank between 1864 and 1914. Years later this became the site of the American Legion. Christina now was the proprietor of a produce stand with Phil as a salesman. They had their first two children - Joseph Prosper and Marie, Michelina being born later. Also living there was Christina's mother, Michelena and five of her siblings. Perhaps Orlando had sold the Monroe Street property?

1930 finds them living at 117 West Main Street in a home they owned. There were nine residents in the home, including the couple with their three children; sister Carmela, her husband, John Palma, their daughter; and another sister, Virginia Terranova. Phil and John were both highway workers, Christina sold dresses. Their son, Joseph Francisco later sold the home to Dominick and Viola Peruzzi.

In 1933 the couple was living at 27 East Liberty Street, later the home of Dominick and Mary Papa. The 1940 census shows them still living here with Phil working in the Felt Shoe, Christina in an underwear factory and son, Joe working in a grocery store, most likely the Acme Market in the old stone building on the corner of East Main and Kingsbury Avenue, where he was employed when he enlisted in the Army.

Believing their son, Joseph would be unemployable due to his severe injuries with his service in the Army, upon his return it was decided they would go back into the grocery and produce business. In late 1943 they purchased the D. Benjamin Youker large turn-of-the-century colonial home with attached store at 27 West Main Street and Mechanic Street that we all have known as Francisco's Market. Records show it was purchased in their son, Joseph's name as his parents had filed bankruptcy in 1935. They did an extensive renovation with the apartments and the store and all lived there for the rest of their lives.

Beginning her work career with employment in her uncles' Carmine and Luciano Terranova's retail and wholesale businesses of produce and olive oil sales, Christina Francisco was able to utilize these skills in her own ventures. In 1918 and at the time of her marriage in 1920, she was the manager of the Terranova Retail Store.

After her marriage, when she decided to venture into business on her own, her first venture was making 7½ dozen cookies to sell. This evolved into adding more items. Being an entrepreneur seemed to be in her genes.

In 1943 the St. Johnsville *Enterprise & News* featured Christina Francisco's recipe for Rice Patties aka Arancini, along with her homemade spaghetti sauce recipe. You'll find the recipes with the Barca Bakery article.

Francisco's Market carried a large array of Italian specialties, fresh cut cold cuts and Barca's Italian bread. Charlie Campione, whose daughter, Anna married Joe, was a big supplier of ripe juicy fresh-off-the-vine tomatoes and other produce from his bountiful gardens in Mindenville. Many residents of St. Johnsville have wonderful memories of stopping at the market after school to pick up a slice of the Barca's Bakery tomato pie aka pizza, or for the purchase of penny candy.

50 years after leaving their hometowns, Phil Francisco and my grandfather, Giuseppe Sindici returned to Italy to visit families in Supino and Torrice, respectively. They returned home to St. Johnsville on May 20, 1960.

Filippo Mastrofrancesco passed away on July 30, 1963, at age 68, suffering multiple injuries from a fatal automobile accident. It was assumed he suffered a heart attack and veered off the road, hitting a tree and power pole near Nelliston.

CHRISTINA MICHELINA TERRANOVA was the daughter of Giuseppe Terranova and Michelina Terranova. She had nine siblings, three of whom passed away as infants.

Her family lived in Canajoharie for several years, where her father, Giuseppe supported them by selling produce. They moved to St. Johnsville when he became ill and passed away. You can read more in the article *La Famiglia Giuseppe et Michelina Terranova*.

Christina Terranova was born August 11, 1902 in Canajoharie and died in March of 1952 at her home after a long fought battle with cancer, shortly after a visit with her brother, Ralph, whom she hadn't seen in years.

JOSEPH PROSPER FRANCISCO born August 28, 1921, spent his entire life in St. Johnsville, other than the two and a half years spent in the military. He was named Joseph after both parents' fathers with his middle name in honor of a cousin, Prospero Napoleone, who was fatally wounded at a young age while trying to break up a fight at his Napoleon Café.

Deeply devoted to his faith, Joseph served as an altar boy for 12 years with St. Patrick's Catholic Church, serving two masses every Sunday besides the daily morning masses. He was selected to be the "master altar boy", instructing and overseeing the others.

Hosting a going away party with other altar boys in attendance, Father Neville gave him resounding praise when he was about to enter military service. Joe later served as a trustee of the church, president of the Holy Name Society and a member of the Knights of Columbus.

Joey graduated from St. Johnsville High in 1939. He began his sales career as the Produce Manager of the Acme Market on East Main Street, which was newly opened. I believe this would be the building known as the "stone building" on Main and Kingsbury Avenue that has since been torn down.

When World War II erupted, Joey enlisted in the US Army, serving from February 4. 1942 to July 28, 1944. While storming Salerno Beach in Italy with his 5th Army troops, Pvt. Joseph Francisco was seriously injured, losing three fingers and receiving numerous shrapnel wounds throughout his body. Brought back to the states, he was a patient in the Halloran General Hospital, Staten Island, which was the largest Army hospital in the world, later closing in the early 1950s. Joey was a recovering patient for many months, before being honorably discharged and allowed to return to his home. After arriving in New York City, he wrote home telling his family, "After eight months I had my first glass of milk, fresh butter, ice cream and a Coca Cola."

Joseph Prosper Francisco received a Purple Heart and became a charter member of the Starr-Colorito VFW Post. He was a recognized 25-year member of the M. J. Edwards American Legion Post.

After his mother, Christina's death, the business continued under the proprietorship of Joe and his father, Phil, with his two sisters assisting whenever able. When his new wife, Ann, joined the family, she prepared many special Italian dishes and cold salads in her kitchen to be sold in the market deli.

Joseph Prosper Francisco married Anna Jane Campione, daughter of Charles Campione and Giovanna "Jennie" Marchese on June 1, 1952. The couple had three children, Philip, who died as a toddler, Christine and Joseph, Jr.

After her husband, Joe's passing on July 28, 1976, Ann and their son, Joey took over the operation of the thriving Francisco's Food Market. After Ann's death, the business was sold to the Licari Corporation as the Little Big M. The home remains with the Francisco heirs.

Anna Jane Campione was born in Frankfort, April 6, 1917. She passed away in Little Falls Hospital on September 7, 2006 at the age of 89. You can read more in *La Famiglia Campione*.

MARIE JOAN FRANCISCO was born February 24, 1924. As an exceptional student, she graduated from St. Johnsville High School and went on to study Nursing at St. Peter's Hospital in Albany, where she worked as a registered nurse for many years.

Marie initiated the school nurses program at St. Catherine of Siena School. She later worked with her husband as office manager at Cotrell and Leonard Inc. They also owned a costume business.

On August 29, 1948, Marie Joan Francisco married Anthony Harden, son of Everett and Mary Julia Harden, Canajoharie. The parents of four children - Patricia, Joseph, Philip and John - they made their home in Albany, where Marie passed away on November 25, 2013.

Anthony J. Harden was born April 22, 1927 and died Christmas Eve, December 24, 2015.

MICHELINA A. FRANCISCO was born May 21, 1926. She was a popular student at St. Johnsville High, participating in various clubs and a member of the cheerleading squad.

After graduation she became engaged to Richard Nalli of Canajoharie, son of Mary Nalli. Apparently, they broke off the engagement, as she later met and married William Pelgrin of Albany, while being employed as a secretary at St. Peter's Hospital. The couple had three children - Christine, Michael and William.

William P. Pelgrin was born February 8, 1920 and passed away at the early age of 54 on June 22, 1974 in Albany NY. A graduate of Siena College, Bill was employed in the banking industry. He was a gracious and kind gentleman.

Francisco's Italian Market

Charlie Campione's Tomato Crop

~ GIOVANNI DeNOVEMBRE FRANCISCO et FILOMENA CACCAVALE ~

GIOVANNI "De Novembre" FRANCISCO, born November 18, 1893 in Supino, was the son of Giuseppe Mastrofrancesco and Maria Demesi. In 1910, he was the first of the three Francisco families to arrive.

It is not clear if his uncle, Lorenzo Mastrofrancesco, adopted him. I was told he was given the name "De Novembre", the month of his birth, to distinguish him from Lorenzo's real son, Giovanni. He was a brother of Filippo Francisco. They had another brother, Victorio, still in Supino.

In the 1910 Census, I found him living in Little Falls as a boarder, working on the Barge Canal. He worked as a fabric cutter with the Luxuray in Fort Plain for several years, then as a leather cutter at the Little Falls Felt Shoe in St. Johnsville, retiring in 1959.

Giovanni Mastrofrancesco lived a long life, passing away on October 25, 1985 at 92 years in the Mohawk Valley General Hospital, Ilion.

FILOMENA CACCAVALE, 17 years old, arrived in Philadelphia, PA on May 6, 1921 from Teano on the way to her aunt Maria Lauro's home on Sanders Street. Maria Lauro was the wife of Antonio Corso. It's unusual for an immigrant, when heading to upstate New York, to not arrive at Ellis Island.

On November 10, 1921 Filomena, daughter of Giuseppe Caccavale and Lucia Lauro, was married to Giovanni Francisco, son of Giuseppe Mastrofrancesco and Maria Demei. Justice of the Peace, Mildred Walrath performed the ceremony, which was witnessed by Evaristo Masi and Filomena's cousin, Rosaria Corso. Her uncle, Antonio Corso, Filomena's guardian, authorized the marriage, as she was only 17. They resided at 13 Sanders Street after their marriage. The couple had one son, Richard. Filomena had a sister, Carmela Gluttone in Supino.

As confirmed by their beautiful wedding portrait, Giovanni and Filomena were later married on February 12, 1922 in a church ceremony.

By 1925, they had made their home at 15 Sanders Street with their son, Richard Joseph. They later moved to 3 Sanders Street, where they resided for the remainder of their lives. Their son, Richard and his family also resided there until moving into their newly built home on Crouse Boulevard on January 4, 1955. It is thought there may have been a second child who died at birth. In researching Prospect View Cemetery records, I discovered a female, Lucia, Filomena's aunt's name, who was buried September 3, 1926. Cemetery records also show a male, Michael Francisco, buried on June 8, 1915, certainly not her child.

Filomena Caccavale was born January 5, 1903 in Teano and died September 1, 1974 in Little Falls Hospital. She was employed at Corso Dress Company.

RICHARD JOSEPH FRANCISCO was born at 15 Sanders Street on April 3, 1923. He graduated in 1942 and was active in high school, played in the school band and was the manager of the high school basketball team. His epitaph in the yearbook states, "a chuckle that cheers anyone who hears." Seems appropriate.

Richard Francisco was drafted into World War II in Utica, serving from January 30, 1943 to September 7, 1945. He served with the Army Air Corps with the 724-bomb squad. After his discharge, records show in 1947 Richard was living at 3 Sanders Street and working at the National Automotive Fibers in Little Falls.

On June 29, 1947, Richard Francisco and Ada Anne Nalli of Fort Plain were married at St. James Catholic Church, Fort Plain. Serving as attendants were Sally Hage, maid of honor, Rose Croce, bridesmaid, Raymond Coco as best man with Richard's cousin, Lawrence Francisco and Rudy Salvagni as ushers. The couple had four children, Richard Joseph, who died May 21, 1948, six days after his birth, Ann Marie, John and Mary Beth.

Although Richard had received a promotion at Little Falls Felt Shoe, on June 2, 1962 he decided to start a new career as a barber on East Main Street in the former Harvey Nellis newsstand. This was the building that once housed Limber's Ice Cream Parlor and Confectionary and the A&P Store, later Herbie Smith's Variety Store. It was torn down and is now the site of the Midtown Estates Senior Housing complex.

Richard moved from that site into the Cap's Cigar Store space across the street, previously occupied by the Snell and Glenar Barber Shop. He later had the opportunity to take over the James Pietrocini Barber Shop. After retiring, his son, Attorney John Francisco, occupied the building with his attorney office. Richard continued to provide his barber skills from his home until the time of his death.

Richard Joseph Francisco passed away March 1, 2006 at Little Falls Hospital and is buried in the Prospect View Cemetery. Ada Nalli Francisco resides in the Palatine Nursing Home at this writing.

* Mary Beth Francisco has contributed to this article. Grazie!

Giovanni di Novembre Francisco et Filomena Caccavalli Wedding

~ GIOVANNI MASTROFRANCESCO (FRANCISCO) et DOMENICA COLETTA ~

Another very familiar Francisco family would be Giovanni "John" Francisco and his wife, Domenica "Mary" Coletta. They were the proprietors of the Bridge Street Bar and Grill, which was located at 36-38 Bridge Street near the New York Central Railroad Bridge. After over 70 years of business services with St. Johnsville and the surrounding towns, the property was purchased and demolished in 1975 due to the construction of the new New York Central Railroad and Mohawk River Bridge. By this time, John had retired and passed away.

A note of interest - when the building was torn down, it had an original oil painting of the Anheiser Busch horses pulling a wagon. It was presented to the business in a contest for having the highest sales of their beers. The current generation of family members would be very interested in knowing who may have purchased the painting?

GIOVANNI "John" MASTROFRANCESCO was born April 5, 1896, son of Lorenzo Mastrofrancesco and Francesca Allessadrini in Supino, Italy. He had four sisters - Maria Rossini, Loretta Mastrofrancesco of Supino, Ines Peroli, mother of Joanne (Ralph) Palombi, and Rosa Iacobucci D'Arcangelis.

As a single man, John arrived in America in 1912, first settling in Little Falls, living with friends and relatives, Vespi and Zuccaro. He worked the night shift for Gilbert Knitting Mills.

On April 5, 1918, his 22nd birthday, while still a resident of Little Falls, he was drafted to serve in World War I. He was a Private with the 310th Ambulance Corps, serving overseas from June 4, 1918 until his discharge May 29, 1919. He served as a medic in France and was in two of the last battles of the war - the Battles of St. Michael and Meuse Argonne.

Giovanni Mastrofancesco was sent out on a mission to a gruesome battle scene to recover injured soldiers. Under gunfire, he returned with four of the six. Another soldier rescued the other two. However, due to John's inability to speak correct English, when asked who had saved them, the other soldier raised his hand and John missed out on a medal. For serving his country he earned his American citizenship and Americanized his name to John Francisco.

On January 26, 1920, John Francisco returned to Italy, where he married Domenica Coletta. He arrived back May 11, 1925 aboard the Conte Verde with his wife and four-year-old daughter, Gilda, the only child born in Supino.

Upon his return to the United States, the family first stopped in St. Johnsville to visit John's sister, Rosa Iacobucci and other friends and relatives. While visiting, Domenica fell in love with the quaint village, saying it reminded her of Supino.

However, they proceeded to Detroit where John worked in the Hudson and Packard Automotive factories for four years. While living there, they had three other children - Lawrence, Palmena and Rocco, all born in Detroit, Michigan.

In 1929 the stock market crashed and John was laid off. While he was waiting to get called back to work, he attended barber school. He purchased a barber chair, put it in the front room of their home and cut hair for ten cents a head. With prospects poor in Detroit in 1930, the family moved to St. Johnsville, where John and Mary remained until John's retirement in Florida after Mary's passing.

Back in St. Johnsville, they rented an upstairs apartment on the corner of Mechanic and Sanders Streets. John set up his barber chair in the front room downstairs and opened for business. He continued his business in this location until purchasing the 36-38 Bridge Street property, where they finally settled.

The Italian history of the 36-38 Bridge Street property dates back to September 1910, when Carmine Terranova purchased the property from Timothy Dineen, St. Johnsville postmaster at the time. Terranova paid $4000 and set up his produce and mercantile business in the downstairs area with living quarters over one section of the building.

In 1935 John Francisco purchased the property for a sum of $1500, including the $1000 mortgage and a $500 down payment, his veteran's bonus for serving in World War I. Paul Salvagni had lived there and conducted his barbershop for a few years in the section that hadn't burned, so John set up his own barbershop and cut hair for 25 cents a head.

I have discovered conflicting information about the ownership of 36-38 Bridge Street from the time Terranova lost it through bankruptcy and the purchase by Francisco. The history of this property is discussed in another article.

When prohibition had ceased, John was approached by Graziano "James" Terricola to rent the vacant side of the building for his Roman Garden Café. After Terricola died in a tragic auto accident, John made some much needed renovations, gave up the barber business, obtained his own liquor license and established the popular Bridge Street Bar and Grill aka the "bucket of blood" in 1937.

John maintained a large grape vineyard in the back of the property, so I assume he made his own homemade wine at times. Many of the Italians including my grandfather brewed their own wines from the fruits of their vines.

A grandson of John told me this story: "One of the Grill's regular customers was John Perfetta. He would take evening walks from his Spring Street home with his wife, Lena and their Springer Spaniel, Ginger. They had purchased her from John Francisco's daughter-in-law, Betty. While Lena would enjoy female conversations and wine with John's wife, Mary, in the comfort of their home, John would sit at the bar with Ginger at his side and order two beers from the tap. The first he would guzzle down, the second he sipped slowly, while visiting with John and the other patrons."

John Francisco was a respected member of the Morris J. Edwards American Legion Post, where he served as an officer. After their meetings, he would invite those in attendance to his restaurant for a home-cooked spaghetti dinner.

Giovanni Mastrofrancisco died July 10, 1970 in Fort Pierce, FL, shortly after his retirement.

DOMENICA "Mary" COLETTA was born in Supino on March 9, 1898 to Rocco Coletta and Luisa Zuccaro. She passed away in St. Johnsville in 1968.

GILDA BUSSONE, born April 13, 1921, was the only child born in Supino. She came to America with both of her parents at the young age of four on May 11, 1925, locating in Detroit, Michigan.

Gilda attended St. Johnsville Schools, worked at the Luxuray in Fort Plain and later at the Corso Dress Factory. She was a member of St. Patrick's Church Rosary Society and St. Johnsville Senior Saints, where she loved to travel with the group. She was a great friend of her neighbor, Yolanda "Viola" Narducci Potenziani.

On May 2, 1943, Gilda was married to Staff Sergeant Frank P. Bussone, Jr., son of Mr. and Mrs. Frank Bussone of Beverly, MA, in St. Patrick's Church. Attending the couple were Grace Croce, maid of honor, her sister, Palmena and friend, Mary Fontana as bridesmaids. Serving as best man was Vincent Bussone with Gennaro Croce and Joseph Peace as ushers. A dinner was served at the Community House with a reception following at the home of the bride's parents on Bridge Street.

Gilda and Frank first resided near the Camp Edward, MA Army Base where Frank was stationed, later settling into their home on East Liberty Street. They had three sons - John, Frank and Richard.

Frank P. Bussone enlisted in the army March 15, 1941. After moving to St. Johnsville, he was employed with the Beech-Nut Packing Company for several years. He was a member of the Morris J. Edwards American Legion Post.

When his father-in-law retired from the Bridge Grill and Restaurant, Frank became the proprietor until the time of his yearlong illness and subsequent death at the Albany Veteran's Hospital on March 11, 1974, at the age of 57. He was born July 6, 1916 in Lynn, MA.

In 2004, accompanied by members of her family, Gilda experienced a life-long dream of returning to her birthplace in Supino and attending the Festa di San Cataldo, stories of which her mother had told her since childhood.

Bishop Cataldo was Irish born. He is celebrated in Supino every May 10th. He invoked protection against epilepsy, paralysis, visual impairment, as well as plagues and droughts. Cataldo's mother, Aclena, while waiting to give birth, had a vision of great light over the rooftops – a sign her child would honor the faith. She died with his birth.

Gilda Francisco, 90 years of age, died on December 2, 2011 at the Loretto Nursing Home in Syracuse with her family at her side. She is buried in Prospect View Cemetery.

PALMENA FRANCISCO was the first child born in Detroit with her parents move from Supino after five years.

She was very active in high school as a member of the Glee Club and serving as a class officer throughout the years. After graduation in 1944, she attended Mildred Elley Business School in Albany. She kept the business records for both her father and husband's businesses.

On Sunday, January 16, 1947, she was married to Albert Leon Dietlin of Little Falls in St. Patrick's Church, the same day as Carlo Polidori and Margaret Cunningham. Albert passed away at the early age of 38 of a sudden heart attack, while conducting business at the Corner Tavern in Little Falls. They had two daughters - Joanne and Claudette.

After retiring in Florida, Palmena married John Edward Slaughter on March 29, 1974. Palmena Francisco was born March 26, 1926 and passed away February 2, 2013 in Raleigh NC.

LAWRENCE RICHARD FRANCISCO was born November 27, 1927 in Detroit and came to St. Johnsville with his family in the early 1930s.

Larry enlisted in the US Army on January 25, 1947, where he served as a Medical Specialist, much like his father, first stationed at Camp Stoneman CA. By July 1947, he was sent to Okinawa, Japan, where he helped prepare casualties for evacuation. While there he played center for the 8th Army Football Chicks.

After his discharge, he married Beatrice "Betty" Love from Little Falls on September 3, 1950 at St. Patrick's Church. They lived in Fincks Basin, Little Falls, where they raised their three sons - Curtis, Glen and Dean.

In 1976 the family moved to Palm Beach Gardens FL. With his retirement Larry and his wife of 60 years moved to Sebring FL. Lawrence Richard Francisco passed away in Sebring FL May 25, 2011.

ROCCO R. "Rocky" FRANCISCO was born on April Fools Day, April 1, 1930. Rocky was quite a unique personality with his winning smile. He graduated four years before me, but I remember him well in high school.

After graduating in June 1949, he enlisted in the Korean War in the US Air Force on January 26, 1950, ready to serve his country. He completed his basic training at Lackland Air Force Base in San Antonio TX. Rocky was later stationed at Hickham AFB in Hawaii, where he met his sweetheart and life's companion, Martha Victor.

Rocco Francisco and Martha Victor were married January 19, 1954 in St. Johnsville. They had six children - Ron, Darlene, Desire, Kevin, John and the youngest, Jon, who died at birth.

Following in the footsteps of his father, John and brother, Larry, Rocky also served in the Air Transportation Squadron with Medical Evacuation, transferring the wounded from the Philippines and Japan to Tripler Army Hospital, Hawaii. In honor of his service, he received many commendation awards - Good Conduct Medal, Korean and United Nations service medals, National Defense, Meritorious Unit Commendation and the Marksman's ribbon.

After his honorable discharge, Rocky and Martha moved from Hawaii back to St. Johnsville. He furthered his education by earning both a bachelor's degree in education and master's degree at Oneonta State College, which commenced his long career as an educator in Ilion for several years. Rocky also taught at two separate Elementary schools in Hawaii, retiring after a very distinguished career of nearly 30 years of teaching.

Rocky was always quite an outdoorsman, enjoying fishing and deer hunting in New York State. While living in Hawaii, he also became a certified scuba diver. He learned to spearfish and managed to catch a barracuda.

Martha Victor was born in Hawaii on April 26, 1933 and passed away before her husband on October 19, 2012.

Rocco R. Francisco died peacefully in his sleep on September 13, 2014. He truly lived his life to the fullest! Like Old Blue Eyes ~ *St. Johnsville Italian Man Did It His Way!"*

* *Curt Francisco and Frank Bussone contributed to this article. Grazie!*

La Famiglia Giovanni Francisco
Giovanni, Domenica Colletta holding
Lawrence, Palmena, Gilda

Bridge Street Grill
36-38 Bridge Street

Supino, Italy

Supino, Italy is a *comune* southeast of Rome, not too far from Patrica. Here is my brief rendering of some interesting tales about Supino, as told by Maria Coletta McLean in her delightful memoirs - *My Father Came From Italy* and *Summers in Supino*.

Storytellers in the village of Supino claim the *comune* got its name over 2,000 years ago when Christ walked the dusty road from Rome to Naples. He was weary and needed rest. Halfway along the route, He paused to look out over a pasture that was covered with clover and buttercups. The late afternoon sun sent a shadow of the Santa Serena Mountain across the valley and into the fragrant meadow where Italian warblers and canaries sang their song. He lay on his back in the soft grass, spreading his arms wide to catch the breeze. Christ slept, later rising and going on His way.

Shepherds came to the field in the early evening to gather their sheep and viewed the imprint of His body impressed into the grasses with two lines intersecting in a giant cross. As He lay supine, His body had extended to the four corners of the valley.

The farmers at the end of the four corners decided to build four churches - one at the base of Santa Serena where He had laid his head; one in the pasture at His feet and one each at the tips of each of His hands near clusters of cherry trees. Christ's imprint lasted much longer than the churches.

At the intersection of the four churches a village was built with two intersecting streets in the shape of a cross, honoring the space Christ had reclined with his face to the heavens. The village was named Supino, the Italian word for supine.

Supino is noted for its yearly festas, especially the first Sunday of May, when they celebrate the *Feast of San Cataldo*, their patron Saint. There is a huge turnout with vendors and participants arriving from all over the outside areas. They are also noted for a festa celebrating the blooming of its fabulous azaleas, which take over the entire village with beautiful fragrant blossoms in various shades of pinks and reds. Everyone participates bringing their own flowering pots to adorn the village streets.

You will find several common names in Supino – Corsi (Corso), Battisti and Tolfa. The Italian name Corsi was derived hundreds of years ago, when the Corsican army making their way to Rome to fight stopped in Supino. They plundered the village, raping the women. Nine months later many babies were born out of wedlock. Not being allowed to give the babies the family names, parents asked the local priest what to do. The priest suggested giving them all a name of their own and he baptized them Corsi for the French island of Corsica in the Mediterranean Sea.

If you have Supinese ancestors, I recommend reading these two delightful memoirs of Supino - its homes, residents, lifestyle and customs vividly portrayed by Maria Coletta McLean.

Wouldn't it be interesting to discover if Maria is related to Domenica "Mary" Coletta, wife of John Francisco, proprietor of Bridge Street Grill?

~ *La Famiglia CAMPIONE* ~

Among the actual farmers who emigrated from Sicily to America were four brothers - Salvatore, Charles, Antonio and Vincenzo Campione, the sons of Vincenzo and Angela Campione of San Giuseppe, Sicily. Passenger manifests have confirmed the father's name as Vincenzo.

It seems Charles came over first on January 4, 1903, and Salvatore arrived on June 11, 1909. Both settled in Frankfort NY. However, I found a January 4, 1903 passenger manifest that shows a Rosario Campione going to join his brother Salvatore in Frankfort. I'm thinking this was Charles, who may have Americanized his name? This is rather confusing considering the dates.

Antonio arrived April 24, 1910 with his new wife, Giovanna Marchese. He also brought Salvatore's wife, Giovanna "Jennie" Tolomeo and two children, Vincenzo and Maria. Their youngest brother, Vincenzo, came on April 24, 1910, but chose to return to Sicily. There was also a sister who moved to the Buffalo area.

The three Campione brothers were the patriarchs and members of a huge very close-knit family. Not only did they all marry wives with the same first name of Giovanna "Jennie", they seem to have also shared the naming of their children going forward into the third and fourth generations. I have found so many first names that are the same. I don't know how they kept them all straight. I've found it difficult! It was an Italian custom, following a definite pattern, to carry on the names of the patriarchs and matriarchs of the family through the generations.

The June 1910 Census records show all three brothers living near each other on farms in German Flatts (Herkimer). Antonio and his Jennie had just arrived. Salvatore, his wife Jenny and three children lived next door. Charles, his wife, Jenny and their son were living in another home with Jennie's father and mother, Giuseppe and Antonia Marchese. There was also their son, Salvadore Marchese and James Campione, a boarder. This was most likely Vincenzo, as he had just arrived.

The brothers were well known as successful dirt farmers in the Mohawk Valley their entire lifetimes. Salvatore remained in Frankfort, Antonio in the Mindenville-Little Falls area and, of course, Charles, who stayed on the same farm in Mindenville for most of his life. I will focus on Charles and Antonio, living most of their lives in St. Johnsville as Italian immigrants.

~ CHARLES T. CAMPIONE et GIOVANNA O. MARCHESE ~

To residents of St. Johnsville, Charles T. "Charlie" Campione is the best known of the brothers. This is the first information I had regarding this couple. Charles T. Campione and his wife, Giovanna O. "Jennie" Marchese, immigrated in 1901 and first settled in Frankfort, purchasing a farm near his older brother, Salvatore, on Williams Road.

With my further search of Ellis Island passenger manifests, I discovered a Giovanna Marchese and her four-year-old son, Vincenzo "James" arriving on August 2, 1912, heading to Ilion to be with her husband, Rosario. I also found Rosario arriving on January 4, 1903 heading to Frankfort. This seems to confirm the couple's voyage and final destination. Rosario may have Americanized his name to Charles? The problem is there is a nine-year difference with their emigration and Vincenzo is only four. I shall leave it to the descendants to decide.

As mentioned earlier, the 1910 Census states the Charles Campione family was living in German Flatts (Herkimer). Sometime between 1920 and 1921, Charlie, his wife and three children decided to move to a farm next door to his brother, Antonio in Mindenville, located across the Mohawk River on the Mindenville-South St. Johnsville Road. I find no records for either family in the 1925 NYS Census. Not unusual; they seemed to have missed many of the Italians that year.

Charlie and Jennie were the parents of six children - James, Lena, Anna, Joseph, Salvatore and Mary. Most of them attended the one-room schoolhouse in Mindenville before transferring to St. Johnsville.

JAMES CAMPIONE aka Vincenzo was born October 15, 1908, in Frankfort NY. He married Rose Finochio; they had two children - Charles and Jennie.

Working with his father, Charlie, as a truck farmer, James passed away at the young age of 32 years on August 27, 1939 in Little Falls Hospital of some type of disease, leaving Rose with two young children to raise. They did reside with James' parents for a while, but it seems Rose may have moved to Frankfort with the children at some time?

As I recall, their son, Charles lived with his grandparents when he attended St. Johnsville High School. He married his St. Johnsville High School sweetheart, Ellen Guhring on October 18, 1952.

LENA CAMPIONE was born November 17, 1914, in Frankfort. On October 26, 1940, she married Frank P. Danna of Elmira. As a Private, he served with the Army Engineers in New Guinea, enlisting September 13, 1943. They had one adopted child, Frank C. Danna.

Lena was like the "welcome wagon" of Francisco's Market, with her always friendly greeting of customers. Residing at Wells House, Johnstown, near the end of her 94 years of life, she passed away on May 2, 2009, the last of the second generation of the Charles T. Campione family.

ANNA JANE CAMPIONE, born in Frankfort, April 6, 1917, married Joseph Prosper Francisco, son of Philip Francisco and Christina Terranova on June 1, 1952. The couple had three children - Philip, who died as a toddler, Christine and Joseph, Jr.

After her husband Joe's passing on July 28, 1976, Ann and their son, Joey took over the operation of the thriving Francisco's Food Market. Ann alone prepared many special Italian dishes and cold salads in her kitchen to be sold in the market deli. She passed away in Little Falls Hospital on September 7, 2006 at the age of 89.

More information about Francisco's Market can be found in *La Famiglia Mastrofrancesco*.

JOSEPH F. CAMPIONE was the first to be born on the Mindenville farm on January 17, 1922. He worked with his father for many years, later becoming self-employed for 43 years as a truck driver.

Joseph Campione married Hazel Young on April 25, 1942. They were the parents of seven children – James, Charles, Joseph, Frederick, Linda, Joanne Lee (Kucharski–Potter), and Sheri Lynn. The latter two daughters died at an early age.

Joanne Lee Kucharski had a son, Robert, who married Sheila Goodbread, daughter of Cynthia Colorito and Carl Goodbread. Cynthia's parents were Joseph Colorito and Josephine Riscica.

SALVATORE "Sam" CAMPIONE was born March 23, 1925, on the Mindenville farm. He married Lena Hall. They were the parents of six children – Peter, Frank, Salvatore, Mary Ann, Diane and Joanne (Bussone).

Sam also had his own farm with a vegetable trucking business. On January 5, 1966, at the young age of 40, Sam experienced what was determined a seizure, while driving along the River Road in Mindenville. He died, leaving his wife to raise the children alone. His wife Lena was notified that he had gone off the road. Upon checking, she found him sitting up with a lit cigarette still in his hand.

Three years after Sam's death, Lena married Albert Dupont, Jr. from Little Falls.

Lena Hall was born May 23, 1928 in St. Johnsville and died March 4, 2013 in Little Falls Hospital.

MARY ANN CAMPIONE was the youngest of the siblings, born May 1, 1933, in Minden. She married Edward Woroby on June 6, 1954. They were the parents of a son, Edward Jr. Mary passed away on September 10, 2004.

From his Mindenville farm, Charlie provided his fresh vegetable products to area stores and individuals for most of his life, right into his late 80s. He took a great deal of pride in his products, especially his luscious red juicy tomatoes. He was the main supplier of produce for his son-in-law Joe Francisco's family grocery store, Francisco's Market, for many years.

Charlie was also known for the Italian "stogie" cigars he always had hanging from his mouth. Perhaps that's why he lived such a long life? I wonder if he also dipped them in rum, like one of the other Italian gentlemen? It seems these were the cheapest cigars available at the time.

Charlie was always plagued with some sort of disaster. In 1930 he had a structure fire, which caused a lot of damage to his barn and its contents. After rebuilding the barn, in 1940 it was again completely destroyed by fire, along with the loss of 19 cows and some equipment, to the cost of over $5,000.00. His son, Joseph had just finished milking and discovered the fire. On July 4, 1946 during a summer storm, which brought huge hailstones and high winds to the area, another new barn was blown down. In April 1950, due to the quick response of the St. Johnsville Firemen, his greenhouse was saved from the ravages of fire. However, it was full of tomato plants, which were destroyed, but he pledged to replant more to keep his numerous customers supplied.

One December evening, he discovered the home of his neighbors, Dominick (Perri) Perry and Domenica "Minnie" Riscica, was on fire. The couple had taken their young son, Frank, to the movies, so no one was at home. Unfortunately, by the time of the discovery and arrival of the St. Johnsville Fire Department, the home had burned to the ground. The Perry's had purchased the farm home about seven years previous from Charlie's brother, Antonio. Perry operated a truck garden there in the summer.

CHARLES T. CAMPIONE was born August 23, 1881 in San Giuseppe, Sicily and died March 1, 1993 at the home of his daughter, Ann Francisco in St. Johnsville. He had recently celebrated his 90th birthday.

GIOVANNA "Jennie" MARCHESE was born about 1891 in San Giuseppe, Sicily. Jennie and Charles were married before coming to America. Although I did find a couple obituary dates for Jennie Campione, it was confusing due to the three wives having the same name.

I found a death date of July 20, 1961 through a memorial notice in the newspaper, which states she is wife of Anthony. However, the information I have about Anthony's wife is much different.

San Giuseppe, Sicilia

The village of San Giuseppe, Sicilia is in the Provence of Palermo. The population of over 8,000 relies on the production of corn, olives and grapes for their livelihood. Every September they hold the *Festa of Grapes and Wine*.

~ ANTONIO J. CAMPIONE et GIOVANINA MARCHESE ~

Antonio Campione first lived on Barringer Road in Ilion where he worked as a laborer, which included the harvesting of ice blocks. After farming in Frankfort for almost ten years, Antonio decided to move to the St. Johnsville area.

On March 25, 1919, Antonio Campione and his wife, Giovanina "Jennie" Marchese, made the purchase of a farm on the Mindenville Road owned for many years by Henry and Addie Fineour, who retired and moved into the village of St. Johnsville. Antonio worked the farm for 10½ years before deciding to sell to Dominick and Minnie Perry in October 1929. The deed shows that the property was sold for $1.00, which seems hard to believe, but times were really tough then with the impending Depression.

Minnie (Ruscica) Perry is a sister of Josephine "Buff" Ruscica Colorito and Lucy Ruscica Fletcher.

After the sale of the farm, the Fineours moved to 16 West Liberty Street. After Mr. Fineour's death, his wife later sold the property to Lillian Mancini Neri and her second husband, Howard Keller. Lillian was a sister of Joseph Mancini, who lived on New Street.

After selling the farm, Antonio and his family moved to the village, purchasing the 10 South Division Street home on the corner of West Liberty, where they lived until 1939. After attending the one-room Mindenville schoolhouse, all of the children completed their education in the St. Johnsville school system.

I had thought Antonio Campione sold the home to my parents in the early 1940s. This was the home where I grew up and lived until my marriage. They had moved to their new farm on Ashe Road between St. Johnsville and Little Falls by then. I checked the entire St. Johnsville 1940 Census and found no record of 10 South Division Street. Perhaps it was vacant at the time? Another point of interest I discovered - around 1915 the property housed the Fisk Laundry.

With some assistance from Fred LaCoppola, the current owner, I have discovered the brick home was built in the 1870s, the original owner being Catherine Bellinger. The latest deed, after Campione, shows Kenneth and Mary Klock deeded the home to my parents, Floyd Perry and Rose Sindici, on September 2, 1947. It apparently was a "rent to own" contract or my parents paid it off by then. We moved there just before World War II.

Noted as belonging to the son James, in March 1933 the large barn/garage at the rear of the property was involved in a fire, consuming a horse, pickup truck, pleasure car, a wagon, some hay and numerous pieces of machinery. The estimated $3000 loss also included about ten thousand berry baskets and crates, which were used in their berry field. Since they didn't own a farm at the time, I'm wondering if perhaps they utilized the spacious side yard on South Division Street and the area behind the garage to grow their berry produce? They must have rebuilt the barn/garage, as it was a 3-stall garage with an expansive upstairs, reached by a wall ladder on the backside, when my parents purchased the property.

It seemed working the land was in his blood, as Antonio gave up his semi-retirement working as a private gardener, and went back into farming in 1939 with the purchase of the Valkenburg farm on Ashe Road off Route 5, between St. Johnsville and Little Falls. Until my recent discovery of this evidence, I had always thought his brother, Charlie, owned this farm.

Antonio worked this farm about 20 years before finally retiring in 1959 and moving into the city of Little Falls, where he lived until his death. Here, he remained very active with his love of the land, raising his own crops.

While still residing in Sicily, in 1906 at age 23, Antonio served in the 54 Reggimento Fanteria at Palerma.

Antonio J. Campione and Giovanina Marchese were married on March 28, 1910 and sailed the Perugia ship from Palerma, Sicily, for America one month later on April 24, 1910. Accompanying them were his brother, Salvatore's wife, Giovanna Talameo and their two children Maria and Vincenzo.

A family member told me that Antonio and Giovanina's marriage was not approved at first, due to her young age, so Antonio actually put a ladder up to the bedroom window of Jennie and they spent the night together. Their marriage was thus approved the next day. Antonio was 27, Jennie 16. On their journey to America, the couple was separated, as was the rule of immigrant travel. Jennie suffered from seasickness, so Antonio would sneak some stale bread to her for relief. Yes, the bread the immigrants were served on these long voyages was always stale. They most likely got the remnants of what was left over from first class passengers' meals.

ANTONIO J. CAMPIONE was born July 8, 1883 and passed away in 1973 at the home of his daughter, Mary Campione Williams, shortly after celebrating his 90th birthday.

GIOVANINA "Jennie" MARCHESE, daughter of Tomaso Marchese and Pietra Pullara, was born May 27, 1894 in San Giuseppe, Sicily. An incredibly resilient lady, she passed away in March 1977 at Little Falls Hospital at 83 years. Have you taken note that Antonio, Charles and their brother, Salvatore, all married women with the same exact first and last names? Jennie and Antonio were the parents of five children - Madelyn, Beatrice, Vincenzo, Mary, and Thomas.

MADELYN "Lena" R. CAMPIONE, born April 9, 1911 in Ilion, married Frank Musella Jr., Dolgeville, on April 8, 1934. Frank was born in Italy in 1908. They had two children - Donald and Mary. Lena died in December of 1988 in Frankfort. Musella was a noted prominent Dolgeville businessman as proprietor of a shoe and repair shop. He suffered a fire with that business. In 1952, he opened another shop on East Main Street, St. Johnsville in the Ollie Kneeskern building.

BEATRICE "Trina" CAMPIONE was born May 7, 1912 in Ilion. I have no date of death. In 1934 she married Anthony Sciortino, who was born in 1910 and died October 30, 1984. They had two children – Joanne Graudons and Marion Guthrie.

VINCENZO "James" CAMPIONE was born August 22, 1914 in Ilion; he died June 29, 1993 in Little Falls. James married Columbia "Cleo" Vespi, daughter of Frank and Elizabeth Vespi, in 1937. Columbia was born March 14, 1916 in Fort Plain and died June 9, 1997 in Mohawk. They had two children – Anthony James and Joanne.

Before his marriage, while living at 10 S. Division Street with his family, James worked with his father, Antonio growing and selling produce to area stores and residents.

MARY ANGELINE CAMPIONE was born September 11, 1916 in Ilion. She married Harry Williams of Dolgeville in 1954. Mary was employed at the Little Falls Dress Company. She passed away February 14, 1991 in Florida. They had no children.

THOMAS ANTHONY CAMPIONE, the youngest and only sibling born in Mindenville was born September 8, 1921. After spending the day picking crops on the farm, his mother, Jennie went into labor. As she was birthing Thomas, the last of their children, the midwife seeing that something might be wrong walked out of the home, leaving Antonio to complete the delivery. Mother and baby turned out fine.

Thomas Campione first married Nancy DeLuisi, daughter of Joseph DeLuisi and Loretta Ciero in 1944. Nancy was born in 1922 in Little Falls, and passed away June 1967 at Little Falls Hospital. The couple had four children – Joanne Lanphier, Loretta Parry, Patricia Wright and Anthony Joseph.

Upon Nancy's death, Thomas married Theresa Burroughs on September 1968. They had a son, Thomas Anthony, Jr.

Thomas, Sr. worked on construction most of his life, serving in the Military in 1943 during World War II. At 89 years of age, he died in Little Falls at the home of his daughter on April 20, 2011. He was buried in the Veteran's Cemetery in Schuylerville, Saratoga County, NY with full military honors.

Thomas Anthony Campione, Jr. has contributed a great deal of information to the Antonio Campione family story. Grazie!

~ *La Famiglia IACOBUCCI ~ PERUZZI* ~

Possibly one of the first Italian families to settle in St. Johnsville was the Iacobucci family. I'm not able to find a positive immigration record for Gaetano Iacobucci, the head of the family. However, I did find a date of March 26, 1896. The old passenger manifests did not give much information that would help determine if you had the correct person.

GAETANO IACOBUCCI was born in Supino, Italy in 1856 and died in St. Johnsville NY on November 11, 1909. His wife, Verginia Perruzzi was also born in Supino in 1853; she died in St. Johnsville on June 15, 1912. They are both buried in Prospect View Cemetery.

    Gaetano Iacobucci and Verginia Perruzzi, daughter of Dominico Perruzzi and Santia Fausta were married in their hometown of Supino on April 15, 1880. They had five children, all born in Supino - Leopoldo, Alberto, Natalino, Torello and Marietta. 1917 City records show that the entire family lived at 20 E. Liberty Street, St. Johnsville.

    On December 4, 1906, Verginia Perruzzi, age 53, immigrated with their daughter, Marietta, 16 years. It seems these are the last of this Iacobucci family to immigrate. It also stated that they were joining the son, Leopoldo. A Gaetano Iacobucci, 18 years, also accompanied them.

    I have located a record of two Iacobucci deaths - a mother, Virginia Iacobucci on August 23, 1913 and her son, Giovanni, three months later on November 23, 1913, both buried in Prospect View. I fail to find any further information on either.

LEOPOLDO IACOBUCCI, the eldest son, was born on October 2, 1881; he died in Troy NY and was buried in the Prospect View Cemetery, St. Johnsville on September 30, 1942.

    On April 27, 1904, at age 23, Leopoldo immigrated from Supino to Palatine Bridge with Lorenzo Iacobucci, Giovanni Iacobucci and Giuseppe Arduini, who stated he was a cousin of Joseph Tolfa. I haven't yet found any relationships with any of these men.

    In my extensive research I've found several claims of immigrants being a cousin of Joseph Tolfa. Sometimes immigrants would mention the name of a friend or someone else's relative. It was necessary that someone be a sponsor for you to enter the United States at Ellis Island. You had to show that either you or someone else could provide for you.

    Leopoldo later moved to St. Johnsville, where at age 29 he married Catallina Cochi, age 20, daughter of Ottavio Cochi and Merinda Veccarelli, in St. Patrick's Catholic Church on February 26, 1911. Carmine and Mary Terranova were the witnesses.

    Carmine Terranova assisted the Italians in many ways. Being one of the very first Italian businessmen in St. Johnsville, he was somewhat of a Godfather to those who followed. You will read much more about him in *La Famiglia Carmine Terranova et Mary Magdelene Napoleone*.

CATELLINA COCHI was born March 1891 in Maenza, Italy. She died in May 1979 in Troy NY. At age 19, she arrived in St. Johnsville on September 1, 1911, with her brother Carlo Cochi, from Maenza, Italy.

    By 1920 they had three children – Elsie, Jeffrey and Ouriposa "Emma" and lived at the 20 East Liberty Street address, along with her brother, Anastasio Cochi. By this time, Leopoldo's parents had passed away and the rest of the siblings were either married or out on their own. Emma was born in 1919 and died December 10, 1924 in St. Johnsville.

    The 1930 Census shows the couple had purchased a home at 10 Kingsbury Avenue, where they lived until moving to Renssalaer NY by 1935. The home has obviously been torn down, as it would have been located at the Kingsbury Avenue entrance to Park Place.

    Leopoldo worked in various positions in factories - a knitting mill, shoe factory and garment factory. Many of the Italians moved to the Troy/Renssalaer area when employment opportunities dwindled in St. Johnsville.

Jeffrey Iacobucci had married Angelina Battisi, daughter of Pietro Battisti, in St. Johnsville before they all moved to Troy. Jeffrey Iacobucci became a Prudential Insurance Agent. They had a son, Jeff. Pietro Battisti was the brother of James Battisti, Romeo's father.

ALBERTO IACOBUCCI aka Tom Boskey was born April 29, 1884. He immigrated to America in 1898 at the age of 14. Alberto died September 9, 1954 in St. Johnsville.

On June 3, 1911, Alberto Iacobucci married Maud Van Allen. He was 27, she 19. Witnesses to the union were Maude and Lincoln Arthur. I found they might have had a child that died at a very young age. There is a gravesite in Prospect View Cemetery for an "Infant Iacobucci", a female who died May 11, 1916.

Maud was the daughter of Jonathan Van Allen and Hattie Clemons. Born June 1, 1892, she died in February 1970 at the Turpin Nursing Home in Gloversville.

The couple lived on Center Street Lane, directly across from Cross Street, next door to the Smullen family home. When Maud passed away the property was sold through her estate to Donald and Cathy Bellen.

Tom Boskey was always available to assist other Italian immigrants as an interpreter. He was active in village activities, serving as a police officer for five years. Along with Frank Colorito, he was sworn in to assist in the impending milk strike of May 1933. Until an illness necessitated his retirement, he was employed at Remington Arms in Ilion.

NATALINO IACOBUCCI, the middle child, was born December 27, 1886 in Supino. After first residing on Liberty Street in 1913, he later lived with his family at the 30 Hough Street home he owned until his passing January 22, 1951 in St. Johnsville.

At age 23, Natalino arrived in the Mohawk Valley on April 3, 1910, first settling in Palatine Bridge NY, where I've found several of the immigrant young men first settled. He probably went there because his brother Leopoldo lived there at the time. He worked in a knitting mill for a time, then later with the New York Central Railroad.

Natalino Iacobucci and his wife, Giuseppina Vallecorso's love story is reminiscent of Romeo and Juliet. They actually met in Patrica, Italy at a celebration that Natalino attended with a friend. It was love at first sight, even though Giuseppina was already spoken for. Like many of the old country Italians, her parents disapproved of their new relationship.

Giuseppina broke off her engagement, left her family, and accompanied by her sister, Concetta, set sail for America to join their brother, Luigi Vallecorso, a barber in Little Falls on June 11, 1910. Unfortunately, Giuseppina's fiancé, Federico had placed a *malocchia* "curse" on the couple when she broke their engagement.

On November 6, 1910, the smitten couple, Natalino and Giuseppina, was married in Little Falls NY with Concetta as a witness. They had two daughters - Viola and Virginia, known as the "doll sisters", as the Vallecorso sisters had also been known in Italy.

GIUSEPPINA VALLECORSO was born in 1889 in Patrica, the daughter of Antonino Vallecorso.

At the age of 26, Giuseppina died six months after giving birth to their second child on January 11, 1915, stricken with a kidney infection that was untreatable at the time.

CONCETTA VALLECORSO, Giuseppina's devoted sister, took over the care of the two daughters and the home. She had moved next door at her brother, Luigi's home, who now lived in St. Johnsville.

Concetta was born in 1887 in Patrica. After leaving Italy she was compelled to adhere to her father's pre-arrangements while she was in America. He committed his daughter to a marriage with Adriano Rotundo, whom she hadn't known. Adriano was an extremely jealous man, who didn't approve of her taking care of her ill sister or the young children.

During the few years of their marriage, Adriano was confined several times in the Albany County Penitentiary due to his abusive assaults on Concetta. Shortly after his release, on Monday noon, July 24, 1916 his jealous rage resulted in the tragic knifing death of Concetta as she stopped on her way home from her employment at Reaney's Knitting Mill on New Street to purchase some groceries at the original Rapacz Meat Market at 28 Sanders Street.

Adriano Rotundo was stealthily waiting by the front door of the market. In front of many other witnesses and their brother-in-law, Natalino Iacobucci, Adriano jumped out, grabbed her by the neck and stabbed her to death. Viola, the traumatized oldest daughter of Natalino, also witnessed the horrific incident.

Adriano then ran off through the streets of St. Johnsville, bloody knife in hand and, unfortunately, after an intensive search of the entire area, wasn't discovered until many weeks later when he appeared back in his hometown in Italy. It seems he had made his way back to the railroad under darkness and eventually returned to Italy, where five years later he was found, charged and hanged for the murder in March of 1921.

After Giuseppina's and Concetta's deaths, both Luigi and Natalino sent correspondence to Ildeconda "Hilda" Montini, a best friend of the two sisters still living in Patrica, informing her of all the recent events and the depression of Natalino. They suggested she come to St. Johnsville to take over the household duties. Residing in a convent due to the recent passing of her fiancé, Bernardo, Hilda was almost ready to take her vows, as she was considered too old for marriage.

Natalino Iacobucci and Ildeconda "Hilda" Montini were married on August 19, 1918. Arriving in America in 1917, Hilda moved into the 30 Hough Street home and raised both of Natalino's daughters as her own.

During those years, when many women died from childbirth, husbands remarried immediately to have someone care for and help raise the children.

ILDECONDA "Hilda" MONTINI lived a long life in the Hough Street home until her passing in January 1975. She was born in Supino on August 31, 1890.

It seems Federico's "curse" haunted Natalino most of his life. First, it was the early death of his beloved Giuseppina, then the witnessing of the horrific murder of her sister, Concetta and, finally, the discovery of his brother-in-law, Antonio Palitti's dead body wedged in the pear tree he had been pruning. It's a wonder he ever survived all these tragedies.

Putting a curse on an enemy, or someone who was felt to have done you wrong, was quite prevalent in Southern Italian culture. Apparently, this created the advent of designing the *cornicello* "little horn" that was worn as protection from *malocchio* "the evil eye". These amulets were quite popular in the Southern Italy area where our Italian ancestors had resided. The women, especially, were very superstitious. The *Benedetta* (blessed one) were gifted with *la forza* (spiritual healing powers) and worked with herbs, plants and other natural elements. If you had grown up in an Italian family you would most likely have been exposed to these traditions.

VIOLA IACOBUCCI was born May 19, 1912 in St. Johnsville. She died October 1, 2009 at the St. Johnsville Nursing Home.

On November 29, 1941, Viola "Boskey" Iacobucci married Stacey "Jerry" Dunton. Their good friends, Lawrence Tolfa and Olga Sackett attended them. They had one daughter, Cheryl Blaydon, who was born October 23, 1943. At this time, they were living on South Division Street.

Before her marriage, Vi worked as a stenographer-clerk for the Montgomery County Welfare office in Fonda. After her marriage she became a hair stylist, this being her craft most of her life. It allowed her to remain at home with her daughter.

I knew Vi my whole life. She was a great friend of my mother's, Rose Sindici Perry. I was also her designated baby sitter for Cheryl. A generous soul, Vi loved to laugh and have fun.

After their marriage, during World War II, I first remember Vi and Jerry living on South Division Street, across from my family homestead. From here they later moved to 20 East Main Street where Jerry conducted a pool and cigar room. Vi set up her hair salon upstairs in their living quarters. After selling the pool hall, they moved further east to their final home at 36 East Main Street around 1952, which had been the Marocco family's St. Johnsville Restaurant serving home cooked Italian cuisine for many years. She continued her hair salon at this site.

Stacey "Jerry" Dunton was a noted businessman in St. Johnsville for most of his life, after serving in the US Army during World War II. His first venture was a variety store in a building next to Cap's Cigar Store. Then, he purchased Cap's, which he operated for several years until opening Jerry's Dinette at 33 East Main Street, now the site of the St. Johnsville Youth Center. Upon his retirement, he sold the business to Peter Ciani in 1967. At this writing, Jerry is still living in a nursing home.

VIRGINIA AGNES IACOBUCCI was born May 30, 1914 in St. Johnsville; she passed away peacefully at the home of her daughter on January 9, 2002 in Troy NY.

A graduate of the class of 1933, "Ginny" went on to graduate Mildred Elley Secretarial School, later taking employment with the U.S. Treasury Department at the Watervliet Arsenal during World War II. She married William S. Sillary in August 1946. They had two children - William Jr. and Natalie.

~ LUIGI VALLECORSO et GENTILINA FOGGIA ~

I have discovered several Vallecorso's, most living in Little Falls in later years. However, Prospect View Cemetery records indicate the burials of Antonino Vallecorso, age 4, on September 7, 1917 and infant Ugo on December 15, 1917. I'm surmising that these may be the sons of Luigi Vallecorso and Gentilina Foggi?.

There are also two Iacobucci infants buried on May 11, 1916 and May 14, 1916, apparently twins, with one-month-old Virginia Iacobucci on August 23, 1913, along with several other Iacobucci family members.

Luigi Vallecorso and his wife, Gentilina Foggia, immigrated together May 31, 1913, coming to St. Johnsville to join his sister, Giuseppina Vallecorso and her husband, Natalino Iacobucci at their home on Liberty Street. This contradicts the previous information of Luigi's two sisters' arrival, unless Luigi had returned to Italy and later came back with his wife.

World War I records of June 5, 1917 show them living at 23 Sanders Street. The family lived in St. Johnsville for several years until finally settling in Little Falls, most likely after the death of both of Luigi's sisters. It also seems the couple had returned to Italy in October 1919 and the early 1920s after the sad events. The timeline is rather confusing. The 1925 Census shows them residing in Little Falls with their two sons - Gino and Anthony.

LUIGI VALLECORSO was born in Patrica on April 4, 1888. He died in Little Falls October of 1966.

GENTILINA FOGGIA was also born in Patrica on June 19, 1888. She died in Little Falls July of 1980.

I recommend the reading of The Memory Keepers by Cheryl Dunton Blaydon, who is the granddaughter of Natalino Iacobucci and Giuseppina Vallecorso. It is a wonderful memoir of her recollections of the history of her family.

~ *Returning to La Famiglia Iacobucci* ~

TORELLO "Toulo" IACOBUCCI arrived in America from Supino at age 16 on June 23, 1905 headed to join his brother, Leopoldo. He apparently later returned to Supino and married Giovanna Porti, as I found her accompanying her husband, Torello Iacobucci to America on February 7, 1911, coming to St. Johnsville. I also discovered another passenger manifest of his arrival on April 19, 1914. Torello and Jennie had two children - Leonina aka Eleanor and Gaetano "Joseph", both born in St. Johnsville.

The 1915 Census shows Torello's family living at 21 Sanders Street, a very popular boarding house for young Italian families and single immigrants.

Torello was born 1890 in Supino, and died at the early age of 26 on March 3, 1917 in St. Johnsville. After Torello's death, Jennie married Celestino Scaccia. Giovanna "Jennie" Porti was born August 25, 1887 in Supino. She died January 1977 in Utica.

Leonina "Eleanor Jane" Iacobucci was born May 26, 1912 in St. Johnsville, daughter of Torello Iacobucci and Jennie Porti. She passed away March 9, 1996 at 83, and is buried in Oak Hill Cemetery, Herkimer.

Eleanor was first married to Michael Massino, a much older man from Coulterville, PA. They had two daughters - Dolores and Michaelina, both born in Coulterville. I knew both daughters well in high school as good friends, attending some fun parties they hosted. Michaelina aka Mickey and I were basketball cheerleaders together.

Eleanor and Michael divorced and she married Andrew "Jumbo" Sands of Nelliston on February 18, 1940 in St. Johnsville. They had two children - Florence and Andrew, Jr.

The 1940 Census of April 18 shows Michael Massino and his two daughters, living at 10 Sanders Street with his wife, Leona. He later moved to Herkimer where he died in 1970.

Andrew Sands, Jr. was born in Nelliston August 5, 1911 and passed away February 1, 1996 in Herkimer; he's buried with Eleanor in Oak Hill Cemetery, Herkimer.

Gaetano "Joseph" Iacobucci was born May 11, 1916 in St. Johnsville, the son of Torello Iacobucci and Jennie Porto. After his father's passing it seems he went by the name Guy Boskey for a short while.

Joseph is mentioned in the Carlo Cochi article, as he is the neighbor customer, who tried to assist Carlo upon his passing in 1940. At this time, he was working on the New York Central Railroad.

He served in World War II from August 28, 1942 until his discharge on December 17, 1945. During this time, he married Florence M. Donatucci of Palatine Bridge in 1944. They had four children.

After raising their children on East Main Street in St. Johnsville, the couple moved to Sharon Springs, where they lived out their lives. Joseph Iacobucci died September 13, 1993. Somehow, his birth years do not compute with the census records.

MARIETTA "Maria" IACOBUCCI, the youngest sibling and only daughter, came to America with her mother, Verginia, arriving December 4, 1906 at age 16. She was born in Supino on March 14, 1892 and lived in St. Johnsville until her passing August 1978.

Mary married Gaetano "Guy" Corso on December 23, 1911 in St. Patrick's Roman Catholic Church in St. Johnsville. Mary's brother, Leopoldo and Guy's sister, Rosa (Corso) Masi served as witnesses. They had four children – Dante, Dario, Guido and Gloria.

You will read more about Mary and Guy Corso in *La Famiglia Corso*.

* *Tom Riley, who recently visited Supino, has contributed information to the Iacobucci family.*

~ *La Famiglia SCACCIA* ~

CELESTINO "Charles" SCACCIA was born in Torrice, Italy, the son of Stefano Scaccia and Magiuseppe Martini. At the age of 19, he first came to America on August 15, 1911 heading to St. Johnsville to join his cousin, Gaetano. I have no last name for his cousin.

There is conflicting information regarding his birth and death dates. His wife, Jennie's obituary states he died in 1961. However, I have discovered an Italian Death Report that could possibly be him. Passenger records show Celestino made at least four trips back and forth to his homeland of Torrice in his later years, spending up to six months at any given time.

Celestino's Social Security and World War I and II records show his birth as the same date as the aforementioned death report. I am concluding that he died in his hometown of Torrice, Italy, on December 16, 1967 and is buried in the Municipal Cemetery of Torrice. This record also shows a Clelia as his wife with two sons, Paolo and Massimo. To prove all of this would take a considerable amount of in-depth research.

GIOVANNA "Jennie" PORTI was born August 25, 1887 in Supino and died January 4, 1977 at a Utica hospital. She was the daughter of Giovanni Porta and Filomena Giammetti.

Employed for many years at the clothing factories in St. Johnsville, during World War II she was employed by National Automotive Fibers of Little Falls, making parachutes.

HERMAN F. "Scottie" SCACCIA was the child of Celestino Scaccia and Giovanna Porti, born December 30, 1920 in St. Johnsville.

Graduating from St. Johnsville High School in the Class of 1939, he was quite an accomplished musician. He performed with James Pietrocini's St. Johnsville Band for several years, later establishing his own band, the "Al Scotty Trio". He provided the music at the Perina Fontana - Dominick DeCamillo and Amelia Palombi - Thomas Logar weddings.

Serving in World War II, Herman entertained Army Troops and formed an Infantry School Band in Fort Benning GA. He had played with the "Sonny" Durham, Ray Keating and Ray King bands. Herman composed a melody, "My Thoughts of You", which was copyrighted.

Herman Scaccia passed away on February 10, 1975 in Duval FL. I find no record of a marriage.

~ *La Famiglia PALITTI* ~

~ ANTONIO PALITTI et MARIA MONTINI ~

ANTONIO PALITTI, the son of Domenico (Dario) Palitti and Domenica Piroli of Italy, was born in 1892. At 22 years of age he first immigrated to Quebec, Canada in May of 1912 and then crossed the border into the United States at Niagara Falls on June 18, 1913. He was naturalized in 1917.

A Veteran of World War I, Antonio entered the service on August 26, 1918. He was a member of a group of 14 enlistees from the area, including Frank Triumpho.

The 1920 Census finds Antonio and his brother, Angelo, living with the Natalino Iacobucci family at 22 East Liberty Street. At this time, Angelo was working in a knitting mill, while the New York Central Railroad employed Antonio.

On July 30, 1921, Antonio Palitti married Maria Montini, sister of Natalino Iacobucci's wife, Hilda. Maria was the daughter of Francesco Montini and Serafina Coretti. Serving as witnesses to the bond were Domenico Iacobucci, a cousin of Natalino's and his wife, Rosa Mastrofrancisco Iacobucci. They had two daughters - Colinda "Clara" and Lena Virginia. I tend to believe this might have been an arranged marriage, Maria being Hilda's sister.

The 1925 Census states that Peter Mastrocco, his wife, Jennie and son, Joseph are sharing the 30 Hough Street 2-family home with Antonio Palitti and his family.

Antonio worked most of his short life on the railroad. At the age of 37, he died on December 2, 1928, as he was pruning the pear tree in the backyard of the 30 Hough Street home, where his family resided upstairs. His brother-in-law, Natalino discovered his body stuck in the tree.

Besides his wife, Maria, he left two young daughters of six and four years old. Natalino was the executor of his estate.

MARIA MONTINI was born in Supino, Italy on September 20, 1902. She arrived in the country in 1920 to live with her sister, Hilda Iacobucci. Maria's family resided in the upstairs apartment at 30 Hough Street their entire lives.

At the age of 62, Mary died on Sunday, May 2, 1966 at Little Falls Hospital. Besides her sister, Hilda, she had another, Ausilia Iocchi in Rome, Italy. Maria Montini and Antonio Palitti are buried in Prospect View Cemetery.

Mary worked in the Little Falls Felt Shoe across from her home. She was a member of the American Legion Auxiliary.

Mary always had a smile with a great sense of humor. I recall sitting in front of her at the St. Johnsville Movie Theater one night. The name of the movie doesn't come to me, but there was a great deal of comedy. She laughed so hard, I was laughing more with her than the movie.

CLARA M. PALITTI, born Colinda, arrived on June 26, 1922 at home. She passed away at the age of 86 on New Year's Eve, December 31, 2008 at Bassett Health Care, Cooperstown.

Clara was employed at the Beech-Nut in Canajoharie most of her life. She had also worked at the Felt Shoe and Luxuray.

Clara had her mother's personality, always making jokes out of a bad situation. She loved to travel with me on my motorcoach trips. Being neighbors, she was a great friend with my mother and aunts - the Sindici girls.

On May 20, 1950 Clara was joined in marriage with Gerald Johnson at St. Patrick's Church. Her friend and childhood neighbor, Philomena Romano Coco was matron of honor, with another close friend, Theresa Papa Dolan as bridesmaid. Her little cousin, Cheryl Dunton was flower girl. Raymond Coco served as best man with Anthony Dolan as an usher. A family dinner was held at the Manor with a large reception at the Central Hotel. The couple had one daughter, Pam and a grandson, Anthony.

Gerald Johnson, brother of Calvin Johnson, who was the husband of Alyce Peruzzi, was born July 27, 1927 in Salisbury. At 41 years, he was stricken with a heart attack on Valentine's Day, February 14, 1969 at the St.

Johnsville Methodist Church, where he was a member and also worked with maintenance. He had arrived at work at 7:30 am and was found on the floor at 3:30 pm by the pastor's son, Durwood Winner.

LENA VIRGINIA PALITTI aka Helen was born on April 23, 1924 and passed away at home on March 19, 2000 at the age of 75. She never married.

Lena worked many years for Harland Devendorf Insurance on West Main in the Beardslee building, where the Failing Ford automobile agency was located.

She was an avid bowler in the Women's Friday Night League, being one of the high scorers. Lena was always very outgoing, but unfortunately, upon her retirement, she became somewhat of a recluse.

ARCANGELO "Angelo" PALITTI was born in 1884. He came to America on July 14, 1906 before his brother, Antonio Palitti, looking for his friend, Antonio Peruzzi. In 1910-1912 he was living in Little Falls and working on the Barge Canal.

1915 finds Angelo boarding at 44 Hough Street with the Carmine Peruzzi family and working at the Gem Knitting Mill. After his brother, Antonio's arrival, they both boarded with the Natalino Iacobucci family on East Liberty Street.

By 1930 and 1940, until his death, he was a boarder at 14 South Division Street with the Amy Castrucci family, now working on the New York Central Railroad. The Census records now state his name as Charles Politilo. The Castrucci's had opened a grocery store at this location. They lived upstairs and, I believe, Angelo had a small apartment downstairs behind the store. I don't find that he ever married.

Living across the street from the store, I remember Angelo as "Charlie Chooch", hanging around or working in the store with his smelly "stogies". I never liked to go there when he was working. I was told he soaked them in rum. Perhaps that was his secret elixir to longevity? Arcangelo Palitti died in October 1982 at 98 years of age.

Angelo was one of the members of the Home Guard Band.

The Palitti's had family in Johnstown that they visited quite often - Alfred Alfini, his wife, Victoria and children, Theresa Ann, Marilyn and Alfred, Jr. I haven't found any additional information on this family, so I don't know the relationship.

~ *La Famiglia ANTONIO IACOBUCCI et MARIA SCHIRIO* ~

I haven't discovered any direct connection with this family and the previous Iacobucci families. It's my belief they may be cousins. Henry Iacobucci was a nephew of Antonio Iacobucci.

Antonio Iacobucci and Maria Schirio arrived in America in 1910 from Supino, Italy, settling in St. Johnsville, where they purchased a family home at 3 Hough Street and resided until their deaths. They had a son – Dominick, who was born in Supino, Italy.

ANTONIO IACOBUCCI was born February 25, 1866 in Supino, son of Dominic Iacobucci and Maria Marchioni. The New York Central Railroad employed him for 39 years. After his retirement, he worked as a gardener. Antonio passed away October 13, 1939 at his home on Route 5, a short distance from the village.

MARIA SCHIRIO was born in August 1863 in Supino. She also passed away at home eight months before Antonio on February 5, 1939. She was the daughter of Mr. and Mrs. Anthony Schirio.

DOMINICK IACOBUCCI, the oldest son, was born February 13, 1871 in Supino and died September 14, 1974 in Schenectady NY. It seems he came over with his parents. Dominick married Rosa Mastrofrancesco (Francisco), sister of Giovanni "John" Francisco, owner of the Bridge Street Bar & Grill. Rosa's parents were Giuseppe Mastrofranceso and Maria Demeis.

ROSA MASTROFRANCESCO was born in Supino on July 2, 1902. She arrived in America in 1921 and married Dominick at eighteen years of age. They had two sons – Mario Lawrence and Antonio. I recall that her son, Antonio lived at the Hough Street residence most of his life.

Rosa later divorced Domenick and married Cataldi "Frank" D'Arcangelis from Fort Plain. He was born in Patrica, Italy on September 27, 1895. Frank arrived in America with his father, Cherubino D'Arcangelis on April 26, 1912 at the age of 16; they settled in Fort Plain. His mother was Natalina Barletta.

Frank had also been previously married and divorced from Nellie Green Garlock; they had a daughter, Viola. Serving his country in two world wars, he died June 11, 1968 in St. Johnsville.

Rosa Francisco D'Arcangelis passed away at her home in August 1991.

Mario Lawrence Iacobucci aka Larry was born February 8, 1921 in St. Johnsville. On October 17, 1942, he enlisted as a Pfc. during World War II in the US Army, seeing action in the Pacific.

On December 15, 1946 Mario Iacobucci married Helen Marie Paluzzi, daughter of Joseph Paluzzi and Florence Rose of Canajoharie. Attending Mario was his brother, Anthony as best man, with friends, Lee Macci and Cus Terricola as ushers. They had two daughters.

I seem to recall that Larry was employed by the Niagara Mohawk Electric Company?

After a lengthy illness, Mario passed away on April 24, 1999 in Canajoharie, where he resided after his marriage, and is buried in Sts. Peter and Paul's Cemetery, Canajoharie.

Antonio L. Iacobucci aka Tony was born June 21, 1923 and died August 20, 1987 in St. Johnsville. Tony enlisted in the World War II military on January 23, 1943, being discharged on December 1, 1945.

On April 30, 1949 Anthony Iacobucci married Theresa Beckel. It seems he lived in Canajoharie for a few years. Tony worked with the New York Central Railroad.

~ ENRICO IACOBUCCI et LENA JACOBUCCI ~

ENRICO "Henry" IACOBUCCI came to America January 31, 1921 at age 17, to join his Uncle Antonio and family. He was born December 9, 1903 in Supino, son of Giuseppe Iacobucci and Loretta Scaredloni.

The 1930 Census shows Henry living with his uncle and other family members at 3 Hough Street. He may have lived in Herkimer before moving to St. Johnsville. It seems shortly after the 1930 Census was taken, he left for Cohassett, Massachusetts, where he married Lena Jacobucci on June 29, 1930. A family member told me they had known each other in Supino.

Henry brought his wife, Lena and two daughters back to St. Johnsville in 1933. The 1940 Census shows them living at 10½ Sanders Street in a duplex home next to the Michael Massino family.

Henry and Lena lived at 10 East Liberty Street most of their lives and were the parents of three children – Livia, Mary and Primo.

The New York Central Railroad employed Henry Iacobucci, retiring as a foreman in 1965. He passed away on December 6, 1998 in Herkimer, NY, where he lived with his daughter, just three days before his 95th birthday.

LENA JACOBUCCI was born November 6, 1913 in Supino, Italy and died June 10, 1999 at St. Luke's Hospital, New Hartford NY. She was the daughter of Giovanni and Pauline Jacobucci. The Little Falls Felt Shoe employed Lena until her retirement in 1962.

LIVIA IACOBUCCI was born in N. Scituate, Massachusetts in 1932. After graduating St. Johnsville High School, Livia married Roland Terricola, son of Giuseppe Terricola and Ausilia Palladini. They had two daughters - JoAnne and Paula. They were later divorced.

Livia's good friend, Mary Spinelli, daughter of Giovanni Spinelli, was married to Livia's cousin, Gabriel Jacobucci of Scituate MA.

MARY IACOBUCCI was also born in N. Scituate about 1934. After her graduation from St. Johnsville High School in 1952, she was married to Salvatore DiChristina of Frankfort on June 16, 1962. They had four daughters - Linda, Diana, Maria and Cindy. Salvatore DiChristina passed away on November 13, 2016.

PRIMO IACOBUCCI was born in St. Johnsville in 1937. When he went to school they sent him home because he couldn't speak English.

Primo was married twice to gals named "Wanda". His first wife was Wanda Masi, daughter of Edward Masi and Wanda Bednarski. They had two daughters - Lori and Carrie.

The Iacobucci's were neighbors and good friends of mine when I grew up on South Division Street. Primo was a bosom buddy of my brother, Joseph Perry for a lifetime. The two of them were part of a special gang along with John Papa and Jon Cairns. They shared a special bond, much like the Sinatra "Rat Pack". Sheriff Ronald "Rush" Emory was also part of these long time friendships. At this writing, Primo Iacobucci is the only remaining member.

I have many fond memories of my friendships with all three of the Iacobucci siblings, including many fun times with Primo through our years of basketball and cheerleading.

* Livia Iacobucci Terricola has contributed to her family's story. Grazie!

~ *La Famiglia PIETROCINI* ~

~ CAMILLO PIETROCINI et DELIA FORCINELLI ~

CAMILLO "James" PIETROCINI arrived in America from Maenza, Italy, in 1907 at age 14, first going to Pittsburgh, where he expected to meet his older brother, Vincent, who had already returned to Italy. In 1910 he was boarding with the Antonio Mancini family on West Main Street and working at a knitting mill. I don't know what brought him to St. Johnsville, except perhaps employment.

Jimmy's work history included first working on the Barge Canal, Lyon's Mill and Engelhardt's Piano Factory, where he became a member of the renowned Engelhardt Band. It seems the band had two different names - Peerless Piano Player Band and Old Regimental Band. The name may have been changed from the latter. The band members were all employees of the piano factory.

Camillo told the story of his name being changed to James by one of his bosses at the Engelhardt Piano Company, who didn't like his birth name. I find no record of his working there, but he may have changed jobs several times in the five years between the Census records. Camille's was the name of the restaurant later opened by his son, Jimmy, daughter, Hilda and her husband John Cairns, on the corner of Bridge and East Main Streets.

In 1912, Jimmy attended Barber School. Noted as the first Mohawk Valley hairdresser, in 1914 he opened his first shop at 32 S. Division Street on the corner of Hough and South Division Streets near Sanders Street. He was at this location for 5 years, later occupied by Rapacz Grocery. (Rapacz purchased the property, tore the building down and built new. They had originally been at 28 Sanders Streets on the corner of South Division.)

The 1915 Census shows Jimmy residing at the 32 South Division location with his partner, Carlo Cochi, his future wife, Delia Forcinelli, her sister Leonina and Ermelinda Cerri as boarders.

The Census states that he and Cochi were partners in a grocery store. Perhaps he had his barbershop somewhere in the back?

On January 16, 1916, Camillo Pietrocini, son of Giuseppe Pietrocini and Loretta Cortese, married his schoolmate from Maenza, Delia Forcinelli, daughter of Gaetano Forcinelli and Luisia Donofrio of Maenza. Carlo Cochi and Delia's sister, Leonina Forcinelli attended them. They had two children - Hilda and James Jr.

His World War II registration of June 1917 also states he lives at the same address and has a wife and child.

The 1920 Census shows both Pietrocini and Cochi with their families living at 21 S. Division Street. This was another of the popular boarding homes at the time, later the Paul Guarnacci home.

Pietrocini became one of the more prominent Italians of St. Johnsville businessmen, not only through his business, but also with his organization and participation in local bands.

Jimmy was a barber for 52 years. In December 1918, he purchased the Bill Wagner Barber Shop in the old Sutherland building at 9 West Main Street. This would have been next to Phil Caponera's Liquor Store. 1928 shows him still located here. He later purchased the Beekman block – 2 East Main, next door to his final location, adding a hair salon in 1923.

In October 1934 he purchased 4 East Main Street, where he remained for 18 years. His daughter, Hilda joined his business after completing a beauty course in New York City in 1935.

Pietrocini was also noted as the manager and conductor of the St. Johnsville Band. It seems there was a conflict over the name, as another band of Roy Bowers also used the same name. Pietrocini seemed to win out with a court decision. Jimmy's band featured younger musicians, who were paid by the village for their performance. In the early 1940s into the 1950s, the band played on Friday nights; first on Bridge Street behind his barber shop, then moving to a much larger location on the lawn of the Methodist Church on Main Street, directly across from his business. 40 years of James Pietrocini's life was dedicated to his music and band.

In 1950, during a return visit to his homeland of Maenza, Italy to visit family, Jimmy had the distinct pleasure of meeting the Pope at the Vatican in Rome. After his return, he shared his visit with the St. Johnsville Rotary Club. He remarked that his airplane flight was much more comfortable than his initial journey to America at the age of 14, when he lived in the ship's steerage section for 17 days.

Jimmy had a brother, Vincent, and sister, Palmira, both in Italy and a cousin Fred, living in Cleveland, Ohio. His wife Delia's sister, Leonina "Lena" married his good friend, Carlo Cochi.

Camillo Pietrocini was born September 29, 1889 in Maenza, Italy. He died in early May 1964, stricken with a heart attack while doing some gardening in the back of his building during his day off.

After his death, his wife, Delia and daughter, Hilda continued the Beauty Shop and rented the barbershop to Richard Francisco. The barber shop was in business for over 50 years.

As was the "old" Italian tradition of mourning the death of a husband, Delia wore black for the remainder of her life after Camillo's passing.

Pietrocini's musical talents were instilled in his grandson, Jon J. Cairns, son of Hilda, who, as I recall, played trumpet and had a wonderful singing talent, performing in his later years at venues where he lived. I'm not sure if it's California or Las Vegas, perhaps both? He passed away in California. After viewing Jim Pietrocini in Sophia Cochi's wedding photo, I see that his grandson, J.J. even looked like him.

DELIA FORCINELLI was born in Maenza on June 20, 1895. She died July 10, 1988 at the age of 93 at the Sunset Nursing Home, Boonville NY, near her granddaughter, Camille.

Delia had two brothers, Francino and Giuseppe, and two sisters, Leonina, who married Carlo Cochi, and Armancia, who was married to Paolo Salvagni. Armancia passed away at an early age leaving two young childen.

In 1913 Delia arrived in America, coming to St. Johnsville with her sister, Leonina, to meet their future husbands.

HILDA L. PIETROCINI was born July 14, 1916 in St. Johnsville. She passed away April 2, 1989. Graduating in June 1934, Hilda was active in the St. Johnsville Players Club, which performed many humorous plays as fundraisers for various organizations. Eugene Ross, my father, Floyd Perry, and my aunt, Helen Perry were also active members of the casts.

In 1935, Hilda completed a beauty culture and hairdressing course in New York City. Her father set up a shop located in the rear of his barbershop, where she worked with her mother, Delia.

Hilda Pietrocini married John Shaw Cairns on April 22, 1936 at St. John's Reformed Church. They had two children - Jon James and Camille, named after her grandfather. They divorced. Later in life, she married Kenneth J. Walrath. John Cairns married Grace Triumpho.

JAMES J. PIETROCINI, Jr. was born July 23, 1920 in St. Johnsville and passed away at his home in Lakeland FL on December 5, 2015 at the age of 95.

As a graduate of St. Johnsville High, Jim was another of the school's stellar athletes, excelling in football, baseball and basketball. The New York Yankees scouted him. Like most of the Italian young men and athletes, Jim was quite the dancer, noted for his impressive twirling of his dance partners around the large dance floor at Sherman's in Caroga Lake. I can still see him moving gracefully around the huge dance floor.

While attending Hartwick College, where he also played on the sports teams, Jim enlisted in the US Marines the day after the bombing of Pearl Harbor. He served for four years and at his passing was buried with military honors at Prospect View Cemetery.

In 1951, Jim and his brother-in-law, John Cairns were co-owners of Camille's Restaurant on the corner of Bridge and East Main Streets. It was named after Jim's father who had purchased the Harvey block in 1945.

On November 3, 1956, James Pietrocini was united in marriage with Mary Louise Braske from Monson, MA and moved to Utica for Jim's employment. They had a son, James M.

While out to dinner with some girl friends Mary Lou tragically choked on a piece of meat and was not able to be revived. Jim later married Natale Scaparo of the Elm Tree Hall in Fort Plain and moved to Lakeland, FL, where he resided until his death.

Home Guard Band ~ 1902

A wonderful article in the *Enterprise and News* on November 11, 1931 relating to the Home Guard Band narrates memories of this impressive group that had formed in May of 1902. The published article reads as follows:

"The Home Guard Band will ever be held in respect and cordial remembrance by the war workers during the strenuous days, incident to raising our quota for the Liberty Loans. The able leadership of J. H. Reaney in putting the various drives "over the top" was loyally seconded by the "Four Minute Men" and the Home Guard Band. Like a fire company, the Home Guard Band was always ready. Through the mud, and darkness, over the country by night or day, they were always on hand. And on Armistice Day! What a Day! And the Home Guard Band! Were they there? They were!

At the first sound of the whistles on that eventful day of the "False Armistice", they literally boiled out of the factory windows, grabbed their instruments and headed the wildest parade ever staged in this quiet old village. And they not only headed the parade, they remained there. Making up in volume for at least three bands, they played until dark and then some, and they were ready on the real Armistice for another day, the likes of which no man has ever seen before or since. The pent up emotion and vocal expression of relief shook the whole village and high above all the others came the notes of the Home Guard Band.

They have scattered since then. Some have gone over the Great Divide. Others are scattered to the four parts of the earth. Some are still with us. But whether here, there or beyond, this community will cherish the memory of the loyal Home Guard Band of 1918."

There was also a photo of the entire band, but the image was so dark nothing was recognizable. The Home Guard Band consisted of at least 21 members, all but one of them being Italian. Though small in size, as you can assume from the news article, the band was strong and tall in its impression.

The Bandleader was Rocco Sugar, with members - Patsy Montoni, Leopold Iacobucci, James C. Pietrocini, Felice Vito, Joseph Tolfa, Carlo Cochi, Angelo Battisti, Pietro Battisti, Tony DeAngelis, Cesare Vito, Luigi Vallecorso, Pietro C. Battisti, Arcangelo Palitti, James Carboni, Vittorio Palombo, Amedeo Palladini, Amy Castrucci, John Francesco and Harry Wagner.

A news article of 1902 says an Italian band has formed, making it three in the village. A May 27, 1908 article mentions the Peerless Band, which was a band formed through the Peerless Piano Company with many Italian employees as members. They were headquartered in Englehardt's Peerless Building, which may have been the old Cheese Factory on Sanders Street behind Rapacz' Grocery.

From 1905 through 1917, when the Home Guard Band came into existence, the "St. Johnsville Band" was recognized. The Home Guard Band was formed during the years of the First World War, 1917-1918. All Italian men in the country, regardless of age or if naturalized, were required to register for the draft. Italy also played a huge part in this war, and the Italians of St. Johnsville were rightly recognized for their efforts.

In 1919, after World War I, this band regrouped and entertained until 1935. I believe James Pietrocini, a popular figure in the village's band era, served as the conductor. Later forming his own band, he was instrumental in entertaining the residents of St. Johnsville at regular Friday night band concerts into the 1950s.

I've seen a picture of Joe Tolfa, proudly wearing his band uniform and holding the cornet he played in the Home Guard Band.

In August 1941, James Pietrocini formed the St. Johnsville Band. There was a lot of controversy and a lawsuit against the band, as there seemed to be another band with the same name. From what I could determine, Pietrocini won the lawsuit. His band played at the Friday night band concerts for about 15 years, first on Bridge Street, right behind the Pietrocini building and later on the lawn of the Methodist Church across the street.

Members of the St. Johnsville Band were also mostly Italians. Selected as the Conductor was James Pietrocini; assistant conductor, Loren Cross, Jr.; president, Peter Battisti; vice-president, Anthony Battisti; secretary, Lee Macci; treasurer, Joseph Tolfa; librarians, Anthony Carroll, Guido Tolfa, Don Nellis, Richard Francisco and Paul Battisti.

In addition, through the years, these young Italians became members of the regular Friday night band concerts: Carl Cochi, John Palma, Jr., Leland Arduini, Joseph Croce, Philip Terricola, Louis Montoni, Carlo

Polidori, Angelo Macci, Edwin Pistilli, Joseph Barca, Paul Salvagni, Lee Macci and Herman Scaccia, who went on to form his own band.

It seems St. Johnsville produced many bands through the years, most membered by Italians. The Ponzi brothers, Zach and Louis both entertained and Herman Scaccia formed his own little orchestra. The Zuccaro (Sugar) brothers also had a small band at one time. There was a great deal of musicality in the immigrant Italian genes that obviously transferred to their children.

Although they did have small Firemen's parades in the early part of the 20th century, it is my impression that the Italians of St. Johnsville may have been responsible for implementing the grand parades that the village of St. Johnsville has always been famous for.

Home Guard Band

~ *La Famiglia COCHI* ~

This couple is the knot that binds the Cochi and Vecciarelli families together.

OTTAVIUS COCHI was born in Maenza in 1860. He came to America and St. Johnsville to join his son, Carlo on December 9, 1913, apparently after the death of his wife, Elemerinda. He died five years later on October 13, 1918 and reposes in Prospect View Cemetery. I find no records of his parents.

ELMERINDA VECCIARELLI, the daughter of Domenico Vecciarelli and Maria Laura Giambattista, was born in Maenza in 1868 and died in her hometown either in 1905 or 1913.

Elmerinda Vecciarelli and Ottavius Cochi had five children – Catallina, who married Leopoldo Iacobucci; Carlo, who married Leonina Forcinelli; Anastasio, who married Anna Belli; Sophia, who married Domenick Fiaschetti, brother of Rosina Battisti; and Amilcare, who married Gina Olivieri.

Carlo, Catallina and Sophia all came to St. Johnsville. Carlo remained here his whole short life. His sisters both moved and resided in Troy for the remainder of their lives, as did the two brothers.

~ CARLO COCHI et LEONINA FORCINELLI ~

The name Cochi stirs memories of St. Johnsville's original convenience store on the corner of East Main Street and Lyon Avenue, near the Soldiers and Sailors Memorial Park. It was a "must stop" after a day of playing or swimming at the park to spend penny allowances on Mrs. Cochi's famous penny candy - or perhaps an ice cream treat. They also carried a selection of Italian specialties and provided gasoline service.

Born August 8, 1893 in Maenza, Italy, Carlo Cochi immigrated to America from Naples, Italy on September 1, 1910 with his older sister, Catallina.

Coming directly to St. Johnsville NY, Carlo joined his good friend, Camillo "James" Pietrocini. They resided together for several years, becoming partners in business at 32 S. Division Street. The 1915 Census confirms that Cochi partnered with Camillo in a grocery store, with Pietrocini apparently setting up his barbershop in the rear. The building was later torn down, rebuilt and became the permanent site of Rapacz Grocery and Meat Market.

Carlo Cochi and his wife, Leonina Forcinelli were both born in Maenza, Italy. Carlo arrived in St. Johnsville before his wife.

Leonina Forcinelli and her sister, Delia, arrived in St. Johnsville together in 1913 and boarded with their future husbands, eventually marrying. I've been told that Mildred Giovampietro Terricola also arrived with the two sisters.

Rev. Joseph A. Thornton, then priest of St. Patrick's Roman Catholic Church, married Carlo Cochi and Leonina Forcinelli on August 29, 1917. Carlo's parents were Ottavio Cochi and Elmerinda Vecciarelli. Leonina's parents were Gaetano Forcinelli and Luisia Donofrio. Leonina's sister Delia, and Carlo's brother Anastasia served as witnesses. They had three children – Ottavio "Oscar", Laura and Carlo, Jr.

By 1920, the Cochi's had located to the Main Street address where they both lived the remainder of their lives. Before opening his store in this location, Carlo was working at a Knitting Mill. Pietrocini had moved his barbershop to a Main Street location.

CARLO COCHI expired suddenly on June 10, 1940, from a major heart attack at the young age of 46, leaving Lena to run the business with the aid of her children. After working in his garden, Carlo was sitting in a chair in his store, with his young son, Carl by his side, reading the newspaper. A customer, Joseph Iacobucci, had come in and was speaking with him. As Iacobucci turned his back, Carlo slumped over in the chair. After trying to make him comfortable, Iacobucci ran to call the doctor, but it was too late. Not everyone had phones and 911 service wasn't even heard of then.

Lena also followed the tradition of wearing mourning black for many years. Carlo's death put a major financial burden on his wife, Lena and their children. Lena was forced to sell off some of the assets. Still in high school, their daughter, Laura spent her time at home handling the bookkeeping, pumping gas and generally assisting her mother wherever she was able.

LEONINA FORCINELLI was born May 29, 1897 in Maenza. Lena died February 15, 1997, just short of her 100th birthday.

OTTAVIO ROBERT COCHI aka Oscar was born December 20, 1918 in St. Johnsville, named after his grandfather Ottavio Cochi. He served as a Captain in the US Air Force during World War II, stationed in India. After graduating from St. Johnsville High School, he attended St. Lawrence University, where he became a teacher, well-respected coach and administrator in the Webster NY school district. Oscar held the honor of being entered into an Athletic Hall of Fame. He died October 20, 1012 in Webster.

On June 9, 1946 Oscar Cochi and Winifred Theresa Whitelaw were united in marriage. They were the parents of five children – Oscar Robert, Stephen, Carla, Chris and Joanne. Winnie passed away in 1996 after the couple had celebrated 50 years of marriage.

LAURA V. COCHI was born in 1925. After graduation, besides assisting her mother at the store, Laura was able to attend business school. She worked at Central National Bank and in later years as secretary to Clarence Oarr, St. Johnsville High School Guidance Counselor.

Given in marriage by her brother, Oscar, on November 9, 1952, Laura Cochi and Dominick Fontana, son of Antonio Fontana and Philomena Baccari, were married in St. Patrick's Catholic Church. Attending the couple were Amelia Tolfa Battisti and Romeo Battisti with Carl Cochi and Philip Terricola as ushers. All four parents were immigrants from Maenza, Italy.

The couple first lived with Laura's mother on East Main Street, and then moved to North Division Street. They had two daughters - Joan and Janice.

After the closing of the popular convenience store, it was remodeled into a home for Leonina. The Fontana's moved to the Cochi homestead, where Dominick maintained a large garden.

Dominick Patrick Fontana was born March 23, 1927 in St. Johnsville. He passed away at the age of 75 on June 15, 2002. You can read more about him in *La Famiglia Fontana et Baccari*.

CARLO COCHI, Jr. was born in 1929. A graduate of St. Johnsville High School, he attended Albany Law School. He first set up his practice with his future father-in-law in Utica NY. Carl has enjoyed a successful career as an attorney for over 60 years.

Carl and his wife, Jackie have five children – Carlina, Nicole, Mark, Michael and Todd.

Carl is another noted Italian athlete of the village, excelling in basketball, baseball and golf.

This strong, hard working Italian family, who suffered personal and financial losses, seem to be proof of how saving "penny candy" income could provide further education and esteemed careers for the talented children of the Italian immigrants of St. Johnsville.

Leonina and Delia Forcinelli had another sister, Armancia, who was married to Paolo Salvagni. She died in Italy after their children, Lola and Florido Salvagni, were born. I found a record of her passage to America, arriving on August 27, 1912. She apparently returned to Italy before the children were born. Paolo remarried and had two more children by his second wife, Adelgesia Pasquale.

Carlo Cochi had three sisters - Catellina, Sophia and Hilda, and three brothers, Giullermo, Anastasio and Amilcare. They all immigrated to America, finally settling in the Troy-Renssalear area.

~ SOPHIA COCHI et DOMINICK FIASCHETTI ~

On June 6, 1926, Dominick Fiaschetti and Sophia Cochi, daughter of Ottavio Cochi and Elmerinda Vecciarelli, were married on Sophia's 21st birthday in a beautiful ceremony at St. Patrick's Catholic Church in St. Johnsville. The couple had three children —Antinio, Dante, and Gloria.

While searching for information on the couple, a priceless wedding photo of the bridal party and family members surfaced. Seen in the photo are Sophia's brother Anastasio Cochi, the best man and his future bride, Anna Belli as maid of honor. Her brothers, Giullermo Cochi, and Carlo Cochi with his wife, Leonina Forcinelli, and their brother-in-law, James Pietrocini, and his daughter, Hilda Pietrocini, also appear in the family portrait. Pietrocini's wife, Delia was not present.

SOPHIA COCHI was born in Maenza on June 6, 1905 and died in February 1971 in Troy NY, where she lived most of her life. Both Sophia and Dominick are buried in Renssaelaer. She was the sister of Carlo Cochi, and aunt of Laura Cochi Fontana. Laura's daughter, Joan, was born on Sophia's birthday, June 6.

DOMINICK FIASCHETTI was born August 12, 1905 in Maenza and died October 22, 1995 in Troy, two days after his sister, Rosina Fiaschetti Battisti's birthday. Rosina was the wife of Antonio Battisti of the Home Town Dairy.

Sophia Cochi et Domenick Fiaschetti Wedding

Front: Hilda Pietrocini, Maid-of honor Anna Belli Cochi,
Groom Dominick Fiaschetti, Bride Sophia Cochi,
Best man Anastasio Cochi, Lee Belli
Back: Benny Grossi, Julia Belli Grossi, Silvano Cacciotti,
Leonina Forcinelli Cochi, Carlo Cochi, Alida Belli Cipriani,
Camillo Pietrocini, Louise Grossi, Guillermo Cochi

~ *La Famiglia BATTISTI* ~

~ ANTONIO BATTISTI et ROSINA FIASCHETTI ~

ANTONIO "Tony" BATTISTI first arrived in New Jersey from Supino in 1912, later coming to St. Johnsville sometime before June 1917, when he was living at 12 Spring Street and working on the State Road in Herkimer.

ROSINA FIASCHETTI arrived in 1919 from Maenza. The daughter of Cataldo Fiaschetti and Gioseffina Ioni, Rosina Fiaschetti married Antonio Battisti on May 17, 1920. Both of their children, Paul and Nancy were born in St. Johnsville.

In 1923 Antonio and Rosina Battisti purchased a dairy farm located on the Mohawk Valley Turnpike, Route 5 just west of the village of St. Johnsville. Tony became the founder of Home Town Dairy, a local company that pasteurized and delivered its own milk in the area for 15 years. It was valued at $3500.

The NYS Census of 1925 shows Tony's brother, Amedeo and his wife, Virginia, living with the Battisti's. Since his occupation is stated as farmer, I'm assuming he was working for Tony. The couple later had a daughter, Gloria.

On May 16, 1928 a devastating fire destroyed the Battisti residence. They lost all of their possessions. Thankfully, the barn and pasteurization equipment across the road weren't involved.

After many years of bottled milk delivery in the St. Johnsville area, in 1958 the Hometown Dairy farm and barn were sold to Adler's Creamery of Fort Plain. It had other owners after that transaction. One of them manufactured their own ice cream to sell from the dairy.

Tony used the sale funds to purchase 40 acres of land surrounding his home from Sam Christi at an auction, enlarging the fields down to the New York Central Railroad boundary. After the sale, the couple remained in the home for the rest of their lives. Their son, Paul and his family occupied the tenant house next door.

Antonio Battisti was born in Supino on September 10, 1895. He died in March 1964 at Little Falls Hospital. I find no records of his parents or affiliation with the other St. Johnsville Battisti families.

Rosina Fiaschetti was born October 20, 1900 in Maenza. She passed away on November 9, 1989 at her St. Johnsville home. Rosina had a brother, Dominick Fiaschetti who married Sophia Cochi, sister of Carlo Cochi.

PAUL ROCCO BATTISTI worked with his father on the dairy farm in the early years of his youth. He was also a highly skilled union carpenter, employed to help build industrial plants and homes with fine cabinetry.

Owning his own Cessna, flying was Paul's passion, which he shared with his friends and family, taking them on aerial excursions along the old Erie Canal, skimming the Great Adirondacks and soaring into the Adirondack Mountains wilderness. He would joke about being lost in the clouds. A proficient pilot, he always knew his way home, except the one time he was lost in Pennsylvania and had to stay overnight. In November of 2015, not too long before his passing, he experienced the thrill of his lifetime with a ride in the new Goodyear Airship with his daughter, Paula.

An accomplished musician, Paul played trumpet in an area New York dance band. He often performed musical solos on his cornet as a member of James Pietrocini's St. Johnsville Band during its concerts in the mid 1940s. In 1941, as a new member of the American Legion, he was appointed their official bugler.

He loved to dance and frequented Sherman's Dance Hall in Caroga Lake, where he met his wife, Anna Quattrocchi from Amsterdam. They would swing the night away for many years thereafter.

On August 26, 1951 at Lady of Mount Carmel Church in Amsterdam, Paul Rocco Battisti and Anna Marie Quattrochi, daughter of Mr. and Mrs. Archimede Quattrochi, were united in marriage. Serving as best man was his friend, Constantino Terricola. Paul previously had served as best man for another friend, Gene Castellucci.

For more than 20 years the couple traveled back and forth to Boca Raton FL as "snow birds", eventually settling there to be close to their children – Paula, Roseanne and Robert.

Anna Marie Quattrocchi was born in 1926 in Amsterdam, one of 10 siblings. She passed away in Boca Raton FL on January 5, 2015 at the age of 89.

Ann worked from home at her trade as a talented seamstress. She was a powerhouse bowler in the Friday Night Women's League. I had the privilege of being her doubles partner in a New York State bowling tournament, which we won.

Paul Rocco Battisti passed away a year after his beloved dance partner, Ann, on June 8, 2016 in Boca Raton. He was born March 27, 1924 in St. Johnsville.

NANCY BATTISTI was born in St. Johnsville in 1927. She married Edward James Leo of Oneida on November 11, 1956 at St. Patrick's Catholic Church. A family dinner was held at Capece's Restaurant, followed by a reception at the church hall. I believe they had children, but I find very little information regarding Nancy.

ITALIANS OF ST. JOHNSVILLE ATHLETES

St. Johnsville has always been noted for producing strong winning teams in every sport they played.

Undoubtedly, the 1930s and 1940s produced many young second generation Italian athletes in their teens - sons of immigrants - that expressed their natural athletic skills on the baseball diamond and basketball court. Some excelled more than others, but the incentive was always there - in the genes.

These are some of the young athletes who were a huge factor during the 1940s in putting St. Johnsville on the winning track. They all were involved in various sports throughout their lives – baseball, basketball, bowling, boxing, football and golf.

Albert "Mag" Battisti, James Battisti, Romeo Battisti, James Capece, Jr., Joseph Capece Sr., Carlo Cochi, Oscar Cochi, Augustio "Gus" Fontana, Dominick Fontana, Angelo Macci, Leondro Macci, Louis Montoni, Aldo Palombo, John Palma, Samuel Papa, James Pietrocini, Eugene Ross, Peter Sackett, Rudy Salvagni, Benjamin Terranova, Giovanni Terranova, Philip Terricola, and Peter Tolfa.

Have I missed anyone?

Of course, the athletic Italian genes trickled down into the third and fourth generations, whom I haven't mentioned.

~ *La Famiglia* FONTANA ~

~ ANTONIO JOSEPH FONTANA et FILOMENA BACCARI ~

As an Italian immigrant, Antonio Joseph Fontana arrived in America in 1906, settling in St. Johnsville. He was born in Maenza, Italy on April 4, 1883, the son of Domenico Fontana and Francesca Olivieri.

Before leaving Maenza at age 23, it seems Antonio had pledged to marry Filomena Baccari. Traveling with her future sister-in-law, Rosa Fontana, Filomena arrived in a group of eleven others on July 19, 1913. The group also included my grandmother, Edvige Sindici and her cousin, Desiderio Coco, Gino Polidori, and Quintilino Olivieri, who may be related to Antonio Fontana, along with several other St. Johnsville Italians who apparently moved on.

Antonio and Philomena had three children - Augustio, Teresa and Dominick. They all continued to reside, marry and raise families in St. Johnsville. Teresa resided in the family homestead her entire life.

FILOMENA BACCARI was born in Maenza on March 17, 1887, the daughter of Luigi Baccari and Constanza Pasquale. She passed away at her Sanders Street home after a long illness, on January 24, 1956 at 69 years of age.

World War I records of September 1918 state that Antonio and Filomena lived at 23 Ann Street and he worked as a USRR Administrator. 1925 NYS census records show they lived at 23 Sanders Street.

By 1930, they owned the 23 Sanders Street home, which I believe was a 2-family duplex, with the Guilio Patrei family residing in the other half. Ascenzo "Vincenzi" Baccari Patrei was Filomena's sister. They also had three brothers - Angelo in Olean NY, and two others in Maenza, Italy.

Census records note that Antonio worked on the railroad, but other records say at Little Falls Felt Shoe. In 1939 he had been employed with the NYS highway department. While trimming trees on a long ladder, a Niagara Freight Line truck crashed into his truck, throwing him to the ground, causing serious injuries. He was awarded $7500.00, a sizeable settlement for the time.

ANTONIO FONTANA died suddenly of a heart attack at the age of 81on March 12, 1965 at home, where he lived with his daughter, Teresa and family, after residing in this country for 54 years.

Antonio had two brothers, James and Salimo in Maenza, Italy. He also had a sister, Rosa, wife of Biaggio Mastracco of Kingsbury Avenue.

AUGUSTIO FONTANA aka Gus was born June 11, 1914 in St. Johnsville. Gus excelled in several sports throughout his high school years and into his adulthood. He was noted as a high scoring bowler, proficient golfer and winning baseball pitcher. Gus was part of the group who formed the St. Johnsville Athletic Association, serving as president.

At one time, Gus owned a shoe store on East Main Street, where young Bob Failing now has his business. He worked at Helmont Mills most of his life and played on their baseball team.

On September 28, 1935, Augustio Fontana joined in marriage with Angelina Rose Vespi from Fort Plain. They had two daughters – Josephine and Carol.

Josephine Fontana was born in 1937 and died on December 9, 2009 in St. Mary's hospital, Amsterdam.

On August 25, 1956, Josephine married Anthony LaCoppola. He preceded her in death in 2002. They had seven children – Robyn, Kimberley, Angela, Kelly, Matthew, Stephen and Christopher.

Carol Fontana was born in Amsterdam on March 28, 1944. She died on August 24, 2013.

She was married to Jon Putman, son of Margaret "Peggy" Putman. They had three daughters - Lorraine, who died at birth, Jennifer and Jaki.

TERESA FONTANA was born in St. Johnsville on February 22, 1921. She lived her entire life at the family homestead – 23 Sanders Street. Tragically, Teresa lost her life on icy roads on Thanksgiving Day, November 28, 1985, in Nelliston, while enroute to her son Tony's home.

Teresa was married to Andrew "Andy" Susi from Canajoharie on December 19, 1942, while Andy was serving in the military. I recall as a young girl, while with my grandmother at the New York Central Railroad station, Teresa was waiting for her train's arrival to go visit Andy, wherever he was stationed at the time.

Pvt. Andrew Susi was a World War II Army Veteran, who was involved in D-Day in Normandy, France and the Battle of the Bulge, the last major German offensive campaign. He was the recipient of the Purple Heart, the Bronze Star and a Distinctive Service Medal.

Originally from a large well-known Italian family in Canajoharie, Andrew Susi was born September 16, 1917 to Frank Nickolas Susi and Agatha Cancellano. He passed away at his home October 20, 1996.

Andy will be most remembered by many of the younger citizens of St. Johnsville as the well-liked Custodian at St. Johnsville High School. They had three sons - Anthony, Andrew and Dominic.

Anthony Susi was the first born at Little Falls Hospital. He attained good marks in school, played basketball and was noted as a winning baseball pitcher. He attended college, and served in the U.S. Navy in Newport RI.

After his discharge, Anthony Susi married Barbara Joyce Battisti, daughter of Angelo and Eleanor Colorito on August 30, 1969 in St. Patrick's Church.

With the assistance of other dedicated veterans and volunteers, Tony is responsible for bringing the Morris J. Edwards Post 168 in St. Johnsville back to life.

SP4/Andrew Paul Susi began his tour of duty on August 6, 1969 and made the ultimate sacrifice in Vietnam on May 27, 1970, when wounded while serving as the Crew Chief on a helicopter mission. He died on May 28. Andy will always be remembered for his bravery, as his name appears on the Vietnam Wall in Washington DC, among all those other brave young men and women who died serving their country, including two other St. Johnsville young men, Dennis Frasier and Lester Ropeter. Andy was awarded several medals, posthumously.

Upon his arrival at the Nellis Airport in Minden, the hearse was met and accompanied by a local veteran's color guard, commencing at the Mohawk River Bridge up Bridge Street, over East Main Street to the C.C. Lull Funeral Home on Kingsbury Avenue. His body was left in repose overnight at St. Patrick's Church until the Mass of Christian burial. He was buried in Prospect View Cemetery, St. Johnsville with military honors.

My brother, Richard Perry, while serving in the Army National Guard, had the extremely emotional duty of standing guard at the casket of his good friend, Andy.

This website - www.army.togetherweserved.com/profile/70782 devotes a complete page to SP/4 Andrew Paul Susi. Andy was also known as a stellar athlete in high school, playing on winning basketball and baseball teams.

Domenic R. Susi ~ On July 18, 1974, tragedy struck this family again. Born December 15, 1956, Domenic R. Susi died a tragic death while enjoying a motorcycle ride with a friend. Coming back into the village of St. Johnsville, they collided with a vehicle. Both of the young men were thrown off the bike with Domenic obtaining the worst injuries. He was transported first to Little Falls, then to a Utica hospital, where he succumbed to his severe injuries. He was 17 years old and would enter his senior year of high school in the fall.

During his short life, Domenic also excelled in high school athletics, playing all the sports – soccer, basketball and baseball. All three of the young sons of Teresa and Andy were stellar athletes during their lifetime and contributed much to the winning teams of basketball and baseball. Domenic was a good friend and teammate of my son, Rodney Palma.

DOMINICK PATRICK FONTANA ~ Athletic genes certainly were strong in the Fontana family. Undoubtedly, the most talented Italian athlete in St. Johnsville, Domenick Fontana was an exceptional athlete, not only in the high school sports of baseball and basketball, but upon his commencement taking up bowling and golf. Dom was one of only three Varsity basketball players who were only 14 years of age. At the time he attended high school in the 40s, most of the athletes were of Italian nationality.

Referred to many times as a "sensational" leading Shortstop in the valley, in 1945 Dom attended the Phillies baseball school in Utica. While under contract with the NYS Professional League's Ball Club in Gloversville NY, he was inducted into the Army, where he continued his love of sports. Pfc. Dominick Fontana played basketball on the Army team in Germany as a guard, contributing to his team's wins.

After his release from active duty, Dom returned to St. Johnsville and joined the St. Johnsville Baseball Team. In later years, golf and bowling became his sports of choice. He was proficient in both, winning many individual awards. He participated in the St. Johnsville Semi-pro bowler's traveling league. If memory serves me, he bowled at least one perfect score of 300.

Most of his working life Dom was a Prudential Insurance Agent, serving the St. Johnsville area. He had previously been employed at Palatine Dye.

Dominick Fontana married Laura Cochi, daughter of Carlo Cochi and Leonina Forcinelli, on November 9, 1952. The couple first lived with Laura's mother on East Main Street, and then moved to North Division Street until the closing of the Cochi convenience store, which was remodeled into a home for Mrs. Cochi. Dom and Laura then moved to the Cochi homestead. They had two daughters - Joan and Janice.

Dominick Patrick Fontana was born March 23, 1927 in St. Johnsville. He passed away at the age of 75 on June 15, 2002.

VINCENZO "James" FONTANA was the brother of Antonio. He was born in Maenza on February 10, 1886 and died in St. Johnsville in March 1973. 1942 World War II records show that he lived at 10 Sanders Street, being employed by Lewis M. Fowler at the New Street knitting mill.

In reviewing death records for Fontana's in St. Johnsville, I discovered several deaths of infants, most stillborn, being buried in Prospect View Cemetery. I also found a Death Index for a James Fontana who died at birth, claiming a death on August 17, 1919. Perhaps a child of Antonio and Filomena?

~ *La Famiglia PATREI* ~

~ GIULIO PATREI et ASCENZA BACCARI ~

Arriving in 1907, Giulio worked on the New York Central Railroad for most of his life. Sadly, he also became a victim of his employment. As a trackwalker, on February 2, 1943 Giulio Patrei was hurled to his death while emerging from the back of a freight train into the path of the "Missourian" passenger train. He was found some distance from the impact, about a mile from the village.

GIULIO PATREI was born in Roccagorga, Italy, on November 11, 1887, son of Guglielmo Patri and Maria Pasquali.

On Halloween, October 31, 1915, Giulio Patrei married Ascenza Baccari, daughter of Luigi Baccari and Constanza Pasquale. She was a sister of Filomena Baccari Fontana, wife of Antonio Fontana. Serving as witnesses for the union were Giuseppe Locorini and Giolitta Marchetti. They had four children - Mario, Albert, Constance and Mary Joan. They both were working in a knitting mill at the time, perhaps where they met?

In 1920 the couple was renting a home on Sanders Street. At this time the Census did not show house numbers. By 1925 the couple were living at 23 Sanders Street, quite possibly the rented home. They would reside here for the remainder of their lives, sharing the duplex of Ascenza's sister, Filomena and brother-in-law, Antonio Fontana. 1930 records show the family owning the home.

ASCENZA BACCARI, the sister of Filomena Baccari Fontana was born in 1893 in Maenza. She died the year before her husband, Giulio, of an unfortunate accident outside her home on a winter night. She had fallen and became frozen into some winter slush. When she was discovered it was necessary to chop her loose. The accident aggravated her current illness and she died a few months later in April 1942. Ascenzo and Giulio are buried in Prospect View Cemetery.

MARIO J. PATREI was born July 30, 1916 in St. Johnsville. He enlisted in World War II with the US Army on May 1, 1945 and was discharged November 3, 1945.

In December 1949, Mario married Christina Acquasanta of Little Falls in the Methodist parsonage there. He lived the remainder of his life in the city, passing away May 16, 1983.

ALBERT FRANK PATREI was born August 18, 1917. He also served his country in the US Army from June 4, 1941 to September 25, 1945. When first enlisting as a Sergeant he was sent to Panama with the Balloon Barrage and was later commissioned a Corporal. He had been in the employ of the Little Falls Felt Shoe Company.

Returning from World War II, Albert Frank Patrei married Marguerite Mingst of Canajoharie on February 15, 1947 at St. Patrick's Church. They had four sons - Ronald J., Robert, Gary Joseph and Brian. They later divorced.

On October 17, 1971, a tragic drowning accident took the lives of brothers Ronald and Gary. While with some friends, their aluminum boat capsized at Stewart's Landing, Stratford NY. It seems neither young men were able to swim. Numeous efforts were made to save them.

A Vietnam Navy veteran, Ronald was born September 5, 1949. A recent high school graduate, Gary was born December 12, 1952. Both were born in Amsterdam.

Albert later married Mary Jane Rockefeller Kucharski. It was the second marriage for both. Mary Jane's husband, Longin Kucharski had passed away at an early age.

Albert was very active with the H.C. Smith Benefit Club of St. Johnsville, often serving as an officer and a member of the kitchen committee. He was a skilled carpenter.

Albert Frank Patrei aka "Paddle" passed away December 30, 1990 in St. Johnsville. Marguerite Mingst was born on January 10, 1914 and died May 11, 2004 in St. Johnsville, where she had lived since her marriage to Albert.

CONSTANCE VICTORIA PATREI was born August 19, 1918, a belated birthday gift to Albert, whose birthday was the day before. She died on April 25, 2013 at the age of 94, at Aaron Manor Rehabilitation and Nursing Center, Fairport NY, where she and her husband of 72 years, "Patsy", resided. She is buried in Sts. Peter and Paul's Cemetery in Canajoharie.

On July 6, 1940, Constance "Connie" Patrei married Patrick "Patsy" Grippe of Canajoharie. Serving in the bridal party were maid of honor Rose Grippe, sister of the groom and bridesmaids - her sister Mary Patrei, friends -Thressa Loccia, Teresa Fontana and Fedora Fiacco. Albert Patrie served as best man. A wedding dinner was held at Marocco's St. Johnsville Restaurant with a reception following at the Odd Fellows Hall on Bridge Street. Music for dancing was provided by a 7-piece orchestra. I'm wondering if this may have been the Henry Sugar Zuccaro ensemble or Herman Scaccia's band?

The couple had two children - Jerome and Barbara. Connie lived most of her life in Canajoharie. She had been employed by the Luxuray, later working as a skilled seamstress altering and making men's and ladies' clothing. For many years she made the Canajoharie basketball cheerleaders outfits.

In her later years, Connie loved to golf, and along with her husband Patsy, won several tournaments at the Canajoharie Country Club. She was also an avid bowler and bridge player.

MARY JOAN PATREI was born April 17, 1920. She lived most of her life at the family home at 23 Sanders Street, before moving to the Palatine Nursing Home, where she passed away on November 4, 1999.
Mary Patrei married Anthony John Pollak of Johnstown on June 27, 1959. She had a daughter, Joanne Patrei.

~ *La Famiglia MASTRACCO* ~

~ BIAGGIO MASTRACCO et ROSA FONTANA ~

The son of Giacomo Mastracco and Teresa Rossi, Biaggio Mastracco was born in Alatri, Italy, on April 26, 1891 and immigrated in 1906 at the age of 15.

BIAGGIO MASTRACCO died October 1976 at his home on 9 Kingsbury Avenue. A long time employee of the New York Central Railroad, he retired in 1955. In his retirement, he worked as the grounds keeper at Margaret Reaney Library. I recall that he always had a large garden at the north side of his home. I don't know of many Italian immigrants who did not have some type of garden to supplement their Mediterranean diets.

ROSA FONTANA immigrated with a group of eleven, including her sister-in-law, Filomena Baccari, Antonio Fontana's wife. My grandmother, Edvige Cacciotti, Desiderio Coco and Gino Polidori were also part of this group. Another passenger, Quintiline Olivieri may have been a relative of Rosa. Their names were together on the ship's manifest. However, I can find no further information of her/him?

Shortly after her arrival on July 19, 1913, Rosa Fontana became Biaggio's wife on October 26, 1913 at St. Patrick's Church. Her parents were Domenico Fontana and Francesca Olivieri. Witnessing the union were Angelo Battisti and Antonia Pelligrina. I'm wondering if perhaps Rosa's brother, Antonio Fontana, may have arranged their marriage?

Biaggio and Rosa had three sons - Vincent Philip, Giacomo and Paul Henry. From what I have discovered, Biaggio had two brothers, Peter Mastrocco, St. Johnsville and another who was Teresa (Mastracco) Colorito's father. He apparently passed away after his wife, Almerina Cacciotti brought Teresa to America.

Born February 7, 1891, in Maenza, Italy, Rosa Fontana died in January 1983 at 91 years of age at the Stone Hedge Nursing Home in Rome, NY. Rosa donated her eyes to the Lions Club Eye Bank.

VINCENT PHILIP MASTRACCO, the eldest of the three brothers, was born February 10, 1916 in St. Johnsville. He died in Spring Hill, FL on December 17, 1998.

Vincent Mastracco married Maria E. Musa, born May 23, 1921. She also died in Spring Hill, FL on May 31, 2015. They had several children.

GIACOMO "John" MASTRACCO was born August 19, 1918. He volunteered for the Navy in World War II and was in my father, Floyd Perry and uncle, Daniel Matis' group that went to Sampson Naval Base on Seneca Lake in New York. I do believe he lived in Gloversville most of his life. I have no further information on Giacomo.

PAUL HENRY MASTRACCO, the youngest son, was born on January 15, 1921. He lived with his parents into his married years. In February 1950 he married Ursula Rich from Little Falls. They had three children - Rosemary, who died at four months in October 1960, Vincent and Robert.

World War II called Paul, where he served in the Army's 3rd Armored Division. He fought in the Battle of the Bulge and was a recipient of the Purple Heart. Paul was active in the Starr-Colorito Post of the VFW, serving as an officer. He was a cousin of James Colorito, son of Gino Colorito and Teresa Mastracco. James Colorito was killed in World War II; the VFW post was named after him.

Like his father, Paul loved flowers and gardening. After returning from armed service, he established a florist business, Paul's Flowers, at the Kingsbury Street home. When I was married in June 1955, he designed all of my floral arrangements, which were very pleasing.

In 1964 the family moved to Camden NY and later to Sacramento CA, where Paul passed away on July 18, 2002 at 81 years of age.

In my search of Prospect View Cemetery records, I found the following Mastracco's:

Francesco 1920-1920; James Frances buried 10/17/1949; Paulo J. 1943-1943; Viginzo 1881-1914; Vincenzo 1914-1915. It was quite common for babies to die at birth or soon after, as many were birthed at home. I've also discovered that cemetery records are not always up to date.

~ MARCELLO PETER MASTRACCO et JENOVINO NALLI ~

Immigrating in 1912, Pietro Marcello Mastracco, brother of Biaggio Mastracco, was born April 26, 1894 in Alatri, Rome, Italy. He died April 24, 1988, in St. Johnsville, 2 days before his 94th birthday.

1917 World War I records show he was single, living at 23 S. Division Street and worked on the New York Central Railroad.

JENOVINO "Jennie" NALLI arrived from Supino to America in 1920 at the age of 19. She was the daughter of Giuseppe and Celelia Nalli, who settled in Fort Plain. She had a brother, William in Fort Plain and a sister, Rosanna in Italy.

PIETRO MARCELLO "Pete" MASTRACCO and Jenovino Nalli were married at Saints Peter and Paul's Catholic Church in Canajoharie on January 28, 1923. Dominic Iacobucci and his wife, Rose Mastrofrancesco served as witnesses. Peter and Jennie had three children - Joseph, Henry and Mary.

They are shown residing at 28 Hough Street with their two–year-old son, Joseph, and the James Battisti family in the 1925 NYS Census. Battisti's owned the home. I don't know of any relationship between the two families.

The 1930 Census records tell that Pete now owns a home at 6 Lyon Place, valued at $2000, where he and his wife, Jenny, lived most of their lives. At this time he was working on the highway.

On October 20, 1935, Yolanda Narducci had been residing with them, when she married Alessandro Potenziani.

From 1937 to 1942, the family lived at 36 Ann Street, while Peter was employed as the grounds keeper at Joseph H. Reaney Memorial Library. June 1942 World War II records show that he moved back to 6 Lyon Place. The Beech-Nut Packing Company in Canajoharie later employed Peter until his retirement in 1959.

In July 1967, Pete was informed by a phone call that he was one of 25 winners in the Marlboro Country Vacation Sweepstakes and had won $1000.

Jenovina Nalli was born in Italy on June 24, 1901 and died November 30, 1987 in Little Falls Hospital where she had been a patient since November 1. Jennie and Peter are buried in the West St. Johnsville Cemetery off Route 5, where their son, Joseph currently serves as caretaker.

She was a member of the Navy Mother's Club in St. Johnsville.

JOSEPH J. MASTRACCO was born August 22, 1924 in Canajoharie, where his parents lived after their marriage and before coming to St. Johnsville.

While in high school, Joe worked as a projectionist at the Smalley Theater on Main Street.

In July 1943, shortly after his graduation from St. Johnsville High School in June, he enlisted in the US Navy, receiving his basic training at Sampson Naval Base. He was sent to Iowa State College in Ames, Iowa for training as an electricians mate. As a Fireman 1st Class, he worked at the Naval Supply Depot, which funneled supplies to the vast Pacific Fleet. It was an important strategy to supply what was needed to batter the doors of Tokyo. He was stationed in Pearl Harbor, where his brother, Henry, met up with him while passing through the Panama Canal.

After returning home, Joe worked at the Beech-Nut Packing Company, Canajoharie, where he was very active in running for various offices with the Beech-Nut Employees Association. He was also a prominent member and officer of the Republicans of the Town of St. Johnsville.

On October 10, 1953, Joseph Mastracco married Rosalie Finch, a sixth grade remedial reading teacher in the St. Johnsville School system, at St. Patrick's Church. They had two sons - Marcus John and Gregory Joseph.

Rosalie Finch was born February 22, 1930 in Plattsburgh. She died June 25, 2007 in the St. Johnsville Nursing Home. Joseph Mastracco is still living at this writing.

HENRY ANTHONY MASTRACCO aka "Hank" was born on December 1, 1925 in St. Johnsville, soon after the family had moved to the village. Hank's obituary states he was born in Canajoharie, but this isn't possible, as the family is listed in the June 1925 Census as living in St. Johnsville.

Hank attended the St. Johnsville Schools. Along with his brother, Joe, he also served as a projectionist at Smalley Theater in St. Johnsville, where he was employed when he decided to serve his country in the US Navy.

Enlisting early 1944, Henry was also recruited in the same group with my father, Floyd Perry and uncle, Daniel Matis for training at Sampson Naval Training Base in Seneca Falls NY. After his training, he was sent to an amphibious training center in Little Creek VA. He served onboard the USS New York LST 914, an amphibious assault craft as a gunner's mate in both the Pacific and Atlantic Theaters. He saw action in North Africa, Sicily and Southern France as part of Operation Dragoon and was at the liberation of Okinawa on April 1, 1945. As Henry remarked, "we were all fools!" He was honorably discharged in May 1946 as a Seaman 1st Class, receiving numerous medals.

Henry Mastracco passed away on November 27, 2017. He would have celebrated his 92nd birthday on December 1. Hank was employed by the Beech-Nut Packing Company for over 25 years.

Henry Mastracco married the love of his life, Mary Croce, whose pigtails he constantly pulled in grade school. They were wed on Armistice Day, June 14, 1953, which they celebrated for 64 years along with their anniversary.

Attending the bridal couple were Lena Barca, maid of honor, bridesmaids Mary Mastracco, Henry's sister, and Leonora Cacciotti, cousin of Mary. Serving as best man was Joseph Mastracco, Henry's brother, with Thomas Croce, brother of the bride and friend John Marocco as ushers. A wedding dinner was held at the Community House with a reception following at the American Legion. They had one son, James.

Mary Croce, the daughter of Pasquale Croce and Mary I. Landolfi, was born in 1926. She also was an employee of the Beech-Nut most of her life, until her retirement. You can read about her family in *La Famiglia Croce*.

MARY KATHERINE MASTRACCO was born on May 30, 1927 in St. Johnsville.

She was married in December 1952 to Howard Trumble of Canajoharie, with a reception following at the Canajoharie Forest, Fish and Game Club. He died in 1976.

On November 1, 1978, Mary married Robert Moyer in California, where she passed away on August 8, 1988. Mary is buried with her first husband, Howard, in the Canajoharie Falls Cemetery.

They had two sons - Steven and David.

While living in California, Mary had graduated in August 1982 with an Associate's Degree in Interior Design.

~ *La Famiglia COLORITO* ~

~ VERGINIO COLORITO et TERESA MASTRACCO ~

VERGINIO COLORITO, son of Raffaele Colorito and Alesandra Ceri, is the younger brother of Frank Colorito. He arrived at Ellis Island from Maenza on April 30, 1909 at the age of 17, looking for his uncle Antonio Carpentiero in St. Johnsville and cousin, Ernesto on May 1, 1909.

In 1910, I found Gino among the 26 boarders on Sanders Street, who worked on the New York Central Railroad. Others noted are John Ponzi, Joseph Zaccho (Sackett), Umberto Sanguine and three Castrucci's – father Antonio and brothers, Gaetano and Filiberto.

Five years later in 1915, Gino was a boarder with the Lewis DeAngelis family at 4 Roth Street. His brother, Frank Colorito later married Rosa DeAngelis, daughter of Lewis.

Gino's World War I record, dated June 5, 1917, shows him married at 25 years old and living at 19 Sanders Street, supporting his wife and father. I found a marriage document showing Verginio Colorito's marriage to Theresa Collannelli, daughter of Costantino Collannelli and Annunziata Panico, on June 21, 1917. Serving as witnesses were Vittorio Palombo and Christina Terranova.

Further research shows that the first Theresa Colorito, who was born in 1896, had died on October 14, 1918 at the age of 22 in St. Johnsville of complications from Influenza, and is buried in Prospect View Cemetery.

Verginio Colorito was born April 15, 1892 in Maenza; he died suddenly of a heart attack at his home on Route 5 east, just outside the village limits of St. Johnsville on April 9, 1957.

Gino worked 43 years of his life on the New York Central Railroad, retiring due to illness. He was a member of the Railroad Brotherhood. Besides his immediate family, Gino was also survived by another brother, Joseph, and two sisters, Assunta Petrosini and Rena Cappodilupo, all still in Italy.

TERESA MASTRACCO was born in Maenza, Italy, on January 16, 1906 and died in Herkimer in October 1984.

At the age of only four, Teresa Mastracco made the voyage to America with her mother, Almerina, arriving on April 10, 1911, headed to Bedford Falls NY to be with her father, Vincenzo. Apparently, Vincenzo passed away a short while later, as Teresa and her mother somehow ended up living in St. Johnsville, where Almerina remarried Salvatore Iannucci, who helped raise Teresa.

Although I find no documents of their marriage, Teresa Mastracco was married to Verginio Colorito for many years. Gino and Teresa were the parents of seven children - Alesandra, James Vincent, Joseph Richard, Elinor, Ruby Marie, Dolores Ann and Mary Jane, all born in St. Johnsville.

The 1920 Census records show Gino, age 26, and Teresa, age 16, living with her parents on Spring Street. Gino worked on the railroad and Teresa in a mill.

In 1925, the couple, with their three children, Alice, James and Joseph, lived at 3 West Liberty Street. The family moved to 22 Ann Street by 1930, next door to the Saverio "Sam" Papa family, and had two more daughters – Elinor and Ruby. By 1940 they were settled into their final homestead, just outside the eastern end of the village on Route 5, across from the Palombi Service Station, with two more young daughters, Dolores and Mary Jane, also born at the Ann Street home.

After Gino's death, Teresa sold the family homestead and moved to Herkimer with her youngest daughter, Mary Jane, to be closer to her daughters, Alice and Ruby.

ALESANDRA "Alice" COLORITO was born in 1922. She married Anthony Aiello from Herkimer in November 1945. At this writing, Alice is still living in Herkimer. They had a daughter.

JAMES VINCENT COLORITO was born in 1923. On December 23, 1942, he enlisted in the US Army of World War II. At age 22, just before giving his life for his country in Germany on March 4, 1945, James received a commendation from his Commander, who praised him for his service in the Harbor Craft Co. and promoted him to Cpl. Tech-5. His body was buried in a European cemetery. At the request of his parents, it was finally brought home to St. Johnsville on May 5, 1949 for a proper funeral and burial in Prospect View Cemetery. Cpl. James Vincent Colorito was met at the railroad station by a color guard that remained with him until his burial with full military honors.

In April 1950, the newly formed Veterans of Foreign Wars Post, aka Starr-Colorito Post VFW, honored his memory with sharing the name of the post with Francis Starr, a casualty of WWI. The post disbanded several years ago, but both veterans are still visible on a prominent wall of honor at the American Legion Post.

In April 1952, his mother, Teresa became involved with the VFW Auxiliary, serving as its president for many years. She also filled other positions. She was a "Gold Star" mother and proudly hung the little flag in her home's front window.

James had been engaged to Dora Palombi, a neighbor and daughter of Harry Palombi and Rosina Capece. She later married Leo Mancini, son of Frank Mancini and Louisa Fiorini.

JOSEPH RICHARD COLORITO was born August 13, 1924; he died January 29, 1991. Joe enlisted as a Private in the US Army on February 26, 1943. As a member of the 11th Battalion, which was the first to enter Japan, he served overseas in New Guinea, Luzon and Okinawa. Joe was the recipient of three battle stars and the Philippines Liberation Ribbon.

After returning from service, Joseph Colorito married Josephine "Buff" Riscica on March 22, 1947, a week after her sister, Lucia "Lucy" Riscica and Homer Fletcher's marriage in Albany. They lived in a home on Thumb Road until the passing of Joe. Joe and Buff had three children - Gene, Richard and Cynthia.

Both brides were daughters of Giuseppe Riscica and Josephine Lopresto, originally from Sicily, who had divorced. With the divorce, Mrs. Riscica and the children went to live with the oldest daughter, Domenica Mamie, wife of Dominick Perry, on their Mindenville farm. They all seemed to have resided there until their marriage. There were also two brothers, Cosimino and Philip.

Joe worked most of his life with the Village of St. Johnsville, under my husband, John "Buttsy" Palma's direction. They were great friends. Joe was a conscientious worker and had a special ingenuity for solving any problem that might arise. Before joining the employ of the village, he worked for Bill Ottman Ford and Failing Ford on the corner of West Main and South Division.

Josephine Riscica was born in Frankfort on August 29, 1918 and died December 27, 2012 in the St. Johnsville Nursing Home. All of her siblings except Minnie were born in Frankfort. Minnie was born in Sicily.

ELINOR COLORITO was born March 30, 1926. She became a dairy farmer's wife on June 25, 1944 with her marriage to Angelo Stanley Battisti, son of Peter C. Battisti and Anna Piniaha, farmers on Averill Hill, Kringsbush. They had six children - Angelo James, John, Barbara Susi, Elizabeth Pachut, Mary Ann Davis and Connie DaBiere.

The couple loved to square dance. Elinor is still living at this writing.

A lifelong dairy farmer, Angelo Battisti was born March 15, 1920 on his parent's farm; he died May 20, 2012 in Johnstown. You can read more about this couple in *La Famiglia Peter C. Battisti*.

RUBY MARIE COLORITO was born July 7, 1929 and passed away after a long illness on March 15, 2001 in Herkimer.

On February 9, 1946, Ruby was married to Robert Dinehart of Ephratah. They had six children - Carol Ann, Robert, James, Dolores, Terri and Richard.

Robert Dinehart was born June 12, 1924 and died December 10, 2009 in Herkimer, where the couple had made their home and lived the remainder of their lives.

DOLORES ANN COLORITO was born June 15, 1932 and passed away after a long illness on November 13, 1983 in Provo, Utah, where she had made her home with her second husband, Clyde E. Ferguson. Dolores and Clyde had three sons - Buddy, Joseph and Eric.

Dolores had first been married at a young age to George Maves of Canajoharie; they had a daughter - Jackie Firmage Carter.

I remember Dolores and her sister, Mary Jane being very close. Both were popular high school cheerleaders and exceptional dancers. They always wore each other's clothes.

MARY JANE COLORITO was born on December 12, 1934 at her parents rented home at 22 Ann Street. She was an active student in high school, a cheerleader, excelling in art and serving as the head Majorette of the high school marching band, later heading the St. Johnsville Fireman's marching band. After graduating St. Johnsville High School, she worked at Palatine Dye.

Mary Jane and I graduated together and were the best of friends in our school years. We shared lots of fun adventures and awesome memories. Not a summer week of four nights went by that we didn't attend the Freddie Clute Orchestra's big band dances at Sherman's, Caroga Lake, followed by the weekly winter Saturday night affairs at St. Anthony's Church Hall, Johnstown. We'd either hitch a ride out to Sherman's or my mom would take us and come back to pick us up after closing the luncheonette. I don't recall ever missing a beat on the Sherman's dance floor or St. Anthony's!

In her senior year, Mary Jane decided she would be a hair stylist. While on our senior trip to New York City, we had some boring free time, so she suggested she cut and style my hair. Well, I left home with very long hair and returned with almost a boy cut, just before our Senior Prom. As I exited the bus upon our arrival home, no one recognized me. She did give me a good haircut!

When Mary Jane's mother sold the family home in 1957, both moved to Herkimer, where she attended the Utica School of Beauty Culture, set up her hair salon and met her husband, John Scialdone, of Herkimer. They were married the summer of 1960. Shortly after their marriage, John joined his partner, attended the same beauty school and together they opened the successful Jo-Mar Beauty Salon in Herkimer for many years, before retiring to Delray Beach FL. They had two children - Teresa and Gino.

ALMERINA CACCIOTTI, daughter of Louis Cacciotti and Antonia Olivieri, was born in 1886 in Maenza. She died in April 1940 in St. Johnsville. She was a sibling of Paolo "Paul" Cacciotti of St. Johnsville, and Ernesta Cacciotti, whom I believe was still in Italy.

Almerina Cacciotti was first married to Vincenzo Mastracco in Maenza, Italy. It seems he passed away shortly after her arrival in New Bedford NY to meet him. She later married Salvatore Iannucci aka Sam Rose, son of Frank Iannucci and Angeline Capozi, on August 10, 1914 at the St. Patrick's parish home. Witnesses were Dominico and Michelina Stagliano.

SALVATORE IANNUCCI was born about 1883 and died in September 1939, being buried in Prospect View Cemetery. He immigrated in 1900.

~ *La Famiglia RISCICA* ~

~ GIUSEPPE RISCICA et JOSEPHINE LOPRESTO ~

On June 15, 1907 at age 24, Giuseppe Riscica arrived from Sicily to America and settled in Frankfort NY. His wife, Josephine Lopresto and four-year-old daughter, Domenica Riscica, joined him in 1909.

GIUSEPPE RISCICA was born in 1881 in Sicily. The 1920 Census shows him living in Frankfort with his wife, and four children - Domenica, Philip, Luciano and Josephine. The couple later had two sons - Cosimino and Philip. Giuseppe Riscica passed away March 23, 1963 in Albany.

From what I've been able to determine, Josephine divorced Giuseppe at some point between 1925 and 1930. After the divorce, Mrs. Riscica and the children went to live with the oldest daughter, Domenica Mamie "Minnie" Perry, wife of Dominick Perry, on their Mindenville farm.

JOSEPHINE LOPRESTO was born in 1884 in Sicily. She passed away sometime between 1930 and 1940 at the home of her daughter, Domenica aka Minnie Perry.

DOMENICA "Minnie" RISCICA was the only child born in Sicily in 1905. At 94 years of age, Minnie passed away at the home of her grandson in Gloversville, after a long and eventful life.

On February 16, 1924, Domenica Riscica was joined in marriage with Dominick Paul Perri, son of Francisco Perri and Genice "Jennie" Raco. They had one son - Frank Francis Perry.

Minnie and Dominick celebrated 50 years of marriage in 1974. It seems they separated after their golden wedding anniversary. Minnie lived alone on Center Street for many years until moving to Gloversville with her grandson.

Throughout her lifetime, Minnie Perry first worked a vegetable farm in Mindenville with her husband for 40 years. She later became the proprietor of a bar and grill, the White Cabins on Route 5S. With her move to St. Johnsville, where she resided for over 25 years, the Green Thumb program employed Minnie as a Refuse Inspector.

DOMINICK PAUL PERRI (Perry) was born in Taormina, Sicily on February 16, 1924.

At six years old, Dominick immigrated on April 11, 1909 with a group of seven heading to Little Falls. His immediate group of four included Filippo Arico, a 34-year-old male (quite possibly his mother's brother?) and two of his siblings, Carmela and Carmine.

The 1915 Census shows his parents with seven children residing in Little Falls.

After Dominick's marriage to Minnie in 1924, the couple lived in Amsterdam. Records also show them living in Little Falls in 1928, before purchasing the farm of James Campione on the Mindenville Road in October of 1929. As per the information in the deed, they paid just $1.00 for the entire package. Times were tough during the Great Depression.

In later years, one December evening while the Perry family was at the movies, their neighbor, Charles Campione, brother of James, discovered a fire at the home. Unfortunately, the home burned to the ground. Apparently, they rebuilt as they did live there for many years.

Dominick Perri passed away in Little Falls in October 1987 and was buried in Fort Plain.

Frank Francis Perry was born in Amsterdam on February 28, 1926. He died on September 5, 2000 in Lakewood, Colorado.

On May 22, 1954, Frank Francis Perry married Yolanda M. Cacciotti, daughter of Paul Cacciotti and Carmela Romano of Sanders Street, the week before Yolanda's birthdate of May 28, 1930. They had six children - Kevin, Carmella, Domenick, Mary Ann, Frank and James. They later divorced and Frank married Betty Lou Smith.

Yolanda M. Cacciotti of Old Meadow apartments, St. Johnsville, passed away at the age of 44 at St. Elizabeth's Hospital in Utica on November 26, 1974 after a lengthy illness.

LUCIA A. "Lucy" RISCICA was born in Frankfort on July 28, 1916. She died February 19, 2002 at the St. Johnsville Nursing Home.

On March 22, 1947, Lucia A. Riscica was united in marriage with Homer Edward Fletcher in Albany NY. They had one daughter, Valerie.

The couple resided at 9 Hough Street most of their married lives. As I recall Homer's mother, Ethel, may have lived with them or perhaps they with her? Homer Edward Fletcher was born November 22, 1925, the son of Homer J. Fletcher and Ethel Dwyer.

JOSEPHINE J. "Buff" RISCICA was also born in Frankfort on August 29, 1918. She, too, died at the St. Johnsville Nursing Home on December 27, 2012 at age 94.

On March 28, 1947 Josephine J. Riscica was married to Joseph Colorito, son of Verginio Colorito and Teresa Mastracco, in Albany the week after her sister, Lucy. They had three children - Gene, Cynthia and Richard. You will find more of Joseph Colorito's story in *La Famiglia Colorito*.

~ FRANCESCO COLORITO et ROSINA DeANGELIS ~

FRANCESCO "Frank" COLORITO, son of Raffaele Colorito and Alesandra Ceri, arrived in America around 1913 and first boarded with the DeAngelis family at 4 Roth Street.

The 1915 NYS Census shows him living in Governeur, St. Lawrence County in a boarding house with John Palma, my father-in-law, and several others. It seems they worked either on the St. Lawrence Seaway in some capacity or with the building of a highway.

By 1920, Frank was back in St. Johnsville, now married to Rosina DeAngelis, with an infant son, Raffaele. The New York Central Railroad now employed Frank. He was the older brother of Verginio Colorito.

ROSINA "Rose" DeANGELIS was the youngest daughter of Luciano DeAngelis and Olympia Narducci, their only child born in America, in Schenectady on October 15, 1904.

After their marriage, I believe they moved next door and boarded with her cousin, Filiberto Castrucci, and his wife, Josephine. Frank had worked on the railroad, but later both he and Rose were employed at the Little Falls Felt Shoe for many years. I also recall Frank worked as a grounds keeper for the Margaret Reaney Memorial Library in his retirement. It seems several Italian immigrant men performed this manicuring task for the library.

After Rose's mother passed away in 1923, her father, Lewis, and sister, Francesca Fiorini and her family all moved to 14 South Division Street, the future home and business of her cousin, Amy Castrucci and family. Lewis DeAngelis had sold the 4 Roth Street home to my grandparents, Giuseppe Sindici and Edvige Cacciotti.

Upon her family's move to Scotia, Rose and Frank moved back in with Filiberto and Josephine. They now had a daughter Celia, born 1926. The couple's first son, Raffaele passed away at age nine on October 24, 1928 in Little Falls Hospital, where he had surgery for an infected bone in his leg. He was born in May 1920. While living on South Division and before purchasing their 17 Ann Street home before 1940, they had another son named Ralph.

CELIA O. COLORITO was born in 1926.

On August 11, 1946 she became the bride of John Donadio, son of Mr. and Mrs. Pasquale Donadio of Little Falls at St. Patrick's Church. Her friend, Palmena Francisco was a bridesmaid. They later settled either in Little Falls or Herkimer. As I recall, at one time they either owned or managed the Mohawk Valley Country Club. John had also been the manager of the Little Falls Bowling Lanes at one time. I have no dates of birth or death for either.

Celia and my Aunt Viola (Sindici) Perry formed a friendship as little girls when they lived next door to each other on Roth Street.

RALPH L. COLORITO, named after his sibling who had passed away, was born July 20, 1931 in St. Johnsville. Many knew him as "Porky", which he carried throughout his school years. He was very active with the Boy Scouts through the years.

Ralph graduated with the St. Johnsville High School Class of 1948. I don't find that he played any sports, but he did serve as the manager of the 1946-47 Section 2 basketball championship team under Coach Ralph Anderson.

Ralph was married twice. His first wife was Beverly Jean Diefendorf from Fort Plain. They had two children, Ralph, Jr. and Laura Rose. I believe both were born in Pittsburgh, PA where Ralph lived for 25 years.

It seems Ralph made a career of the Army, being promoted to Corporal. As a Private he was stationed at Fort Dix, NJ. While stationed in Stuttgart, Germany, Cpl. Ralph L. Colorito had a few days furlough and traveled to Rome to visit relatives. He spent a few days in Maenza with his father, Frank Colorito's sisters and brothers. From there he returned to Rome where he visited James Pietrocini's sister, Mrs. Palmina DeCamille and family.

On May 7, 1988, Ralph married his second wife, Sonia in Travis TX. They had no children.

Ralph passed away on September 20, 2013 in Austin TX, where he had lived for over 34 years.

FLORENCE A. COLORITO was born January 17, 1935 in St. Johnsville. She passed away at the Kingway Arms Nursing Center, where she was employed for 37 years, retiring at age 75.

Beginning her nursing career through studies at Russell Sage College and Ellis School of Nursing, she first worked at two different New York City hospitals.

Florence and I were great friends and classmates from kindergarten to our senior year, when she qualified as Valedictorian and I as the Salutatorian of the Class of 1953. We had a lot of fun times through the years. In high school, Florence was very active in extracurricular activities.

The night before our Senior trip to New York City, I stayed overnight with her and we were room-mates during our stay in the Big Apple.

On August 9, 1959, Florence Colorito married Patrick La Porta in St. Anthony's Church, Schenectady. They had two children - Michele and Patrick.

~ *La Famiglia DeANGELIS* ~

~ LUCIANO DeANGELIS et OLYMPIA NARDACCI ~

LUCIANO DeANGELIS and his wife, Olympia Nardacci were from Maenza, Italy, and immigrated to the United States sometime between 1902 and 1903. They had been married in Italy in 1889 and were the parents of three children born in Maenza – Frank, Francesca and Anthony. Their fourth child, Rosina was born in Schenectady where they first lived, according to the 1910 Census.

By 1915, the family had moved to 4 Roth Street in St. Johnsville, where they took in boarders - Erasmo Fiorini, Antonio Ettore, Verginio Colorito, brother-in-law Antonio Castrucci, his sons Filiberto and Amadio, and Olympia's brothers, Nicola and Rocco Nardacci. The residents also included their daughter Francesca, now married, her husband, Antonio Fiorini and their two-year-old son, Columbus for a total of 15 residents.

In 1920, the DeAngelis family still resided at the 4 Roth Street address, which he purchased with a mortgage. His two daughters and their families lived with them, Frances, her husband and son, Columbus, and Rosina, her husband, Frank Colorito and their son, Raffaele. At this time, they housed no boarders.

OLYMPIA NARDACCI passed away on September 25, 1923 at their home at 4 Roth Street. She was born April 29, 1873 in Maenza, Italy.

After her death, Lewis sold the home to my grandparents, Giuseppe Sindici and Edvige Cacciotti. His family moved in with his nephew Amadeo "Amy" Castrucci and family at 14 South Division Street for a couple years. He later moved to Scotia to live with his daughter, Frances Fiorini and family, where he died on December 28, 1930 at an Amsterdam Hospital. Luciano DeAngelis was born in Maenza on March 10, 1871.

FRANK DeANGELIS, born in Maenza in 1895, was the oldest child. I don't locate any information about him after he is listed in the 1910 Census living with his parents in Schenectady. He most likely remained in Schenectady when they moved to St. Johnsville or passed away?

FRANCESCA DeANGELIS, the first daughter, was born in Maenza, Italy in 1899 and came to America with her parents in the early 1900s. She married Antonio Fiorini from Rocia, Italy, son of Jack Fiorini and Geldinia Felippi, on October 12, 1913 in St. Patrick's Church, St. Johnsville. Witnesses were Alberto Iacobucci and his wife, Maud. They both worked in a mill, perhaps where they met. She was 17, he 23. They were the parents of two children - Columbus A. and Dora. Francesca DeAngelis died November 27, 1979 in an Amsterdam hospital.

Antoino Fiorini was born June 3, 1890 and died 1968 at Ellis Hospital, Schenectady at 77 years. Both are buried in Prospect View Cemetery. Their son Columbus "Russ" is also buried there. I discovered a small stone nearby for a child, Roland that only states 7 months. I'm assuming he was another child of Francesca and Antonio's?

COLUMBUS FIORINI aka Russ, as he was better known, was a musically talented man. When he was ten years of age, his family moved to Scotia. While attending Scotia-Glenville High School, he played the violin in the orchestra. Russ later became interested in playing a tenor saxophone and a clarinet. He sure played a mean sax. I loved to listen to him. Music was the love of his life!

After training at the Sampson Naval Base, Seneca Lake and serving in the US Navy from February 16, 1943 until November 5, 1945, it seems Russ settled in Geneva NY after his discharge.

Besides performing quite often with his band, he was also manager of a bowling alley in Ovid NY. I'm not sure when he formed his own orchestra, whether before or after his service in World War II. He was still living in Ovid into the early 1950s before moving back to the Amsterdam area, where he worked as the manager of the Windmill Bowling Lanes. Russ was also an exceptional bowler. And, he continued to blow his horn at many events.

I knew Columbus "Russ" Fiorini quite well in his later years when he joined my family as a companion to my Mom, Rose Sindici Perry, after my father passed away. They had known each other as playmates in their early years, when Russ lived at 4 Roth Street, where he was born. At the time my mom, Rose, lived around the corner at the end of Hough Street.

I always heard of his wife, Dorothy Clark and his two daughters, whom my Mom thought well of. However, I did not know he had been married before until researching him. I have discovered that Russ was first married to Antoinette Nuzzaco of Schenectady on Sunday, February 27, 1938. A news article about a bridal shower confirmed it as his mother and sister were in attendance.

I also found an article about Antoinette being a singer and entertainer, possibly how she and Russ met. After their divorce, she married two other men. I'm assuming she and Russ divorced before he entered the Navy. I can't find a record of his marriage to Dorothy to figure out a timeline and confirm which wife was with him in Geneva. It was most likely Dorothy as one of their daughters was born in 1953 at the time Russ was a resident. They had a son, Robert, and two daughters, Toni and Sarah.

Ironically, Russ' grandfather, Luciano DeAngelis, sold the home to my grandparents, where they lived out their lives. My family all thought well of Russ. In my mom's final days, he was there continuously, assisting with her care and giving us comfort.

Columbus Fiorini was born November 2, 1914 at the 4 Roth Street home. On March 2, 1995 he passed away peacefully after doing what he loved the most, entertaining a group with his amazing sax and music. He returned home to his apartment, sat in his rocking chair and reposed in harmonic sleep forever.

DORA FIORINI ~ I find no information regarding Dora.

ANTHONY N. DeANGELIS was born June 6, 1900 in Maenza, the second son of Lewis and Olympia. He was employed at General Electric, Schenectady, before serving in World War I.

It seems at the age of 19, as stated in the 1920 Census, Anthony was the owner of his own grocery store in St. Johnsville. In his later years he became an Insurance Agent, first in Schenectady, where he lived after his marriage.

On June 28, 1927, Anthony DeAngelis married Concetta "Helen" Massari, a daughter of Antonio Massari and Angelina Augustina from the town of Minden, in St. Patrick's Church. Attending the couple were James Sanguine, neighbor of Anthony, and Emma Massaro, sister of Helen. Rose Fiacco served as flower girl. I don't know who the flower girl's parents were? Helen's oldest sister, Mary Massaro Fiacco had four daughters, but none with this name.

By 1940 the family had moved to Canajoharie where Anthony continued his insurance business. Anthony passed away June 2, 1980 in Canajoharie.

Concetta Massari was born January 3, 1907 in the town of Minden and died September 7, 2000 in Delmar NY. The couple had three children - Dorothy, Richard and Donald. Richard was a graduate of St. Lawrence University. Donald David graduated from Albany Law School and married Mary Kathryn Dunnigan.

Most residents of St. Johnsville are more familiar with Rose DeAngelis.

ROSINA "Rose" DeANGELIS was the youngest daughter and only child born in America in Schenectady on October 15, 1904. She married Francesco "Frank" Colorito, older brother of Verginio. He had been a boarder at the DeAngelis home in 1913, when he first arrived.

Many times when Russ Fiorini came to see my Mom he would also visit his Aunt Rose.

You can read more about Rose and Frank in *La Famiglia Francesco Colorito et Rosina DeAngelis*.

~ *La Famiglia CASTRUCCI* ~

~ ANTONIO CASTRUCCI et ERSILIA NARDACCI ~

Castrucci is a well-known name in the village of St. Johnsville. There were three brothers who seemed very close, Filiberto, Augustino and Amadio. They were sons of Antonio Castrucci and Ersilia Nardacci from Maenza, Italy.

Both Antonio and his wife, Ersilia Nardacci, immigrated to St. Johnsville, where they lived out their lives, usually residing with one of their children. They lived with their son, Amadio "Amy" in their final years.

Ersilia Nardacci died at Amadio's home on January 16, 1937 at the age of 63, and was buried in Prospect View Cemetery. She was born November 13, 1868 in Maenza.

I didn't find an exact date of birth or death for Antonio. As of the 1940 Census he was still living with Amy and Mary at 14 South Division Street. However, in checking the photos that I had taken of the gravestones in the Prospect View Cemetery, I found he was born in 1885. He died in 1951 and is buried next to his wife, Ersilia.

The 1910 Census shows the father, Antonio Castrucci, his oldest son, Filiberto, age 19, and Augustino, 16, living in a home on Sanders Street among 26 boarders. Antonio worked on the Barge Canal, his two sons in a knitting mill.

By 1915 Antonio, Filiberto and the youngest son, Amadio, were boarders at 4 Roth Street with the Luciano DeAngelis family. I didn't find Augustino. Antonio Castrucci and Luciano DeAngelis were brothers-in-law, both being married to sisters, Ersilia and Olympia Nardacci, respectively.

The 1920 Census shows Filiberto was renting the home next door at 6 Roth Street, where he was now living with his father and two brothers. By 1930, he was the owner. I think this was the last home built on the street.

On December 18, 1921, two of the Castrucci brothers shared a double wedding, which had originally been planned to be a triple wedding ceremony in St. Patrick's Catholic Church. Augostino married Filomena Iagnacco. Amadeo married Maria Zolli.

It was said the three marriages were all pre-arranged.

ANTONIO CASTRUCCI was born April 10, 1863 in Maenza, the son of Francisco Castrucci and Theresa Rozetelli. He died November 7, 1951 in Little Falls Hospital.

ERSILIA NARDACCI was born November 13, 1868 in Maenza, the daughter of Antonio and Constina Nardacci.

~ FILIBERTO CASTRUCCI et GIUSEPPINA GRANTI ~

At age 17, on April 12, 1907, Filiberto Castrucci immigrated, first joining his uncle Salvatore Nardacci in Oneonta. By 1910, he was living on Sanders Street with his father, Antonio and brother, Augostino and working in a knit factory.

His 1917 World War I registration shows Phil living at 4 Roth Street, working at Lion Manufacturing. He claims a wife and child and that he had served 2½ years as a Private in the Italian Infantry. However, the information he gave doesn't fit his timeline!

Applying for a passport on March 7, 1922, Filiberto returned to Maenza, where he married Giuseppina Granti shortly after arriving there. Giuseppina was not allowed to immigrate in time for them to share a triple wedding with his two brothers. Phil returned with Josephine to St. Johnsville via Fonda on July 1, 1922. They were the parents of a son, Paul, born July 10, 1934.

I recall hearing they had a daughter who died shortly after birth. I located a small gravestone of Leonora, who was buried May 30, 1924, which says she was daughter of Filiberto. I also found in the Prospect View Cemetery records, Paul A. Castrucci, an infant born in May 1929, living only nine hours, and also buried there.

Since they did have a son, Paul, born in 1934, I'm assuming it was their son. Italians always named the next child of same sex after a previous one that had died, as did other ethnicities in those days.

By 1920, Filiberto was renting the 6 Roth Street home. 1925 shows Phil, his wife Josephine, his parents, Antonio and Ersilia; his brother, Amy with wife, Mary and their son, Joseph all living at that address. The 1930 Census shows he owned the home. Residents were the Castrucci couple and Frank and Rose Colorito with their daughter, Celia. The Colorito's first born, a son Raffaele, died at a very young age in Little Falls Hospital.

Filiberto toiled on the railroad most of his life. In his free time, he cultivated an immaculate huge garden that took up more space than his home. He was so proud of his harvest and was quite selective about whom he would let take a short cut to go from Roth Street to West Liberty Street. The whole yard was fenced in.

I don't know of one Italian family who did not have a thriving garden in their backyard, whether large or small. Italians were so proud of the harvest they reaped every summer for consumption, providing luscious tomatoes for their Sunday sugo "sauce" all winter long and other home-grown vegetables they canned to hold them over until the next harvest. Some used their gardening skills as a means of bringing in more income.

Many years later, after selling their homestead to a nephew, Paul Vacca, son of Marguerite (Castrucci) Vacca and grandson of Amy and Mary Castrucci, Filiberto and Josephine moved to the home of their son, Paul in Burlington VT, where they both passed away.

FILIBERTO CASTRUCCI was born November 5, 1890 in Maenza; he died in 1991 in Burlington VT.

GIUSEPPINA GRANTI was born March 12, 1900 in Maenza; she died November 1, 1978 in Burlington.

PAUL P. CASTRUCCI was born to Filiberto Castrucci and Giuseppina Granti on July 10, 1934 at their 6 Roth Street home. Having parents who were much older, especially his father, didn't make his childhood very easy. The discipline paid off. They certainly raised a very accomplished man.

Living next door to my grandparents, he was one of my very first childhood playmates and a good friend throughout our school years. Although he was in the graduating class one year before me, we shared math and science classes together in high school. He played on the basketball team, was active in extracurricular activities, holding office on the Student Council for four years and was an exceptional student, culminating in Salutatorian of his class.

I have many memories of fun times with Paul back in the late thirties, early forties. Life was simple. We didn't have the toys, bikes, electronic instruments, etc. that kids have today. We played hide-n-seek and kick-the-can under the one dimly lit streetlight in the unpaved cul-de-sac of Roth Street. Or we just sat on my grandparents' front steps and told stories. Paul loved to show off his hobby of tracking homing pigeons to my cousin Pauline (Matis) Smith and me. To be honest, I really didn't like being around the dirty pigeons, but I was impressed how they always came home to roost. Paul always possessed an inventive gene, which he utilized in his adult years. There were no other kids his age on the street or the surrounding area of Hough Street.

After graduating in the class of 1952, Paul continued his education at Union College, Schenectady NY on a scholarship with a major in physics. After graduation he worked for IBM before serving two years as an officer in the Air Force. After his discharge, he returned to IBM, where he made them famous for several inventions through his research. It's my understanding that he never received full credit for his accomplishments.

Paul P. Castrucci held 24 U.S. patents, including basic patents for integrated circuit memory devices and semi-conductor process manufacturing. He also had a patent for the Smart Card. During his 30-year career with IBM Corporation in Burlington Vermont, Paul invented the first 16-bit memory chip used in a computer for IBM in 1965 and also some type of silicone wafer. He held many major technical accomplishments.

With his retirement from IBM in 1988, he served as COO at SEMATEC, a government-sponsored consortium of 14 semi-conductor firms. After leaving there, Paul formed his own consulting firm and assisted many of the top semi-conductor companies around the world. A down to earth, rather typical Italian man, Paul was well known and respected in the Silicone Computer Industry. This is all Greek to me, but I can truthfully say, "I am so proud and honored to have known this fine man." He has made the *Italians of St. Johnsville* and entire village proud.

Paul married his high school sweetheart, Margaret Davis, daughter of Edward Davis and DeEtta Ottman, who were the proprietors of Ottman's Grocery Store and Soda Fountain on West Main Street. They had four children. Margaret was also a friend; we were on the basketball cheerleading squad together.

Paul P. Castrucci passed away at his home on June 22, 2013, one month before his 80th birthday.

It has come to mind that I recall from my youth that Paul Castrucci, Filiberto's son, and Florence Colorito, Rose Colorito's daughter were cousins.

~ AUGUSTINO CASTRUCCI et FILOMENA IAGNACCO ~

AUGUSTINO "Gus" CASTRUCCI was the middle son of Antonio and Ersilia. He was born April 11, 1894 and died May 1, 1977 at the age of 83 in Little Falls Hospital.

As a veteran of World War I, where he served in the Calvary Division of the European Theatre, he was a 55-year member of the Morris J. Edwards American Legion Post. He was discharged August 14, 1918. He was also a member of the Brotherhood of Railroad Employees, as a railroad worker most of his life.

On December 18, 1921, Augostino Castrucci, 26, married Filomena Iagnacco, 23, daughter of Francisco Iagnacco and Erselia Condinti, of Maenza, Italy, in a double wedding ceremony with his brother, Amadeo and Maria Zalli. Attending Augustino and Filomena were Augustino's cousin, Frances DeAngelis and her husband Anthony Fiorini. Gus and Filomena celebrated 55 years of marriage.

Gus and Filomena resided at 4 Lyon Place most of their lives, where they raised two daughters, Ersilia "Elsie" and Allesandra "Alicia", who was employed as a Medical Secretary for an Ophthalmologist in New York City.

Elsie was an avid reader and constant visitor to the Margaret Reaney Memorial Library. She had a massive collection of her own books. She invited me to see her collection, which was so large she ran out of bookcase space and had them piled neatly on the stair steps of her home.

FILOMENA IAGNACCO was born August 19, 1897 in Maenza, Italy and died in St. Johnsville on April 1, 1985 at the age of 87.

~ AMADIO CASTRUCCI et MARIA ZALLI ~

AMADIO CASTRUCCI was born April 18, 1899 in Maenza, Italy, to Antonio Castrucci and Ersilia Narducci.

As business owners, Amadio "Amy" Castrucci and his family are undoubtedly the best-known members of the Castrucci family.

They settled into a two-story building at 14 South Division Street on the corner of West Liberty, where they converted the downstairs into a thriving Italian Grocery Store, even surviving the Great Depression.

My strongest memory of this store was during World War II, when my dad was in the Navy. My mom would often send me across the street to purchase the fresh-out-of-the-oven Barca's Italian bread minutes after it was delivered. I can still visualize the interior and smell the fresh bread aroma. Add a slice or two of salami and we had lunch.

The living quarters were upstairs, where Amy and Mary lived most of their lives, sharing their home with Amy's parents and a gentleman, whom I remember as "Charlie Chooch".

Charlie's real name, as I've discovered, is Arcangelo Palitti aka Charles Polito. He was the brother of Antonio Palitti. Sometimes he helped out in the store. Charlie always had an Italian cigar, which he probably rolled, hanging out of his mouth. I have heard he soaked them in rum. They were so gross! You'll read more about Charlie in *La Famiglia Palitti*.

On December 18, 1921, Amadio Castrucci, 22 was united in marriage with Maria Zalli, age 17, sharing the double ceremony with his brother Augustino Castrucci and Filomena Iagnacco. Serving as their attendants were Francesco Colorito and Amadio's cousin, Rosina DeAngelis Colorito. Amadio's parents authorized the marriage due to Maria's age. The only record I find of Maria's parents is the name William Zalli on the marriage certificate.

Amadio's mother, Ersilia had brought his bride, Maria, age 14, to St. Johnsville on March 22, 1920, when she emigrated. Obviously, it was a pre-arranged marriage. They had gone to meet Ersilia's husband, Antonio Castrucci, a boarder at her sister's 4 Roth Street home.

The two couples also celebrated their 50th wedding anniversary together with a large gathering of friends and relatives. Amy and Mary only celebrated 52 years together with Amy's passing on December 29, 1972.

It seems Amadio immigrated in 1914, going first to Schenectady, then St. Johnsville, where he was employed at age 16 at Union Knitting Mills. A business man most of his life, Amadio, better known as Amy, was also employed with General Electric and on the New York Central Railroad at one time.

Amadio also served in World War I in 1917-18, as a Commander in the Army. While in the Army, he became a naturalized citizen on August 14, 1918 in El Paso, Texas. He was exceptionally active in the Morris J. Edwards American Legion Post, where he was honored with a life membership. Amy Castrucci was the first St. Johnsville veteran to receive a 50-year pin. There was a flagpole erected in his honor.

Both the 1920 and 1925 Census records state that Amy, his wife, Maria and their son, Joseph, were living with his oldest brother, Filiberto, his wife Josephine and the mother and father, Antonio and Ersilio at 6 Roth Street.

By 1930 the Castrucci's had opened their Italian Grocery Store at 14 South Division Street, which they owned for 20 years before turning it over to Dominick and Mary Papa in June 1949. At this time, he became the proprietor of Amy's Service Station at the western end of the village, along with his son, Joseph. He was a member of the St. Johnsville Merchant's Association.

MARIA ZALLI was born on December 7, 1906 in Maenza and died on November 1, 1985.

JOSEPH A. CASTRUCCI, the son of Amadeo Castrucci and Maria Izzo, was born March 28, 1923, most likely at the 6 Roth Street home of his uncle Filiberto, where his parents were residing.

On December 18, 1945, Joseph A. Castrucci married Mizpah June Woodward of Carthage NY, daughter of George Woodward and Laura Schell. His parents remodeled the back portion of the grocery store into an apartment for them. They had three children - Eleanor, Albert and James.

When his father opened the Texaco Service Station, Joe worked for him. After Amy's retirement in 1964, Joe continued the business with his wife, June. At 46 years of age, Joe died on October 1, 1969. He had been in ill health for four years and had his foot amputated.

His son, Albert conducted the business until his untimely death in 2010; his fiancée Lois Thomas continues with the business today.

Joseph A. Castrucci was very active with the Fire Department, as a member of the St. Johnsville Volunteers and the Montgomery Fire Advisory Board, where he served as Deputy Fire Coordinator. His wife, June, was also active as a member and officer of the St. Johnsville Firemen's Auxiliary. She suffered a heart attack at her home at West Main Street and died November 1, 1975 at the age of 48.

MARGUERITE C. CASTRUCCI, an exceptional student and honor roll member throughout high school, went on to graduate from Oneonta State Teacher's College, Oneonta NY with a Science in Education degree. Upon graduation, she taught in Van Hornesville for a few years before returning to her hometown, serving as the second grade teacher for 35 years at the David H. Robbins Elementary School.

Marguerite C. Castrucci joined in marriage with Felix A. Vacca from Middletown CN on July 3, 1955 at St. Patrick's Catholic Church. They were the parents of two sons, Paul, who passed away five years after Marguerite on September 5, 2012, and Peter.

Marguerite C. Castrucci was born November 1, 1925 and passed away at the St. Johnsville Nursing Home December 29, 2007.

Slightly older, Felix A. Vacca was born August 28, 1912 in Connecticut and passed away March 3, 1998. He worked with Amy's as their service repairman with furnaces and fuel delivery.

~ *La Famiglia CACCIOTTI* ~

~ PAOLO CACCIOTTI et CARMELLA ROMANO ~

PAOLO "Paul" CACCIOTTI immigrated to America on January 7, 1921, first settling in Westfield MA, although the passenger's manifest stated he was going to his sister, Almerina Cacciotti Rose's in St. Johnsville. He also had another sister, Ernesta, still in Maenza.

On January 20, 1926, Paolo Cacciotti married Carmella Romano in St. Patrick's Catholic Church with John Fiacco and Mary Massari serving as witnesses. At the time of the marriage, Paul was living in Westfield. This is confirmed by not only the marriage certificate, but also 1926 city records, which also state he was a laborer. They had two daughters - Leonora and Yolanda.

The 1930 Census shows the couple and their young daughter, Leonora, living at 23 Ann Street with his sister, Almerina, and husband Sam Rose aka Salvatore Ianucci. There was also a boarder, Arcole Cicevardini. Paul was a laborer on the highway, as was his brother-in-law, Sam.

By 1940 they had moved to 3 Sanders Street. In the early morning of February 13, 1949, as Paul was leaving for work, he noticed the duplex across the street at 10½ Sanders Street was on fire. He quickly alerted the Frederick Smith family, who climbed out on the roof from their bedroom, and then dropped to the ground. There was extensive interior and smoke damage, which also permeated to the attached home of the Giuseppe Terricola family.

The son of Andrea Cacciotti and Antonia Oliveri, Paul was born in Maenza on July 18, 1900. At the age of 50 years, he was stricken at home, transferred to Little Falls Hospital and died January 6, 1951 upon arrival. Paul worked on the New York Central Railroad most of his life.

CARMELLA ROMANO was born January 29, 1902 in Baia e Latina, the daughter of Thomas Romano and Maria Filomena Itri. She was the sister of Giuseppe "Joe" Romano, Antonio Romano, and Guilia "Julia" Romano Laurora. Antonio Croce was her cousin; their mothers were sisters.

On September 14, 1974, while shopping in Amsterdam with her daughter, Leonora, Carmella was stricken and succumbed to a heart attack. Just two years before, at 70 years of age, she had become a U.S. Citizen at the Supreme Court in Schenectady.

LEONORA "Lee" CACCIOTTI was born in 1929, when her parents lived at 23 Ann Street. She graduated with the St. Johnsville High School Class of 1945.

On October 25, 1953 Leonora Cacciotti was joined in marriage to William Gutowski of Amsterdam at St. Patrick's Catholic Church. Given in marriage by her uncle, Joseph Romano, she was attended by three cousins, Crestina Croce Smith as matron of honor, Philomena Romano Coco and Mary Jane Colorito as bridesmaids, along with her sister, Yolanda Cacciotti. Prior to the reception at the Klock's Park hall, a dinner was served at the Manor.

Italians were noted for having a dinner for family and bridal party members prior to the reception. I found it interesting that there were guests from Westfield MA? Perhaps Cacciotti family?

Upon returning from their honeymoon, the couple resided on Sanders Street with Leonora's mother, until their move to 97 West Main Street. They later moved to their newly built home on Rockefeller Drive. They had two sons - Paul and David.

William Gutowski was born in Amsterdam on June 24, 1927 and passed away at the St. Johnsville Nursing Home on October 27, 2007 at the age of 80. Bill was a World War II Veteran. Upon moving to the village, he became very active in St. Patrick's Church and community affairs. He entertained with the piano and taught Polka lessons. Bill and Leonora were avid polka dancers, traveling all over the area to attend events.

YOLANDA CACCIOTTI was born on May 28, 1930, living a short life of 44 years. She was married to Frank Perry, son of Dominick Perri and Dominica "Minnie" Riscio. She had six children with him - Carmella, Mary Ann, Domenick, Frank, Kevin and James. Carmella and James have both passed away. They divorced, and Frank married Betty Lou Smith.

Yolanda Cacciotti died at St. Elizabeth's Hospital on November 24, 1974 after a lengthy illness.

~ *La Famiglia CROCE* ~

Ambrogio Maria Croce and Maria Carmina Itri, both from Latina, Italy, were the parents of eight children. At least three of them came to America – Antonio and Pasquale to St. Johnsville, Salvatore to Schenectady.

Immigration records seem to show Ambrogio arriving alone on February 1901 at the age of 38 years. Born May 24, 1862, Ambrogio died September 1951 in Latina, Italy. He apparently returned to his home country. Maria was born April 28, 1864 in Latina. Her death is unknown. She may have passed before Ambrogio came to America.

~ ANTONIO CROCE et ROSALIA GINOCCHI ~

ANTONIO CROCE was the first of the siblings to arrive in the United States at the age of 16, coming directly to St. Johnsville to join his father, Ambrogio on May 7, 1903. I found him in 1910 living at 23 Sanders Street in a group of 24 immigrants. I also found him at age 35 in a passenger manifest arriving August 5, 1922 with his younger brother, Salvatore. Judging from the birth dates of his children, Antonio must have made the voyage several times. Three of them were born in Italy.

Antonio was born May 11, 1887 in Latina, Italy. After a long life of 93 years, he passed away at the home of his daughter Christina (Croce) Smith on September 12, 1980. He worked most of his life on the New York Central Railroad.

ROSALIA GINOCCHI was born on January 3, 1891 in Latina, Italy. On September 21, 1928, she immigrated to St. Johnsville, bringing their three oldest children with her - Maria, 13 years, Gennaro, 9 years and Maria Grazia, 7 years. After the family came to St. Johnsville, Tony and Rosalia became the parents of Christina.

Rosalia passed away at the young age of 48 years on February 9, 1939, leaving Christina to be raised by her older sisters.

The 1930 Census shows Antonio and Rosalia own the 18 East Liberty Street home and live there with Antonio's brother, Pasquale's family. In 1940 they resided at 19 Sanders Street, before eventually purchasing their home on Mechanic Street. According to his World War II registration, the family lived at 15 Center Street in 1942.

MARIA CARMINA CROCE, the oldest child, was born in Latina, Italy and came to St. Johnsville with her mother, Rosalia to join the father, Antonio.

Maria was born March 31, 1906 and passed away at Albany Medical Center March 30, 2015, the day before her 90th birthday. She joined in marriage with Peter V. DiGiacomo May 11, 1947. They lived most of their lives in Mohawk, Peter's hometown. He passed away in 1982.

They had a son Peter, who had been married to Margaret LaCoppola of St. Johnsville.

GENNARO JAMES CROCE, known by most as Jerry, was born December 15, 1919 in Latina, Italy and emigrated with his mother, Rosalia and two sisters.

On February 9, 1942, Jerry enlisted in the Army during World War II, where he quickly had three promotions. He was honorably discharged as a Sergeant on November 5, 1945, serving in the Infantry in the European Theater.

Upon his return home, he was united in marriage with Mary Ellen Van Valkenburg from Fort Plain on May 11, 1947. They had two daughters - Judith and Patricia.

Jerry worked as the head mechanic at the Fort Plain Bus Garage until his retirement. He died of a heart attack at 59 years old on February 4, 1979 in Fort Plain.

Mary Ellen Van Valkenburg was born in 1926 and passed away in 2010.

MARIA GRAZIA "Grace" CROCE came to America at the age of seven, along with her mother and two other siblings in 1922.

Born in Latina, Italy on October 24, 1921, Grace passed away September 25, 1996. She was married to Harold J. TenEyck of Mohawk NY.

CRESTINA PATRICIA CROCE was the only child born in America, sometime around 1930. Crestina's mother, Rosalia passed away when she was nine years old.

On October 4, 1953, Crestina Croce married Charles Augusta Smith from Amsterdam. Attending her were cousins - Leonora Cacciotti as maid of honor and Mary Croce Mastracco as the bridesmaid. A reception was held at the American Legion rooms, preceded by a dinner at the Manor. They had two children - Charles, Jr. and Rosalie, obviously named after her grandmother.

Crestina worked at the Luxuray in Fort Plain, Charles at GE in Schenectady. The couple made their home with her father on Mechanic Street until building a new home on Timmerman Avenue, where they lived until Charles' passing.

Charles A. Smith was born May 22, 1928 in Troy. He died February 29, 1996 in St. Johnsville.

~ PASQUALE CROCE et MARY L. LANDOLFI ~

PASQUALE CROCE was born in Italy around 1890. He passed away July 7, 1967 in St. Johnsville.

Pasquale aka Patsy first came to America on May 3, 1910 at the age of 18, joining his older brother Antonio. According to the 1910 Census, Tony was one of the 24 Italian immigrant men who were living at 23 Sanders Street in the Italian Quarters. Patsy was employed in a knitting mill.

The 1915 Census shows Patsy as a boarder at 34 Hough Street with the Joseph Romano family.

Patsy apparently lived in Herkimer, as shown on his World War I application, where he also worked in a knitting mill before moving back to St. Johnsville permanently.

Being inducted into World War I on May 27, 1918, he served overseas from July 24, 1918 to April 21, 1919. Pvt. 1st Class Pasquale Croce was in the 51st Pioneer Infantry and Army of Occupation. Over fifty years later, the Morris J. Edwards Post American Legion, St. Johnsville, honored him for a half-century of membership in the Post. He was among the few St. Johnsville Italian immigrants who served in World War I. Upon his discharge, Patsy apparently returned to St. Johnsville to join his brother, Antonio.

On August 12, 1919, he applied for a Passport stating he had lived in St. Johnsville since 1910. It seems he returned to his homeland after the war and married Mary L. Landolfi. On April 5, 1921, Patsy, at 28 years of age, emigrated with his wife, Mary, and their two-month-old daughter, Theresa.

They first lived at 34 Hough Street before eventually purchasing their 18 East Liberty Street home, where they lived out their lives with other children. They were the parents of five children - Theresa, Rose Marie, Joseph, Mary and Thomas.

MARY LANDOLFI was born May 3, 1899 in Latina, Caserta, Italy, daughter of Pasquale and Esther Landolfi. Mary passed away at the St. Johnsville Nursing Home August 18, 1993 at the age of 94. Mary had survived a serious accident when she was knocked down by a Village of St. Johnsville pickup truck that was backing up, the driver not seeing her. She suffered serious leg injuries.

THERESA CROCE, at the age of just two months old, came to America with her parents from Latina, Italy. Born New Year's Day, January 1, 1921, she is most likely the youngest immigrant coming to St. Johnsville. The only child born in Italy, she passed away October 25, 2009.

Theresa married Genario Candella from Little Falls. They had a daughter, Diana Marie.

ROSE MARIE CROCE was the first-born child in St. Johnsville on March 29, 1922, most likely at 34 Hough Street. She married Lawrence Joseph Connor from Green Island NY on October 17, 1953. Lawrence Connor was born in Troy in 1926 and died 1979 in Green Island NY. Rose Marie Croce passed away April 15, 1999 in Troy.

JOSEPH CROCE was the oldest son, born June 17, 1923.

On January 23, 1943, Joe enlisted in the US Army Air Corps of World War II. He was sent to North Africa and Europe, where he was in the British Army Signal Corp., learning how to build and operate radar information centers. He used this knowledge for the construction of the French School of Radar, being cited by the free French government for his achievement.

After returning home, Joseph Croce married Erma M. Osborn from Fort Plain on September 1, 1946. They had two children - Mary Ann and David.

In 1949 Joe joined the Bauder Oil Co., Fort Plain, where he worked in the heating and air conditioning industry for many years before retiring and moving to Zephyhills, FL with his wife, Erma. He passed away there at the age of 85 on September 19, 2008.

MARY CROCE is the youngest daughter, being born in 1926, most likely at 18 East Liberty Street. Mary joined in wedlock with Henry Mastracco, son of Marcello Pietro Mastracco and Jenovino Nalli of St. Johnsville, on June 14, 1953. You can read more about Mary and Henry in *La Famiglia Mastracco*.

I vividly remember Mary and her sisters always being so well dressed. I admired them when they attended church, all decked out. They seemed to be the best customers of my neighbor, Anna House, a noted seamstress on South Division Street. Many were the times I saw them going there with clothes to be altered.

THOMAS JOSEPH CROCE, the youngest child and son, was born in 1933. As a junior in high school, Tom was selected by the St. Johnsville American Legion to represent them at Boy's State. After graduating in 1951, he attended both Oswego and Albany State Colleges, studying Science.

At 22 years of age, Tom entered the service in November 1954, serving in the Vietnam War as a Pfc. in the 504th Field Artillery Battalion. Upon his return home, in 1958 Tom was hired by his alma mater to teach Junior High Science. He later taught High School chemistry and became the head of the Science department. He taught in St. Johnsville for several years until his retirement.

Thomas Joseph Croce married Barbara Ann Wheeler from Gloversville in July 1972. They both are very involved with the St. Johnsville Senior Saints group, Tom serving as president for many years, with Barbara using her creative skills to plan various events. Tom was always involved in extracurricular activities and served as an officer in many of his high school clubs.

~ *La Famiglia ROMANO* ~

~ GIUSEPPE ROMANO et CARMELLA DiLEMBO ~

GIUSEPPE "Joseph" ROMANO was born January 25, 1886 in Baia e Latina, Caserta Italy, the son of Thomas Romano and Philomena Etri. He had two sisters, Carmella Romano, wife of Paul Cacciotti, and Guilia Romano, wife of Silviano Laurora, both living in St. Johnsville. His brother Antonio never emigrated from Italy.

Joseph arrived in America March 16, 1903, at the age of 18. In 1912 he was single, living at 10 Center Street and working on the New York Central Railroad.

Giuseppe Romano married Carmella DiLembo, at St. Mary's Church, Little Falls. I am assuming they met in Little Falls, where Carmella was living with her sister, Congetta. She was the daughter of Nicholas DiLembo and Raffaela Liotti, from Molise, Campabasso, Italy. They had five children - Thomas, Maddelena, Fred, Peter and Philomena.

The 1915 Census shows the couple already living at 34 Hough Street with their 1-year-old son, Thomas, and a boarder, Pasquale Croce, who was a cousin to Joseph. Their mothers were sisters. Joseph worked at a knitting mill. They are still residing here in 1920, with the first three children and John Ponzi as a boarder, also working at a knitting mill. John Ponzi married Carmella's sister, Stella.

In 1925, the couple was still living at 34 Hough Street, where they both lived out their lives. They had their last child, Philomena, but had recently lost their first daughter, Maddalena, one month before the census. Joseph was now working again on the New York Central Railroad.

Giuseppe Romano died April 21, 1960, in Elmira NY at the home of his son, Tom, who had been home for Easter. Joe had returned with him for few days' visit.

CARMELLA DiLEMBO was born in 1886 in Molise, Italy. She died May 13, 1956. Carmella spent Christmas of 1908 onboard the ship bringing her to her new home, arriving the day after Christmas, December 26, 1908. She went to Little Falls, where a cousin and sponsor, Vittorio Giarusso lived. Besides Estella DiLembo Ponzi, she had a sister, Congetta, living in Herkimer.

MADDALENA "Lena" ROMANO was born March 8, 1910 in St. Johnsville. She died 15 years later in March 1925. Apparently, Maddalena was a sickly child. At the age of 11 years, it seems she was sent alone to Baia e Latina, her father's hometown in Italy. The January 24, 1921 temporary passport application states she is going there due to illness and will return in six months; she returned on November 3, 1921. Her father made out the application, but I don't believe he accompanied her. I find no records of his return and he did not include his name as a traveler on the application. Perhaps the family felt she would recuperate better in the arid climate of Italy and sent her there to be with family?

THOMAS R. ROMANO was born August 15, 1913 at the Hough Street home. He died January 20, 1996 in Elmira, where he lived most of his life. He never married. Tom enlisted in the Army of World War II on April 16, 1941. After his discharge, he graduated from Clarkson College, Potsdam and taught Business subjects in Elmira schools.

FRED CHARLES ROMANO was born January 7, 1917 at home. In May 1943, Fred Romano married Jennie Colangelo of Little Falls, daughter of Louis Colangelo and Angela Zambri, at St. Joseph's Church, Little Falls. They had three children - Madeleine, Laraine and Robert.

Fred attended Defense Training School and became a qualified licensed electrician, employed by the government, retiring in 1984. In 1947 he moved to Phoenix AZ, where he lived his life with his first wife, Jennie, until her passing on November 10, 1963. Jennie Colangelo was born in Little Falls on January 27, 1922.

On February 12, 1967, Fred married Maxine Doris Zuege of Phoenix. Fred Charles Romano followed his brother, Peter in death on October 12, 2003 at 84 years. He is buried with his first wife, Jennie in Phoenix.

PETER P. ROMANO was born July 10, 1921 and passed away June 9, 2003 in a Utica hospital at 81 years of age.

He graduated from St. Johnsville High School in the Class of 1940.

On September 19, 1942, he married Angelina Rizzi, daughter of Vito and Concetta Rizzi of Little Falls, at St. Joseph's Catholic Church, Little Falls. They had two sons - Peter, Jr. and Dr. James Romano.

Five days after his wedding, Peter entered the US Army, serving in the Coast Guard in New Orleans and Panama. He was honorably discharged on October 25, 1945 and went on to become a master plumber, a career that expanded 45 years. He was a member of the DeCarlo Staffo VFW Post of Little Falls.

Angelina "Angie" Rizzi was born in 1920 in Little Falls. She passed away on October 14, 2016 at 96 years, at the home of her son, Dr. James Romano in Victor NY, where she had resided the last 13 years.

Many who shopped at the Boston Store in Little Falls, where she worked over 25 years, would know Angie. She was the employee who greeted you with a congenial smile. She was not one to push the inventory on a customer, as the owners would. I most always found whatever I was shopping for in that store, but preferred the assistance of Angie.

PHILOMENA MARIE ROMANO was the center of a New Year's Day celebration with her birth January 1, 1924 in St. Johnsville. She was the daughter of Giuseppe Romano and Carmella DiLembo. I've been told that Philomena weighed only two pounds at birth and her mother would use the oven as an incubator to keep her warm and alive. It certainly worked!

Phyl passed away on September 19, 1998 at age 74, at the 16 Hough Street home, where she and her husband, Ray, lived out their retirement years. This was the home of Ray's parents for all of their years. I'm assuming Ray was born here?

On April 29, 1947, Philomena Marie Romano was united in marriage with Raymond Peter Coco, son of Desiderio Coco and Carmelia Corso. Attending the couple were Clara Palitti, maid of honor; cousin Leonora Cacciotti as bridesmaid; best man Richard Francisco and usher Joseph Francisco. The ceremony was followed by a dinner at Henry's Restaurant in Little Falls, with a reception in the St. Johnsville American Legion rooms. They had one son, Raymond, Jr., born in September 1948.

The couple resided at the home of the groom's parents at 16 Hough Street for many years before moving to an apartment over their business on West Main Street, where they resided while in business.

Phyl was a 1941 graduate of St. Johnsville and was first employed at the F.S. Dress Company of Little Falls.

Renato (Raymond Peter) Coco was born July 25, 1921 in the family home at 16 Hough Street in St. Johnsville. After graduating in 1940, he served two years in the US Marine Corps as a Sergeant from March 31, 1943 through March 19, 1946, in the Pacific Theater.

In 1950, Ray and Phyl purchased the St. Johnsville Hardware Company from long-time owner, Claude Bottomley. Phyl and Ray refurbished the upstairs apartment. The Coco's later purchased the brick portion originally owned by Charles McCrone, from Michael Galuski. It was originally a paint and wallpaper store for many years. It now serves as the American Legion Post organization's home.

In 1995, Phyl and Ray sold the business property and enjoyed a much-deserved retirement. They had moved back into the Coco home on Hough Street with Carmelia after Desiderio's death. Ray became employed with the village of St. Johnsville at the St. Johnsville Housing development off Averill Street for several years. Ray died on March 28, 2002 at 81 years of age, while on his walk home following a daily breakfast get-together with friends at Lamanna's Restaurant.

~ *La Famiglia LAURORA* ~

~ SILVIANO VINCENZO LAURORA et GUILIA ROMANO ~

SILVIANO VINCENZO LAURORA aka James Laurora arrived in America at the age of 34 on June 12, 1907. He claimed a friend, Antonio Mancini, sponsored him. Sylviano was born in Terracina, Italy on May 13, 1873 to Francesco L'Aurora and Maria Giuseppina Riccardi.

GUILIA "Julia" ROMANO followed her husband to America on December 4, 1910, bringing their three daughters, Domenica, age 9; Giovanna, age 8; and Rosaria, age 3, from Terracina. Born in 1886 in Baia, Latina, Guilia was the daughter of Thomas Romano and Maria Filomena Itri. She was also a sister of Giuseppe Romano, St. Johnsville and Antonio Romano in Italy.

Silviano Laurora and Guilia Romano were married in Italy. They had already settled into their 24 Sanders Street home by 1917, when James registered for the World War I draft. At the time he worked on the New York Central Railroad in an administrative position.

By 1920 they owned the home and had three more children - Mary, Perminio and Frank. Julia was working in a knitting mill. It seems apparent that daughters Domenica and Rosaria may have died during the Influenza epidemic. I find no record of them after their arrival.

Their daughter, Giovanna aka Nina, was also living with them with her husband, Guerrino Salvatore Fontana aka Kain Fontana, and two of their young daughters - Teresa and Perina.

In 1925, Census records show only James, Julia, Perminio and Frank, no Mary. 1930 records show a Maria born at a later date. It's a little confusing with the Mary and Maria; they both have different birth years. I've been unable to find any further data. Perhaps they both died at birth? Also, it was quite common to name the next child after one who had recently died.

By 1930 the couple was now living at the 28 Sanders Street property they had purchased around 1924 from Michael Rapacz for $4500. Julia initially continued with the grocery store.

An October 20, 1937 article states Angelo Tolfa and Gus Heitz obtained a liquor license for 28 Sanders Street. Perhaps they were renting part of the business area?

By 1940 Julia had established the New York Central Grill, specializing in food and drinks. James was listed as the owner / proprietor with Julia as cook. Their son, Perminio was still at home. He worked for the St. Johnsville Post Office. They also had a boarder, Anthony Sicilian.

Silviano Vincenzo Laurora died at his home, 28 Sanders Street, on May 8, 1945, just short of his 75th birthday. He worked his entire life on the New York Central Railroad. Only two of his children were survivors - Nina and Perminio.

Guilia Romano passed away September 4, 1953 after several months of illness, a resident of Charlotte's Nursing Home in Little Falls.

The Laurora family would be related to Phyl Romano Coco's family.

~ GUERRINO SALVATORE FONTANA et GIOVANNA LAURORA ~

GUERRINO SALVATORE FONTANA aka Kain, the son of Antonio Fontana and Teresa Ulgiati, arrived from Terracina in 1907. It seems he went directly to St. Johnsville. I find no connection with Antonio Fontana on Sanders Street who was from Maenza.

On June 13, 1915, Guerrino "Kain" Fontana married Giovanna "Nina" Laurora, daughter of Sylviano Laurora and Guilia Romano, in Little Falls. Nina was just 16; Kain was quite a bit older at 29 years. Her parents signed for her. It was quite common in those days for older men to marry teenage girls. Witnesses to the marriage were Evaristo Masi and Rosaio Corzi (Rosadia Corso.)

In 1920, the couple was living at 24 Sanders Street with Nina's parents, and had two young daughters, Teresa and Perina. Kain was working on the railroad. By 1925 they lived at the same address, renting the home, and now had a son, Roggiero. Nina's parents, the Laurora's, had moved to 28 Sanders Street.

1930 shows them still renting the home and Kain working as a garage mechanic. By this time they had their third daughter, Mary. By 1940 they had apparently moved and were again renting 26 Sanders Street. Kain worked as a dredge man on construction. I'm assuming this was with the Erie Canal system?

They moved again when Kain's wife, Nina inherited and took over the New York Central Grill, when her mother became ill and later passed away. Her parents had purchased the 28 Sanders property on the corner of South Division Street. This would have been the first Rapacz Meat Market. In June 1953, Nina applied for a liquor license under the business name of The Friendly Tavern.

My cousin, Dan Matis tells the story of going there with our grandfather, Giuseppe Sindici. My grandmother would insist that Dan accompany him, ensuring Grampa wouldn't drink so much. Usually sitting on Grampa's knee, Dan said he slid off one time and landed in the spittoon. It was quite a popular watering hole and restaurant, especially for the dairy farmers after they had dropped off their milk supplies nearby and gone to Rapacz' for groceries.

At the age of 80, Guerrino Salvatore Fontana lost his life in yet another tragic train accident on a Thursday morning of October 17, 1963. He had been tending his garden located across the railroad tracks behind the train station. Upon attempting to make his way home by crossing the tracks in front of his home, Kain was killed instantly by a New York Central freight train, suffering a fractured skull and multiple fractures. As one train passed by, he thought another was on a different track than where he was positioned. He had previously worked for the NYCRR and later retired from the Allegro Shoe Company in 1953.

GIOVANNA "Nina" LAURORA was born in Terracina on December 23, 1901, the second born child of Silviano and Guilia Laurora, and one of only two who survived to adulthood. She came to America with her mother on December 4, 1910 at the age of eight. She died on July 6, 1980 at the age of 79. The newspaper stated 75, which seems incorrect, given her birthdate.

Nina was quite active throughout her life. She was a member of St. Patrick's Altar Rosary Society, Navy Mother's Club and St. Johnsville Senior Saints. Giving up her restaurant/bar business, she became employed by the Allegro Shoe Company. After retirement in 1963, one could find her in the kitchen at her daughter, Perina Fontana DiCamillo's Century Tavern.

TERESA GENEVIEVE FONTANA, the first child of Kain and Nina Fontana was born January 26, 1916 in St. Johnsville. She lived her whole life on Sanders Street. On September 18, 1937, she married Bennie Bommarito of Frankfort. Following the service, a wedding breakfast and dinner were served at the home of her parents, followed by a reception at the Ukrainian Club Rooms, just a short walk away, behind the Rapacz Meat Market on South Division Street. They had one daughter, Olivia.

The couple first lived at 24 Sanders Street most of their lives. They later downsized, turned the home over to their daughter, Olivia and purchased a mobile home situated across the street.

Teresa graduated from St. Johnsville High in the Class of 1934 with my Mom, Rose Sindici Perry. She passed away on April 11, 1993.

PERINA FONTANA was born November 11, 1919 at the family home on Sanders Street, where she eventually retired. She graduated from St. Johnsville High with honor roll recognitions.

On September 30, 1939 Perina Fontana was joined in marriage with Dominick J. DiCamillo of Frankfort, son of Lawrence DiCamillo and Josephine Dee, in St. Patrick's Catholic Church. They had two sons - Lawrence and Ronald. I'm assuming Perina may have met Dominick through her brother-in-law, Bennie?

While Dominick aka Durkee was serving in World War II, Perina lived with her parents at 28 Sanders Street. Perina received her restaurant training assisting her mother at The Friendly Tavern. An October 1942 news article states Dominick DiCamillo had obtained a liquor license under the New York Central Restaurant.

Employed at the Beech-Nut Packing Company, Durkee joined the Armed Services on January 30, 1943. He was first stationed in Hartford CN. As a Pvt. 1st Class, he was sent to the European Theatre and honorably discharged in January 1946. Coincidentally, Durkee met up with Perina's uncle, Perminio in Europe, as noted in Perminio's life story following.

In 1947 upon Durkee's return to civilian life, he and Perina became the proprietors of the Century Tavern in Mindenville, across from Erie Canal Lock 16. They conducted the famous cocktail bar until 1965, when they both retired and sold the business. Sandwiches and light fare were always available, usually prepared by Nina, Perina's mom. They also catered small events. The family lived in the upstairs apartment.

As I can attest, this was undoubtedly the most popular venue in the area for dancing the night away on Fridays and Saturdays to the big band sounds resonating from the jukebox selections. The memories of spending many wonderful date nights with my husband in the friendly ambience of the Century Tavern, aka Durkee's, are forever embedded in my heart.

Durkee was also employed for 20 years by the New York State Department of Transportation in a day job at this time. During the ownership of the Century Tavern, he served as president of the Liquor Dealers Association of Montgomery County and Sergeant-at-arms of the NYS Liquor Dealers. Locally, he was a member of the American Legion, H.C. Smith Benefit Club, a board director of the St. Johnsville Greater Health Center and a member of the Civil Service Employees Association.

Dominick J. DiCamillo was born November 21, 1916 and passed away on December 7, 1977 at the 23 Sanders Street home, where the couple had retired. He suffered a heart attack and was pronounced dead on arrival at Little Falls Hospital. He was 61 years old.

Employed at Corso Dress Company for several years, Perina acted as an employee representative at the ILGWU, AFL-CIO meetings. Perina was a member of the Ladies Auxiliary of the American Legion and an active member of the St. Johnsville Business Girls. She was also very creative and designed unusual "egg head" dolls, dressed in various attire. Her Christmas Santa dolls were the most popular. Her dolls would be displayed for sale on the back bar of the tavern.

From their teen years, Perina and my mom, Rose Sindici Perry, were the best of friends. After the deaths of their husbands, with both loving to dance and enjoy life, they would get all "dolled up" and venture out on a Saturday evening to an Amsterdam venue, where they would enjoy dancing to the big band sounds of Columbus "Russ" Fiorini and his combo. Another lady friend, Mary Jones, would accompany them.

One evening, Perina became acquainted with a gentleman from Amsterdam. She and Al Moore were later married and relocated to Largo, FL to live out their active lives. Every time I hear their song "Strangers in the Night", I think of Perina.

Perina enjoyed life to the fullest. She traveled to Hawaii with my mom, Rose, Aunt Lena and Mary Jones, where they donned their grass skirts, colorful floral leis and joined in the festivities of the island, enjoying the company and music of Don Ho. I have some memorable photos of them.

Two weeks after her 90th birthday, Perina Fontana DiCamillo Moore passed away on November 24, 2010 in Largo FL. Four years before her death, Perina lost her first grandchild, Michael DiCamillo, son of Ronald DiCamillo and Cheryl Gabriel. He died unexpectedly at age 38.

ROGGIERO FRANCIS FONTANA aka Roger was born December 23, 1923, in St. Johnsville, but lived most of his life in Houston TX.

Like his uncle Perminio, he served his country in World War II in the U.S. Marine Corps. Receiving his boot training February 2, 1942 at Parris Island NC, he was assigned to Jacksonville FL as a machinist mate in the Marine Corps Air Wing. He later was assigned to Santa Barbara, then on to the Pacific Theater. Roger was one of the first waves of Marines who landed in Okinawa and other Pacific Islands. He had a brief stint in Japan before his discharge in December 1945. He also served several years in the Merchant Marines.

Roger later returned to Japan, where he married Kayoko Sano (Kay Tisshu) on November 18, 1965. He was employed as a carpenter in a housing construction company in Houston TX.

At the age of 56, Roger Fontana was stricken with a major stroke. He lived in a coma state until his passing in the Veteran's Hospital in Houston on November 23, 1980.

MARY FONTANA, the youngest of the siblings, was born February 16, 1926.

An active student, Mary graduated with the St. Johnsville High School Class of 1943. She was a member of the Glee Club, Secretary of the Drama Club and a Basketball Cheerleader. Her group had the honor of being selected for a 2nd place medal of honor in a cheerleading contest. Mary's yearbook photo mantra states, "Take life seriously and what have you?"

On March 18, 1946, Mary Fontana married Carl Donadio, son of Mr. and Mrs. Patsy Donadio, Little Falls. A wedding dinner was held for family members at Casa Loma, Little Falls, with a reception following at the St. Joseph Catholic Church hall. It seems they were married at St. Joseph's? Celia Colorito served her good friend as maid of honor, with her future husband, Carl's brother, John as best man. Mary later was maid of honor in Celia's wedding. Palmena Francisco was the bridesmaid. Mary was also a bridesmaid in Gilda Francisco's wedding.

Mary went on to become a hairdresser for most of her life. She was employed at Catherine's Beauty Salon, Little Falls. Carl worked at Read's Florist. After her marriage she set up her own business - Mary's Beauty Salon in an area of her mother's downstairs restaurant and bar business.

Mary later moved to Houston TX. I'm not certain if Carl moved with her; they subsequently were divorced and Carl moved back to Little Falls, later remarrying. Mary married twice more in Houston - Glen Burgess and John Gudelman. I don't find any record of Mary having children. I did discover that she also went by Mary DeStefano in 1959?

Mary Fontana Gudelman passed away in Missouri City TX on December 5, 2013 at age 87.

This completes the Kain Fontana – Nina Laurora family.

PERMINIO S. LAURORA was born in St. Johnsville on January 21, 1915 and died in March 1986 in St. Petersburg, FL, where he had lived and retired after his stint in the US Army. He was one of the two surviving children of James Laurora and Julia Romano.

Before entering the service, he had been a substitute mail carrier with the St. Johnsville Post Office. Perminio was inducted into the Army on February 12, 1941 receiving his training at both Camp Hulen TX and San Diego CA. In March 1943 he attended Officer Candidates School at Camp Davis in North Carolina, where he was commissioned a 2nd Lieutenant on May 27, 1943. He was sent overseas that November.

Perminio was the first local man inducted into the Army after the Selective Service became effective. He was one of the many soldiers who landed at Normandy, France. While in Europe, Perminio met up with Cpl. Dominick DiCamillo, his niece Perina's husband, in a small town on the Swiss border.

While in England, prior to the European invasion, he met and married his wife, Eileen Barnes, on May 8, 1944. She had lived near the Army base where he was stationed. Perminio later became an instructor in the Coast Artillery at Camp Davis.

FRANK LAURORA lived a short life of 16 years after contracting pleura-pneumonia. He was born January 14, 1918 and died at home on February 16, 1934. Attending his sophomore year in St. Johnsville High School, Frank was a popular student. He was the youngest son of James and Julia Laurora.

~ *La Famiglia PONZI* ~

~ GIOVANNI PONZI et MARIA STELLA DiLEMBO ~

At 18 years of age, Giovanni "John" Ponzi made the long journey to America on April 1, 1907, finding his way to St. Johnsville to work on the New York Central Railroad, where he worked most of his short life. He became one of the 16 boarders in a house filled with 23 residents on Sanders Street aka the Italian Section. The 1912 City Directory shows him living at 15 Sanders, probably the same house.

Maria Stella DiLembo arrived on November 22, 1911 going to her sister, Carmela Romano's home in St. Johnsville. They shared a sister, Concetta, who married Michelangelo "Michael" Giarusso.

On May 15, 1913 Stella DiLembo and Giovanni Ponzi were married and had their first-born son, Angelo in 1915.

As stated on John's enlistment papers of July 23, 1918, he had a wife and child. He was living at 21 Sanders Street. John served in the First World War as a Private in the Army. While stationed at Camp Fort Dix, he was naturalized on November 30, 1918. When serving in the war, Italians automatically received their citizenship papers.

After his discharge, the 1920 Census shows only John residing with his in-laws, Giuseppe Romano and Carmela Di Lembo at 34 Hough Street and working in a knitting mill.

October 11, 1920, John applied for a passport to return to Italy to visit his mother. It also stated he was to bring back his wife and boy, but that was crossed off? On May 30, 1923, he returned with his wife, "Mariastella", as stated on the manifest, and son, Zaccaria only eight months old. They were not listed on the original passport application. Apparently, Stella had returned to Italy alone.

Besides the two sons, Angelo and Zachary, the Ponzi couple had four more children - Mary, Louis, Regina, and Renalda. By 1930 they had purchased their final residence at 7 Spring Street. By this time John had returned to working on the railroad.

GIOVANNI PONZI was born in Norma, Italy on July 2, 1889, to Zacharia and Louisa Ponzi. He died March 24, 1948, yet another tragic victim of the New York Central Railroad, shortly after enjoying lunch with his co-worker and friend, Alexander "Alec" Vecciarelli. The men were walking back to the freight house, when a train that had been sitting idly on the track before the lunch break, started backing up slowly. Neither of the men heard it. John died instantly, while Alec was caught under the engine. Alec's legs were both severed below the knees and he lost a lot of blood. After valiant efforts by Dr. Raymond Wytrwal and the staff at Little Falls Hospital, he succumbed to his injuries. The accident happened a short distance from the Vecciarelli home at 10 Sanders Street. The railroad company settled with Mrs. Ponzi and John's children for the sum of $8500.

MARIA STELLA DiLEMBO was born around 1894 in Molise, Italy, the daughter of Ernesto DiLembo and Raphaele Liotti. It seems she never worked outside the home, only caring for their six children. I'm convinced her marriage was arranged through her sister, Carmela DiLembo Romano.

Stella DiLembo passed away on September 12, 1955 in St. Johnsville.

ANGELO P. PONZI was the first of three sons born to John and Stella on February 25, 1915. It is not clear if he was born in Italy or St. Johnsville. Due to the timelines of his parents, I'm guessing St. Johnsville. He died in June 1971 in Little Falls. Angelo was married to Florence Agnes Peckover of Little Falls.

ZACHARY J. PONZI was born on August 3, 1922 in Italy, while his parents were there for three years on a visit. His brother, Angelo is not listed on the returning passenger list, so I wonder who may have taken care of him while his parents were gone? Perhaps Stella's sister, Carmella Romano?

Zach was married twice. In 1942 he married Antoinette Zazzero. On March 3, 1991 he married Judy Phillips. Zach was very musical, entertaining throughout his life with his guitar and mouth organ. He died November 20, 1999 in Gloversville.

MARY A. PONZI, the oldest sister, was born in 1925 in St. Johnsville. On May 5, 1956, she was married to Richard C. Groshans of Caroga Lake and Gloversville. I find no date of death or further information.

LOUIS PONZI, the youngest son, was born in St. Johnsville, January 5, 1928. He died in November 1976 at St. Mary's Hospital, Amsterdam.

Louis also married twice, the first time to Louella Mosher of St. Johnsville. They had six children - Barbara, Louise, Marie Colorito, Mary Ann, who died in a tragic automobile accident while in high school, Mary Lou and a son, John.

Louis later married Lucy Conti from Canajoharie. At one time he was the proprietor of the Boulevard Tavern in Canajoharie.

REGINA PONZI was born June 18, 1930 in St. Johnsville. She passed away in Stafford Springs, CN on June 10, 2011, just days before her birthday. On December 8, 1951 Regina married Frederick Rivenburgh of St. Johnsville in Bennington VT.

RENALDA PONZI was the youngest of the six siblings. She was born December 28, 1931. She passed away on September 18, 2017.

Renalda Ponzi was joined in marriage with Marvin Culver of Johnstown after graduation. Although a few years older than me, I remember her in high school as a varsity cheerleader, while I was on the junior varsity squad and also as a great dancer. She was very warm and outgoing.

It seems that Zach and Louis Ponzi were both quite proficient with the guitar, forming a group and even recording a demo record. They played at Cap's Cigar Store at times. There seems to be a lot of musical talent in this family among Zachary, Regina, Renalda, Louis and some of his daughters.

~ *La Famiglia GIARRUSSO* ~

The Giarrusso and DiLembo families were both quite extensive, with each producing numerous children. With the joining of the two families, many more heirs were added to their family tree. Both have links to the St. Johnsville immigrants.

The bulk of the Giarrusso family lived in Little Falls. None of their immigrants settled in St. Johnsville. However, there are ties to some of the St. Johnsville families.

First, we have the marriage of Michael E. Giarrusso to Lillian E. Massari of St. Johnsville. Margaret Primer, wife of Frederick Giarrusso, was a sister of Stanley Primer who married Rosa Battisti, daughter of Peter and Anna Piniaha Battisti.

Sisters, Carmella DiLembo Romano and Stella DiLembo Ponzi, were sisters to Concetta DiLembo. The DiLembo family in my research thus far dates back to 1775. A great deal of in-depth Genealogical research would be required to clarify all their descendants.

~ MICHELANGELO GIARRUSSO et CONCETTA DiLEMBO ~

Michelangelo "Michael" Giarrusso and Concetta DiLembo were both born in Campolieto, Moline, Italy, where they were joined in marriage on New Year's Eve, December 31, 1872. Several of their children were born there and came to America, either with their father in 1888 or their mother in 1905.

The family initially lived in Canajoharie before moving to Little Falls. According to 1905 NYS Census records, Michelangelo was living with his son, Vittorino and family at 9 Mohawk Street in Canajoharie, where both worked as bartenders. I believe this is now the large corner parking lot, which was the previous site of the Hotel Wagner.

Concetta DiLembo came over after the 1905 Census. On April 21, 1905, she and two of her children, Carmela and Giuseppe seemed to have been turned back, their names being crossed off the ship's manifest. Concetta returned again on June 23, 1905, alone.

By 1910, the Giarrusso's were residents of Little Falls, where they lived the remainder of their lives. Michelangelo Giarrusso was born July 22, 1847 and died in Little Falls sometime before 1920. Concetta DiLembo was born December 10, 1850 and died in Little Falls sometime before 1930.

~ VITTORINO GIARRUSSO et FILOMENA ALDI ~

This is where we have another connection to the *Italians of St. Johnsville*. Vittorino "Victor" Giarrusso married Filomena "Florence" Aldi in 1898 in Little Falls. Filomena had arrived October 28, 1898 at the age of 20, first going to Gloversville. The couple had ten children, all born in Little Falls. It seems one of them died at an early age, as there were two with the same name. It was common to name another child after one who had passed away.

VITTORINO GIARRUSSO was born in Campolieto, Molise, Italy on October 29, 1873. He passed away on August 28, 1967 in Phoenix AZ, where several of the Giarrusso's had eventually moved.

FILOMENA ALDI was born in 1878 in Caserta, Italy. I find no death records.

MICHAEL EDWARD GIARRUSSO, the oldest sibling, was born in Canajoharie on January 11, 1900. His family moved to Little Falls where he attended schools and lived until his marriage. He passed away on October 19, 1986 at St. Elizabeth Hospital, Utica, living in St. Johnsville at the time.

On Christmas Eve, December 24, 1923, Michael Edward Giarrusso and Lillian Massari, daughter of Antonio Massare and Angeline Sausto, applied for a marriage license. The wedding took place at St. Patrick's Church in St. Johnsville on January 6, 1924. William Lucas and the groom's sister, Stella Giarrusso, were witnesses.

The couple first lived in Little Falls, where their two sons - Harold and George were born. Tragically, at the age of 21, Harold was killed when colliding with a car while riding his motor scooter in Caroga Lake on August 8, 1946. I found his name in a Montgomery County list of deceased veterans who were buried in Prospect View Cemetery. He may have recently returned from service.

When they celebrated their 50th Anniversary in 1974, the couple was living in Fort Plain. From what I can determine they lived there at least until 1983, then moved to St. Johnsville. After Michael's death, Lillian moved to Phoenix AZ in 1991 to be with her son, George.

From November 11, 1919 to August 20, 1921, Michael had served in the U.S. Navy during World War I. He worked as a security guard at Remington Arms during World War II, later at the H.P. Snyder Bicycle Manufacturing Co. and a policeman in Little Falls. Lillian was a factory worker.

Lillian E. Massari was born on February 22, 1905 at her family home on the River Road in Minden. She passed away on November 28, 1995 at St. Joseph's Hospital, Phoenix AZ, where she had resided with her son, George since 1991.

FREDERICK A. GIARRUSSO, seventh child and son of Vittorino Giarrusso and Filomena Aldi, was born April 27, 1911 in Little Falls. He passed away in Phoenix AZ on November 19, 1963 at 52 years of age.

Margaret Elizabeth Primer, daughter of John Primer and Jenny Frances Lonchar, was born in Manheim, Herkimer on November 29, 1917. While living in St. Johnsville, she passed away on October 4, 1970.

The couple was married around 1933 and lived in Little Falls during the early years of their marriage. They had two children - Frederick and Francine, both graduates of St. Johnsville High School. Young Fred was salutatorian of his class of 1954.

In 1940 Fred was working as a welder at the H.P. Snyder Bicycle Manufacturing Co. and Marge worked in a dress factory.

Eventually the couple moved to St. Johnsville, where they purchased property on Route 5 West across from the intersection of Kennedy Road, from Fred's uncle, Louis Amarosa on November 23, 1943. It consisted of a small house and garage. Fred built an addition to be used for Margie's roadside food stand. When his family moved to Phoenix in 1952, this property was sold to Fred's cousin, Louis Ponzi and his wife, Louella Mosher.

In the late 1940s, Fred also built a large concrete block building next door, which he used for his auto repair shop. In June of 1951, his sister, Helena "Lena" and her husband, Leon Youker, purchased the building and added an upstairs apartment, where they lived until moving to Phoenix AZ in 1955, selling the property to Christian Schumacher and his wife. They in turn must have sold the block building to Floyd Snell, Sr.

I have a great deal of interest in this block building, as my husband, John Palma and I were the proud owners from October 1971 until February 1986, purchasing it from the estate of Floyd Snell, Sr. We auctioned all of the piled high "stuff" and refurbished the building into an Arts and Crafts Consignment Shop for me. Three years later it became The Red Palette Bridal Center after a disastrous fire in 1973 caused by squirrels eating into the electrical wires caused considerable damage to the upstairs area. John also developed Serenity Mobile Home Park, a lovely site in the rear of the building with spacious lots for our tenants. Sadly, the building no longer exists, destroyed right to the ground by a careless inferno a few years ago.

* Francine Giarrusso Wigton contributed to this article. Grazie!

~ *La Famiglia PETER C. BATTISTI* ~

~ PETER C. BATTISTI et ANNA PINIAHA ~

PETER C. BATTISTI was quite well known as someone active in the dairy farming industry for many years. Sometime between 1915 and 1917, Peter and his Austrian, wife, Anna Piniaha, moved to the Kringsbush rural area of St. Johnsville, where they were renters of a dairy farm. By 1932 they had become the proud owners, successfully establishing their life long livelihood.

Born May 8, 1890 in Supino, Italy, Peter C. Battisti was the son of Egidio "Lewis" Battisti and Rosa Cevitini. He had a brother, Angelo, who also came to America and lived in St. Johnsville.

I located a passenger manifest of June 15, 1905, that seemed to match Peter. It shows a Pietro Battisti immigrating at age 15. This young man was going to connect with a cousin Umberto Vespasiano in New York City? That's the closest I could find. It is unbelieveable how many Pietro Battisti's I have found. Battisti was quite a common name, especially in Supino.

I do find Peter in the 1910 Census at 20 years old, working in a knitting mill and living with his mother, Rosa and brother, Angelo, age 16, at 9 Spring Street. Other boarders were Master Mastrofrancesco, who most likely was John Francisco, Richard's father; Guy Gong and Antonio Sundree. It is my assumption that Peter's father had passed away in Italy and his mother, Rosa Cevitini (Cortini), brought both boys to America to begin a new life.

ROSA CORTINI was born in 1864 in Italy; she passed away on September 12, 1920 in St. Johnsville.

On November 21, 1912, Peter C. Battisti and Anna Piniaha, daughter of Thomas Piniaha and Katherine Yendryka, were joined in marriage at St. Patrick's Catholic Church, where they became devout lifetime members. Witnessing their union were Ettore Polamki (Palombi?) and Maria Palombi. They became the parents of ten children and an adopted son, Anthony Korniat. They also raised their grandson, Rosario Primer, after his mother's untimely death at the time of his birth.

1915 shows that Peter, his wife Anna, their first child, Rosa and his mother, Rosa, were four of the 19 residents living at 12 Spring Street, in later years the home of the Giaquinto family. Others included his cousin, Joseph Tolfa's family of three; the Sam Ross (Iannucci) family of three and six boarders – brothers Cataldo "Guy" and Rocco Zuccaro; brothers Pietro and Edjidio Battisti; Julio Coggi, Jimmy Colonna, and John and Philip Mastrofrancesco (Francisco). Peter was still employed at a knitting mill.

Peter C. Battisti's World War I record of June 1917 states that he lived in a rural area, had a wife and four children to support. It had to be shortly after 1915, when he began renting the dairy farm on Kringsbush Road.

By 1920, Peter and Anna had definitely settled into their home and dairy farming business, where they would spend the rest of their lives. At this time they had four children of their own - Rosa, Fiorino, John, Joseph, and an adopted son Anthony Korniat. Also living with the family were Anna's sister, Josephine Yestremski and her four children - Anthony, Stella, Caroline and Mary. Stella married Paul Matis.

The 1925 NYS Census shows the family living on what they called State Road, but I'm certain it was Kringbush. By now they had added four more sons to their growing family - Egidio, Angelo, Americo and Albert. Two more daughters - Anna and Gina arrived by 1930 and they were now the proud owners of their prosperous dairy farm that was valued at $29,000. All of the Battisti siblings received their early education at a country school. Besides his dedication to his family and dairy farm, Peter was also active in St. Johnsville community activities. Known as "red headed Pete" to many of his friends, Peter was one of the standard bearers of the St. Johnsville bands. He played the tuba. In 1917 he was one of the performers with the Home Guard Band, mostly made up of Italians. He served as President of the St. Johnsville Band when it was formed. This group also boasted mostly Italian musicians, who served on the board. The band headquartered at the old firehouse on Center Street.

Both Dairy Farmers of note, Peter and his friend, Thomas Triumpho acted as spokesmen for other farmers in the St. Johnsville Township. During 1939-1940, there was a major milk strike. Fearing there might be violence and serious damages, the two men approached the Town Board requesting they shut down the Dairymen's League plant until the strike was over; their plea was denied. Peter also served as a director of the Schenectady Production Credit Association.

Peter C. Battisti died on April 28, 1943 in Little Falls Hospital of complications of pneumonia close to his 53rd birthday. He is buried in Prospect View Cemetery. His sons continued with the dairy farming business.

ANNA PINIAHA arrived in America in 1911 at age 14, as stated on Census records. I find no confirmation of her arrival. She was born in Austria on November 27, 1887. She had six siblings, two of note being Josephine, married to dairy farmer, Peter Yestremski, and Veronica, first married to R.W. Edwards and later dairy farmer, Jay Settle after Edwards' death.

After Anna's father, Thomas, had died in 1916 of bleeding ulcers, her mother, Katie brought their other seven children to America from Austria to begin a new life. Initially, she lived with her daughter, Josephine Yestremski on her family farm. Katie was born November 20, 1870 in Yaroslaw, Austria and died of a stroke at the home of her daughter, Anna Battisti on October 5, 1942.

It seems the extensive Battisti property was registered in Anna's name. I've found this was quite common in those days, perhaps in the event of bankruptcy? In May 1948, after Peter's death, she deeded acreage to her children, Fiorino, Angelo and Gina, all living nearby on some of the plots.

The children didn't stray too far from the family homestead, even though they established their own farming businesses. It was a very close-knit family.

After 50 years of residency in St. Johnsville, Anna Piniaha Battisti, age 64, passed away on August 27, 1961 in Little Falls Hospital, like her mother, the victim of a stroke.

The Battisti Dairy Farm legacy continued to live on through the efforts of five of the couple's sons - Fiorino, Joseph, Angelo, Americo and Albert. Fiorino, being the oldest, inherited the original family farm, where his mother, Anna continued to live with Fiorino's growing family until her passing.

ROSA BATTISTI, the eldest of the ten siblings, was born November 12, 1913. On November 25, 1934, Rosa became the bride of Stanley W. Primer of Little Falls in a lovely ceremony at St. Patrick's Church. 2½ years later on April 21, 1938, she passed away giving birth to their son, Rosario.

Stanley W. Primer was born April 30, 1911 in Little Falls and died in Prescott AZ on April 18, 1994. His sister, Margaret Elizabeth Primer was married to Frederick A. Giarrusso.

FIORINO PETER BATTISTI aka Floyd was an early family Christmas gift, born December 23, 1915. He died November 17, 2000.

Floyd served a short time as a Tech-4 in the US Army from February 7, 1943 to July 9, 1943. He may have been discharged early due to his father's illness and subsequent death.

On October 22, 1949, Floyd Battisti married Adelaide LaCoppola. They had nine children - Francis, David, Robert, Jean, Carol Ann, Dorothy, Joan, Mary and Rose.

The legacy of Peter C. Battisti still lives on with Fiorino's son, Francis taking over the original family farm. I believe all of the other properties have been sold.

JOHN BATTISTI lived a very short life. He was born March 14, 1916 and passed away suddenly on August 28, 1918 at the age of 2½, attributed to an accidental drowning.

JOSEPH W. BATTISTI was born March 9, 1918 and died May 6, 1985. Joe was an outstanding student at St. Johnsville High School, on the honor list attaining high Regents honors in arithmetic and spelling.

Joseph W. Battisti was married to Violet Elizabeth Miller, daughter of Wilfred and Lillian Miller. Violet Miller was born February 25, 1919, in Stratford NY. She died November 17, 2004. They had seven children - Joseph, Jr., Peter, Anthony, Paul, Dennis, Rose, and an infant daughter who died shortly after birth.

Joe also followed the family tradition of dairy farming, purchasing property with Violet on the Old Mill Road near Fort Klock.

In my research, I discovered a notable article in the June 1, 1976 edition of the *Courier-Standard-Enterprise* newspaper. Lying in a pasture, located on the Joseph Battisti farm, was an old limekiln at least 200 years old. Prior to the American Revolution, it had been constructed near a quarry. It was believed to have provided rock for the construction of nearby Fort Klock. It had definitely been used to draw rock for the Erie Canal and the building of the Brooklyn Bridge. George Matis, another dairy farmer and current Supervisor of the Town of St. Johnsville, at the time was instrumental in restoring the site, with the aid of local boy scouts.

ANGELO STANLEY BATTISTI was a life long dairy farmer, working with his father from an early age. He was born March 15, 1920.

On June 25, 1944 Angelo married Elinor Colorito, daughter of Verginio Colorito and Teresa Mastracco. They had six children - Angelo James, John, Barbara, Elizabeth, Mary Ann and Constance.

In his free time, Angelo took pleasure in working on his woodworking projects. He and Elinor were avid polka dancers and perhaps square dancers, traveling to area events frequently in their later married years.

A devoted family man and the last remaining sibling, Angelo Stanley Battisti passed away at Wells House, Johnstown, on May 20, 2012.

Elinor Colorito was born March 30, 1926. She still survives her husband. She sold the farm and moved to Johnstown four years ago.

EGIDIO FRANCIS BATTISTI was the only son who didn't become a career dairy farmer. He resided with his family on Baum Road, just a short distance from the family homestead. The Peter C. Battisti children lived pretty much in a cluster. I seem to recall that Egidio worked for the Beech-Nut Packing Company in Canajoharie?

During World War II, Egidio served his country for three years. On January 24, 1945, as a Private 1st Class, he was presented with the Bronze Star for meritorious achievement and the Combat Infantryman Badge for his participation in the "Rainbow" Division Campaign in France and Germany. He was later stationed in Austria.

On December 22, 1946 Egidio Battisti married Lois Rockefeller, daughter of Mr. and Mrs. John Rockefeller of St. Johnsville. They had three daughters - Darlene, Diane and Donna.

Lois Rockefeller Battisti was quite active with her church, overseeing bible classes and other programs, and also in other organizations involving young people. The couple served as hosts to "Fresh Air" children during the summer months.

Egidio Francis Battisti was born July 21, 1921. He passed away on March 28, 2001 in Little Falls Hospital. I believe his wife, Lois survives at this writing.

AMERICO BATTISTI for 50 years worked his dairy farm on Thumb Road, just a short distance down the road from the family homestead. The prominent location overlooked St. Johnsville and the beautiful Mohawk River valley. In 1955 the St. Johnsville High School Board approached him to purchase some adjoining land so they could expand the current school building. After approval by taxpayers, the deal was settled at $8000 for 18 acres.

On December 6, 1984 the farm building suffered a devastating fire, which consumed 65 cattle, some equipment and stored hay. Americo immediately planned to rebuild but realized the cost of labor alone would amount to $25,000. With his brother, Angelo leading the way other family members and neighbors pitched in to help him raise a new barn before the Christmas holiday.

On April 7, 1945, Americo Battisti was united in marriage with Julia Stefanie Bilobrowka, daughter of Onofre Bilobrowka and Tekla Noberezna. They were the parents of four children - Edward, William, Michael and Eileen.

Julia Stefanie Bilobrowka was born July 25, 1924 in St. Johnsville and passed away October 7, 2016 at Homelife at Folts, Herkimer. She was a sister of Anne (Peter) Tolfa, Mary Wadin and John Bilobrowka. I believe the Battisti's and Tolfa's may have been cousins?

Americo Battisti was born November 20, 1922 on the family farm and passed away October 1, 1997 in Deatsville AL, as stated on his Social Security record. This seems questionable, unless it was the home of one of his children?

ALBERT PETER BATTISTI, the youngest son, also lived most of his life as a dairy farmer. In 1955 he and his wife, Alberta purchased the farm of Emmett and Hilda Mosher in Crum Creek.

It seems he had been engaged to Anne Papa, daughter of Sam Papa and Madelina Giaquinto of Ann Street in September 1944? The engagement obviously was broken off, as both married others.

On October 6, 1946, Albert Battisti and Alberta L. Cook, daughter of Clarence Cook and Hattie Smith, were united in marriage at St. Patrick's Church. A wedding dinner was held at the Ideal Restaurant, Route 5 East with a reception following at the Ukranian Hall on South Division Street. They had five children - Albert Jr., Richard, Susanne, Lawrence, and Stephen.

Albert Battisti was born on the family farm on October 6, 1924. He died on May 14, 1993. Alberta L. Cook was born March 30, 1928 and passed away on October 23, 2012.

ANNA BATTISTI, named after her mother, was born on February 16, 1927.

On June 21, 1947 Anna Battisti married Olin Hart of rural St. Johnsville. Mary Mastracco, daughter of Peter and Jennie Mastracco, attended the bride as maid of honor, with Anna's brother, Angelo as best man. The couple had seven children - Olin III, Charles, Anne Marie, Sarah, Mary Ellen, Theresa, and an infant daughter, Carolyn, who died shortly after her birth.

Suffering a long illness, Anna Battisti Hart passed away on December 16, 1972 at her home at 34 North Division Street. Although I didn't know her personally, I remember her as a neighbor just two doors away. The home was vacant for several years after her death and eventually torn down. The Olin Hart family had lived on Bolster Hill Road, the former home of her aunt and uncle Veronica Piniaha and R.W. Edwards for many years before moving to the village.

Born May 29, 1929 in the town of St. Johnsville, Olin Hart Sr., son of Olin J. Hart and Sarah Kretser, died on March 5, 2017 in Nathan Littauer Hospital, Gloversville. He was 88 years old.

GINA M. BATTISTI, the youngest of the ten siblings was born on Memorial Day, May 31, 1929. She passed away on May 27, 2006, just four days before her 75th birthday in Edison NJ, where her oldest daughter, Bonnie resided.

On October 27, 1946 Gina M. Battisti married Clifford Heroth from Ephratah at St. Patrick's Catholic Church. A reception followed at the Ukranian Hall on South Division Street. They had five children - Bonnie, Claudia, Charlene, Clifford and Gregory.

They lived almost their entire lives on Kringsbush Road on one of the plots of the Battisti property, just a short walk up the road from the family homestead. Both were devoted parishioners of St. Patrick's Catholic Church.

Clifford Heroth, the son of William Frederick Heroth and Ethel Christman, was born in 1926 in Ephratah. He passed away in Edison NJ on January 10, 2009 at 83 years of age. Clifford was a member of the St. Johnsville Town Board for several years.

ANTHONY THOMAS KORNIAT was a half-brother to all of the Battisti siblings. He was born in Austria on March 10, 1908. Apparently, Peter and Anna adopted him when he came to America as a young boy in 1913 along with his aunt Veronica, Anna's sister.

On February 2, 1932 Anthony married Helen Yokubrit in Renssalear. Their daughter, Jean Marie Korniat, married young Kenneth Watkins from St. Johnsville.

Anthony retired as a custodian from the Fort Plain School system. He died in St. Johnsville, town of Minden, on March 28, 1992.

~ ANGELO BATTISTI et FILOMENA VITA ~

ANGELO BATTISTI, brother of Peter C. Battisti was born on Christmas Eve, December 24, 1893, in Supino, the son of Egidio Battisti and Rosa Cortini. He arrived in America 1909 at the age of 15.

I've encountered several Angelo Battisti's with my research, making it difficult to keep them all in line. Seeming a popular name for the family, it must date back further in the tree than I'm able to connect. When a first name is used so much in one family, it is usually done to honor one of the previous ancestors. This applies to other ethnicities, as well.

In 1910 Angelo lived on Spring Street with his mother, Rosa and brother, Peter. He worked in a knitting mill. The 1915 NYS Census shows Angelo and his mother as two of the 19 residents residing at 12 Spring Street, later the home of the Giaquinto family.

On April 22, 1917 Angelo Battisti was joined in marriage with Filomena "Flora" Vita, age 17, daughter of Lewi Vita and Louisa DiContessi. Serving as witnesses were Gaetano Corso and his wife, Mary Iacobucci. His occupation was farmer. They had three children - Herman, Elio and Leona.

Shortly after his marriage, on June 5, 1917 Angelo registered for World War I, stating he was living at 12 Spring Street, and was a farmer working for his brother Peter. He supported his mother and wife.

By 1920 Angelo owned a dairy farm on Krings Bush Road in the town of Oppenheim and had his first two children, Herman, 3 years and Elio, 6 months.

In 1925, Angelo had moved back to 12 Spring Street with his family, adding another child, Leona, 4 years old. Flora's parents, Luigi and Louisa Vito with their son, Antonio were living with them. Angelo had given up the farm and opened a grocery store on the premises.

The 1930 Census shows Angelo owning the 12 Spring Street property valued at $4000 and employed as a retail grocer. His in-laws may have passed away. I don't think he continued his business here as he sold the property to Frank Giaquinto and his wife, Jennie Campagni sometime early 1930. Jennie continued the grocery business for several years.

I guess dairy farming was also in Angelo's blood. Something drew him to Schodack, Rensselear, where he had moved his family by 1940. He once again owned his own farm and employed a hired hand, Ercola Giarabina. His son, Elio had married a girl named Mary and lived with him.

At 79 years of age, after a seemingly full life, Angelo Battisti died instantly on November 1, 1972 with injuries from a car accident. He failed to make a right turn into a street in Castleton-on-the-Hudson, where he resided and struck a tree. Flora had died in January of the same year.

FILOMENA "Flora" VITA was born in Rome on December 19, 1892. She passed away on January 11, 1972 at Castleton-on-the-Hudson at 80 years of age. She had immigrated in 1910.

* Grazie to Brian Abeling, great-grandson of Veronica Edwards Settle, for contributing information to the Peter C. Battisti family story.

~ La Famiglia JAMES J. BATTISTI ~

~ JAMES JOSEPH BATTISTI et SECONDINA (ENRICA) ARDUINI ~

From what I've come to learn, there were at least four, perhaps five, immigrant Battisti families in the early years of the Italians of St. Johnsville history. So many Italian families are connected to others. This particular Battisti family has many ties.

James Joseph Battisti and Pietro Battisti share the same parents - Francisco Battisti and Lucia Lucidi from Supino. This story is about these two Battisti brothers and their families. One is better known than the other. One brother was quiet and retiring, the other outgoing and adventurous. There was also another brother, Angelo, not the one in the previous article. I believe Peter C. Battisti, the farmer is a cousin.

JAMES JOSEPH BATTISTI was born in Supino on January 17, 1891, the son of Francisco Battisti and Lucia Lucidi. He immigrated to St. Johnsville in 1910.

SECONDINA "ENRICA" ARDUINI, aka Henrietta was the daughter of Severino Arduini and Giuseppina Dolessandri. She arrived in St. Johnsville on May 26, 1914 at age 19, coming to join her brother, Enrico Arduini. I believe this to be Dominico, who had arrived in 1913. She had a sister, Antionette in Italy and four brothers in the United States - Lorenzo, Joseph, Auborno and Dominico of St. Johnsville.

Secondina aka Henrietta Arduini later met James Battisti and they were married on June 23, 1917 at St. Patrick's Church. Serving as witnesses were Cataldo Zuccaro aka Rocco Sugar, and Elizabeth Triumpho, his future wife. James and Henrietta became the parents of three children - Lidia, Romeo and James, Jr.

Reverend J.A. Thorton of St. Patrick's was kept quite busy that summer. He also blessed three other unions - Angelo Battisti and Filomena Vita on April 22, 1917, Celestino Scaccia and Giovannina Porti on June 9, 1917, and Verginio Colorito and Teresa Colomelli on June 21, 1917.

The couple first made their home with his brother, Pietro Battisti and family on upper Averill Street, where their daughter, Lidia, was born in 1920. Others boarding with them were the two Sugar boys, Guy and Rocco, claimed as cousins. James worked as a box maker in a knitting mill.

Five years later, the 1925 Census shows the family living at 28 Hough Street, where James and Henrietta lived out their lives, nestled between the Carmine Peruzzi and Natalino Iacobucci families. By now, Romeo had joined the family. In 1930 they owned the Hough Street home, both worked in the "shoe shop" (Felt Shoe) across the street and they were the parents of their second son, James.

The World War II registration of 1942 for James shows him working for Dainty Maid Company in Dolgeville. In 1957, Henrietta was employed at the P&K Dress Corporation in Little Falls.

James Joseph Battisti passed away on July 10, 1979 in his adopted hometown of St. Johnsville.

Secondina "Henrietta" Arduini was born in Supino October 29, 1895 and died on January 18, 1982.

LIDIA L. BATTISTI was born in 1920. She attended St. Johnsville High School, where she was a stellar student and active in various activities. In 1940 she was employed as a stenographer for a private firm. Lidia married a gentleman with the last name of Roberson and lived in Wilmington, DE. I have no further information.

ROMEO JOHN BATTISTI is by far the most well known of the Battisti families. Most remember him as the Supervising Principal of St. Johnsville Central School. I remember Romeo as my teacher, mentor and friend.

After graduating with the class of 1938 from St. Johnsville High School, Romeo went on to graduate from St. Lawrence University in 1943. He enlisted in the Army Air Corps on April 5, 1943, serving his country through October 21, 1945, when he was honorably discharged.

Having graduated as a Corporal in the Aerial Gunnery unit, he served as a B-17 Bombardier with the 8th Air Force in Europe, where for four days he survived his Bomber being forced down behind German lines. When he returned to his unit, his clothes had been disposed of from his locker. They had given him up for dead.

One of his greatest thrills of World War II was meeting up with his younger brother, James, age 19, who was also stationed in England. They were just 72 miles apart and able to visit and talk on the phone at least twice a week.

Romeo surprised his future wife, Molly, with an engagement ring on her 27th birthday the day after Christmas, December 26, 1947.

On May 16, 1948, Romeo John Battisti and Amelia A. Tolfa, daughter of Joseph Tolfa and Loretta Coggi, were married at St. Patrick's Catholic Church. Laura Cochi served as maid-of-honor, with Lena Barca and Veronica Wytrwal as bridesmaids. Romeo's brother, James was best man with ushers, James Pietrocini and Constantino Terricola. Molly and Romeo served as maid-of-honor and best man at the union of Laura and Dominick Fontana.

They made their first home with Molly's parents before renting a home from James LaLone and Rose Carroll (Carelli) on West Liberty Street for several years. They later purchased the 10 John Street home, where they lived out most of their lives. The couple had four children - Lorraine, Tina, Christa and Richard.

In the fall of 1949 in my freshman year, I had the privilege of being one of Romeo's very first students, when he was hired by his alma mater to teach Junior High School Social Studies. He peaked my interest in the Civil War. Romeo also served as our Class of 1953 advisor for four years. He was respected and loved by all my classmates. We honored him twice with the presentation of a watch, once when we graduated and later at our 50th class reunion in 2003. He told us he still had the original watch.

Romeo also coached the varsity basketball and baseball teams, later becoming Vice-Principal, Principal and Superintendent of Schools for many years. After his retirement in 1976, he was called back to temporarily fill the position until a replacement was found. He also filled in at other area schools for the next 10 years.

Romeo spent his final "retirement" years working part-time for the St. Johnsville Post Office as a rural mail carrier and at the pro shop of the Nick Stoner Golf Course through 2006. He, too, was one of the stellar Italian athletes, playing baseball and basketball through high school, later bowling and playing golf in his adult years.

Romeo John Battisti, the son of James Joseph Battisti and Secondina "Henrietta" Arduini, was born September 5, 1921 and passed away at his home, peacefully, on Easter Sunday, April 8, 2007. Living his entire life in St. Johnsville, he wasted not one moment of time. He was a gentleman and a scholar, who was greatly respected by all who knew and served him.

Amelia "Molly" Tolfa was born as a late family Christmas gift on December 26, 1920 at the family residence over the Central Hotel. She is the last surviving sibling at this writing, now residing in a nursing home in Little Falls.

As a young girl of six years, Molly traveled to Supino, Italy, the natal home of her parents, along with her mother, sister Clara and two brothers, Peter and Guido, returning in 1926.

A graduate of St. Johnsville High School, Molly was active in various activities, such as cheerleading. In her adult years, she was a high scoring bowler in the Friday Night Women's League at the Masonic Temple; also an avid golfer in a Women's League at Nick Stoner's Golf Course. For many years, Molly worked from her home at 10 John Street, where she provided Electrolysis hair removal services.

I had the pleasure of socializing with Molly and Romeo on numerous occasions for many of my adult years. We became good friends; I bowled with Molly. It was fun to be in her company.

JAMES JOSEPH BATTISTI, Jr. is best known as the Honorable Judge James Battisti of Catskill. His extensive resume in the judicial system and in his lifetime is much too extensive to mention here.

He graduated from St. Johnsville High School at 17 years of age in 1943. Like his brother, Romeo, he served as a Bombardier in World War II, and attended St. Lawrence University. He taught in the Dover Plains NY School system.

Jimmy seemed to follow in his older brother, Romeo's footsteps. Ironically, in his Junior year, he was recognized in one of the St. Johnsville high school newsletters as a "second Romeo". If one didn't know this was his brother's name, they might have misinterpreted the comment. He was handsome enough to be a Romeo.

Staff Sergeant James Battisti gathered quite a record with his U.S. Air Force war service from October 16, 1943 to October 26, 1945 in the 3rd Air Division. He racked up 31 combat missions with the 447th Bombardiers, receiving an Air Medal with four oak leaf clusters, a European Theatre Ribbon with four battle stars, plus a Presidential Unit Citation.

After graduating St. Lawrence University, James went on to graduate Albany Law School, which he attended with his friend, Carl Cochi. In 1974 he was appointed Greene County Judge, later elected to the position in 1975. He served two ten-year terms. He was notably active with civic organizations throughout his life in Catskill, where he settled after his first marriage.

As a judge, most of his interests involved the Foster Care system. In a noted landmark decision he "pounded the gavel" and gave the responsibility of fostering Mike Tyson, the boxer and then resident of Catskill, to legendary trainer D'Amato. This allowed Tyson to leave institutional living and concentrate on his boxing career. Judge James Battisti also made some other controversial decisions.

An avid outdoorsman, James loved to golf, fish, ski, hunt and play tennis. In high school, he, too, was an exceptional athlete as a member of the baseball and basketball teams. Sadly, one fine sunny day, while the Honorable Judge James Joseph Battisti, Jr. was enjoying the sport of fishing, his boat overturned and he drowned.

The youngest son of James Joseph Battisti and Secondina Arduini, he was born August 7, 1925 and passed away at 78 years on May 11, 2004 in Catskill. His second wife, June Faulkner-Crossman, and Dr. Amanda Battisti and Stacey Battisti, two daughters by his first wife survived James.

James was laid to rest in the Prospect View Cemetery, overlooking his hometown. His gravestone is as prominent as he was in his extraordinary life.

~ PIETRO BATTISTI et GUGLIELMINA COLONNA ~

Pietro Battisti's family isn't as well known to many of us, as they moved from St. Johnsville to Hartford CN in the early 1940s. However, if you had been a settler in the early 1900s, he definitely would have left an impression.

Arriving in America on May 16, 1913 in advance of his wife, Guglielmina, Pietro Battisti came to the village of St. Johnsville in search of his brother, James.

Pietro Battisti, son of Francisco Battisti and Lucia Lucidi, had married Guglielmina Colonna, daughter of Antonio Colonna and Domenica "Rosa" Zuccaro of Supino, in 1912 back in their hometown of Supino before coming to America. Domenica Zuccaro's parents were Francesco Zuccaro and Francesca Tomei.

The couple had four children - Angeline, born in Supino and three sons, Frank, Anthony and Joseph James, all born in St. Johnsville.

The 1915 Census shows him boarding with Joe Tolfa, his wife and son, Larry at 12 Spring Street, along with Pietro's brother-in-law, Jimmy Colonna; the two brothers Cataldo "Guy" and Rocco Sugar (Zuccaro); also Sam Rose, his wife and step-daughter Teresa Mastracco. Also listed were noted farmer, Peter Battisti, his wife, Anna, two of their children and Peter's mother, Rosa. Brothers, Philip and John Mastrofrancesco, were claimed as boarders for a total of 19 persons in one home. This later became the Giaguinto homestead.

Pietro's wife, Guglielmino "Wilhemina" Colonna, had arrived with their three-year-old daughter on December 17, 1916 headed to 16 East Main Street, the home of the Joseph Tolfa family.

From intensive research I have been doing, I found that Pietro Battisti had been either renting or managing the Napoleon Café at 20 East Main Street later known as Caponera's Cigar Store. Prosper Napoleon had been shot and killed at the location over the 1915 Memorial Day holiday. Suffering from extensive wounds, he died on June 1, 1915 and his brother-in-law, Carmine Terranova, served as executor of his estate.

I believe Pietro had been employed by Napoleon and had been asked to continue the business with a purchase option. Perhaps this arrangement didn't work out, so he bought the property next door. It has become quite the mystery! At this time, Pietro had already begun his future career in dealing with "spirits." He was a saloonkeeper.

There is an October 1914 real estate transfer from F.D. Brown to Pietro Battisti. Apparently, this was the 24-26 East Main Street property, which he owned for several years. Some of the information is rather confusing.

A February 1916 newspaper article reports a fire, which had been caused by a faulty furnace pipe, gutting the Battisti's café. His brother Angelo, who lived upstairs with his wife, discovered the fire. His wife, along with two others, jumped out of the second story window. They suffered no injuries and were all taken to the St. Elmo Hotel across the street. On this frigid, 8 degrees below zero evening, the Mohawk Chief Hose Co., the Rescue Hose Co. and Protection Hook & Ladder quickly responded. Merchants pitched in with R.B. Beekman opening his doors to hand out gloves, mittens and rubber boots. Ralph Perry brought hot coffee in pails from his luncheonette on Bridge Street. I believe this may have been my grandfather, Floyd Perry, not Ralph.

There was a disastrous fire at the Napoleon Café around this time so I've assumed that the above refers to the Café? Confusing! I believe I'm being haunted by the spirits.

Pietro's World War I application of June 1917 states he was living on Main Street and employed by his wife. Records show that she was listed as the owner of his business. I also discovered that Guglielmino had employed Joe Tolfa. It states that he had been a Corporal in the Italian Infantry for three years.

1920 Census records show the couple now on upper Averill Street with two sons, Frank and Anthony, plus the two Zuccaro (Sugar) brothers, Guy and Rocco, whom I've determined were cousins of Guglielmino. By now, Pietro owned a liquor store and was a bartender.

In 1925 the Pietro Battisti family was residing at 24 East Main, where they were the proprietors of a lunchroom, selling soft drinks. This was the time of Prohibition. In 1930 they were the owners and restaurant proprietors of 26 East Main Street, which was connected to the #24 address for which they had paid $2,000. A 1935 Liquor License shows Guglielmina as the owner at 26 East Main Street.

24 and 26 East Main Street, which I refer to, would have been on the eastern side of the Caponera building. There is a long history of many changes of ownership with both properties.

Once again, in May 1932, the family lunchroom suffered a slight fire. In part of the building, a garage housed an Essex sedan, which was saved by Officer William Mac Mahon. From the numerous news articles I have read, it seems these Italian immigrants kept Officer Mac Mahon pretty busy. He was the father of Melanie "Tiny" Mac Mahon Shuster.

1934 was an enterprising year for Pietro. Prohibition was over. The country was beginning to come out of the Great Depression. On September 5, 1934 through the First National Bank, current owners of the Pyramid Dance Hall outside the western end of the village limits, Pietro was able to purchase the popular dance hall. He made some minor repairs and opened the dance hall ten days later on Saturday, September 15.

Professor George T. Snell had built the property and conducted dances. Snell was a noted dance instructor beginning his career as a young man in Syracuse before returning to St. Johnsville. I recall my parents and others of that era talking about the dance hall and how much fun they enjoyed. Many romances began at the popular entertainment venue from all over the valley. In his later years, Snell had given up his profession. I vividly recall Prof. Snell delivering the delicious homemade pies his wife baked daily for my father's luncheonette.

Before this purchase, Pietro had constructed a new dance hall next to his East Main Street restaurant business. The U.S. Postal Service of St. Johnsville also used it as an office. Mr. and Mrs. Oliver Wolcott of Center Street purchased the building, having it towed to the west end of the village to be used as a residence. This may be the small home that sits next door to Amy's Service Station?

By 1940 Pietro Battisti, his wife and three sons had moved to Hartford CN, where they were the proprietors of Pete's Package Store. His 1942 World War II application and a City Registry confirm this information. Two of his sons, Anthony and Frank were in the military service. The daughter, Angeline, had been married in 1935 and moved to Troy with her husband, Jeffrey Iacobucci and his parents.

Around 1946, Weaver's Cigar Store, which had been renting next door, purchased the Battisti property. The Kenneth Watkins family lived upstairs. Later, George Thomas took over the property, where George opened a luncheonette, with family living quarters upstairs.

PIETRO BATTISTI was born June 29, 1887 in Supino. After living part of his life in Hartford CN he passed away July 15, 1963 at 76 years old, in Port Orange, FL, where the couple had retired.

GUGLIELMINA "Wilhemina" COLONNA was born May 17, 1893. She preceded Pietro in death on January 29, 1962 in Port Orange FL. She was 69.

ANGELINE A. BATTISTI, born in Supino on July 22, 1913, came to America with her mother, Guglielmina, on December 17, 1916 at three years old. An exceptional student of the St. Johnsville High School graduation class of 1932, she spent her entire childhood in St. Johnsville. After graduation, she became employed with the Clark Bros. Paper Company in New York City.

On April 11, 1937, Angeline Battisti and Jeffrey Joseph Iacobucci, son of Leopoldo Iacobucci and Catallina Cochi, were married at St. Patrick's Catholic Church. Jeffrey's sister, Elsie Iacobucci Irwin served as maid of honor, with Angeline's brother, Frank Battisti as best man. A reception was held at the Leopoldo Iacobucci family home on Kingsbury Avenue.

Graduating from Troy Catholic School, Jeffrey Iacobucci had attended the St. Johnsville schools until his senior year. He became a Prudential Insurance agent in Troy. His parents were both former residents of St. Johnsville. Leopoldo Iacobucci was the oldest sibling of Natalino, Alberto, Torello and Marietta (Corso). Catallina was a sister of Carlo Cochi.

It seems young Jeffrey Iacobucci had been designated the executor of the Alberto (Tom Boskey) and Maud Iacobucci estate. In 1970 there was a transfer of property from him to Donald and Kathy Bellen. This is the little home at 7½ Monroe Street hidden behind Center and Monroe Streets, where Tom and Maud had resided. The street was originally noted as Center Street Lane.

Angeline and Jeffrey had four children - Jeffrey Joseph, Jr., Wilma, Ronald and Russell.

In 1940, the family was living with Jeffrey's parents, Leopoldo Iacobucci and Catallina Cochi in Troy.

FRANK BATTISTI was the first-born son in St. Johnsville in 1918. He graduated with the Class of 1935. A 1942 Hartford CN City Directory shows he was in the Army during World War II, but I don't find any documents to confirm this.

He also seemed to have resided in Port Orange FL, where he was buried. He apparently resided with his parents at the time. A document states he died in Kings County, Washington on April 22, 2000.

ANTHONY P. BATTISTI, Sr. was born March 21, 1919 in St. Johnsville and died on September 25, 1986 in Westerfield CN. He served in the US Navy from January 3, 1942 until April 3, 1945. He married Michelina Mary "Mickey" Scavullo from Hartford CN. They had a son, Anthony.

JOSEPH JAMES BATTISTI was born in St. Johnsville on April 2, 1921 and passed away in the state of Washington on February 18, 1998. In the early 1940s he had married Carmela Ann "Connie" Cagno, whom he divorced in January 1973 in Los Angeles CA. Their daughter, Barbara Ann, was born in 1945 and died in 1995.

~ *La Famiglia ARDUINI* ~

~ DOMENICO ROCCO ARDUINI et JOSEPHENE RALVINI ~

DOMENICO ROCCO ARDUINI arrived in America on March 13, 1913 at age 21. He was naturalized on September 3, 1915 in Boston MA. The son of Sevenino "Joseph" Arduini and Giuseppina Dolessandri, he was born July 29, 1892 in Supino. Secondina "Henrietta" Battisti, wife of James Battisti, was his sister. He also had three other siblings, Antoinette, Auburno, and Joseph.

JOSEPHENE "Ida" RALVINI arrived seven years later on August 3, 1920, going to meet her husband, Domenico in Utica. Ida was born February 18, 1893 in Supino, Italy. Her mother's first name was Mary. It is said she was adopted; therefore I find no father's name.

In 1917, Domenico's World War I registration record shows him living at 34 Hough Street, married and working at the Lion Manufacturing Company. He stated that he had served three months as a Private in Construction Engineering, while living in Italy.

As per Josephene's passenger manifest, Domenico and she had been married in Italy before she came to join him in America. I don't find either of them in the 1915 or 1920 Census, which isn't unusual. They had four children, sons Leo and Leland, born almost exactly a year apart, a son, Silvestro, born 1921 and daughter, Angelina, born 1924. The latter two died shortly after birth.

In 1925, the family was living at 14 Sanders Street with Egisto Loccia and his wife, Emelia Vicciarelli and their five children. By 1930 they were the owners of the family home at 23 East Liberty Street, where the couple lived out their lives. The Little Falls Felt Shoe Company on Hough Street employed Domenico as a machinist for 40 years.

Domenico Rocco Arduini passed away shortly after being admitted to Little Falls Hospital on June 26, 1964. Josephene "Ida" Ralvini had also died at the hospital on September 19, 1963, less than a year before Domenico. She also worked at the Little Falls Felt Shoe.

LEO R. ARDUINI was the second-born son on July 26, 1922 in St. Johnsville. Silvestro was the first. Leo passed away January 27, 2005 in Fort Plain, where he resided most of his adult life. As I recall, he worked at the Beech-Nut Packing Company in Canajoharie.

Leo had served his country in the U.S. Navy as a 2nd Class Seaman, stationed in Memphis TN. As a 1st Class US Naval Reservist, he was a port waist gunner on a Liberator of the US Atlantic Fleet Air Force, under the command of U.S. Naval Forces in Europe. As patrol planes of the Fleet Air Wing, they were successfully hunting German U-boats in the English Channel and Bay of Biscay.

In May 1943, Leo became engaged to be married to Frances Acovangelo. She was the daughter of Michael Acovangelo and Elizabeth Roberts. I don't find a wedding date. The couple had one son, Michael.

Frances Acovagelo was born in Canajoharie on January 18, 1925 and passed away in Austin TX on October 26, 2014. She was a registered nurse. Leo later married Jacqueline A. Drobish in 1973. She died in 1998.

LELAND R. ARDUINI aka "Lee" was born almost exactly one year after his brother, Leo, on July 20, 1923. He is still living at this writing.

Lee served his country as an anti-aircraft machine gunner with Battery B481. Serving in Germany, England and France, he was involved with D-Day. He was the recipient of the American Service Medal, European-African-Middle Eastern Service Medal, World War II Victory Medal and the Good Conduct Medal in Germany. He had the distinct honor of personally meeting General Patton during his tour of duty.

Lee's working career included the Beech-Nut Packing Company, the Little Falls Felt Shoe and Johnstown Knitting Company as a machinist.

Leland R. Arduini married Antoinette Patricia "Pat" Regusa. They had seven children - Leland Jr., Dominic, Frank, Lance, Lucille, Mary Jo and Toni Rae. Leland and Pat made their permanent residence with Leland's parents at 23 East Liberty until retiring to Florida.

Pat Arduini worked at the Beech-Nut Packing Company and was quite active in the employees' organization, Beech-Nut Nutrition, serving as a trustee. She was born in New Jersey, daughter of Maurice "Mario" and Lucia "Lucy" Ilardi. Her mother, Lucia was only 14 when she married Maurice, age 26.

Antoinette Patricia Regusa passed away on April 27, 2007 in New Smyrna Beach FL, where she and Lee had retired.

LORENZO ARDUINI immigrated on the same ship as Domenico. However, I find no confirmation of his relationship to Domenico. It was stated in the manifest that his wife's name was Antonia Pietrandrea and he was going to join his Uncle. I think the blurred writing read Francisco Pietrandrea? He was blind in his left eye. He may be a cousin of Domenico and a connection to the Pietrandrea family.

Antonia Pietrandrea's parents were Angelo Antonio Pietrandrea and Mary Marocco. I believe she is a link to the Marocco family for Arduini and Pietrandrea families.

*   *Shelley Johnson Arduini contributed to this article. Grazie!*

MORRIS J. EDWARDS AMERICAN LEGION POST 168
~ Italians of St. Johnsville Members ~

In 1970 the following Italian Veteran members were given Awards
for service to their country and membership in the Post.

45-year pin and certificate – Amadeo Castrucci. He was also a member for over 50 years.

25-year pin and certificate – Louis Barca, Arminio F. Caponera, Joseph L. Caponera, Anthony J. Carroll, Raymond P. Coco, Joseph Colorito, Dario Corso, Guido L. Corso, Angelo Giaquinto, Armand B. Mancini, Victor Paluzzi, Louis Salvagni, Constantino J. Terricola, Lorenzo Tolfa and Peter Tolfa.

Others who were members for 50 years or more: Augustino Castrucci – 55 years. Pasquale Croce – 50 years.

I apologize if I've missed any. Most of this information was printed in the *St. Johnsville Enterprise & News*.

In January 1921, the body of Morris J. Edwards arrived in St. Johnsville for burial. He was the first village hero killed in World War I. Thus, the new American Legion Post was named after him.

~ *La Famiglia PIETRANDREA* ~

I shall commence this story with Joseph Paul Pietrandrea aka Peters, who lived most of his adult life with his own family in St. Johnsville on North Division Street. The Pietrandrea family initially settled in Rotterdam Junction. However, I have discovered they have ties to other St. Johnsville Italians.

Family members recall, "when relatives visited them from Canada, they would visit the Arduini family and Ralph Palombi", with perhaps a connection to his wife, Joann, who was a Piroli and niece of Rose Mastrofrancesco Iacobucci D'Arcangelis. It is also recalled that Joe often remarked he was related to the insurance salesman, Albert Nalli from Fort Plain and the Marocco family in Little Falls. And, of course, the Zuccaro family shows up once again.

I believe I have discovered a connection to the St. Johnsville Marocco family. On October 24, 1964, three of the Marocco sisters, Paris Papa, Irene Vespi and Louise Starna attended the Robert Pietrandrea - Diane Grecynski wedding in Amsterdam. James Papa, Paris' son, served as an usher. Robert was the son of Louis Pietrandrea, who was most likely a cousin of Joe. I believe the Marocco connection would be with Joe Pietrandrea's paternal grandmother, Mary Marocco. However, I'm not able to make a definite connection without in-depth research.

I may also have found the link with the Arduini family. Joe's father, Rocco Pietrandrea had a sister, Antonia, who married Lorenzo Arduini, who may be a cousin of Domenico Rocco Arduini and Henrietta Arduini Battisti, who was the mother of Romeo Battisti.

JOSEPH PAUL PIETRANDREA aka Peters was the son of Rocco Pietrandrea and Louisa Battista from Supino, who came to America and settled in Rotterdam Junction near Schenectady in the early 1900s.

Joe was born in Rotterdam on June 30, 1919. As the youngest, he had two brothers, Agostino and Angelo, both born in Supino and two sisters, Vera and Mary, born in Rotterdam.

Rocco Pietrandrea's parents were Angelo Antonio Pietrandrea and Mary Marocco. Louisa Battista's parents were Dominick Battista and Virginia Nalli. Arriving on August 29, 1913, with their two sons, Louisa had two brothers, Giovanni and Luigi, and two sisters, Felicia Madeline and Elizabeth. There seem to be connections to the Marocco family and Nalli family, and, perhaps Battisti? Battisti is a popular name in Supino.

On August 31, 1946, Joseph Paul Pietrandrea married Ruth Elizabeth Babcock from Oneonta. They had two daughters - Louise and Margaret.

Joe was first employed by Arkell Smith, Canajoharie and later by MDS, Herkimer, for many years until his retirement. Upon his retirement he worked for the village of St. Johnsville as the caretaker of the Soldiers and Sailors Memorial Park under the supervision of my husband, John Palma. In November 1981, Joe received a plaque from the village recognizing his service.

Joe Peters and John Palma were great friends. Joe loved to cook. Whenever he made homemade gnocchi he would deliver some to our home. On his return trips from visiting his sister, Vera in Rochester, he would bring us a fresh stick of pepperoni from the Italian grocery.

Joseph Pietrandrea passed away at the home of his daughter in Herkimer on January 8, 2000.

Ruth died December 23, 2008 in St. Elizabeth's Hospital, Utica. Until their closing, Corso Dress Company employed Ruth for many years.

* Louise Pietrandrea Wiernicki has contributed to this article. Grazie!

~ *La Famiglia CORSO* ~

~ ANTONIO CORSO et MARIA LAURO ~

As head of the St. Johnsville Corso family, Antonio was born in Teano, Caserta, Italy in 1858. He married Maria Lauro, born September 11, 1874 in Teano. They had six children, all born in Teano - Rosina, Dominico, Gaetano, Rosadia, Carmelia and Antonio, Jr. I've also discovered there may have been another son, Vincent, still in Italy.

It seems strange they would name two children with almost the same name - Rosina and Rosadia. This was often done in the 1800s and earlier in all the ethnic groups, if the first had died before the second was born.

Except, when they decided to come to America, Italian families didn't move around much. They usually lived in the same town and once they settled into a home they had purchased, they were there for the remainder of their lives. They usually did not rent for very long.

Antonio immigrated to St. Johnsville in June 15, 1917 landing in Boston, Massachusetts, before making his way to his daughter, Rosina's home at 23 S. Division Street, St. Johnsville. Antonio's passenger manifest stated a diagnosis of "permanent senility", which seemed rather unusual.

The 1920 Census shows Antonio, his wife, Maria, Carmelia and Tony living on Sanders Street, with Antonio, Sr. working in a knitting mill. In 1925 they are sharing a duplex at 16½ Hough Street with only Tony, Jr. still residing with them. Carmelia had married and lived next door with her husband, Desiderio Coco and young son, Raymond. Antonio had returned to Italy where he died, shortly after the 1920 Census was taken.

ANTONIO CORSO returned to Italy before his wife, Maria passed away. Records show that he died in Italy in 1925. It was said he was very mean and beat her quite often. It seems Carmelia was the designated caretaker of the aging parents.

MARIA LAURO passed away in April 1928 at the home of her daughter, Carmelia Coco. Maria's gravestone shows 1869 as birth year, but this may be incorrect. Documents show that she was born September 11, 1874 in Teano.

The first of the family members to arrive was Gaetano "Guy" in 1908, at the age of 17, going to Amsterdam NY before later settling in St. Johnsville. Rosina came in 1910, their brother, Domenico in 1913, the father, Antonio, in 1917, and finally, the mother, Maria, on March 31, 1918, along with the two youngest children, Carmelia and Antonio, Jr., landing in Boston. They were headed to 36 Bridge Street, St. Johnsville to join Antonio. I don't find an accurate record of Rosadia's voyage.

ROSINA C. CORSO, the eldest, was born May 24, 1889 in Teano, Italy. She immigrated to America on November 26, 1910, joining her brother Gaetano "Guy" in Amsterdam, shortly before moving to St. Johnsville and residing at 23 South Division Street.

On February 4, 1912 Rosina "Rose" was married to Vincenzo "James" Masi and living at the 23 South Division Street home. Witnesses to the union were Fedeli and Filomena Sarelli.

The 1915 Census shows they now have their first two children - son, Doloris and daughter Mary. Later came two more sons, Walter and Edward.

Rosina worked most of her life in one of the silk mills. She passed away March 3, 1964 in Utica.

Vincenzo Masi was born January 15, 1886 in Maenza, Italy. He came to America on April 8, 1910. Living in Minden across the Mohawk River from St. Johnsville, he was a farmer for the greater part of his life. Vincenzo (James) passed away October 9, 1968 in Utica.

You can read more about Rosina and Vincenzo Masi in *La Famiglia Masi*.

DOMINICO CORSO arrived in America at the age of twenty-one on April 2, 1913. The passenger ship's manifest claims that he was going to his brother, Gaetano's at 23 Bridge Street, St. Johnsville. He was born January 10, 1892 and was a shoemaker.

On June 5, 1917, Domenico registered for World War I, while living at 23 S. Division Street, where it seems many of the Corso family members resided at one time or another. It was also another of the popular boarding houses for immigrants, later owned by the Paul Guarnacci family.

Right after signing up, Dominic moved to Herkimer for work, where he was struck with the Spanish flu. He died at the Masonic Temple there, which was a temporary hospital and morgue at the time. Domenick is buried in an unmarked grave in Prospect View Cemetery, St. Johnsville. He died about 1918, younger than 26 years.

GAETANO "Guy" CORSO was born August 11, 1892 in Teano, Caserta, Italy, son of Antonio Corso and Maria Lauro. He passed away on June 10, 1969, stricken with a heart attack at his home.

MARIETTA "Mary" IACOBUCCI came to America December 4, 1906 with her mother. She was born March 14, 1892 in Supino, Italy to Gaetano Iacobucci and Verginia Peruzzi. She had four brothers, Leopoldo, Alberto, Natalino and Tuolo. Mary passed away in August 1978 at the home of her daughter, Gloria Corso Laraway.

On December 23, 1911 Gaetano Corso and Marietta Iacobucci were married. Their attendants were Leopoldo Iacobucci and Rosina Corso. They had four children - Dante, Dario, Guido and Gloria, all well known in the community. All have passed away.

Since the age of eleven, Guy had been trained in the tailoring business in Italy. In October 1911, after settling in St. Johnsville, it seems he opened his first tailor shop at 9 Bridge Street. In 1915 he and Mary lived at 23 Mechanic Street with their son, Dante, while Guy worked as a superintendent at a Knitting Mill. His World War I documents of 1918 show him living at 38 Bridge Street. By 1920 he had moved to 29 Bridge Street, where he may have opened a tailor shop.

By 1930 Guy had purchased the 2-story brick home at 18 Bridge Street from Fred Guhring, who conducted a popular bakery in that location for many years. Assisted by his wife, Mary, Guy conducted his "Fashion Shop", specializing in designing and altering men's suits.

The 1940 Census shows that Guy still had his tailor shop. Sometime after, he apparently gave up the tailoring business and opened Corso Dress Factory. I believe he had this new shop in the building that also housed the Palatine Dyeing Company on the corner of New and Bridge Street. I do recall a Dress Factory there, but perhaps not his? I'm not able to confirm anything between 1940 and 1947. There was a Cozzolino Dress Factory there at one time. Perhaps Guy took over that business?

In 1947, Guy purchased the Leek building near the Zimmerman Creek off Smith and Church Streets and moved the Corso Dress Factory to this site. Hough, Riggs & Adams had originally established the property in 1840 as the St. Johnsville Woolen Mills. There were several buildings - a storehouse, a dye house and the mill, where the products were manufactured. Sydney Smith and his family took over the property during the Civil War and produced flannels, horse blankets and various custom orders from the wool.

Many of the second-generation Italian ladies worked at the Corso Dress Factory for many years, turning out high quality brand name dresses for New York City fashion companies, such as Jonathan Logan. My mother Rose (Sindici) Perry worked there most of her life as the hemmer. Other Italian ladies I recall were Bertha (Pedro) Mastromoro, Gilda (Francisco) Bussone, Mary (Gagliardi) Papa, Mary (Iozzo) Stagliano, Jennie (Gagliardi) Guarnacci, and my aunt, Susie (Sindici) Corso, who worked as a floor girl at the time. In later years, Guy's daughter, Gloria (Corso) Laraway and Emma (Bovino) LaCoppola joined the company.

At some point in his business career, Guy partnered with Paul De Simone, who had moved to St. Johnsville with his family after 1940 and lived at 3 Roth Street, where the Sanguine family had resided for years. I don't know exactly what they collaborated on. I'm sure it had to do with the tailoring or dressmaking business.

As a businessman, Guy became a prominent figure in the St. Johnsville community, also serving in several positions of the Republican Club. He was active in forming the General Pershing Italian Club and assisted many of the immigrants in securing their citizenship papers.

Guy was very generous, always treating his employees to special parties and donating prizes to various events in the village. In 1934, the village held an event at the Soldiers and Sailors Memorial Park, which featured several running races. My father, Floyd B. Perry, Jr., won 1st place for fastest runner - single men. He and my mom, Rose

Sindici, engaged to be married, also won the necktie race. I'm trying to imagine what that looked like. They both won free alterations and dry cleaning from Guy's business.

DANTE CORSO was the oldest child of Guy and Mary. He was born January 11, 1913 in St. Johnsville and died in September 1981 in Oneonta NY.

Expanding on the tailoring skills of his father, in 1932 Dante attended the New York Design School in New York City, where he learned the trade of clothing design. He returned to St. Johnsville and drafted patterns for the St. Johnsville Leather Coat Company. In 1955 Dante moved his family from their home in Royal Place to Oneonta, where he worked for the C&M Dress Company.

On June 29, 1934, Dante Corso married Marion Putman of Sharon Springs NY. They lived in St. Johnsville and had a daughter, Marilyn (Alger), who was born July 19, 1935 at the Guy Corso home. Marilyn graduated from St. Johnsville High School a year after me.

Dante served as best man at the marriage of his brother, Guido to Susie Sindici.

Marion Putman was born August 31, 1914 in Sharon Springs NY. She died in Oneonta at the age of 96 on January 27, 2011.

DARIO JOSEPH CORSO worked with his father from the early age of eleven and also became very proficient in the art of tailoring. He worked at the Palatine Dyeing Company before entering the armed services.

Dario served as a Pfc. in the Army Infantry during World War II between January 1, 1943 and November 20, 1944, receiving a Good Conduct medal with a medical discharge.

On May 13, 1946, he opened a Men's Store at 21 West Main Street, Corso Cleaning and Clothing, between the Palmer (Palma) Grill and Francisco's Market. Corso's buildings have since been torn down.

Working alongside Dario was his wife, Sofia Kozlowski of St. Johnsville, whom he married in 1934, and his brother, Guido. They resided upstairs with their daughter, Carol, until building a new home on Rockefeller Drive.

Dario not only utilized his tailoring knowledge, but also offered a Dry Cleaning Service – Valley Cleaners. In later years, he expanded the business into an adjoining self-service Dry Cleaning and Laundromat. Dario claimed the distinction of being the first dry cleaning plant in St. Johnsville. Previously, there had been numerous Laundry businesses since the early 1900s.

As an active member of the community, Dario was instrumental in forming the St. Johnsville Businessmen's Association in February 1956, where he served as president. He was also a Rotarian and served as a Chaplain in the Morris J. Edwards American Legion Post, being active for many years. He was involved in politics as a Republican. His civic accomplishments are too numerous to mention here.

Dario Joseph Corso was born April 9, 1919 in St. Johnsville and died July 21, 1991 in Pasco, Florida, where he and Sophie spent their retirement years. While living there, Dario earned extra money as the popular "handy man" in their retirement community.

Sophia Kozlowski was born May 27, 1918 in Amsterdam and lived on Ann Street with her parents before their marriage. She passed away November 9, 2010 at the home of their daughter, Carol in Prescott AZ.

After Guy's death in June 1969, Mary continued to live at the 18 Bridge Street home, later residing with her daughter, Gloria until her passing in August 1989. Their son, Guido and his wife, Susie Sindici, sold their home on N. Division Street, moved into the Bridge Street home and also took over the business for many years. Susie continued to manage the business into the early 1990s, after the death of Guido.

GUIDO LEWIS CORSO was born October 6, 1920. He passed away at the young age of 58 on August 31, 1979. On June 15, 1940 Guido Corso married Assunda "Susie" Sindici, daughter of Giuseppe Sindici and Edvige Cacciotti, in St. Patrick's Catholic Church, followed by a family reception at the Sindici home on Roth Street. Attendants were Mary (Papa) Stankewich and Dante Corso, Guido's brother.

Lenz Hardware employed Guido at the time and they offered the newlyweds their camp at Canada Lake for their honeymoon. Since Guido didn't own a car, Susie's neighbor, Fred Sanguine offered to taxi them back and forth. The couple moved into an apartment over the Sanguine home next door and lived there until Guido was called into service and before they purchased a home on North Division Street.

From October 16, 1943 to December 1945, S1C Guido Corso served in the US Navy during World War II in Northern Ireland. Shortly after he left for Naval service, their son, Peter was born on November 17, 1943.

After his release from the Navy, Guido returned as a plumber for Lenz Hardware & Son. He later became employed with his brother, Dario's Dry Cleaning and Clothing Store. Upon the death of his father, he changed his work status again and took over the management of the dress factory.

Assunda Sindici was born August 11, 1920 and passed away at the age of 92 on January 22, 2012. You will read more about Susie in *La Famiglia Sindici*.

GLORIA CORSO, the only daughter and youngest child, was born in St. Johnsville on September 4, 1929 and passed away on May 1, 2012 at the Faxton-St. Luke's Hospital in New Hartford NY. She was nicknamed "Georgie".

On January 31, 1950, Gloria Corso married Jack Laraway, her high school sweetheart. They were classmates and graduated together in June 1949. Gloria and Jack had two children - Dennis and Dawn. When first married, they lived in the downstairs apartment at 18 Bridge Street, formerly Gloria's father's tailoring shop. They later built a home in the new development on Rockefeller Drive on the hill off William Street and Failing Avenue.

The Laraway family enjoyed traveling the country. On August 23, 1971, along with their daughter, Dawn, they took a 3-week trip to Italy and other Mediterranean countries.

Gloria was active during her high school years participating in plays and as a basketball cheerleader She worked most of her life in her father's dress factory as a presser and helped wherever needed. After the factory closed, the Beech-Nut Packing Company in Canajoharie employed her until her retirement.

Jack Laraway was born July 19, 1930, most likely in Schenectady, where his parents were residing according to the 1930 Census.

This concludes the Gaetano "Guy" Corso family history.

ROSADIA CORSO - Please refer to *La Famiglia Masi* for Rosadia's story.

CARMELIA CORSO See following article *La Famiglia Coco*.

ANTONIO CORSO, JR., the youngest of the Corso family unit, was born on June 13, 1911 in Teano, Italy. He made the long journey to America and St. Johnsville with his mother, Maria and sister, Carmelia, at the young age of almost seven, arriving in Boston, MA on March 31, 1918.

On June 30, 1934, Tony married Mildred F. Heiser from Fort Plain NY. They had four children - Anthony, Jr., Robert, Linda Lee and Joyce Lee.

His first wife, Mildred Heiser was born March 7, 1915 in Fort Plain; she died February 10, 1964 in Little Falls Hospital at 47 years of age. In 1969, Anthony married Lillian Salisbury Hollenbeck.

Millie was a sister of Minnie (Heiser) Caponera, wife of Armenio Caponera, and Anna Mae (Heiser) Caprara, wife of Peter Caprara. Another sister Alma Heiser married John Warn, a local Mechanic Street resident, who lived most of his life among the Italians.

A World War II veteran, Tony was employed at Palatine Dyeing Company. The family lived at 29 Mechanic most of their lives. Tony passed away July 1, 1971 in St. Johnsville.

Anthony Corso was born around 1936 in St. Johnsville. I don't find much information about Tony, except he seemed to have married twice.

On May 2, 1959, he married Geraldine Brennan of Canajoharie. I also found another marriage on October 22, 1962 in Elkton MD to JoAnne Miller of Dolgeville.

I knew Tony growing up. He and my cousin, John Perry, were the best of friends. They would get together and experiment with their chemistry sets. At one time, as I recall, John blew off part of his finger. I think that was the end of the chemistry sets. Tony would also come to my house to play with my brother, Joseph "Jo Jo" Perry.

Robert Gifford Corso was born March 19, 1941 in Little Falls Hospital. He was an active member of the St. Johnsville Volunteer Fire Department, joining in 1966. Bob was awarded Fireman of the Year twice. As Captain of SAVAC, he received the "Stork Pin" for delivering a baby. Bob was also a member of the H.C. Smith Benefit Club and Ephratah Rod & Gun Club.

He retired from the Beech-Nut Packing Company in 2004, after 37 years of employment. Bob purchased the Henry Iacobucci home at 24 E. Liberty Street.

On May 16, 1959 Robert Corso was married to Norma M. Johnson at St. Patrick's Church. After 41 years of marriage, she passed away on April 1, 2001, and he married her sister, Irma Johnson Service, on August 3, 2002.

Bob and Norma were the parents of four sons - Robert Gifford 1961- 1964, who died at three years of age, Wade died at birth in 1963, Anthony and Michael.

On Tuesday, February 28, 2006, Robert Gifford Corso passed away at St. Mary's Hospital in Amsterdam.

Linda Lee Corso died at birth in 1943. She is buried in Prospect View Cemetery, St. Johnsville.

Joyce Lee Corso, the youngest child, was married to Lester L. Buddles at St. Patrick's Catholic Church on June 23, 1962. Her cousin, Norene (Masi) Rockefeller was one of her attendants.

~ *La Famiglia COCO* ~

~ DESIDERIO COCO et CARMELIA CORSO ~

DESIDERIO "Sam" COCO was born in Maenza, January 30, 1896, son of Lewis Coco and Giovannia Cacciotti. His mother was a sister of Francesco Cacciotti, Edvige Sindici's father.

Sam still has family members in Maenza, whom I met while visiting in June 2013. His niece, Luigia Crudetti told me that he would send them each a dollar three times a year - Easter, Christmas and another Italian holiday. I also have photos of his family that Luigia shared with me.

Desiderio arrived on July 19, 1913 coming directly to St. Johnsville with a group of eleven immigrants. I find no record of him in the 1915 Census, which isn't unusual, as I found there are several other Italians who were not recorded, my grandparents included.

CARMELIA CORSO arrived in Boston, Massachusetts on March 18, 1918 with her mother, Maria Lauro and youngest brother, Antonio. The last members of the Corso family to arrive, they joined her father in St. Johnsville.

Within two years of her arrival, Carmelia Corso met and married Desiderio Coco on October 3, 1920. Serving the couple as witnesses were her sister, Rosina Corso and her husband, Vincenzo Masi. They had one son, Renato (Raymond Peter).

The 1925 Census shows Sam and Carmelia living at 16 Hough Street with their son, Raymond. They both lived their entire lives in the home until their passing. At the time, Carmelia's parents, Antonio and Maria Corso, along with her brother, Anthony shared the duplex home with them.

Sometime after the June census, Antonio left St. Johnsville and returned to Maenza, where he passed away. His wife, Maria died on April 23, 1928 at the home of her daughter, Carmelia.

Desiderio served in World War I from August 7, 1918 to February 6, 1919. He was an active member of the American Legion, receiving numerous awards from the post. When his son, Raymond purchased the St. Johnsville Hardware, Sam was a visible helper.

Carmelia and Sam both worked in a knitting mill and also an underwear factory, which I seem to recall as the Luxuray in Fort Plain. I remember Carmelia for her wonderful sense of humor and friendly personality. She and my grandmother Edvige Sindici were the best of friends.

Carmelia Corso was born December 13, 1903 in Maenza, Italy and died April 26, 1991 in St. Johnsville. Desiderio Coco died October 27, 1985.

RENATO "Raymond Peter" COCO was born July 25, 1921 in the family home at 16 Hough Street in St. Johnsville. He served two years in the US Marine Corps as a Sergeant from March 31, 1943 to March 19, 1946 in the Pacific Theater.

Upon his return home, on April 29, 1947, Raymond Peter Coco was united in marriage with Philomena Marie Romano, daughter of Giuseppe Romano and Carmella DiLembo, who lived at 34 Hough Street.

Philomena "Phyl" Romano was born on New Year's Day, January 1, 1924 in St. Johnsville. She passed away on September 19, 1998 at age 74, at their Hough Street home. She and Ray had one son, Raymond, Jr. born in September 1948.

In 1950, Ray and Phyl purchased the St. Johnsville Hardware Company from long-time owner, Claude Bottomley. They carried an extensive line of hardware items, paint, wallpaper and brand name appliances, with Ray always available to service them. Phil watched over the store, did the bookkeeping and lovingly displayed the vast array of high quality beautiful lamps and gift items they had added for home decor. At one time they carried toys for the Christmas season. Customers came from surrounding towns. Travelers passing through the village were also attracted to the lamps hanging in the store windows inviting them in.

The complete wooden part of the building, where they had the original store, is now torn down. My grandfather Perry had rented an apartment in that part of the building when Bottomley's owned it. Phyl and Ray refurbished the apartment and lived there for several years.

The Coco's later purchased the brick portion from Michael Galuski. First owned by Charles and Mabel McCrone, it was originally a paint/wallpaper store for many years. It is now the American Legion Post organization's home.

Being one of their best customers, I can boast of many fabulous decorative pieces of cranberry glassware, Fenton lamps and numerous other home items that were available at St. Johnsville Hardware and displayed at my home. I still enjoy most of them. As I moved, so did they. All of the Maytag and Whirlpool appliances in my home were purchased at the store.

In 1995, Phyl and Ray sold the business and enjoyed a much deserved retirement. They had moved into the 16 Hough Street home with Carmelia after Desiderio's death. Ray became employed with the village of St. Johnsville at the St. Johnsville Housing development, off Averill Street for several years.

One spring morning, Ray was stricken while walking down South Division Street to his Hough Street home, following a coffee get-together with friends at Lamanna's Restaurant on Main Street. He died on March 28, 2002 at 81 years of age. Ray would be my distant cousin.

I discovered an Antonia Coco, who had emigrated with Velina Giovampietro Macci from Maenza on June 25, 1914. She was joining her sister, Rosa Coco.

ANTONIA COCO, born 1893, married Vincent Petronzio on December 13, 1914 at St. Patrick's. Their witnesses were Antonio and Julia Palombo.

ROSA COCO, born 1888, had married Angelo Patronzio, a merchant, on September 14, 1913 at St. Patrick's Church with Antonio Fiorini and Frances DeAngelis as witnesses. They were shown living at 10 Mechanic Street in both the 1913 St. Johnsville Directory and 1915 NYS Census.

Both Antonia and Rosa were the daughters of Perfetto Coco and Liberta Pietrocini. Though it seems the husbands were also brothers, they had different parents. Angelo's parents were Nogenie Patronzio and Dominica Forcinelli. Vincent's parents were Innocenzio Petronzio and Damenacca Torgilla. It is quite possible the husbands' fathers were brothers. I find no further information of these two couples.

I do find these familiar surnames most interesting - Coco, Pietrocini, Forcinelli. With them all originating in Maenza, perhaps they may also be linked somehow with each other, other than the Pietrocini / Forcinelli union?

~ *La Famiglia MASI* ~

~ TOMASSO MASI et MARY COCO ~

Tomasso Masi and Mary Coco were the parents of the Masi brothers, Vincenzo R. and Everisto, who came to St. Johnsville and married Corso sisters, daughters of Antonio Corso and Maria Lauro. Both sons were born in Maenza, Italy and immigrated separately to St. Johnsville, Everisto being the first to leave his homeland. There was also another brother in Italy. I don't know if there is a familial relationship with Desiderio Coco.

~ VINCENZO R. MASI et ROSINA C. CORSO ~

VINCENZO R. "James" MASI was born in Maenza, Italy on January 15, 1886. On April 8, 1910 he immigrated to America to join his younger brother, Everisto.

ROSINA C. CORSO was born in Teano, Italy on May 24, 1889. She came to this country alone at the age of 21, arriving on November 26, 1910, when she joined her brother, Gaetano in Amsterdam. Shortly after her arrival they lived in St. Johnsville at 23 South Division Street. Before this became the home of the Paul Guarnacci family, it seemed to be another popular boarding place for the Italian immigrants.

On February 4, 1912, Vincenzo R. Masi and Rosina C. Corso were married. She was the oldest child and daughter of Antonio Corso and Maria Lauro. Attending them were Vincenzo's cousin, Fedele Sarelli and his wife, Filomena, who lived in St. Johnsville for a short time.

The couple first lived at the 23 South Division street address where they had their first two children. By 1920 they had settled into farming life in Mindenville, just over the Mohawk River and New York Central Railroad Bridges.

James became the proud owner of the farm, where they lived most of their lives. By this time, they had four children – Doloris, Mary, Walter and Edward. Rose also worked in a knitting mill. It seems she worked most of her life outside the home, along with raising the children.

When the NYS Thruway took their farm, James and Rose moved to Utica, NY, where they both passed away. They purchased a home with pink shingles, which Rosina viewed as reminiscent of the homes in Naples, Italy, where the soft pink colors were like the inside of Conch seashells.

Rosina Corso died in her sleep on March 3, 1964 of heart issues. She had suffered seven heart attacks. Vincenzo Masi died in the hospital of pneumonia on October 19, 1968.

DOLORIS J. MASI, the oldest son, was born November 8, 1912 in Minden and died February 1, 1982 in the town of Danube. His godparents named Doloris after a French General.

On July 28, 1934, Doloris Masi married Doris K. Horender, daughter of Fred Horender and Goldie Christman. They had seven children - Doloris, Diana Katherine, Rosemary, David Joseph, Elizabeth, Johanna Dolores, and Patricia Dolores, all born in Little Falls Hospital.

Doris Horender was the daughter of a family that could trace their roots back to 1625. Some of her relatives fought in the Revolutionary War. Besides raising a large family, Doris has quite an interesting profile and active resume. She qualified to be the Valedictorian of her graduating class at Fort Plain High School, but politics came into play when three other graduates had fathers and a family friend on the school board. Doris was dropped down to fourth place, but her teachers stepped in and selected her for the important prizes. She worked her way through high school babysitting a prominent Fort Plain attorney's family. Owning only two cotton dresses, she would wear one while the other was drying on the clothesline.

A noted Mohawk Valley author, Doris Horender Masi was fluent in French, Spanish, German and Italian, learning Latin in high school. She considered herself one-tenth Italian as one of her ancestors had come to America in 1625 from Venice, Italy. Doris wrote mostly about her life on the farm, the local history surrounding her, and even Saltsman's Hotel, a well-known eatery in Ephratah. Doris Horender was born February 6, 1916 in Minden; she died April 1, 2004 at Valley Health Services in Herkimer at the age of 88.

Both Doloris and Doris worked at the Luxuray Mill in Fort Plain. He was paid well for his cutting skills with the underwear; she worked in the office. Due to his extraordinary cutting skills and ability to read blueprints, Doloris Masi was sent to Binghamton to cut dresses for a movie star.

In 1939, following in his father's footsteps, Doloris and Doris purchased the Loyal Creek Farm on Fiery Hill Road in the town of Danube, Herkimer County, where they lived most of their lives. The Loyal Creek Farm had the very first bulk tank able to store milk in Herkimer County.

Doloris J. Masi, Jr., the couple's first-born son, died at birth on August 15, 1935. West St. Johnsville Cemetery records show him buried on August 16, 1937.

Diana Katherine Masi, the oldest daughter, was born July 1, 1937. She died in Newville, Herkimer County on September 18, 2016. Diana married Keith L. Cagwin of Little Falls on April 21, 1957 at the St. James Catholic Church, Fort Plain. Keith was born in Little Falls on April 1, 1935 to noted Antique dealers, Andrew and Evalyn Cagwin. He died in New Hartford NY October 26, 2008.

Rosemary Masi was born July 10, 1940. She attended Oneonta State Teacher's College and later taught in the Elementary Schools of the Ilion and St. Johnsville school systems. In 1968 Rosemary Masi and James A. Casadonte of Mohawk were united in marriage in St. James Catholic Church, Fort Plain. Her sister Elizabeth served as maid of honor. Rosemary and Diana both had red hair.

David Joseph Masi, born August 14, 1942, married Barbara Ann Blencoe from Fort Plain.

Elizabeth Masi was born October 1, 1947.

Johanna Delores Masi also died at birth on May 27, 1949.

Patricia Deloris Masi was born the day after Christmas on December 26, 1950.
She married Roger Stock of Little Falls. Patricia did her student teaching in Canajoharie and served on the faculty of the Oppenheim-Ephratah Central School.

Following are the other children of Vincenzo Masi and Rosina Corso

MARY MASI was the only daughter of Vincenzo and Rosina. Mary was born May 17, 1914 in St. Johnsville. She was a graduate of St. Johnsville High School, Class of 1934, with my mother, Rose Sindici. They were good friends for many years.

Headlines of the announcement of the marriage of Mary Masi and Albert J. Rollman claimed that they were a most popular couple in both St. Johnsville and Fort Plain, Albert's hometown. They were married at St. Patrick's Catholic Church on January 16, 1935, a cold and blustery day. Sisters Agnes and Clara Massari, who were neighbors and best friends of Mary, attended her. Her brother, Doloris Masi was best man, with Victor Gordon, Little Falls as usher.

The couple had two children - Elaine and Donald. Elaine worked many years as an assistant to Dr. Robert Keba, DDS in St. Johnsville. I recall first meeting her in our teen years at the Canajoharie Youth Center.

Mary and Albert made their home on Willett Street, Fort Plain, where Mary later conducted a Ceramics business with classes. Both worked at Luxuray Mills in Fort Plain.

Mary Masi passed away in Herkimer on November 19, 1993. Albert Rollman was born September 1, 1911 in Fort Plain; he died February 8, 1974 in St. Mary's Hospital, Amsterdam.

WALTER MASI was born March 9, 1916 on the family farm in Minden. He died March 11, 1992 in Fort Plain.

On April 12, 1942 Walter married Florene D. Avery, daughter of Trivin and Blanche Avery from Fort Plain. Ella Chiodo was maid of honor, Marie Francisco, bridesmaid with Raymond Coco serving as best man. They had three sons - Barnard, Edward, Vincent and a daughter, Noreen Elizabeth. They lived on the River Road in Mindenville before moving to Fort Plain.

After Walter's passing, Florene often traveled with me on Cora Lee Tours. I believe she is still living.

Barnard is the owner of Masi's Auto Body Shop, St. Johnsville. Vincent married Sharon Ross from Fort Plain. I have no information regarding Edward.

Norene married Charles Brian Rockefeller of St. Johnsville at St. Patrick's Catholic Church on Saturday May 20, 1962. Attending her cousin as maid of honor was Rosemary Masi. Bridesmaids were Joyce Lee Corso and Lovina Suits, both cousins, and Sandra Bower, friend. Robert Peruzzi served as best man with Frank Schwasnick, Harold Countryman and her brother, Vincent Masi as ushers. The ring bearer was Norene's brother, Edward Masi.

EDWARD T. MASI, the last child of Vincenzo "James" Masi and Rosina Corso, was born in June 1918 on the farm in Minden and died in 1944 in Rome NY at the young age of 26, shortly after his daughter, Wanda was born. He was married to Wanda Bednarski, who was born January 10, 1919. Edward's wife, Wanda later married John Keba. She died November 20, 2009 in Gloversville.

Edward grew up working with his father, James on the family farm in Mindenville. Before joining the US Navy during World War II, he was a welder in Schenectady. He was sent to Sampson Naval Base for training. Edward was unable to swim but was forced to try everyday in Seneca Lake. He developed Quincy, which was difficult to treat. Edward died at Rhodes Hospital, now Utica College, three weeks after Christmas of acute Leukemia.

James Masi and Wanda Bednarski's daughter, Wanda Masi was married to Primo Iacobucci, son of Henry and Lena Iacobucci on August 19, 1961 at St. Patrick's Church. They had two daughters, Lori and Carrie. They were later divorced and Primo married another gal named Wanda.

~ EVERISTO MASI et ROSADIA CORSO ~

EVERISTO MASI aka Harry was born in Maenza, Italy on July 21, 1890. Arriving in 1909, he came to St. Johnsville where his older brother, Vincenzo joined him on April 10, 1910. I don't find either in the 1910 Census, which isn't unusual.

On October 18, 1914, Everisto Masi, 24, married Rosadia Corso, 18-year-old daughter of Antonio Corso and Maria Lauro and sister of Rosina Corso, at St. Patrick's Catholic Church. Mr. and Mrs. Louis Amoroso attended them. At this time, Harry was working at a knitting mill.

ROSADIO CORSO was born in Teano, Italy, August 9, 1893. She emigrated either November of 1900 or in 1913. It gets rather confusing with two daughters in one family having almost identical names. Her sister, Rosina married Everisto's brother, Vincenzo.

The 1915 NYS Census shows the couple living at 28 Mechanic Street. They had five children. Carmalia, most likely named after Rosadia's sister Carmelia, was born about 1916. Thomas Anthony was born August 6, 1917, Vetero "Victor" about 1920, and Orlando, May 4, 1921, all in St. Johnsville. A daughter, Jean may have been born in Hartford CN.

1920 Census records show Everisto and Rosadia living on Bridge Street.

On August 25, 1924, Everisto applied for a passport to return to Italy for a visit with his parents after living in the U.S. for 15 years. The application shows that he had lived in both St. Johnsville and Massachusetts.

By 1930 the family had moved to Hartford CN, where they lived the remainder of their lives.

Everisto Masi died in July of 1968 in Hartford CN.

Rosadia Corso living to be 84 years, passed away on January 18, 1978 in New Haven CN.

Patricia Masi Stock provided some information about the Masi families. Grazie!

Sanders Street was noted as the "Italian Section" in early Census records. With easy access to the New York Central Railroad and adjoining the Mohawk River, people could exit the train and omit going over the river bridge, a much longer trek, especially with luggage. I recall crossing the tracks on Sanders Street, at the end of South Division, with my grandmother many times to make the train trip to Little Falls.

The 1910 Census does not publish the house numbers, but it does list six homes on Sanders Street alone that were bursting at the seams with boarders. One boasted 16 male boarders with James Harrod listed to be the "head". A second home had 23 male boarders, plus a James Bell as "head." These are some of the names I recognize as boarders: John Ponzi, Verginio Colorito, Antonio Castrucci, Joseph (Zaccho) Sackett, Tony Boskey, and Rocco Giovampietro.

It seems that from 1900 to 1915, 21 Sanders Street was treated as a boarding house for many single Italian men and women, who worked on the railroad and in various textile mills in the village. It seemed to be the best place to find living arrangements, especially for single Italian men at the turn of the century. It was listed on ship manifests numerous times as a final destination in St. Johnsville NY, referred to as Box #88.

Many of the male immigrants came here to work, earn their wages and then return to Italy, or they moved on to another area to find employment. Some went back and forth to their homes in Italy with seasonal employment and were considered "birds of passage." I can't imagine making the voyage over the Atlantic many times.

Built around 1900, records I've found claimed 21 Sanders Street to be a four bedroom duplex. The 1914 village directory for St. Johnsville showed this address to house a grocery store with Domenic Stevens, proprietor. He lived next door at 19 Sanders. Two years previous in 1917 he was listed as a laborer, living at 17 Sanders. There was also a Sanders Grocery Store located on Main Street in 1890. Perhaps Sanders Street was named after him?

The 1915 NYS Census claims 15 residents living at 21 Sanders Street, which include three families plus three boarders. Listed are: Torello Iacobucci family of four; Garneo Laurora (Nina Fontana's father) with family of six; and Vincenzo Cerri and wife. Boarders were Guerrino Fontana (Nina's future husband), Vincenzo Cortesi and Ignaggio Polidori.

My Nonna, Edvige Cacciotti, when coming to America in 1913 lived at 21 Sanders Street. I'm assuming she shared a room with her sister Marcianna Cacciotti and husband, Giuseppe Narducci, who lived there at the time?

After Nonna and my Nonno, Giuseppe Sindici married in February 1914, they continued to live there for a few years. This was the birthplace of my mother, Rose Sindici Perry born in May 1915. I believe her sister, Lena Sindici Matis was also born there in May of 1917.

However, the Sindici family didn't show up in the June 1915 NYS Census. Although extremely helpful with research, I have discovered Census records to have numerous oversights and errors, especially with the spelling of Italian's names. WWI registration records for my grandfather showed them living there in June 1917.

21 Sanders Street and several other properties that were inhabited by early Italians hosted numerous boarders. This helped the homeowner or renter pay their living expenses during the hard times. Even those with large families somehow found space for boarders.

My grandparents were later shown renting a home at 44 Hough Street in the 1920 Census. They took in three male boarders - Pasquale Montoni, Desiderio Coco and their brother-in-law, Giuseppe Narducci.

Between 1920-1925, the Italians had pretty much settled into their own homes. Many times they took in another family as boarders, usually relatives. The 1925 Census does not show many residents as boarders. The huge influx of Italians had subsided by this time.

A current view of 21 Sanders Street does not look like it could have been a duplex at any time, let alone able to house a store. The explanation is: in January of 1926 when it was owned by the John Pedro family, the home experienced a devastating fire that consumed all of its contents. There were several Italian families, most likely boarders, who were left homeless in the dead of winter. To add to the drama, the fire alarm failed and church bells had to be sounded to alert the firemen. This wasn't the first time the failure had occurred. Due to the lack of a quick response, it spread to the home next door owned by Antonio Fontana and Giulio Patrei. It was suspected that an overheated stovepipe caused the wall behind it to catch fire.

There were so many births at 21 Sanders Street, Joyce Peruzzi Politt has suggested it be called the "St. Johnsville Birthing Center".

I hereby also declare Sanders Street *"Official Little Italy of St. Johnsville NY."*

~ ST. JOHNSVILLE WATER ~

Sanders (Sauders) Street was one of the very first streets to have village water available to them. In 1879, the Village Board formed a water board to oversee furnishing water to the village residents.

There were springs on the land of H.D. Sauders, which the village could utilize. The water system originated from the "Cox Spring" to the corner of Main and Union Streets. I believe the spring may have been somewhere near the Zimmerman Creek on Union or William Street?

Recipients of the water were initially charged a minimum $3.00 per family per month. Rents varied according to the number of families or tenants residing in the homes. There were very strict restrictions for its use at the time.

This is most likely the reason so many of the Italian ladies took their laundry to the Mohawk River and Zimmerman Creek. I cannot imagine how these women struggled to wash the clothing and then lug the heavy wet clothes home to hang out to dry.

In 1880, the north side of Sanders (Sauders) had water connections. By 1890 Sanders was connected to Mechanic, Hough and South Division. They did have village sewers in 1912 and also lighting. Of course, there were fees for their use, as today.

Bertha Pedro et Elenterio Caponera Wedding

Standing: Ushers Eugene Ross, August DeLibro; Best man Joseph Palombi; Groom Larry Caponera Mastromoro
Ushers – Unknown, Guido and Larry Tolfa
Seated: Bridesmaids Yolanda Narducci, Anna Barca; Matron-of-honor Mary Palombi Caponera; Bride Bertha Pedro
Bridesmaids Lola Salvagni, Enelda Loccia and Lavena Loccia
Flower girls: Gilda Caponera, Dora Palombi, Rena Caponera. Ring bearer Louis Palombi

~ *La Familia PIETRASANTI (PEDRO)* ~

~ GIOVANNI PEDRO et IDA SALVAGNI ~

GIOVANNI "John" PIETRASANTI aka PEDRO was born in Maenza, Italy in 1887, the son of Alexandro Pietrasanti and Angela Onorati.

IDA SALVAGNI was born in Maenza, Italy on June 17, 1886. She was the daughter of Lewi Salvagni and Maria Benedetti. Ida immigrated alone from Maenza at the age of 29 on April 18, 1912. She is the sister of Paolo Salvagni.

C.W. Lambert, a Justice of the Peace in St. Johnsville NY, married John Pedro and Ida Salvagni on May 23, 1916. Serving as witnesses for the couple were Pasquale Montoni and L. Terranova, whom I'm assuming is Luciano. He was an uncle of Carmela Terranova Palma.

The couple had four children together - twins Bertha and Guila, Victoria and Alexander. Ida had a son, Eugene, from her previous marriage to Francisco Rossi in Italy.

On November 7, 1913, Ida's mother, Maria Benedetti Salvagni, age 57, arrived in America with her two grandsons, Giovanni Salvagni, age four, and Eugene Luigi Rossi, age two. The manifest stated that Iacsento Rossi was Eugene's father. His mother was Ida Salvagni. Giovanni Salvagni's father was Paolo Salvagni.

1920 shows the Pedro family living at 23 South Division Street, another popular boarding house. There were two boarders, Angelo Battisti and Vincenzo DiBrigida. As an example of errors that the Census employees made, the entire Pedro family is listed as Battisti. Nothing like confusing a future Genealogist!

The 1925 NYS Census lists the John Pedro family and their five children living with Ida's mother, Maria Benedetti Salvagni at 26 Sanders. Ida's brother, Paolo "Paul" Salvagni, his wife, Adelgesia and two sons, Florido and Luigi lived next door at 24 Sanders. Maria Salvagni was also Paul's mother. I could not locate a record of 21 Sanders in the 1925 Census.

Apparently after the 1925 Census was taken, John Pedro and Ida Salvagni purchased the 21 Sanders Street home on the railroad side of the street. In January 1926, the home was consumed by fire, as per the previous article.

On August 8, 1928 a news article stated that John Pedro was living at 21 Center Street when he reported for work at 11 pm and discovered a fellow West Shore Railroad "track walker", Anthony Morlando had been struck by a passing train. The family may have resided at the Center Street home while their home was being rebuilt?

Ironically, John Pedro lost his life within the year on June 9, 1929 at the young age of 42 when he also worked the night shift as a trackwalker, a job he held for eight years. When he didn't return home from his shift the next morning, an alert was put out with a search. They found his body in the Little Falls canal, which ran parallel to the tracks. It is assumed he stepped too close to the canal and fell in, being hindered by having only one arm and most likely not able to swim. A rather lengthy inquest determined he had drowned. Another tragic victim of employment with the railroad!

His great-grandson, Larry Mastromoro, shared the story that John, even though hampered by the loss of an arm, had built a small garage next to his 21 Sanders Street house just before he died.

The 1930 Census shows four non-Italian boarders with the current Pedro family members - Ida, Bertha and Larry Caponera aka Mastromoro, Victoria, Alexander and Eugene.

BERTHA PEDRO was born a twin to Guila "Julia" on March 6, 1913. She died December 6, 2003, while at a nursing facility in Herkimer NY.

On September 15, 1928, Bertha Pedro married Larry Caponera in a beautiful setting at St. Patrick's Catholic Church with a large bridal party of 16 attendants. Besides the maid-of-honor and best man, there were five bridesmaids, five ushers, three flower girls and a ring bearer. With much research, I believe I've been able to determine the identity of most of the bridal party members. Their names are listed in order under their accompanying gorgeous wedding photo.

Bertha and Larry lived with her mother, Ida, a few years, and eventually purchased a home at 9 Mechanic Street, where she and Larry both lived out their lives. They had three children – John, Norman and Nora Jean. Their son, John now resides in the home, owned by their grandson, Larry.

ELENTERIO "Larry" CAPONERA immigrated on October 27, 1920. He was born in Fumone, Italy on April 21, 1903, son of Francesco Mastromoro and Elnora Caponera, as shown on the marriage certificate. Listed on the ship's manifest as Elenterio Caponera, he was traveling with Alessandro Potenziani, Francesco Potenziani and Philip Caponera, a friend, who headed to Rome NY. Larry remained friends with him for years. Philip is not the same one who settled in St. Johnsville and owned the liquor store.

14 years after his arrival Larry became a U.S. citizen on September 10, 1934. On June 15, 1937, Elenterio Lawrence Caponera was granted his request to change his last name to his father's – Mastromoro - by Montgomery County Court Judge George C. Stewart in the County Court Chambers in Amsterdam, NY.

Larry Mastromoro died at his home in St. Johnsville on March 31, 1985. Census records show he worked as a gardener/landscaper most of his life. He had an inborn talent of working with concrete. The New York Central Railroad also employed him as a laborer and cook. Upon his retirement, he took a custodial job at the St. Johnsville Central School. His granddaughter shared this, "Someone would knock on his door at 4 am. He had to be ready to work at 42 cents per day."

Larry was very proud of his own garden, selling and sharing the fruits of his labor with neighbors. Larry was an excellent cook, going into the woods to pick just the right mushrooms, and sometimes simmering his sauce on the fireplace he had built in his backyard. His wife, Bertha claimed Larry was a much better cook than she.

Working first in the Little Falls Felt Shoe factory, Bertha was employed by the Corso Dress Factory most of her life. She also sold movie theater tickets for her brother, Alex Pedro.

Bertha loved to play Bingo at the American Legion Hall every Saturday night. Her son, John tells how she could "smell" a bingo game 100 miles away. He has so many humorous stories about his mother with her three bingo friends, Martha Pedro, Catherine Mentis and Kathleen Keller and their antics over their passion of bingo, which was a first and foremost necessity in their lives. Bertha's grandson, Larry, has fond memories of the Saturday night Bingo games he attended with her at the American Legion and how he "looked forward to his hot dog and sauerkraut every week with Gramma." How these fanatic bingo players handled so many cards at once still amazes him. This includes my Mom, another avid Bingo player.

John Mastromoro is a noted piano and keyboard player, entertaining at many local events and still sharing his gift with nursing homes and senior centers. John has a natural talent, playing "by ear" at a very young age. We took piano lessons from Mrs. Mildred Walrath on John Street. With the use of his computers, he currently composes and sells his piano-keyboard selections on CDs. His keen musical ear was helpful with the recent tuning of the St. Johnsville Reformed Church chimes.

After graduation in 1954, John enlisted and served in the U.S. Navy for four years. He had the opportunity to visit most of the European and Mediterranean countries, being assigned to the USS Coral Sea CVA43 for 15 months.

With his honorable discharge, John served first as a Printer apprentice at the Enterprise & News, then the Little Falls Times, Utica Observer and White Plains newspapers. He owned a small job shop in Daytona Beach FL. John later worked 27 years for the Conrail Railroad as a clerk in the Utica station, 10 years in Syracuse and finally at the Selkirk yards near Albany, retiring in 1999 with the new ownership of CSX.

John has shared so many wonderful humorous stories with me from the many times he spent with his father, Larry and other Italian men as they sat around on Sunday, smoking their stogies, playing cards and swearing in their distinct dialects when they lost. They used wine and "goodies" as their wagers.

John told me, *"The old Italians were pretty strong on becoming good American citizens. At one of their card-playing sessions they remarked that they would never speak Italian to each other in front of anyone that didn't understand it, because it would have been an insult to them. Also, they would never consider accepting welfare or like assistance as long as their arms and legs still moved."* Italians are a very proud culture!

Attorney Norman Lee Mastromoro was admitted to the New York State Bar in 1981. At this writing, he has been in his law practice over 38 years, his office being located in Little Falls. He has served as both the town and village attorney of St. Johnsville for many years and was a Town Justice at one time. He was very active in village and town politics, once serving on the Urban Renewal Commission.

In 1962 Norman graduated from Bryant College in Providence RI, where he majored in Business Administration and Accounting, going on to SUNY at Albany. He received his "Juris Doctor" law degree from Western New England College, Springfield MA. Norman currently lives in Broadalbin with his wife, Gail.

Norman was also gifted with musical genes, playing guitar and singing in a few local bands. Musical talent is obviously in the Mastromoro Italian genes!

Nora Jean Mastromoro graduated St. Johnsville High School as an honor student and attended Albany Business College. As a young woman, in July 1973 she had a wonderful 2-week experience of touring London, Paris and Rome with a friend.

Nora was united in marriage the following year with John R. Gentile of New York Mills NY on August 3, 1974. Her brother, Norman served as an usher and brother, John provided the wedding music. A reception followed at the Manor, Route 5 West St. Johnsville.

GUILA "Julia" PEDRO, a twin to Bertha, was born in St. Johnsville on March 6, 1913. I believe Bertha was the first-born.

Julia Pedro resided in Ithaca NY after marrying August De Libro of Ithaca on August 11, 1928, one month before her sister, Bertha's wedding. The ceremony was performed at St. Patrick's Catholic Church with Lavena Loccia as maid-of-honor and Lorenzo Tolfa as best man. In attendance as bridesmaids were Bertha Pedro, Anna Barca, and Lola Salvagni. Ushers were Lawrence Caponera aka Mastromoro, James De Libro and Eugene Ross. Mary Francisco and Romalia "Molly" Tolfa were flower girls. A reception with a wedding dinner was held at the Odd Fellows temple on Bridge Street. The couple had two children - Dora and Gerald.

VICTORIA PEDRO was born August 11, 1917 in St. Johnsville. She passed away in April 1982.

On June 13, 1936 Victoria Pedro married Francis Fitzgibbons of Little Falls. After first living with her mother for several years, the couple resided most of their married life in Little Falls. They had two children - Jacqueline and David.

By 1940, only Ida, as the head of the household, lived with her son, Alexander and mother, Maria Salvagni in the 21 Sanders Street home. They rented part of the home to Dominick Peruzzi and Viola Nobili, along with their two oldest daughters, Mary Ann and Barbara. Their third child, Joyce was born in this home.

ALEXANDER "Alex" PEDRO was born November 12, 1919 at the family home, 21 Sanders Street. He died on March 26, 1999 at the home of his birth.

In November 1942, while serving in the Army Air Force, Pvt. Alexander "Alex" Pedro married Martha Cherry from Herkimer. They first lived in Baltimore MD, where Alex was stationed. He was reassigned to Amarillo AFB, Texas, where he received technical training as a fuel supply specialist. Alex was inducted February 26, 1942 and honorably discharged December 12, 1945.

Alex and Martha resided in Amsterdam during their early marriage, where Alex worked in a movie theatre as a film projectionist. While serving his country, Alex worked at his trade as a motion picture projectionist. The Army Air Force sent him all over to entertain the wounded troops with movies, which was important to their morale. During this time, he had the great pleasure of meeting and having his photo taken with Mickey Rooney and another entertainer. They were part of a group of 100 entertainers, who traveled with the troops. The story goes that Mickey Rooney borrowed $20 from Alex that was never repaid.

In January 1947, Alex and his friend, John Francisco were managers of the Fonda Movie Theater. In later years, Alex purchased the Smalley's Theater in St. Johnsville, along with several others in the Mohawk Valley. He also partnered with his brother-in-law, Francis Fitzgibbons and his two friends, Arminio Caponera and John Francisco at various times in the film industry. I was told this John Francisco was owner of the Bridge Street Grill.

Alex and Martha had two children, a son Richard, who married Carol Richard, daughter of Fedora Fiacco and James Richard, and a daughter, Linda Pedro, who married John "Gene" Maher, who has passed away.

Richard Pedro was born August 2, 1944 in Amsterdam NY. He died June 18, 2014 in Gloversville.

To my knowledge, the 21 Sanders Street home remained in the Pedro family until Alex' wife, Martha Cherry passed away March 29, 2016. The daughter of Angelo and Antionette Cherry of Herkimer, Martha was born on Halloween, October 31, 1921.

EUGENE LOUIS ROSS was born November 24, 1911 in Maenza, son of Francisco Rossi and Ida Salvagni. He immigrated to America on November 7, 1913 with his grandmother, Maria Benedetto Salvagni and his cousin, Giovanni Salvagni.

Eugene died March 10, 1989 in Ithaca, where he had lived since his marriage to Josephine A. Funari. They had two daughters - Mary and Barbara, both married to brothers, John and William Crowley, respectively.

In 1929 Eugene was quite active in school activities at St. Johnsville High as a starring member of both the football and baseball teams. He was elected Captain of the football team under Coach McIntosh and played shortstop in baseball.

He grew up and played sports with my father, Floyd B. Perry. The two of them were also part of the cast for the playlet, "What Annie Brought Home" presented at the Masonic Temple as a benefit for St. Patrick's Church on February 8, 1934.

Eugene continued his love for baseball while managing the championship baseball team for the Morse Industry Association and the Hook Wilse team in Ithaca.

John Mastromoro and his son, Larry Mastromoro, have contributed to this article. Grazie!

~ *La Famiglia SALVAGNI* ~

Self-employed most of his life as a barber, Paolo "Paul" Salvagni was born October 14, 1884 in Maenza, Italy to Lewi Salvagni and Maria Benedetti. He was the last survivor of 13 siblings.

MARIA BENEDETTI was born in Maenza in 1855. She passed away April 30, 1944 in St. Johnsville. I find no information regarding Paul's father, Lewi Salvagni. He may have passed away in Italy.

Maria Beneditti came to America and St. Johnsville on November 7, 1913, bringing with her, Paul's son Giovanni, age 4 and her daughter, Ida's son, Luigi Rossi, age 2. Luigi aka Eugene was the son of Iascento "Francisco" Rossi. Luigi was raised in the Pedro household, where Maria resided from the time of her arrival until her passing. Ida (Salvagni) Pedro was Maria's daughter.

PAOLO "Paul" SALVAGNI apparently emigrated back and forth several times from his home in Maenza to his home in St. Johnsville. Census records state he first came over in 1908. He may have gone to Pennsylvania first.

ARMANCIA FORCINELLI arrived on August 27, 1912, meeting her brother Giuseppe Forcinelli. Obviously, Paolo and Armancia met in St. Johnsville. She was also a sister of Delia Pietrocini and Leonina Cochi.

Paul Salvagni and Armancia Forcinelli were married in St. Patrick's Roman Catholic Church, St. Johnsville. The couple apparently went back to Maenza, where she gave birth to a daughter, Lola and son, Florido "Floyd". Armancia passed away in 1918 of Influenza, shortly after another child's birth and death. She was a sister of Leonina (Cochi), Delia (Pietrocini) and Giuseppe Forcinelli.

While back in Maenza, Paolo Salvagni served in the Italian Army from 1915 to 1918. 54 years later, he finally received his medals and certificate.

Leaving behind his two children from his wife, Armancia Forcinelli, on July 3, 1920 at the age of 36, Paul emigrated again to live with his mother at 36-38 Bridge Street. During this time he began his tonsorial career, opening a barbershop on Sanders Street for 11 years.

Paul again returned to Maenza and married Adelgesia Pasquale. Perhaps Adelgesia was caring for his first two children after their mother's death with Paul back in St. Johnsville? They had a son, Luigi "Louis", whose twin brother died at birth.

I have found conflicting information regarding Paul's immigration and his business ventures. Therefore, some of his story may not be completely accurate.

From what I've determined, it seems Paul, being married three times, was the father of seven children; two of which died at birth

ADELGESIA PASQUALE came to America on October 21, 1922 with the three children, Lola, age 9, Florido, age 5, and Luigi, age 3, who had been hospitalized upon arrival. They later had another son, Rudolph born in St. Johnsville.

The May 24, 1924 manifest shows that Paul was detained due to his wife's hospitalization, but they later continued their journey. He and Adelgesia had apparently returned to Italy and were now returning to his home at 26 Center Street, as stated on the ship's manifest. This seems to be an error; according to family members they had gone to the family home at 26 Sanders. It was rare that any Italian resided north of Main Street in the early part of the 20th century.

Also onboard the ship with Paolo and Adelgesia were Michelangelo Iagnocco and his wife, Beatrice Vicciarelli. They were headed to 4 Roth Street, where Michalangelo apparently was a boarder at the time. I do not find him in the 1920 Census or any trace of him thereafter until the 1940 Census, which shows the couple living in Utica with their children. Beatrice was a sister of Elena (Vicciarelli) Montoni.

Unfortunately, in the early years of immigration there seem to be no records of the immigrants' journies back to Italy, so it's difficult to determine their passage back and forth. In later years they were required to apply for a passport.

The 1925 NYS Census shows the Salvagni family living at 24 Sanders Street, next to Paul's mother and the Pedro's, his sister, Ida's family. There seems to be an oversight as Louis is missing and Floyd is listed as a daughter. (Sometimes the Census takers missed a person and wrote their names in later on another page.) The record shows Paul being employed by the Railroad in 1925?

Before setting up his Ideal Barber Shop at 7 Bridge Street, Paul apparently conducted his business at several other locations in the village. Records show at one time he had set up his barbershop at 36-38 Bridge Street, where he lived with his mother.

In 1918 a fire destroyed the 36-38 Bridge Street buildings owned by Carmine Terranova. Paul had his barbershop in the General Pershing clubrooms at that time. In 1920, Salvagni had temporarily moved to Sanders Street. 1924 finds him again renting a barbershop at 36 Bridge from John Francisco, who had purchased the property. When Paul moved, Francisco continued the barbershop, until opening the Bridge Street Bar and Grill.

1928 finds Paul located at 38 East Main. By 1933, Paul had his Barber Shop at 7 Bridge Street, the final location, purchasing the former Beekman property. He retired on January 8, 1952, after 35 years of providing haircuts for male residents of St. Johnsville. His son, Louis, continued the business.

I discovered that in 1918 the Italian Society aka General Pershing Club had its headquarters at 36 Bridge, when it burned. Paul was very active with this group, being one of its founders. During the 1930s, he was also quite active in village politics as a Democrat, serving in different positions.

It has been noted that at one time there were six barbers in the village, all doing well.

Paolo Salvagni passed away October 1986, just before his 102nd birthday at the Van Allen Nursing Home, Little Falls and is buried in the family plot in Prospect View Cemetery.

GIOVANNI (JOHN) SALVAGNI arrived in America at the age of four years with his grandmother, Maria and cousin, Luigi Rossi on November 7, 1913. He was born in Maenza, Italy in December 1909 to Antonia Palmystri and Paolo Salvagni.

John Salvagni married Linda Sanguine from St. Johnsville on August 23, 1930. She was born on February 24, 1911 in Italy, daughter of Umberto "Bart" and Angeline Sanguine. The Sanguine family lived at 3 Roth Street.

John died in Fort Myers, Florida on June 16, 1990. Linda passed away September 4, 1975 in Fort Myers, Florida. Both are buried in Calvary Cemetery, Herkimer.

1935 city records show John living in Waverly, Oneida County. According to 1940 Census records, it seems they made their home in Utica, where they became the parents of three children - Angeline, Jean, and Patrick. Another daughter, Annette was born sometime around 1950. They apparently retired to Fort Myers, Florida, where they both passed away.

After Linda's passing, John married Genevieve Rose Arra August 31, 1984 in Fort Myers FL.

LOLA SALVAGNI was born in St. Johnsville, as per Census records on March 10, 1914, daughter of Paolo Salvagni and Armancia Forcinelli, shortly before their return to Maenza, Italy. Another daughter was born in Italy between Lola and brother Florido, but did not survive.

At seven years of age, Lola came back to America on October 22, 1921 with her stepmother, Adalgesia, brother Florido and half-brother Luigi.

On August 18, 1940, Lola married Michael Lesa of Johnstown NY in Saint Patrick's Catholic Church, St. Johnsville. A wedding shower was held in the Ukranian Hall given by her attendants, which included Gilda (Francisco) Bussone and Mary Fontana, among others.

Lola served as a bridesmaid in her brother Giovanni "John" Salvagni's wedding to Linda Sanguine. Always the bridesmaid, she also served in both Julia and Bertha Pedro's weddings.

Lola lived most of her life in Whittier, California, where the family moved in 1953. They had two sons, Leon and Michael.

Lola Salvagni passed away in Whittier CA on May 10, 2007 at the age of 93 of a lung disease.

On a personal note: I discovered that Lola was one of the hostesses at a bridal shower for my mother, Rose Sindici, who had just been married to my father, Floyd B. Perry. Other hostesses were Mary Wolinski, Contance Patrei, Teresa Fontana and my mom's cousin, Viola (Narducci) Potenziani. It was held at the American Grill Restaurant on New Street, owned by Sadie Palombi.

FLORIDO SALVAGNI, second son of Paolo, was born in Maenza on August 11, 1917, sharing the same mother with his sister, Lola – Armancia Forcinelli. He also came to America with his stepmother, Adelgesia, his sister, Lola and half-brother, Luigi.

Floyd, aka Fat, followed in his father's footsteps and worked as a barber most of his life. He worked for his father before and after his World War II service. Floyd later opened his own shop in Fort Plain until his retirement, when he worked part-time with his daughters, Barbara and Mary Ann at the Ideal Hair Fashions.

A much-decorated hero of World War II, Floyd was presented the Bronze Star for a valorous deed on D-Day on the beachhead of Normandy, France on June 6, 1944. He had contracted malaria during his time there and recuperated in a hospital in England. He was a private in the Army fighting in eight battles. Floyd had the distinction of being the first St. Johnsville serviceman to go overseas.

On June 16, 1946 upon his return from service, Floyd Salvagni and Esther Balderston from Little Falls were married in St. Mary's Catholic Church, Little Falls. Together they had a son, Robert and two daughters, Barbara and Mary Ann. After his marriage, the family lived upstairs in the building that later housed his daughters' Ideal Hair Fashions.

Robert Salvagni married Carol Burns of Utica. Barbara married Dominick Stagliano; Mary Ann married Gary "Dart" Jones, both local young men.

Robert Salvagni followed in his father's footsteps with military service. The girls also followed the tradition of hair care and opened Ideal Hair Fashions at 8 East Main Street, the building owned by their parents. Later, Mary Ann left the beauty salon and became employed by the St. Johnsville branch of the U.S. Postal Service.

LUIGI Louis SALVAGNI, also born in Maenza on December 19, 1919 was the son of Paolo Salvagni and Adelgesia Pasquale. He arrived in America on October 21, 1922, coming to St. Johnsville with his half-sister, Lola and half-brother, Florido, along with his mother, Adelgesia. Louis had a twin brother, who didn't survive his birth.

The St. Johnsville Dress Shop employed Louis from 1936-1940 before he entered the service.

On December 5, 1940, Pfc. Louis Salvagni joined the U.S. Army as a rifleman. He was sent overseas in July 1942 where he was taken prisoner by the Italians in North Africa. He was confined to Italian and German prisons for 18 months. The story Louie related to his nephew, Bob, is "the German prison guards left the prison because they thought the United States and its allies were closing in. Louie heroically led the rest of the prisoners in their escape. He found an Italian family who helped them hide. Louie hid his dog tags and wore civilian clothes. He fit right in with his fluent Italian. When the U.S. Troops finally came by the farm, they didn't believe his story until he went to the barn and got his dog tags."

After hiding behind enemy lines for nine months, Louie returned to active duty on June 25, 1944 and was honorably discharged November 2, 1944 after serving his country for four years. I understand he had numerous stories to tell of his internment. It was an experience he seemed to struggle with the rest of his life.

Like his father, Louis worked in the barber trade most of his life. With his discharge he attended the Henry Ford Trade School in Detroit, MI and worked in New York City before relocating back to St. Johnsville, where he joined with his father at the Ideal Barber Shop, continuing the barber tradition the remainder of his life. Louis passed away at his place of business on January 16, 1986.

On August 24, 1954 in St. Patrick's Catholic Church, Louis Salvagni was joined in marriage with Susan Gretna Guarnacci, daughter of Paul Guarnacci and Jennie Gagliardi.

Susie was born in St. Johnsville on August 14, 1929. She died October 10, 1998.

Susan Gretna Guarnacci was noted for her dedication to St. Patrick's Catholic Church as the musical director, organist, soloist and choir director for many years. She provided the music for numerous funerals and weddings throughout her lifetime. This included my wedding in 1955 and my daughter's in 1982.

RUDOLPH SALVAGNI as the youngest of the siblings was the only child of Paul's born in St. Johnsville in 1927. At this writing, he is still living. Deciding not to follow the family tradition of serving as a barber, in 1959 he attended Albany Business College in Albany NY.

Upon graduation, he set up his own bookkeeping and tax preparation business for several years. If memory serves me, he also worked in the office of Palatine Dyeing Company on New Street and later the Beech-Nut Packing Company in Canajoharie.

As a stellar athlete, Rudy is most noted for his outstanding skills and sportsmanship throughout high school into his retirement years. He was referred to as a "speedy centerfielder" in baseball. There wasn't a sport he played that he didn't excel in. After high school, he played in baseball and bowling leagues. In his retirement he was an avid golfer, winning many awards at the Canajoharie Country Club. So many of the second-generation Italian young men seemed to have a God-given talent for sports. Certainly embedded in the strong Italian genes!

On Labor Day weekend, September 1951, Rudolf Salvagni joined in marriage with Rose Marie Ianiello from Canajoharie. Born June 28, 1931, she was the daughter of Ernest Ianiello and Carmela Palm. Carmela Palm Ianiello is a cousin of Carmela Terranova Palma and the entire Terranova families that settled in St. Johnsville and Canajoharie. Rudy and Rosie had a daughter, Sherrie.

Rosie's parents would be noted as proprietors of Ernie's Tavern on Mohawk Street, Canajoharie for many years. Rudy and Rosie took over ownership for a while after his retirement. Rose Marie Iannello passed away January 17, 2013.

Robert Salvagni shared his uncle Louis Salvagni's war story. Grazie!

~ *La Famiglia SANGUINE* ~

~ UMBERTO SANGUINE et ANGELINA DiPINTO ~

Umberto "Robert" aka Bart Sanguine, listed as Sanguigni on the ship's manifest, and also on his marriage certificate, arrived on March 24, 1904 headed to Palatine Bridge to meet Antonio Mancini, who would later become his brother-in-law.

Sometime before the 1910 Census Umberto Sanguine married Angelina DiPinto. They were listed as living with the large group of immigrants on Sanders Street with their two oldest sons, James and Emilio. In 1912 they are living at 34 Mechanic Street; Bart works on the railroad.

By 1915, he had purchased the 3 Roth Street home where he and his family lived until the early 1940s. It was a 2-family home and only one on the dead-end street that had a garage and driveway.

UMBERTO SANGUINE was born October 7, 1879 in Terracino, Italy, the son of Petre Sanguine and Carolina Corsi. He died New Year's Day, January 1, 1940 in St. Johnsville. Married twice, he had seven children with his first wife, Angelina DiPinto. The eldest was James, then Emilio, Linda, Joseph, John, William and Fred.

ANGELINA DiPINTO was born in Terracino, Italy on January 27, 1885, the daughter of Giovanni DiPinto and Maryanna Mastrocola. After a 15-month illness with tuberculosis, she passed away on December 29, 1920, leaving seven young children motherless.

On September 2, 1905, Angelina and her sister, Concetta DiPinto, arrived in America together with their brother, Francisco and Concetta's son, Giuseppe Mancini. Concetta was the wife of Antonio Mancini. This would be the connection to the Joseph Mancini and Lillian Mancini Neri Keller families.

After Angelina's death, Umberto Sanguine married Teresa Olivieri to assist in the care of his young children. The ceremony took place on December 11, 1921 at an Amsterdam Catholic Church with witnesses Francesco and Sophia Salvagni. They had no children together. Theresa was the daughter of Rocco Olivieri and Rosa Vecciarelli. Teresa was living at 10½ Sanders Street at the time of their marriage.

I recall the Sanguine family very well, as they lived next door to my grandparents, Giuseppe Sindici and Edvige Cacciotti at 4 Roth Street. After Umberto's death, Teresa lived there with the youngest son, Fred. She worked in the dress factory doing hand sewing.

From my recent discoveries and checking the timeline I have determined that after Umberto's death, Teresa was seeing John Spinelli. When visiting my grandparents, I would go there to play table games with John's daughter, Mary Spinelli, whom I had always thought was Teresa's niece. Research proves her not to be a niece, but stepdaughter. I mostly remember Teresa to be a rather fun lady.

I also remember that Teresa loved her wine. The story I always heard is that she would give my Aunt Viola a quarter with a glass canning jar to fill with wine from my grandfather's vat in the cellar. He made his own wine from the bountiful grapevine in his backyard.

My Aunt Susie Sindici and Uncle Guido Corso rented the upstairs apartment of 3 Roth Street after their marriage, until purchasing their own home.

VINCENZO "James" SANGUINE was born December 3, 1907 in St. Johnsville. James was the oldest of the seven children born to Umberto Sanguine and Angelina DiPinto. He lived most of his life in St. Johnsville until retiring to Port St. Lucie FL, where he passed away on January 6, 1989.

As an employee of the Little Falls Footwear, James was a director of the 30-year club. He was a very active member of the St. Johnsville community, always serving in some official capacity as a member of an organization. He served with the Auxiliary Police, was an active member of the Harry C. Smith Benefit Club and involved with local politics.

On April 26, 1930, James Sanguine married Eness Battico. They purchased a home at 15 Church Street in 1934. Many years later he sold the home to Rose Papa and her husband, Burton Dolan.

In his retirement, James and his second wife, Lucille Van Vranken built a home in Allen Heights, St. Johnsville, right next door to his lifetime friend, Dominick "Maymo" Peruzzi and his wife, Viola Nobili. James and Maymo lived around the corner from each other in their childhood.

Eness Battico died from a heart ailment at the young age of 33 years. She was born in 1908 and died November 25, 1941 at Cooperstown Hospital. She left two very young daughters, Dolores and Patricia.

Dolores married Vernon Stone, her high school sweetheart. Patricia is married to Russell Sitterly from Canajoharie. Russell served in the Paratroopers in Germany.

On April 16, 1942 James joined in marriage with Lucille Van Vranken at St. Patrick's Catholic Church. Perina Fontana and Dominick DiCamillo attended them.

James and Lucille kept themselves busy with catering dinners for organizations and various events, as well as working as dedicated members of the Benefit Club. They hosted many Sanguine family reunions at their home, with as many as 35 in attendance.

Lucille Van Vranken was born in Johnstown on October 27, 1915 and passed away at Cooperstown Hospital on July 4, 2008.

EMILIO "Bob" SANGUINE was also born in St. Johnsville in 1909. He passed away in February 1975 at Albany Medical Center.

On November 14, 1932 Emilio was married to Mary Ann Chirico. It seems they moved to Albany after the marriage. They had a son, Robert.

LINDA SANGUINE was born February 24, 1911 in Terracina, Italy. Linda Sanguine doesn't show up in the 1915 NYS Census records. Her obituary says she was born in Italy and came to America as an infant. She was born when her parents had returned to Italy for a visit. She was the only girl in the family of six boys and only child not born in America. Her marriage certificate shows her mother's name as Antoinette Di Venti, which seems rather odd.

Linda Sanguine married Giovanni "John" Salvagni from St. Johnsville on August 23, 1930 at St. Patrick's Church. Serving as maid of honor was Nellie Loccia and best man Henry Sugar, with bridesmaids, Lola Salvagni, Bertha Caponera (Mastromoro), Terese Salvachio, and ushers, Eugene Rossi, Joseph Sanguine and James Campione. A reception was held at the General Pershing Italian Club rooms at 36 Bridge Street.

Giovanni "John" Salvagni arrived in America at the age of four years with his grandmother, Maria Benedetto Salvagni and cousin, Luigi Rossi on November 7, 1913. He was born in Maenza, Italy, the son of Paolo Salvagni and Antoinette Palmyjohn, on December 2, 1909 and died in Fort Myers, FL on June 16, 1990.

After their marriage the couple moved to Pennsylvania, then to Utica in 1937. Upon retirement, the couple moved to Florida in 1972. Linda passed away September 4, 1975 in Fort Myers, FL. Both are buried in Calvary Cemetery, Herkimer. They were the parents of four children - Angeline, Jean, Patrick and Annette.

After Linda's passing, John married Genevieve Rose Arra on August 31, 1984 in Fort Myers.

JOSEPH A. SANGUINE was born February 24, 1913 in St. Johnsville and died in Clinton NY on December 21, 1992.

He was first married to Genevieve Pendrak of Fort Plain. They had a daughter, Joyce Ann, who died early May 1939, shortly after her birth in 1938. In 1940 the couple lived at 30 Ann Street with the Dominick Papa family. They later divorced.

Joseph enlisted in the Army on December 23, 1942 and was discharged on May 13, 1943.

Genevieve Pendrak was born October 27, 1917 in Fort Plain. She died January 26, 1990 in St. Johnsville. She is buried with her daughter, Joyce Ann in the West St. Johnsville Cemetery.

On October 13, 1945 Joseph Sanguine married Adele Harr in Utica. They had four children - Jean and Kathleen, who may have been twins, Robert who died at birth, and Bettyann, who died at age three.

JOHN P. SANGUINE was born in St. Johnsville on April 11, 1914. John lived most of his life in the village. On May 27, 1939 John P. Sanguine married Gertrude Smith. They boarded at 2 Cottage Street for a couple years, but lived most of their lives on Mechanic Street. They were the parents of four children - Sandra, Jack, Ronald and Michael.

John worked at the Little Falls Felt Shoe Company, then later at Palatine Dyeing Company. The couple moved to Fort Herkimer in 1974, where they purchased the Starlit Inn. Shortly after, John became ill and passed away on November 1975 at the age of 61.

Gertrude Smith was born August 31, 1921 and died January 3, 1999. After John's passing, she married Walter Nourse of Oppenheim in July 1978.

WILLIAM SANGUINE lived a very short life. He was born in 1916 and passed away in 1922 after the passing of his mother. He is buried in Prospect View Cemetery.

FRED P. SANGUINE, the youngest of all the children and six sons, was born in St. Johnsville on February 10, 1918, most likely at the 3 Roth Street home. His mother, Angelina passed away within two years of his birth.

He was raised by his stepmother, Teresa Olivieri most of his life and knew only her as his mother. He was still living with her after his father passed away in early January of 1940.

After high school, he worked for a short time at the Little Falls Felt Shoe Company, just around the corner from his Roth Street home.

During World War II, Fred enlisted in the U.S. Army August 12, 1941 and was released with honors two years later on September 15, 1943. He was injured and received the Purple Heart. The St. Johnsville *Enterprise & News* features photos with an article about him and his brother, Joseph, who also served at the same time.

A later article reports about a parade and war bond rally that Silver Star recipients Arminio Mancini, Joseph Francisco, John Wolinski and Fred Sanguine were involved with. They estimated that one thousand people turned out for the event. There was $168,500 pledged in bond purchases, which is quite a substantial amount for the mid-40s and the small village of St. Johnsville. James Pietrocini conducted the band concert, which accompanied the event. Fred asked to have the privilege of purchasing the very first war bond at the rally. Investments in war bonds were used to support the military funding of the war.

When Fred returned from the war, he married a girl named Mary from Herkimer. They had a daughter, Linda. Mary was born in 1917 and died in 2001. Fred died May 29, 1999. Fred and Mary are buried together in Calvary Cemetery, Herkimer.

The 3 Roth Street home was sold to the Paul Desimone family (not Italian) breaking the chain of mostly Italians living on the small cul-de-sac type street called Roth

~ *La Famiglia SPINELLI* ~

GIOVANNI "John" SPINELLI was born in 1894 in Bari, Italy. He died of a heart attack on June 15, 1972 at the home of his daughter, Mary Spinelli in Scituate, Mass.

John came to America at the age of 19 in 1913. In 1920 he was registered as a boarder at the home of Carmine Peruzzi at 24 Hough Street. He was 26 and working at a knitting mill. The New York Central Railroad later employed him for 34 years until his retirement in 1958.

John Spinelli was married to Martella "Martha" Marcucci, who was 18 years older. The 1940 Census shows her age at 62 and John's daughter, Mary at age 8, born in 1932. 1935 records show Martha living in Cortland NY. It is my determination that Mary's birth mother had died and John met and married Martha to help raise his daughter.

Martella Marcucci, the daughter of Raphael Marcucci and Checi Cachael of Campagnia, was born September 28, 1877 and died in Little Falls Hospital on January 20, 1944.

I don't find a record of his first wife, but it seems John Spinelli was married three times. After Martella's passing, John married Teresa Olivieri Sanguine to help raise his daughter, Mary.

THERESA OLIVIERI was born in Maenza on February 16, 1894, the same *comune* as my grandmother, Edvige Sindici. The daughter of Rocco Olivieri and Rosa Vecciarelli, she passed away on May 15, 1958, leaving a brother, Louis and a sister in Italy. You can read more about Teresa Olivieri in *La Famiglia Sanguine*.

MARY SPINELLI was born on March 1, 1932. After graduating in 1949 from St. Johnsville High School at age 17, she went on to become a member of the largest class of nursing students at Ellis Hospital's School of Nursing in Schenectady. She worked as a registered nurse at the Cardigan Nursing Home in Scituate, Mass.

Mary Spinelli was married to Gabriel Jacobucci, who was born October 10, 1929. The couple had four children. Mary passed away at the age of 78 on September 3, 2010 in Scituate MA.

Gabriel Jacobucci was a cousin of Lena Jacobucci, Livia's mother. Mary was a best friend with Livia Iacobucci.

Roth Street – Another Little Italy

In 1889, the Engelhardt and Roth Peerless Piano Player Company, once located on Hough Street next to the railroad tracks, was the manufacturer of the very first American coin-operated pianos. At the height of the business three thousand pianos per year were shipped worldwide. Mr. A. P. Roth was a partner until 1908, when Frederick Engelhardt bought out his share.

As the piano business prospered, more employees were needed. From information I can gather, Roth apparently invested in developing the dead-end graveled cul-de-sac across from the piano manufacturing firm to provide homes for their employees. He named it Roth Street.

I'm unable to find exactly when Roth Street was actually developed, except it had to be shortly before 1905. I did find in the 1905 NYS Census that the Dewitt "Colonel" Nellis family resided at 4 Roth Street. Colonel Nellis was employed with the piano company for about 20 years until his retirement. I assume he was the first tenant.

1912 City records show residency by all Italians on Roth Street. I also found that 6 Roth had been built in 1918. This became the home of Filiberto Castrucci.

The four large homes that graced the street, numbered 2–3–4-6 remain there to this day. Only Italians inhabited Roth Street for at least 25 years. The only home I recall being occupied by a non-Italian was 3 Roth Street, where the Sanguine family had lived for years. Teresa Sanguine had sold it to Paul DeSimone.

Census records show that from 1915 to 1940 the same Italian families resided in the same homes for years. This has continued on for up to 60 years later with a third generation family member still residing on Roth Street. Giuseppe Sindici and Edvige Cacciotti, my grandparents, lived at 4 Roth Street most of their lives, from 1924 until their passings in 1973 and 1957, respectively.

My Mom and I experienced the great pleasure of having a Peerless Piano Player in our home for many years. My first introduction to this amazing piece of art was the pretense of being a noted concert pianist by pumping the pedals that motivated the pre-programmed paper piano rolls to emit wonderful sounds for everyone's enjoyment. In later years, I was allowed to participate in piano lessons, as had my Mom.

~ *La Famiglia MANCINI* ~

Ranking #15, the Mancini surname is one of the most popular in Italy. Not too far behind is Fontana at #22. I found no other St. Johnsville Italian names in the "Top 100 List."

There were two Mancini families who settled in St. Johnsville at the turn of the century. I had always thought that Joseph Mancini and Frank Mancini were brothers. As I recall, Frank's family is related to a Mancini family in Fonda. Here are their stories.

~ ANTONIO MANCINI et CONCETTA DiPINTO ~

Arriving from Italy in the very early 1900s, Antonio Mancini was born June 18, 1873 in Terracina, Italy, to Francesco Mancini and Angela Ceraso.

Before coming to America he married Concetta DiPinto of Terracina, daughter of Giovanni DiPinto and Marianna Mastrocola, the wedding taking place at a summer resort in the Mediterranean on November 14, 1894. Their son, Giuseppe was born in Italy. They later had a daughter, Yolanda, born in St. Johnsville.

In 1910 the couple first lived at 50 West Main with their children, Giuseppe "Joseph" and Yolanda "Lillian". Antonio was the owner of a grocery store, where he was assisted by one of their boarders, Amadeo Capponi. They also had three other boarders living with them at the time – Laudo Capponi, Fedele Sarelli and Canerella (Camillo?) Pietrocini.

By 1918 Antonio was living at 9 New Street and working on the railroad, as stated on his World War I enrollment. The 1925 census has only their daughter, Lillian with them, along with Victor Palombo and I believe his wife, Biacini. Lillian was married later that summer.

Antonio and Concetta owned the home at 9 New Street, where they were living in 1930 with their son, Joseph, his wife, Myrtle and two children - Bernard and Helen.

In January 1931, Antonio Mancini became a naturalized citizen in Fonda. Sharing the ceremony was another St. Johnsville Italian immigrant – Giovanni Palma, my father-in-law.

ANTONIO MANCINI died in 1977 in the Canajoharie Nursing Home at the age of 95.

CONCETTA DiPINTO was born January 31, 1878; she died July 15, 1965.

On September 2, 1905, Concetta and her sister, Angelina DiPinto arrived in America together with their brother, Francisco and Concetta's son, Giuseppe Mancini. Angelina was the wife of Umberto Sanguine. This would be the connection to the Sanguine family.

GIUSEPPE ANTONIO "Joseph" MANCINI was well known in the village of St. Johnsville for all the community service he was involved with throughout his life. As a lifetime member of the Sir William Johnson Council Boy Scouts of America, he served as a Scout Master of Troop 71, St. Johnsville for over 35 years. He received numerous awards, including the highest honor Silver Beaver award and the prestigious National District Service Award at an Order of the Arrow ceremony in Johnstown. He was involved with numerous Boy Scout activities such as the summer camporees at Woodworth Lake Scout Reservation. Many St. Johnsville scouts participated in this every summer, including my brother, Joseph Perry.

Joe Mancini was an excellent student while attending the St. Johnsville school system. He utilized these skills as president of the Community Chest and Village Recreation Commission, along with his memberships with the Rotary Club and Starr-Colorito VFW, where he received a service award. Joe's employment was as an agent for Metropolitan Insurance Company.

On March 19, 1921, Joseph Mancini married Myrtle Nancy Loucks of St. Johnsville.

Myrtle Nancy Loucks was born July 28, 1896 in St. Johnsville and died March of 1984 at their 9 New Street home.

Giuseppe Antonio Mancini was born September 23, 1899 in Terracina, Italy and came to this country as a young boy of six years. He died in January 1984.

BERNARD J. MANCINI was gifted with a great mentor. Following in his father's footsteps, he also worked with the Boy Scouts for many years, and served his community with representation in some of the same organizations as his father. He served on the St. Johnsville School Board for several years. Bernie was a dedicated member of St. Patrick's Catholic Church and its organizations. His religion meant a great deal to him.

Besides being very intelligent, Bernie was also quite the handyman, making repairs wherever they were needed, not only for himself, but also for others in his circle.

On June 7, 1941, Bernard Mancini married Ellen Mary Coso in Catskill, NY. They shared 40 years together before Ellen's passing. They had one daughter, Vicki. Vicki had been married to Richard Chiodo, son of Louis Chiodo and Ella Montoni.

Bernard J. Mancini was born February 4, 1920 in Syracuse and passed away September 8, 2008 at 88 years of age. Ellen Mary Coso was born January 31, 1918 and died April 11, 1981. She was a pleasant presence behind the desk at the Margaret Reaney Memorial Library for many years.

After Ellen's passing, Bernie shared his life as the companion of my aunt, Susie Sindici Corso until the time of his death.

HELEN A. MANCINI was born in 1925. After graduating from St. Johnsville High School, she registered with the Nurse's Training School in Utica. Helen was very musical, playing the piano and vocalizing in duets and trios during her school years with her friends, Mildred Walrath and Kay Corte Davis.

In August 1948, Helen Mancini was joined in marriage with Claude M. Bottomley, son of Claude H. Bottomley and Gladys Miller, the owners of Bottomley's Hardware Store on West Main, where he worked. The Bottomley's later sold the business to Raymond and Phyl Coco.

Helen and Claude moved to Arizona after their marriage, where they resided the remainder of their lives. They had four children.

Claude M. Bottomley was born March 31, 1926 in Auburn and passed away suddenly on February 1, 1967 in Phoenix AZ, at the young age of 41. I believe Helen is still living.

YOLANDA "Lillian" MANCINI was born in St. Johnsville, the daughter of Antonio Mancini and Concetta DiPinto, on July 26, 1908. At the time the family was living at 50 West Main Street.

Lillian was an accomplished musician, playing the organ at St. Patrick's Catholic Church and entertaining with her solos for various occasions. Her daughter, Marianne inherited her mother's musical talents.

Lillian was married twice. At the young age of 17, she married her first husband, Vincenzo Nirri on August 16, 1925 in Millbrook NY. Serving as witnesses were Raymond Evangelist of St. Johnsville and Madaline Galli of Millbrook. The marriage certificate states that Vincenzo's father was Pietro Vespasiani; no mother listed, and that he lived at 4 Roth Street at the time. They had two children - John and Marianne.

Vincenzo "James" Nirri, age 41, was killed August 27, 1939 in a horrific auto accident right in front of Dr. Raymond Wytrwal's home and medical office, while driving east on Main Street in the late evening. Another vehicle pulled out from John Street and hit his driver's side, slamming him against the steering wheel and crushing his heart. His passenger friends, Paul Salvagni, Anthony Montegeorgio, and Lester Rivenburg all survived. He was carried to the office of Dr. Wytrwal, but to no avail. Vincenzo Nirri was born in Italy April 10, 1898. He was employed at Little Falls Felt Shoe.

On July 7, 1943, Lillian Neri married Howard Keller, who adopted Marianne, only about five years old at the time of her father's death. Howard's sister, Jennie Keller, came to live with them and helped raise Marianne after Lillian's passing.

Not long after her marriage to Howard, Lillian became quite ill with leukemia and passed away at Little Falls Hospital in 1946. She was a member of the Navy Mother's Club and Montgomery Rebekah's Lodge.

JOHN ANTHONY NIRRI was born October 23, 1926 in St. Johnsville. John was intent on joining the U.S. Navy, desperately trying to sign up before the age requirement. Finally on October 23, 1943, his 17th birthday, he went to tell Uncle Sam, "Today I am a man." As a birthday gift, he received the distinction of being the first St. Johnsville boy to be assigned to the new Sampson Naval Training Station at Seneca Lake NY. This was the first place any Navy enlistee was assigned, including several young men from St. Johnsville.

John had decided, since the attack on Pearl Harbor during World War II, that he wanted to serve his country and made quite a career of his enlistment, graduating as Seaman 2nd Class from Torpedo School in Newport RI and submarine school at New London CN. As T.M. 3rd Class, he was part of a task force at Guantanamo Bay, Cuba.

After his discharge, he returned to complete a post-graduate course at St. Johnsville High School, along with Louis Palombi. He was a member of the American Legion and St. Johnsville Sportsman's Club Ski Patrol in 1947. He later entered the service again, serving in the Air National Guard September 10, 1978 through October 30, 1989.

John Anthony Neri married Fern Marilyn Sponable on April 2, 1948. She was the daughter of Jay Sponable and Catherine Miller. Fern was born December 2, 1927 and died December 26, 1977 in Burlington VT. John died in Tillamook, OR on November 20, 2008.

MARIANNE NIRRI KELLER was born in 1934, the daughter of Lillian Mancini and James Nirri. After her father's tragic death, Howard Keller, her mother's second husband, adopted her.

Marianne graduated with the Class of 1952 in St. Johnsville and was a soloist with the Glee Club and the St. Patrick's Church choir. She inherited her mother's musicality with a beautiful singing voice and piano playing. We took piano lessons together for a few years.

After graduation, she attended the NYS University of Agriculture and Home Economics in Cobleskill.

In August 1957, Marianne Keller married Gordon Douglas of Little Falls, residing there after the marriage. "Gordie" has passed away. He was an exceptional athlete.

Marianne lived down the street from me at 16 West Liberty when I was living at 10 South Division Street. I have fond memories of Marianne as a playmate. I loved to go to her home as she had her own separate playroom attached to her bedroom, like a large walk-in closet, which I thought was awesome. And her mother always offered me the most delicious piece of apple pie. The first time she made the offer, I said, "I don't care", so she interpreted that I didn't care for any. I quickly learned to say yes. I was very shy in my younger years.

~ FRANCESCO MANCINI et LOUISA FIORINI ~

Many of us know Frank Mancini as a Custodian at the St. Johnsville High School for 25 years or more. The teachers and students held him in the highest esteem. When he retired he was celebrated as an Honorary Member of the Teacher's Association. They presented him with an engraved gold wristwatch. He was always the smiling gentleman, ready to assist anyone.

FRANCESCO "Frank" MANCINI immigrated to America in 1905 from Roccagorga, where he was born September 14, 1891. He was the son of Oreste Mancini and Maria Attore.

LOUISA FIORINI, daughter of Giovanni Fiorini and Gerdentz Felippe, Roccagorga, was born March 3, 1894. She arrived in 1914.

The couple was married shortly after Louisa's arrival, on July 4, 1914 at St. Patrick's Church with Joseph and Carmela DiLembo Romano as witnesses. They had three children - Mary Louise, Leo, and Armando.

This may have been a pre-arranged marriage. I find no record of Frank from the time he came here in 1905 until the date of their union.

The 1915 Census shows the couple living at the Romano's 34 Hough Street home after their marriage. They were both working at a Knitting Mill. Frank later went to work at the Felt Shoe before joining the school system. Louise also worked at the Felt Shoe.

Louise was the sister of Antonio Fiorini, who married Frances DeAngelis, sister of Rose DeAngelis Colorito. 34 Hough Street was just around the corner from the DeAngelis home at 4 Roth Street.

Within five years, in 1920, the couple had saved enough money to purchase at least half of a duplex at 61A East Main Street and had their first child, Mary. By 1925, Frank's brother, Pio Mancini was living on the other side of the home at 61 East Main Street.

After her two son's military enlistment, Louise was very active with the Starr-Colorito VFW Post Auxiliary.

With Frank's retirement from the school system, they moved to Hollywood FL, along with their daughter, Mary. They returned to St. Johnsville several times to visit and celebrate their wedding anniversaries. Both passed away in Hollywood, Florida - Louise in August 1968 and Frank in 1969.

MARY LOUISE MANCINI, a member of the 1934 graduation class of St. Johnsville, was a graduate of the Edward J. Mayer Memorial Hospital School of Nursing in Buffalo. She worked as a private duty nurse.

As her mother, Louise, Mary was very active with the Starr-Colorito VFW Post Auxiliary. In 1957, she moved to Hollywood FL with her parents.

In January 1960, Mary Mancini married Peter O. Mandra of Hollywood, FL, who had a daughter, Janette, from a previous marriage.

Mary Louise Mancini was born in 1918 and died August 29, 2001. She was a loving daughter, always caring for her parents, especially in their retirement years.

LEO T. MANCINI was born February 19, 1920. Graduating from St. Johnsville High School, he attended the Albany School of Business, receiving an associate degree in business administration and accounting. After graduation, the General Electric Company, Schenectady employed him as a cost accountant.

Beginning as a teller with the First National Bank of St. Johnsville, Leo was later promoted to Senior Vice-President when the First National Bank became Central National Bank. He was responsible for procuring new banks and all large industrial loans. Leo worked with Olga Sackett Tolfa as his assistant for many years.

After his retirement in 1975, Leo worked for the Montgomery County Economic Development Department, being responsible for developing many new businesses, such as the St. Johnsville Nursing and Rehabilitation Facility, which opened in 1990.

In 1941, Leo enlisted in the US Army Air Corps, serving in the European Theatre and Morocco, flying more than 65 missions over enemy lines. Serving in the military until 1945, he was awarded the Air Medal with Seven Clusters in recognition of his many missions, as well as many other medals for his bravery.

On July 5, 1947 Leo Mancini married Dora Amelia Palombi, daughter of Ettore "Harry" Palombi and Rosina Capece. They had two sons - Leo Gregory and Michael H.

The day after the wedding, Dora's father, Harry, was stricken with a fatal heart attack. They were on their honeymoon in Canada and unable to be reached by either the NYS State Police or Canadian officials. The body was held for burial upon their return home.

Leo was very active in community activities with the St. Johnsville Businessmen's Association, Rotary Club and Morris J. Edwards American Legion Post, who honored him and his brother, Armand in a Memorial Day Parade. Leo was an honored member of the American Legion Post for 72 years.

In 1960, Governor Nelson Rockefeller appointed Leo to the Advisory Board of Utica Hospital in Marcy NY. He was a lifelong member of St. Patrick's Church, where he served as an altar boy until age 16. He was an avid golfer.

At the age of 97, Leo T. Mancini passed away on September 27, 2017 at the home he had worked to develop – St. Johnsville Nursing and Rehabilitation Facility.

Dora Amelia Palombi passed away May 25, 2003.

ARMANDO B. MANCINI was born March 19, 1922 in St. Johnsville. His death occurred in Little Falls Hospital, April 14, 2016, shortly after celebrating his 94th birthday.

A graduate of St. Johnsville High School, he worked most of his life with Chicago Pneumatic in Utica as a Milling Machine Operator.

Armand also had a very active career with the US Army Air Corps, joining his brother with enlistment on July 14, 1941. He was sent to the South Pacific, participating in the Battle over Rabaul, New Britain. Armand was presented with the Silver Star at Griffiss Air Force Base, Rome NY as a result of the bombing raid. He was a corporal at the time of the mission when he suffered serious injuries. He received an honorable medical discharge.

On January 5, 1943 he was a Ball Turret Gunner on a B-17, which was bombing the Japanese installations. He was wounded in five areas of his body from a burst of flak that hit the plane. Though suffering from pain, and with his gun shattered by the explosion, Corporal Mancini took over another unmanned gun and fought off an attacking Zero plane, causing it to flee. His plane was forced down at sea with motor trouble on its return to its home base. The crew was cared for by friendly natives along the coast and later rescued by the British Royal Air Force. After being hospitalized in Brisbane, Australia and San Francisco, he carried the flak in his body for the rest of his life.

Like his brother, Armand was a lifetime member of the American Legion and also the Fort Plain VFW. He was an outdoorsman, enjoying both hunting and fishing. As with many Italian men, he was noted for his meticulous garden, which he truly enjoyed.

Armand Mancini and Margaret Bazanski shared a blessed union of 70 years, being united on August 25, 1945 at St. Patrick's Church. They had two daughters - Carol and Joann.

In 2014 Leo Mancini and Armand Mancini, together, received World War II proclamations from NYS Senator Cecilia Tkaczyk, when both Veteran brothers were honored in the annual Memorial Day parade, sponsored by Morris J. Edwards Post American Legion.

Columbus "Russ" Fiorini would be a nephew of Frank and Luisa, his father being Luisa's sister.

~ PIO MANCINI et ANNA ZUCCARO ~

PIO MANCINI came to St. Johnsville to join his brother Frank on July 3, 1920. He was born September 15, 1897 in Roccagorga, the son of Oreste Mancini and Maria Attore.

On September 30, 1922, Pio Mancini married Anna Zuccaro, daughter of Antonio Zuccaro and Mary Ciampini, at St. Mary's Catholic Church in Little Falls. They had one son, Richard. Anna was a sister of Jennie Zuccaro Marocco, Rocco and Henry Zuccaro (Sugar).

After their marriage the couple moved to 61 East Main Street, in the adjoining duplex of Pio's brother, Frank Mancini and his wife, Louisa Fiorini. Pio worked at the Little Falls Felt Shoe most of his life.

1930 Census records show the three family members living at 101 East Main with Anna's brother, Rocco, and his son Harold, whose mother Elizabeth "Lucia" Triumpho was confined to a hospital at the time. In 1940 Pio's family was still living at this address; Rocco and Harold had moved to Little Falls.

Pio Mancini died June 3, 1982 in Milton FL, where he had retired after Anna's death.

ANNA ZUCCARO was born in Supino on September 15, 1904. She immigrated at age 17 to St. Johnsville with her brother, Enrico "Henry" Zuccaro on August 10, 1921.

Anna was an active member of the St. Johnsville Navy Mother's Club of America, serving as a color bearer. As a member of St. Patrick's Church, she was also active in the Altar Rosary Society.

Anna Zuccaro Mancini died January 19, 1945 at Little Falls Hospital at 40 years of age. She had recently become a US citizen in 1940.

RICHARD MANCINI was born in 1924 in St. Johnsville. In 1941, while in high school, he participated on the basketball team. After graduation, he went on to graduate from the Cooks and Bakers School in Portsmouth VA.

In 1945, while serving in the US Navy aboard the destroyer escort U.S.S. Deede, he was promoted from Ship's Cook 2nd class to 1st class.

He married his wife, Ann in 1957. They had three children. Richard was living in Pensacola FL in 1958. I assume that's where he passed away on June 4, 1971.

~ *La Famiglia VECCIARELLI* ~

These St. Johnsville Vecciarelli families date back to great-great grandparents, Domenico Vecciarelli and Maria Laura Giambattista, who lived in the *comune* of Maenza, Italy, in the 1800s. Domenico and Maria were the parents of four children - Nicola Antonio, Elmerinda, Alexander and Giovanni.

There are various spellings of the Vecciarelli name. To avoid confusion, I shall use only this spelling.

My focus will first be on the son, Nicola Antonio Vecciarelli. Born in Maenza in 1873, he died there in 1964. He was married to Palma Monescalchi. They had three children - Luigi, Maria and Emelia.

Luigi Vecciarelli was married to Alessandra Mazza of Maenza. They were the parents of Elena Vecciarelli Montoni and Beatrice Vecciarelli Iagnacco, who emigrated to St. Johnsville.

Elena Veciarelli settled in St. Johnsville and married Pasquale Montoni. Beatrice married Michelangelo Iagnacco and eventually moved to Utica.

Emelia "Elsie" Vecciarelli married Egisto Loccia and settled in St. Johnsville.

Maria Vecciarelli immigrated to Herkimer and married Anthony Nobili. Emelia Loccia and Maria Nobili were sisters.

The Nobili's were the parents of Viola Nobili Peruzzi, wife of Dominick Peruzzi, son of Carmine Peruzzi and Maria Paluzzi. Viola will be recognized in *La Famiglia Peruzzi*.

In summary, sisters Elena Vecciarelli Montoni and Beatrice Vecciarelli Iagnacco and their siblings in Italy, Viola Nobili Peruzzi and her siblings, plus the entire Loccia family siblings are all cousins.

We also have Elmerinda Vecciarelli Cochi and Alexander Vecciarelli coming into the familial web. Elmerinda was a sister of Nicol, Alexander a brother. Elmerinda married Ottavius Cochi and the mother of Carlo Cochi. Therefore, the Cochi family is related to all of these families. You will read more of Elmerinda in *La Famiglia Cochi*.

~ PASQUALE MONTONI et ELENA ALBINA MARIA VECCIARELLI ~

ELENA ALBINA MARIA VECCIARELLI was born a twin on January 12, 1901, alongside her brother, Lamberto Fulgenzio Vecciarelli who died at birth, in the medieval hilltop *comune* of Maenza in the province of Latina. Her parents were Luigi Vecciarelli and Alessandra Agnese Maria Mazza, a young unwed couple of 27 and 23, respectively.

Being married on April 14, 1902, Alessandra was already seven months pregnant with their third child, Beatrice Anna. Five more children were later added to their household - Eraldo Rodolfo Giuseppe, Caterina Margherita, Lamberto Saverio Mario named after the deceased twin, Giuseppe Antonio Maria and Palma, who was stillborn. Only Elena and Beatrice came to America.

To support their growing family, Luigi, like his father Nicola who often worked as a *nettorbino* cleaning the village streets, worked many odd jobs around the village including *agricoltore* (farmer) and *mulattiere* (mule driver) early in life, to a simple *bracciant* (laborer) and *cantoniere*, the latter being employed to clean and maintain the roads leading to and from Maenza. His wife, Alessandra, the daughter of Baldassare Mazza, one of the village's tailors, worked as a housewife, raising the six of her eight children that survived childhood.

Having lost two children to the hardships of Italy, Luigi and Alessandra would lose two more to the mass migration to America occurring at the time. Their two eldest children, Elena and Beatrice left for America in 1921 and 1924 respectively, to help support their family in La Terra Maledetta - *The Cursed Land* - as Italy was known at the time. They first settled in the village of St. Johnsville, where many of their *compaesani* (townspeople) had already settled, and would both go on to raise families in Upstate New York. Elena remained in St. Johnsville; Beatrice moved to Utica.

While her youngest son, Giuseppe was still in his early teens, Alessandra Mazza passed away on November 26, 1925 at the young age of 48, predeceasing her husband by almost exactly 40 years. Luigi Vecciarelli passed away at over 92 years old on November 14, 1965 in his son's home in Piazza del Duomo in Maenza.

With little land to work and even less hope of a future in Italy, Elena Vecciarelli's stay in her ancestral homeland would be brief. Arriving at Ellis Island on August 19, 1921 at the age of 20, Elena traveled aboard the S.S. Europa under the watch of two men from the neighboring village of Roccagorga, who were on their way to Binghamton NY. One of them accompanied her to St. Johnsville. Elena's passenger manifest first stated she was going to Herkimer to join her aunt, but that was crossed off with St. Johnsville added. It is not known if she went to her Aunt Emelia Loccia or her good friend, Edvige Cacciotti Sindici's home.

After her arrival, she met fellow immigrant, Pasquale "Patsy" Montoni. Patsy and my grandfather, Giuseppe Sindici were best friends, both coming from the village of Torrice located about 20 miles southeast of Maenza in the bordering province of Frosinone. I'm wondering if my grandparents played "match-maker"? Neither of the two couples had previously known each other. The Sindici's had also met in St. Johnsville.

It was love at first site! Elena and Patsy were married almost three months later on November 6, 1921 by the priest at St. Patrick's Church, with Carlo Cochi and Leonina Forcinelli as witnesses. Carlo was a cousin of Elena's. They were both living at 14 Sanders Street at the time. The Montoni's had three children together - Ella, Nello Peter and Luigi.

In 1925 the Montoni's were boarders at the newly purchased home of their friends, Giuseppe Sindici and Edvige Cacciotti at 4 Roth Street. The Sindici's had four daughters. The two youngest, Susie and Viola became best friends with Ella through the years. I have a treasured photo of my Aunt Susie holding me as a baby, with Ella Montoni at her side, taken at my grandparent's home in 1936.

The 1930 Census shows the family living at 22 Sanders Street. By this time Louis was almost two years old. It looks like they were sharing the home with the Gino Polidori family. Elena and Gino may have known each other in Maenza.

By 1940 the Montoni's were settled into their own home at 5 Hough Street, where they lived out their lives. Both worked in the Little Falls Felt Shoe, a short walk down the street.

I have vivid memories of this beautiful couple and the many visits I had at their home as a young girl. Elena was such a sweet little lady. I always referred to her as Zia Elena, and thought our families were related. Patsy was my baptismal godfather.

I recall visiting Elena when she was recuperating at home from gall bladder surgery at Little Falls Hospital. Making a humorous story of her surgery, Elena was showing us the removed gallstones that had been saved in a jar. This was soon after Patsy had passed away and Ella's family was living with her.

Elena was widowed at just 51 years old, when her dear husband, Patsy passed away in 1952. Before passing away in her home on February 22, 1972, Elena became not only a grandmother, but also had returned to her place of birth to see her father once again - visiting both Maenza and Torrice during her two month stay.

In July of 1965, Elena's sister, Beatrice Iagnocco joined her on this journey back to their roots to visit their 92-year-old father, Luigi, three brothers and a sister, whom they hadn't seen in 44 years. Flying in style out of Kennedy Airport in New York City, it certainly didn't compare to the stressful journey they experienced when coming to the land of promise in steerage.

PASQUALE "Patsy" MONTONI was born in Torrice, Italy to Dominici Montoni and Bernardina DeAngelis on July 23, 1894. He came to America alone in 1910 at the age of 16.

Patsy served as a Private in World War I from September 17, 1918 to July 5, 1919. His 1917 application shows him living at 21 Sanders Street, along with Giovanni "John" Ponzi, who was also called up the same day. Other Italians "called to colors" from St. Johnsville on that day were Domenico Iacobucci of 2 Hough Street, Alexander Holfi, 2 Roth Street and Adanio Corsi, 13 Sanders Street. Patsy was working in the Lyon's Knitting Mill at the time.

In 1917 he was also a member of the Home Guard Band, which had organized at the beginning of the war.

As so many of the Italian men, Patsy was very handsome. He served as baptismal godfather for my christening.

ELLA JOSEPHINE MONTONI was born March 3, 1923 to Pasquale Montoni and Elena Vecciarelli. She graduated with the St. Johnsville High Class of 1941. Ella had a beautiful voice, harmonizing with others to entertain various groups in the village and vocalizing with the St. Patrick's Church choir.

After graduation she went on to become a nurse at the Caledonia Hospital in Brooklyn. While working there she met her husband, Louis Chiodo. They were married in a ceremony on June 22, 1947 in St. Patrick's Church, followed by a family dinner at the Antler's Restaurant, west of St. Johnsville with a reception at the Central Hotel.

The couple returned to Brooklyn for a few years, before finally residing in the Montoni homestead at 5 Hough Street, where they raised their three children - Richard, Christa and Patsy.

Ella Josephine Montoni passed away at the Palatine Nursing Home, Palatine Bridge on July 12, 2001, where she lived her final days.

Louis Chiodo lived his early years in Brooklyn, the son of Joseph Chiodo and Mary Rose. He was born September 9, 1922 in Brooklyn and passed away November 7, 1994 at Little Falls Hospital.

He served his country in the Marines and was employed for many years by American Airlines. Upon his move to St. Johnsville he became employed by the NYS Department of Transportation as Canal Structure Operator – Lock 15. One day his crew rescued him when he had become caught in a sidewall of the canal.

Louis also became very active in community affairs, working as a Cub Scout Den Master and President of the Holy Name Society of St. Patrick's Church. He was also one of the high scoring bowlers in the Men's League. He fit right in with the other Italian piasani in the community.

NELLO PETER MONTONI was born February 26, 1924 in St. Johnsville. He graduated from high school in June 1942 and enlisted in the U.S. Navy during World War II on October 8, 1942, stationed in the Philadelphia Navy Yard. Serving in the South Pacific combat zone on Parris Island, he was an aviation machinist mate 3rd class, later promoted to Seaman 2nd class, and was discharged October 31, 1945.

Nello Montoni became engaged to Ada Palombo in March 1943. While home on furlough, he married Ada, daughter of Antonio Palombo and Tuillia Montegeorgo on June 18, 1944. His sister, Ella was maid of honor with Margaret Christiano, sister-in-law of Ada's from Gloversville, as bridesmaid. Louis Montoni was best man for his brother, Angelo Macci, an usher. They had two children - Gary Anthony and Tracy Ann.

In January 1949 Nello and Ada purchased the brick home of Vincent and Lucy Constantino at 15 South Division Street, across the street from the 10 South Division Street home where I grew up.

The Constantino's had lived downstairs during the 1940s with Viola Iacobucci and Jerry Dunton occupying the upstairs apartment, where Vi had her hair salon. Lucy conducted a children's clothing business in the home, later having a small building built at the end of the driveway to accommodate the growing business.

At the time of the Montoni purchase, the Constantino's also sold the small building to Harvey and Mary Rackmyer as an addition to their home at the intersection of Averill Street and Monroe Streets. The building was transported from the South Division site easterly through the business district to the Averill Street location. Nello and Ada later built a home on Mill Road, where they lived most of their lives. It seems they sold the brick home to Ada's cousin, Victor?

As a member of the Masonic Temple bowlers and the Mohawk Valley Traveling League, Nello was one of the top bowlers in the area carrying a consistently high average over 250. He also enjoyed games of softball, playing on the Palma Grill team in the Community Softball league with his teammates John Palma, Jr. and James Capece, Jr.

For most of his life, the Beech-Nut Packing Company, Canajoharie, employed Nello. He passed away on March 25, 2008.

Ada Palombo was born June 10, 1924 in St. Johnsville. She died October 5, 2008 in the St. Johnsville Nursing Home, nine months after her husband, Nello.

Ada worked at the Little Falls Felt Shoe and later as a personal assistant to Mrs. Mabel Fowler. Ada was most noted for her excellent cooking and baking skills that she generously shared with others. She was also a high scoring bowler in the women's Friday night league.

Gary Anthony Montoni lived a very short life. He was born June 15, 1945 and died at the age of 14 of a brain tumor January 22, 1960, shortly after the birth of his sister Tracy. In April 1957, Mayor Wilfred Kraft proclaimed a "Gary Montoni Day" as a fundraiser to assist with his medical expenses.

LUIGI P. "Louis" MONTONI was born June 21, 1928 in St. Johnsville.

Louie was another stellar Italian athlete, excelling in basketball and baseball just short of a "No Hit Pitcher" to be entered into a hall of fame in 1946. He was an avid New York Yankees fan, baseball player and golfer. He also volunteered as an EMT while living in Canajoharie.

After graduation he entered the U.S. Army in June 1948, and was stationed in Tokyo, Japan during the Korean War. As a Private 1st Class, Louie served with the 8th Army in Nagai, Japan, where he played on their winning regional softball team as a right fielder and was presented with an award by his commander. He was honorably discharged in 1953.

Louis furthered his education with an Associate's Degree in Business Administration and Accounting at Albany Business College, Albany, where he was elected Sports Editor for the college yearbook. He was employed as an accountant with Luxor Textiles, Fort Plain, and Kraft Brand Foods Company in Canajoharie and Memphis, Tennessee.

On April 19, 1952, Louis Montoni and Janet Sponable, daughter of Milburn and Beatrice Sponable of St. Johnsville were married in St. Patrick's Church. Janet's sister, Jean and Louis' friend, Dominick Fontana attended them. They had two children - Jeffrey and Claudia.

Janet Freda Sponable was born September 21, 1931. She passed away August 18, 2004.

Louis P. Montoni died at the age of 84 at Bush's Personal Care Home, Kunkletown PA, near his daughter, Claudia, on October 23, 2009.

BEATRICE ANNA COSTANZA VECCIARELLI was born June 24, 1902, just two months after her parents were officially wed. Like her sister Elena, Beatrice's life in Italy was very brief.

At the age of 22, after marrying Michelangelo "Charles" Iagnocco, who had recently returned to Maenza from America to take her as his bride, they boarded the S.S. Conte Verde, arriving at Ellis Island on May 24, 1924, heading to 4 Roth Street, where Michelangelo had been residing as a boarder with the Sindici family. Traveling with them was Paul Salvagni with his new wife, Adelgesia, also returning to Paul's St. Johnsville home.

They had four sons - Pierre, Guido, Frank and Mario. By 1927 the couple had moved to Utica, where they resided for the remainder of their lives. Charles worked in a knit mill.

Beatrice passed away in Whitesboro in September 1982. Michelangelo "Charles" Iagnocco was born in 1895 in Maenza, the son of Mr. and Mrs. Francesco Iagnocco. He died March 9, 1956 in Utica. Charles was the brother of Filomena Iagnocco, wife of Augustino Castrucci.

Richard Brown and Elena's granddaughter, Tracy Montoni, have contributed a great deal of information to the Montoni and Palombo articles. Grazie!

~ ERSILIA VECCIARELLI et EGISTO LOCCIA ~

ERSILIA "Elsie" VECCIARELLI, aunt of Elena Montoni and the third child of Nicola Antonio Vecciarelli and Palma Monescalchi, married Egisto Loccia in Maenza, Italy, where they had their first child, Apresa. I cannot locate Egisto Loccia's parents, but I did locate a brother, Francesco.

Ersilia Vecciarelli and Apresa, age 11, arrived March 18, 1910 going to St. Johnsville to meet Egisto. Also traveling to St. Johnsville on the same ship were Verginio Colorito, Giovanni Polodoro and Antonio Surelli. After Elsie arrived in America, the couple had six more children - Enelda, Lavena, Eralia, Raymond, Natalina and Theresa.

Egisto Loccia first arrived on May 16, 1903, going to Albany to meet his brother, Francesco. He claims being a carpenter, working on building construction. Apparently, he returned to Maenza, as I found him again immigrating on April 25, 1907. Sometimes the husband would come over first, decide if he wanted to bring the family here and earn money for their trip.

I'm not able to locate the Loccia family between 1910 and 1920 in Census records. Egisto's World War I records, dated September 12, 1918, state he lives at 14 Center Street, is married and works at the National Music Roll piano factory on Hough Street.

The 1920 Census shows the couple with four children - Lavina, Nellie, Raymond and Natalino. Apresa is not listed; she may have passed away during the 1918 Flu Epidemic. Egisto still works at the piano factory.

By 1925 they were living at 14 Sanders Street. Their son Raymond does not show up, but they now have a daughter, Thressa. It seems they were sharing the home with the Dominick Arduini family. 1930 records state they own the home.

1940 records show them living next door at 16 Sanders Street with two remaining children, Natalino and Theresa. Their son Eralio and wife, Mary Loccia are now living at the 14 Sanders Street address. At this writing in 2017, the home has stayed in the family for over 60 years with Eralio's son, Robert Loccia's family as the current owners.

1942 World War II records state Egisto worked for New York State on road construction.

According to her obituary, Ersilia Vecciarelli was born June 21, 1877 in Neanva, Italy. I believe this should have been Maenza, as I don't find the town of Neanva and she lived in Maenza before coming to America. Unless they immigrated, most Italians usually lived their entire lives in the *comune* where they were born. Ersilia Vecciarialli died March 15, 1947 in Little Falls Hospital.

EGISTO LOCCIA pre-deceased his wife on July 19, 1944. He was born November 18, 1877 in Maenza.

APRESA LOCCIA was the only child born in Italy in 1899. She does not show up in the 1920 Census and I find no record of her family in the NYS 1915 Census. As per my previous determination, she may have passed away before 1920 during the Influenza epidemic.

LAVENA LOCCIA was born on December 14, 1910 in St. Johnsville and died in March of 1978 in St. Peter's Hospital, Albany.

On February 15, 1931, Lavena Loccia married Ralph Compani, son of Frank Compani and Jennie Aldi of Fonda, in a ceremony at St. Patrick's Catholic Church. In the bridal party were maid of honor, Rose Sugar, bridesmaids Florence Sugar, Virginia Terranova and Lavena's sister, Enelda. Carmen Compani, brother of the groom, served as best man. A reception was held at the General Pershing Italian Club located at 36 Bridge Street.

Lavena worked at the Little Falls Felt Shoe. The New York Central Railroad employed Ralph as an Assistant Foreman. They moved to Fort Hunter, where they became the parents of three sons - Ralph Rodney, Rodney Richard and Francis E.

Ralph C. Compani, Sr. was born March 18, 1904 in Fonda; he passed away in February 1984.

A well-known resident of the Fonda-Fultonville area, their son, Ralph Rodney Compani, Jr. was active in local politics. He was noted mostly as the promoter of the Fonda Speedway dirt track racing, where he devoted many years. Ralph was born November 26, 1937 and died on May 2, 2016 in Palm Desert, California, where he retired.

Rodney Richard "Ron" Compani was born June 20, 1941 and died September 1, 1995 in Volusia, Florida. He had also been affiliated with his brother in the Fonda Speedway.

My son-in-law and many dirt track drivers from St. Johnsville raced the track under the Compani ownership.

I find no information for Francis, the third brother.

ENELDA FRANCES "Nellie" LOCCIA was born December 28, 1911, during the Christmas holiday. She died February 22, 2006 at the St. Joseph Nursing Home in Utica, where she had resided after her marriage.

Enelda Loccia and Michael Plescia were married September 2, 1931. They had three children - Sandra, Michael and Gary. A fireman, Michael Plescia was born in Italy on April 29, 1908. He died January 14, 1995 in Utica.

ERALIO P. "Rattio" LOCCIA and his family are probably the most well known in the Loccia family. Remaining in St. Johnsville through his lifetime, Eralio was born November 4, 1912.

Eralio Loccia married Mary T. Covuoto of Dolgeville, daughter of John Covuoto and Angelina Politi, on October 8, 1938. They had three children - Robert, Sharon and Janet.

Mary T. Covuoto was born October 2, 1914 in Dolgeville and passed away July 24, 2009. Their daughter, Janet Pollak, predeceased her. Mary had two sisters, Lucy Enea, wife of the undertaker, Harry Enea, Herkimer and Rose Darling, Dolgeville.

Eralio served his country in World War II, enlisting April 25, 1944 where he was stationed at Fort Dix as a Private in the U.S. Army. With his discharge on January 28, 1946, he had been promoted to Tech 5. Eralio and his brother Natalino were featured in the St. Johnsville *Enterprise & News* Servicemen's column in January 1942. At the time Eralio was stationed at Spokane, Washington with the Air Corp Engineering Aviation Crew and Natalino was in Italy with the Air Corp Grand Crew. Both had worked at the Little Falls Felt Shoe before their enlistment.

Eralio P. Loccia passed away in Little Falls Hospital October 8, 1998. I haven't been able to find any information about his employment after being discharged.

Robert "Bob" Loccia, the only son of Eralio Loccia and Mary Covuoto, was born January 14, 1942 in Little Falls Hospital. Bob passed away December 2, 2015.

Bob had quite an active work and military history. He was employed for 26 years as the Maintenance Supervisor with the St. Johnsville Housing Authority. Previous to this, both the Village and Town of St. Johnsville had employed him, along with MDS and Momentum Tech in Herkimer. He was a licensed electrician.

Cpl. Robert Loccia served in the U.S. Marine Corps from August 31, 1961 to December 17, 1965. In 1976 he joined the New York Army National Guard and continued as a member until his illness. He was active in the Morris J. Edwards Post American Legion, the Earl Stock VFW Post, Fort Plain and the Marine Corps League of Herkimer County. He resided in the original family home with his wife, Sherry, and two children.

Sharon Loccia Flanders is still living at this writing. Janet Loccia Pollak has passed away.

NATALINO LOCCIA was a special Christmas gift for the Loccia family, born December 25, 1913.

On August 21, 1937, Natalino Loccia married Carmen Maddeloni, daughter of Mr. and Mrs. Ralph Maddeloni of Little Falls, in St. Patrick's Church. Thressa Loccia attended her sister-in-law as maid of honor with Perminio Laurora serving as best man and his brother, Eralio Loccia as usher. The groom's family hosted a breakfast for the wedding party at their home, with the bride's family hosting 200 guests at their home in Little Falls. I find no children from the marriage. The couple later divorced before Natalino entered the military.

Natalino enlisted in the U.S. Army Air Corps of World War II on January 7, 1942. He served four years with over a year and a half spent overseas, part of the time in Foggio, Italy. While stationed at Walnut Ridge, AK he was noted as a high scoring bowler. Natalino received a sharpshooter medal for pistol shooting and the Good Conduct Medal.

After his discharge from service, Natalino married Mary Carmel Franchino from California in 1947. He passed away on May 30, 2001 in Palm Desert, Riverside, California.

THRESSA Theresa Y. LOCCIA was the youngest sibling, being born September 8, 1916. She passed away a week after her sister, Lavena on March 11, 1978 in a Cobleskill hospital. She is buried in Prospect View Cemetery, St. Johnsville. All of the records I've found show her name as Thressa.

Thressa Loccia married Kenneth Fleck, moved to Fonda in 1967 and Johnstown in 1973. The couple had two sons - Marine Cpl. Kenneth, Jr. and Terrance T. and a daughter, Shawn. I discovered Terrance in the Prospect View Cemetery. With further research, I found he was killed in an automobile accident while riding with some friends on Hickory Hill in Fonda. He was born in 1950 and died in 1968 in St. Mary's Hospital, Amsterdam, shortly after being admitted.

Thressa had lived in Fonda at the time, also in Gloversville and Phoenix AZ in 1947. I find no information regarding her husband, Kenneth Fleck.

~ *La Famiglia ALEXANDER VECCIARELLI* ~

This would be the Vecciarelli family younger generations in St. Johnsville are familiar with. Alexander, Nicola, Elmerinda (Cochi) and Giovanni Vecciarelli were all siblings. Nicola was the father of Marie Vecciarelli Nobile, Elsie Vecciarelli Loccia, and Luigi Vecciarelli. Luigi was the father of Elena Vecciarelli Montoni and Beatrice Vecciarelli Iagnacco.

ALEXANDER VECCIARELLI was born in Maenza on August 26, 1894, the third child of Vinnauza "Domenico" Vecciarelli and Maria Laura Giambattista. At the age of 15 he arrived in America on May 5, 1910 with Angelo Iagnocco, husband of Beatrice Vecciarelli, who was his niece.

While serving in the military during World War I from September 21, 1917 to January 10, 1919, Alexander became naturalized on December 19, 1918.

The Reaney Knitting Mill had first employed Alexander before his employment by the New York Central Railroad.

On October 29, 1924, at St. Joseph's Catholic Church, Little Falls, he married Jennie Lawrence, an Italian. She was the daughter of Anthony and Mary Lawrence from Little Falls and Italy. They began their married life in St. Johnsville at 7 Sanders Street and had one son, Anthony Vincent.

Alexander had two brothers, Nicola Antonio and Giovanni, who lived in Rensselaer and a sister, Elmerinda Vecciarelli, who was the wife of Ottavius Cochi. Giovanni had originally lived in St. Johnsville.

Alexander Vecciarelli gave his short life to working for the New York Central Railroad, not too far from his home at 5 Sanders Street. On March 26, 1948, at the age of 56, he died at Little Falls Hospital from a horrific accident that had occurred a couple days earlier. Alexander, with his friend and co-worker, John Ponzi, was walking along the tracks, heading back to work after a lunch break. Both were struck by a slow moving locomotive. While Alexander lost both legs, he was more concerned about them retrieving his friend, John from underneath the engine. After extensive surgery and many blood transfusions from his co-workers, Alexander Vecciarelli succumbed to his serious injuries within a few days. John Ponzi had died instantly.

The Vecciarelli home was under extensive renovations at the time, so the funeral was held at the C.C. Lull Funeral Home on Bridge Street. It was an Italian custom to wake the body at the home, with a religious service at the church before burial.

Alexander Vecciarelli had served his newfound country in the U.S. Army during World War I and was a member of the Morris J. Edwards American Legion Post. Known as an industrious and generous man, he was also a member of the Railroad Brotherhood.

With the death of her husband, Jennie was left to raise her son, Anthony alone. She was employed in an underwear factory.

GIOVANNA "Jennie" LAWRENCE was born in Little Falls in 1906; she died in 1984.

ANTHONY VINCENT VECCIARELLI was born in Little Falls Hospital on June 9, 1926. Like his father, he was employed most of his life by the New York Central Railroad. He resided on Sanders Street his entire life, later moving with his family to 15 Sanders.

Anthony was a veteran of World War II, stationed for a year and a half at Fort Dix.

On June 23, 1951 Anthony married Arlene Risedorf, daughter of Mr. and Mrs. Clarence Hotaling of Herkimer, at the Grace Congregational Church in St. Johnsville. A reception was held at Henry's Tavern, upper North Division Street. They had six children - Sandra, Theresa, William, Anthony, Vincent and Deborah, who passed away at a young age.

Anthony Vincent Vecciarelli passed away April 16, 2001.

Arlene Risedorf passed away September 27, 2002 at the age of 74. She was born in the town of Danube on August 29, 1928. Arlene worked most of her life in the Little Falls Shoe Company.

~ *La Famiglia GIOVANNI VECCIARELLI* ~

GIOVANNI VECCIARELLI was born February 4, 1896 in Maenza, son of Vinnauzo "Domenico" Vecciarelli and Maria Laura Giambattista. It is claimed he immigrated in 1917. I find no passenger manifest records.

In 1917, when he registered for World War I he was living at 32 South Division Street. He went on to spend time in the Infantry from May 27, 1918 to June 18, 1918. He was later transported several times overseas and suffered an accidental injury on October 13, 1918. His World War I record of service declared he had a sister Rosa Misi, who lived at 44 Bridge Street. I find no record of Rosa. She may have been a border at the Kate Wilson home next to 36-38 Bridge Street.

While serving in World War I, on June 22, 1918 he was naturalized in Spartanburg SC. Many of the immigrants would become American citizens while serving their new country. Their immigrant wives and children automatically became citizens with this procedure.

On September 27, 1919 he applied for a passport, which stated his intention to bring back a wife and sister. He married Giovanna DiVito of Maenza. The couple lived most of their lives in Renssalaer. I don't find a record of his return, but do know that both lived most of their lives in Renssalaer, where his sister Elmerinda Cochi resided.

Giovanni Vecciarelli died on August 9, 1963 in Renssalaer.

Giovanna DeVito had passed away years earlier on April 13, 1940.

~ ELMERINDA VECCIARELLI et OTTAVIUS COCHI ~

This couple is the knot that binds the Vecciarelli and Cochi families together in the Web.

ELMERINDA VECCIARELLI, the daughter of Domenico Vecciarelli and Maria Laura Giambattista, was born in Maenza in 1868 and died in her hometown either in 1905 or 1913. She was married to Ottavius Cochi. They had five children – Catallina, who married Leopoldo Iacobucci; Carlo, who married Leonina Forcinelli; Anastasio, who married Anna Belli; Sophia, who married Domenick Fiaschetti, brother of Rosina Battisti; and Amilcare, who married Gina Olivieri.

Carlo, Catallina and Sophia all came to St. Johnsville. Carlo remained here his whole short life. His sisters both moved and resided in Troy for the remainder of their lives, as did the other two brothers.

OTTAVIUS COCHI was born in Maenza in 1860. He came to America and St. Johnsville to join his son, Carlo on December 9, 1913, apparently after the death of Elmerinda. He died five years later on October 13, 1918 and reposes in Prospect View Cemetery. I find no records of his parents.

In summary of the Vecciarelli families:

Domenico Vecciarelli and Maria Laura Giambattista were the parents of Nicola Antonio, Elmerinda (Cochi), mother of Carlo Cochi; Alexander and Giovanni.

Nicola Vecciarelli and Palma Monescachi were the parents of Emelia (Elsie) Loccia, Luigi and Maria (Nobili), mother of Viola (Peruzzi).

Luigi Vecciarelli and Alessandra Agnese Marie Mazza were the parents of Elena (Montoni) and Beatrice (Iagnacco), plus several other children who didn't come to America.

I have conferred with descendants of the Elmerinda Vecciarelli Cochi family, who have graciously shared their family tree data with me. Grazie, Nicholas and Stacey Toma and Tom Riley.

GIOVANNI VECCIARELLI

I've mentioned this Giovanni Vecciarelli in my article, Searching My Roots, when I visited his bar/café in Maenza. Some may recall that he would visit the Andrew Susi – Theresa Fontana family on Sanders Street.

Giovanni's parents were Qualtiero Vecciarelli and Franca Baccari. Franca's father was Rocco Baccari, who I have determined may have been the brother of Theresa's mother Filomena Baccari Fontana and Ascienza Baccari Patrei, wife of Giulio. All three shared the same parents – Luigi Baccari and Constanza Pasqueli.

From what I've been told, Giovanni would be a distant cousin of the Vecciarelli families mentioned above.

~ *La Famiglia PALOMBO* ~

~ ANTONIO PALOMBO et ASSUNTA TUILLIA MONTEGIORGO ~

ANTONIO "Fred" PALOMBO arrived in America in 1911 from Bassiano. The Palombo's seem to be the only family that originated from there. Born on September 25, 1888, he was the sixth child of nine born to Pietro Palombo and Nicolina Onari. Besides Antonio, only two others survived to adulthood, his brother, Vittorio and sister, Clarice, who remained in Italy.

ASSUNTA TUILLIA "Julia" MONTEGIORGO arrived from Maenza, a year after Antonio, on January 13, 1913 and came directly to St. Johnsville. On November 30, 1913, Assunta and Antonio were married at St. Patrick's Church. Carlo Cochi and his future wife, Leonina Forcinelli, attended them. I'm wondering if this was somehow an arranged marriage?

In 1917 Antonio's World War I registration shows the couple living at 9 New Street with the Antonio Mancini family. He was working on the Railroad.

By 1920 they had moved to 30 Ann Street and had their son, Aldo. Antonio's brother Vittorio, single, and brother-in-law, Alessandro Montegiorgo's family was also living at the residence. The 1925 NYS Census shows Antonio and brother-in-law, Alessandro still living on Ann Street with their growing families. Antonio and Julia now have a daughter, Ada. He claims to be a carpenter. Vittorio aka Victor Palombo is married to Bianca Pasquale and living at 9 New Street, sharing the home of the Antonio and Joseph Mancini families.

By 1930 Antonio and Julia have moved from 30 Ann to 17 Ann Street into a home they had purchased, valued at $1800. Only Antonio's family was living here. I think there were errors in this census, as the names and ages of the two children are not correct. This was confusing at first, as it had looked like they had another son. As I've stated before, there were many errors in the Census records, as the scribers weren't familiar with foreign names and language.

When working on family trees, it's necessary to carefully consider the information you have. What is in the Census records, Passenger Manifests and even Obituaries is not written in stone. This even includes information inscribed on our gravestones. There may be something missing in the translation – or the memory.

By 1940 the Antonio Palombo family had moved into a cute little home at 23 East Liberty Street, where they lived the remainder of their lives. 1942 finds Antonio working at the Felt Shoe Company on Hough Street. His obituary states he was a carpenter, so he most likely used this skill as a sideline.

Antonio Palombo died suddenly in Little Falls Hospital, where he was confined for a few days, in March of 1958, the year after his wife, Julia's death.

Tuillia "Julia" Montegiorgo was born September 5, 1886 in Maenza, Rome, Italy to Liberatore Montegiorgo and Teresa Taggi. She passed away on February 21, 1957 and is buried in Prospect View Cemetery with Antonio.

I also discovered a Rinaldo Palombo, born in 1914 and buried on May 14, 1915 at this cemetery. He may be a first-born son of Antonio and Julia, named after one of Antonio's siblings?

ALDO ALFRED PALOMBO was born on June 6, 1918 in St. Johnsville. He passed away on October 14, 1991 in Fontana CA and is buried at Forest Lawn, Glendale CA.

An active student of St. Johnsville High, he participated in baseball, basketball and boxing.

Aldo enlisted in the US Army March 19, 1941 as a Sergeant, leaving for Iceland, where he served for a year. He was also active in the European Theater. Before his discharge he was promoted to Corporal.

Upon his return, Aldo Palombo married Margaret Cristiano of Gloversville on April 14, 1945 at Mount Carmel Catholic Church. They had two daughters - Sandra and Angela. He lived most of his adult life in Gloversville before moving to California around 1964.

Margaret had a brother, George, whom I knew. He was one of the best dancers at Shermans, Caroga Lake and St. Anthony's in Johnstown. He dated my friend, Janet Castellucci.

ADA PALOMBO was born June 10, 1924 in St. Johnsville. She worked at the Little Falls Felt Shoe and later as a personal assistant to Mrs. Mabel Fowler.

In March 1943 Ada Palombo became engaged to Nello Montoni, son of Pasquale Montoni and Elena Vecciarelli. On June 18, 1944, while Nello was home on furlough, they were married. Nello's sister, Ella was maid of honor with Margaret Cristiano, Ada's sister-in-law as bridesmaid. Louis Montoni was best man for his brother, with Angelo Macci, an usher. They had two children - Gary Anthony and Tracy Ann.

Ada was most noted for her excellent cooking and baking skills that she generously shared with others. She was also a high scoring bowler in the St. Johnsville Masonic Temple's Women's League. She died October 5, 2008 in the St. Johnsville Nursing Home, seven months after her husband.

Nello Peter Montoni passed away on March 25, 2008. He was born February 26, 1924 in St. Johnsville.

He graduated from high school in June 1942 and enlisted in the US Navy during World War II on October 8, 1942. He was stationed in the Philadelphia Navy Yard and served in the South Pacific combat zone on Parris Island. For most of his life, the Beech-Nut Packing Company, Canajoharie employed Nello.

In January 1949, Nello and Ada purchased the brick home of Vincent and Lucy Constantino at 15 South Division Street. They sold it to Ada's uncle, Victor before moving to their new home on Mill Road. You can read more about Nello and Ada Montoni and their son, Gary in *La Famiglia Vecciarelli ~ Montoni*.

VITTORIO "Victor" PALOMBO was the youngest brother of Antonio and a twin to Arrigo, who died within hours of his birth. They were born just before Christmas, December 22, 1892.

Victor also arrived in America on February 25, 1911, perhaps with his oldest brother, Antonio? His plans were to go to Ithaca NY, where many of his *compaesani* (townspeople) were already living. He was naturalized in 1919.

New York State Marriage Records show that Victor, age 25, had married Teresa Mastracco, age 14, on June 22, 1918. The marriage did not last for very long; they had no children.

The NYS 1925 Census shows Victor living with his wife, Bianca Pasquale at 9 New Street with the Antonio and Joseph Mancini families. Although the name is the same, I'm not able to determine if Bianca is a sister of Adelgesia Pasquale, wife of Paul Salvagni. Bianca came here from Maenza, as did Adelgesia.

By 1926, Victor had finally moved to Ithaca, where he worked as a barber.

On June 14, 1955, Victor and Bianca were returning from Paris, France, via the Trans World Airlines. I'm assuming they had been visiting family in Italy.

Shortly after his visit to his homeland, Vittorio Palombo passed away in 1956 at age 64.

Bianca Pasquale was born in 1892 and died in 1982. I believe both died in Ithaca. They are buried in Prospect View Cemetery near Vittorio's brother, Antonio and wife, Julia. I don't find any children.

ALESSANDRO GIOVANNI MONTEGIORGO was born in Maenza in 1881, the brother of Julia Montegiorgo. He emigrated to America, coming to St. Johnsville in 1909 via Boston MA. Also, as a passenger was Gino Castellucci, age 16, coming to join his brother, Vincenza.

On May 7, 1916, Alessandro Montegiorgo married Felicita Loccia, born in 1887 and daughter of Fortunato Loccia and Antonnina Cesaroni. Serving as witnesses were Carlo Cochi and Leonina Forcinelli. The Cochi's were related to the Loccia families.

The 1915 Census shows Alessandro Montegiorgo and his then future wife, Felicita Loccia, boarding with his sister, Julia and her husband, Toma "Tony" and Julia Polops "Palombo" at 12 Spring Street. Included, as boarders were Lovigi Voli and Vitore Paloprri aka Victor Palombo. Sometimes one has to use common sense to interpret Census records.

In 1920, the couple lived at 30 Ann Street with Alessandro's sister, Julia and her husband, Antonio. They had a one-year-old son, Antonio. 1925 finds them still residing on Ann Street with their son, Antonio and a new addition, daughter Antoinette. I find no further information about this couple.

ANTONIO MONTEGIORGO aka Montegero, the son of Alessandro Montegiorgo and Felicita Loccia was born about 1919 in St. Johnsville.

During World War II Antonio was wounded in action in the Mediterrean, according to an April 3, 1944 news article in the Rome Sentinel.

He died April 19, 1976 and was buried in the Fort Plain Cemetery with full honors by the Mohawk Valley VFW Post of Fort Plain. Only his sister and two cousins survived. I find no record of marriage.

ANTIONETTE MONTEGIORGO, the daughter, was born April 24, 1920 in St. Johnsville. She passed away on August 10, 1990 in Johnstown.

In 1940 Antoinette was a boarder at 12 Kingsbury Avenue with Carroll and Marie McMorris. She worked as a presser at an underwear factory. From my research, I am assuming it was the Luxuray in Fort Plain. She may have met her husband there.

The following year in September 1941, she was known as Antoinette Cassell and lived in Fort Plain. She later moved to Fonda and was a member of the American Legion Auxiliary.

Although I am unable to locate any marriage records, it seems Antoinette had been married twice. In February 1953, I locate her again as Antoinette Walker, living in Johnstown. I don't find any children.

Richard Brown has contributed to this article. Grazie!

Domenick Peruzzi et Viola Nobili Wedding

~ *La Famiglia* PERUZZI ~

In Piazza della Signora, the popular historic center of Florence, next to the Ufizzi Museum, which houses the famous statue of Michelangelo's David, is found a building featuring "The Code of Arms" of several Italian families. In this display is the *Peruzzi* Code of Arms, which features "pears", symbolic of the first part of the name. Not too far from this famous plaza is a smaller area - Piazza dei Peruzzi. Seems Peruzzi was a popular name in the *Fiorenza* area.

Being among the leading families in the 14th century, the Peruzzi families amassed their wealth in the textile business and as bankers in Florence. The family members, who immigrated in the early 19th century, settled in Pennsylvania and founded the Peruzzi chain of automobile dealerships and the Planters Nut and Chocolate Co.

~ CARMINE PERUZZI et MARIA PALUZZI ~

CARMINE PERUZZI, the son of Domenico Peruzzi and Lumiata "Alyce" Masetti of Supino, immigrated to America in May 1902, first settling in Little Falls. He later moved to St. Johnsville, where most of the family lived out their lives.

Carmine was born January 13, 1884. He became a citizen on February 8, 1926, which naturally included his wife, Maria.

MARIA PALUZZI, the daughter of Louis Paluzzi and Rosa Battisti, arrived from Supino in 1907. She was born December 8, 1882.

Carmine Peruzzi and Maria Paluzzi were married in Little Falls on January 18, 1908, shortly after Maria's arrival to America. Witnesses to the union were Luigi Belli and Martha Rozzie. They were the parents of seven children. Two of them, Dargiza, a year and a half, and Linda, 2 months, were born while living in Little Falls before the 1910 Census. Carmine was working at an electrical light company. Antonio and Mary Tucci were boarders.

The St. Johnsville 1913-1914 Directory shows that Carmine, as head of the household, was living at 46 Hough Street and working on the railroad. This would be the very last home on Hough Street near the Zimmerman Creek. My grandparents later rented the home for a few years.

Living at 26 Hough Street was Lorenzo Peruzzi as head and John Peruzzi as his boarder. I'm not certain if they are related to Carmine.

Carmine's World War I registration records of September 12, 1918, show the family living at 24 Hough Street, with him working on the New Yotk Central Railroad. By 1930 the Peruzzi's were the owners of this home, which they purchased from C.C. Bellinger.

By this time, Dominick, Roosevelt, Rose, Joseph, Antonio and Alyce were born. Dargiza was not living there and Linda had passed away in December 1917 as a very young child.

As most other Italian immigrants, every summer Carmine reaped a huge vegetable garden, which was located on the right side of the old river bridge, near Sanders Street. Besides feeding his family with the fruits of his labor, he would drive his buggy pulled by his horse, Tom, to Little Falls to sell his produce to vendors. Tom also helped with the plowing in the garden. It is said it was most helpful that Tom knew the route home from Little Falls in the event that Carmine and his helper friends had too much to drink. Italians were quite noted for imbibing after a hard day of labor.

As told to me, there were two family curses that trickled down through the generations. The superstition that first transpired resulted from a curse by a snake charmer, who died in the act of a Peruzzi constable arresting him. A struggle with a knife caused the charmer's death and before he died cursed the family saying, "One member of each generation would die from a snake bite." The curse seemed to end years ago. However, two members of the current generation have experienced snakebite deaths with their animals – a dog and a horse. Another curse seemed to occur when four in the family lost part of, or their entire finger - Carmine, his son Dominick, granddaughter Joyce, and a grandson.

Working on the railroad until his retirement, Carmine was a member of the Railroad Brotherhood. After a lengthy illness, he passed away October 5, 1959 in Little Falls Hospital at the age of 75.

Apparently, Maria never worked outside the home, except in the summer when she would take her husband's produce to Main Street to sell. She was a caring mother and grandmother, raising not only her own children, but also some of her grandchildren who lived with her at times - Dargiza's children and Alyce's daughter, Margaret, who considered her a second mother.

Maria quite frequently socialized with her close neighbors. I do know she was a good friend of my grandmother, Edvige Cacciotti Sindici, who lived around the corner on Roth Street. On occasion several of the ladies in the neighborhood would gather and share the latest news, many times at the home of Hilda Iacobucci, as portrayed in Cheryl Dunton Blaydon's memoir, *"The Memory Keepers".*

Granddaughter, Joyce Peruzzi Politt told me this story, "Maria would lug her laundry down to the western end of Hough Street, where the Zimmerman Creek flowed to the Mohawk River. Her children were always there to assist her with the washing. One day, as she was on her hands and knees scrubbing clothes on a rock, her son Dominick, asked for a penny for candy. She replied, "no", and he pushed her into the water." I didn't hear the final outcome; surely he learned his lesson.

The Mohawk River area near the railroad tracks and Sanders Street was also a popular site to do laundry. In the early part of the century, they did already have access to village water and sewer, but had to pay for its usage. I'm sure there were other Italian women in that area that may have done their laundry in the creek to save money on their water billings. Italian women were very frugal.

Maria Paluzzi died of a heart attack at Little Falls Hospital, January 1, 1967 at the age of 59.

DARGIZA PERUZZI aka "Dodgie" was the oldest of the eight siblings, born November 30, 1908 in Little Falls. She left the family home early when she met and married Giovanni "John" Donaldo Dannible, originally from Abruzzo, Italy, and moved to Pennsylvania. Giovanni worked on bridge construction.

The 1930 Census shows the couple living in Aliquippa PA with two children - Anthony Lewis and John, Jr. Rosemary was also born in Aliquippa.

By October 1933, Dargiza had moved back to St. Johnsville. I'm assuming the couple divorced, as I discovered a later marriage for Giovanni Dannible. She later had two more sons - Lewis and Raymond.

In May 1939, Dargiza and four of her children were living in Quincy MA. When they returned to St. Johnsville, they resided at 20 Sanders Street, according to the 1940 Census.

Leading a rather adventurous life, Dargiza "Dodgie" Dannible passed away on May 30, 1987 in Utica at 79 years.

LINDA PERUZZI was born March 12, 1910 and passed away at the young age of seven on December 3, 1917. She may have been the victim of the Influenza epidemic?

DOMENICK "Maymo" PERUZZI, the oldest son, was a well-respected member of not only the Italian community, but also the entire community of St. Johnsville. An article in the June 16, 1966 issue of the *Enterprise & News* newspaper has numerous quotes lauding his accomplishments. He was described as "just a regular guy", being noted as someone always there to assist those in need.

Maymo, as he was better known, was active in many village and town organizations, as well as in local politics as a Republican. He served as a St. Johnsville Town Councilman, a special police officer with the Auxiliary Police, and a fire warden with the St. Johnsville Fire Department.

As a member of the Starr-Colorito VFW Post, he was appointed Sergeant of the VFW drill team. He was involved with others in the organization of the Little League Baseball Team, including my father, Floyd Perry.

Maymo was active in the Boy Scouts, at one time going out on a snowshoe rescue mission to retrieve some scouts, who were stranded at a nearby camp by a severe snowstorm. I'm thinking this camp would have been at Klock's Park?

With his vast experiences as a carpenter and working most of his life on construction, Maymo assisted in the building of the new altar railing for St. Patrick's Catholic Church and worked on the construction of the Canajoharie School. He was involved in rebuilding the grandstand and fundraising for new lights for the baseball field at Soldiers and Sailors Memorial Park.

Without Maymo, there may not have been a Harry C. Smith Benefit Club, where he served as vice-president and was most active in all their fundraising activities. Maymo and his brother, Joe, were granted lifetime memberships. In 1962 Maymo had a contract with the village of St. Johnsville, then owners of the original transient camp building at Klock's Park. He purchased the property for $1,000 with the intention of razing the deteriorating building. He was planning to utilize the lumber in the construction of his new home on Crum Creek Road nearby.

This well-known building has quite a history, dating back to the 1930's Great Depression era when it was a camp erected by the Federal Government. Referred to as the "Transient Camp", it was utilized as a haven for homeless youths and men. Having been built on village owned land, the property reverted back to the village when the Federal government released control. During the 1940s, it housed Mexican Nationals who were brought to the area to work on the New York Central Railroad to replace the workers who were serving in World War II. This was the era when "Mexican Hots" made their debut in St. Johnsville.

After that, the building was used by various organizations for their affairs. The Auxiliary Police used it for their headquarters, hosting clambakes and renting the spacious downstairs area and sparse kitchen for weddings and parties. I had my Italian wedding reception at the site in June of 1955, as did numerous other couples.

The grounds surrounding the building were popular for family picnics. To walk the tree-lined paths down to the falls area, where the Zimmerman Creek flowed over large shale rocks into the village, was an exhilarating experience. The Zimmerman Creek was the source of water for the entire St. Johnsville village, flowing down from the reservoir in Lasselsville into the Mohawk River.

In August 1962 the newly formed H.C. Smith Benefit Club approached Dominick to purchase the building. After he had torn down the wings of the building, James Sanguine and Leo Kraft assisted him in refurbishing the middle section for use. For 56 years to this date, the club is still active with fundraising to assist those in need. It is stated in the sales agreement that if the Benefit Club should disband, the property will revert back to the Dominick Peruzzi family.

On June 5, 1930, Domenick Peruzzi was joined in holy wedlock with Viola Nobili of Herkimer. She was the daughter of Anthony Nobili and Maria Vecciarelli. Attending the couple were Maymo's sister, Rose Peruzzi and her future husband, James Minosh. Maymo's friend, Dominick Papa's wife, Mary, had worn Viola's wedding gown and graciously offered its use to Viola.

Viola's mother, Maria, was a sister of Emelia Vecciarelli Loccia and aunt of Elena Vecciarelli Montoni. Knowing what I do about both families, I have determined that Maria Peruzzi and Elena Montoni played matchmakers for Maymo and Viola. Elena lived in the same neighborhood on Hough Street as the Peruzzi family.

Domenick and Viola were the parents of seven children, including two sets of twins - Mary Ann, Barbara, Joyce, twins Elizabeth "Betty" and Robert, and twins Bonnie and Ronnie. They were always totally devoted to their family, instilling qualities of good values and respect.

Before finally settling into their own home, the family moved quite often. After their marriage, they lived with Dominick's parents on Hough Street. This was the custom of many young newlyweds. They later moved to 22 Sanders Street on the corner of Mechanic. (This seemed to be another popular boarding house.) 31 East Main Street became the birth site of their first child, Mary Ann. Shortly after, they moved back to 10 Sanders Street where Barbara was born.

In 1940 they were renting part of the Pedro home at the popular 21 Sanders Street home with their two young daughters. Their daughter, Joyce, was born there, but didn't show up in the Census.

Joyce and I have decided to call 21 Sanders Street, the "birthing place", as so many babies first entered the Italian world of St. Johnsville there. My mother, Rose Sindici and her sister, Lena, were both born at the home many years before. And the list goes on and on.

The first set of twins, Betty and Bob were born in Little Falls Hospital, when the family lived at 30 Ann Street, next door to the Papa family.

Dominick Peruzzi served his country in World War II in the Marine Corps from October 20, 1942 until his discharge on November 10, 1945. With Maymo's enlistment, Viola and the children moved to Utica, to be closer to her Nobili family.

Upon Maymo's arrival home, they settled into their home at 117 West Main Street, which they purchased from Joseph Francisco. The second set of twins, Bonnie and Ronnie were born at Little Falls Hospital during this residency.

Viola was very much involved with the children's school activities, acting as a chaperone for many events. After the second set of twins was born, she hosted a Home Economics class at her home, discussing the responsibilities of being a parent and demonstrating to the students how to attend to babies, such as diaper changes, bathing and feeding.

While living next door to the family for two years with my own new baby, I always admired her ability to multi-task. Her second set of twins was just a few months older than my son. Viola was symbolic of the perfect housewife. I found her to be a remarkable mother, loving wife, exceptional Italian cook and meticulous housekeeper. Her heart was full of generosity! She always had something baked for her children's friends and even the transients who came off the railroad in the 1940's.

One time, while they were living at 117 West Main Street, a young couple with three small children, had broken down while traveling through the village and stopped at Amy's Service Station, where Maymo was working as a mechanic. While the repairs were being made, Maymo brought the family to his home nearby, where Viola graciously prepared a spaghetti dinner for them and invited them to spend the night in the warmth of their home.

After his retirement in 1964, Maymo commenced building a home next to his friend, James Sanguine, on Crum Creek Road, where he and the love of his life lived out their lives.

Viola Nobili was born May 25, 1916 in Herkimer and passed away March 1984 at home, after a courageous battle with cancer.

Dominick Peruzzi was born April 26, 1913 and died January 13, 1994 before his 81st birthday. He was "just a regular Italian guy!"

ROOSEVELT W. PERUZZI was born August 25, 1914. He died suddenly in May 1978 at 88 years of age at his home in Canajoharie, where he lived most of his life.

On October 14, 1939, Roosevelt Peruzzi and Stella Tiberio, daughter of Joseph A. Tiberio and Marie Delganeo, were married in Canajoharie. They had a daughter, Mary and three sons - Carmen, Joseph and John.

Roosevelt was a Navy Veteran from World War II. He was cited as a Lieutenant with the Canajoharie Police. He worked as a self-employed mason.

Stella Tiberio was born July 29, 1917 in Canajoharie and died October 1, 2001 in Herkimer.

ROSE PERUZZI was born April 11, 1916. She passed away September 16, 2005 in Frankfort, where she lived most of her life.

Rose Peruzzi was married to James S. Minosh from Frankfort on July 25, 1936. They lived with her parents for a few years before moving to Frankfort. They had four children - Mary, who died at birth, Joseph, Ann and Sam. I believe Mary and Joseph were born at her parent's home?

James S. Minosh was born September 23, 1916 in Frankfort and died in November 1975.

Living in the same Italian neighborhood, Rose and my aunt, Lena Sindici, became great childhood friends. In September 1933, when they were teenagers of 16 years, they apparently were both unhappy at home or were curious to see what the world was like outside of St. Johnsville. They came up with a plan to run away to live on their own in the city.

Early one Sunday morning, the young ladies left their homes, most likely crossed the railroad tracks, and boarded the local train to Albany. They quickly found a place to room and jobs as waitresses. They even changed their names, acting as sisters. Their families reported them missing to the local police. However, Lena decided to send a postcard to her boyfriend, Daniel Matis, later her husband, telling him of their whereabouts. Perhaps she was having second thoughts? Receiving the card the following Monday, Dan immediately shared the information with the distraught parents. Rose's brother, Domenick and Lena's sister, Rose, accompanied St. Johnsville Police Officer MacMahon to Albany to locate the girls and bring them home - after some considerable convincing by their siblings, I heard.

JOSEPH LOUIS PERUZZI was born August 7, 1918 at home. He died June 13, 2004. As a youth of 15, Joe assisted his father, Carmine with his vegetable garden.

Joseph Peruzzi was married to Helen Lucille Jones of Ames on December 13, 1947 in Pittsfield MA. They moved to Canajoharie and had two children - Joseph, Jr. and Joan.

Wounded in the Viet Nam War, he received the District Service Cross and Purple Heart.

March 3, 1972 was a gloomy overcast day for most, but a bright rainy day for Joe Peruzzi. Working as a bricklayer for Elmer F. Kelly Construction Co, Johnstown, Joe was relaxing at home due to the inclement weather. An unexpected knock on his door came with Bob Snell of Snell's Tavern informing him of his winning fortune of $50,000 from a ticket purchase for the NYS Lottery. Carlo Polidori had sold him the winning ticket from the Thriftway Super Market and was seen congratulating Joe in an *Enterprise & News* article.

Retiring in 1973, Joe was employed for several years by C.J. Burgess in St. Johnsville. He was a lifetime member of the H.C. Smith Benefit Club and the Union Workers of Masons.

Helen Lucille Jones, daughter of Eric and Jennie Jones, was born March 30, 1924 in Ames and passed away February 17, 1975 in Little Falls Hospital. She had worked as a forelady with Palatine Dyeing Co.

ANTONIO PERUZZI lived a very short life. He was born June 4, 1921 and died July 5, 1935 at 14 years of age. While recovering from an appendectomy, he contracted pneumonia and died in Little Falls Hospital.

ALYCE ELIZABETH PERUZZI was named after her grandmother, Lumiata "Alyce" Masetti. She was born December 30, 1921 and passed away January 25, 2005 at home after a lengthy illness.

Alyce Elizabeth Peruzzi married Calvin Christopher Johnson, son of Burt Johnson and Freida Perkins. His brother, Gerald was married to her good friend and neighbor, Clara Palitti. They had three children - Gary, Calvin Jr., and Kelly. She also had a daughter, Margaret.

Along with Dennis Shay, Cal later became a hero with the saving of the life of a young girl while she was fishing at the Fishing Derby site in the Zimmerman Creek next to the Palatine Dye Upper Mill on North Division Street. The girl had fallen into the six feet of water and was unable to swim. Shay jumped in to pull her out, but she kept fighting him, so Cal went in to bring both of them out.

Calvin Johnson was born May 10, 1925 in Stratford and died July 17, 1991 at Cooperstown Hospital. He served in the US Navy in World War II.

* Joyce Peruzzi Pollit has contributed a great deal to this story. Grazie!

~ *La Famiglia TOLFA* ~

~ GIUSEPPE TOLFA et LORETTA COGGI ~

GIUSEPPE "Joseph" TOLFA, aka Joe House, arrived in this country in 1913. Loretta Coggi, his wife, arrived on May 26, 1914 with their first-born child, Lorenzo, who was nine months old. They were on their way to 28 Bridge Street, where Joe was residing.

The June 5, 1917 World War I records later show that Joe and his family were living at 11 Ann Street. Guglielimina Battisti, who would be the wife of Pietro Battisti, employed him as a laborer, most likely at the bar/liquor store Pietro owned. I've found that Battisti is a cousin of Joe's, and also a brother of James Joseph Battisti, father of Romeo. So, I guess that forms a connection.

I also have found through my extensive research that two of the Sugar (Zuccaro) brothers, Rocky and Guy were also cousins of Joseph Tolfa. The Zuccaro family had numerous connections to the immigrant Italians of St. Johnsville.

By June 1917 the couple's daughter, Clara had been born. I have not been able to find the family listed in the 1920 Census records. This isn't uncommon.

For a few years, the Reaney Mills employed Joe Tolfa, before becoming the proprietor of the popular Central Hotel, where he worked until his retirement. For 60 years the Central Hotel, under the Tolfa family's ownership, was a favorite "happy hour" gathering place for many of the village men before heading home from their day's work. They catered numerous parties including stag parties, wedding dinners, bowling banquets, and more. After the Tolfa family moved to their home at 8 William Street, they rented the upstairs rooms to boarders.

One March 1915 news article states that Charles La Rose sold his Café to a firm of Italians. Another article of March 20, 1915 states that Joseph Tolfa had purchased the property.

On August 26, 1924 Joe and Loretta paid $8250.00 to Josephine Sneck, an elderly widow, to purchase the 16 East Main Street property, where they not only conducted a restaurant, but had their living quarters upstairs for many years. I believe all the children but Lorenzo were born there. From the information I've found, I'm assuming Tolfa may have been renting the property for the first couple of years. The timeline is rather confusing.

It seems Joe purchased the Central Hotel before the Prohibition era of 1920-1933 went into effect. In April of 1922, during the Prohibition years, Joe was cited for having an illegal pint of whiskey behind his bar. He posted a $1,000.00 bail bond, quite a huge sum for that period of time. He was not the only one cited; there were several other saloonkeepers in the village. I have heard many stories and found numerous citations of others during those strict early years. How can you own a saloon without alcohol available? The Prohibition act went into effect from 1920 to 1933 with the intent of eliminating domestic violence and other social injustices.

The 1925 Census shows the Tolfa couple still residing at the East Main property with all of their children - Lorenzo, Clara, Peter, Amelia, Guido, and Jessie. Joe's cousin, Angelo Tolfa was also living with them. In the 1915 Census I found an Acilo Torfa, age 22, as a boarder at 44 Hough Street, working in a knitting mill. I believe this would be Angelo.

On January 16, 1926 Loretta and four of her children, Clara, Pietro, Amelia and Guido arrived in New York City from Naples, Italy. They all had traveled on Loretta's passport, apparently returning home from visiting family in Supino.

1930 and 1940 show the Tolfa's still living over the hotel. However, the address is shown as 25 East Main. Again, quite often there are errors made by the Census takers. Sometime after 1940 they moved to a large home at 8 William Street. Their daughter, Clara, was the last Tolfa to live in the residence with her husband, Paul Frezza, before building their new home on Rockefeller Drive.

According to information I have discovered, in 1934 the Central Hotel, with Joseph Tolfa as proprietor, was originally known as the High Hat Restaurant. Several parties were held at the site. The St. Johnsville High School Commercial Club held parties there. Joe feted nine members of the Dolgeville Spofford Hose Company baseball team to a spaghetti dinner for their celebration.

Joe House was an active well-respected citizen of St. Johnsville. As a cornet player, he was instrumental in forming the St. Johnsville Military Band during World War I. On April 3, 1947, a new St. Johnsville Band was formed with Leondro Macci as president, Edwin Pistilli, vice-president, Richard Hillegas, secretary, and Joe Tolfa as treasurer. James Pietrocini was the director/librarian, assisted by Joe, with Joseph Croce serving as property manager. By 1949, Joe Tolfa was the director of the band. It seems they had their own band rooms in the old firehouse on Center Street.

I have discovered there were several bands formed in the early 1900s. It gets confusing trying to keep them straight. I'm sure Joe Tolfa was evident in all of them. There was some controversy, which led to a court decision in favor of the mostly Italian band led by James Pietrocini. (More about this in another article about the bands.)

In November 1938, Joe was also a trustee in the newly organized St. Johnsville Citizens Club, where approximately 25 Italians were involved in its formation.

Within a few months of Tolfa doing some extensive redecorating, the Central Hotel experienced a damaging fire. In September 1948, a shortage in some wiring surfaced in the building when a battering storm blew through the village, causing a massive electrical outage. Fortunately, it occurred during daylight hours. As the village alarm system was inoperable, some men in the immediate area of the hotel were able to run to the churches and firehouse on Center Street and ring the bells to alert firemen. There was a loss of $3,000 to the Tolfa building and some smoke and water damage to the adjoining American Legion rooms. In earlier years, a smaller fire occurred behind the building when young Guido and his friends were in their makeshift clubhouse. It was cold outside, so they lit a fire, which overcame the clubhouse. Fortunately, none of the young boys were injured.

Giuseppe "Joseph" Tolfa, the son of Lorenzo and Victoria Tolfa, was born November 17, 1888 in Supino. He passed away unexpectedly at Little Falls Hospital at the age of 86 on June 20, 1975. He led a long, productive and musical life. Though small in stature, Joe House was a huge presence in the community of St. Johnsville.

LORETTA COGGI was born August 16, 1887 in Supino to Lorenzo Coggi and Maria Nicodimo. After moving to the William Street home, she became quite ill and passed away at Little Falls Hospital on April 4, 1954 at age 66.

Besides raising her large family, Loretta worked with her husband in the hotel, cooking and serving home prepared foods from her sparsely equipped kitchen.

Loretta had a brother Julio Coggi. He lived in St. Johnsville in 1915 as a boarder with the Tolfa family. I believe he returned to Italy.

LORENZO "Larry" TOLFA, at only nine months old, experienced the long voyage over the Atlantic to St. Johnsville with his mother, Loretta. They arrived at Ellis Island on May 26, 1914, going directly to 28 Bridge Street to join his father, Giuseppe.

Larry worked most of his life as a bartender at the Central Hotel, first as an employee with his father, and later, when his father retired, in a partnership with his brother, Peter.

From 1937, Central Hotel had been operated with Larry's name listed on the Liquor License. This was one of the oldest licenses issued by the Montgomery County Alcoholic Beverages Board. This may have been the time the name was changed from High Hat Restaurant to Central Hotel.

On October 20, 1940, Lorenzo Tolfa and Olga Sackett, daughter of Joseph Sackett and Clara Giovampietro, were united in marriage at St. Patrick's Catholic Church. A wedding dinner was served at the Central Hotel, followed by a reception at the Odd Fellow's Hall on Bridge Street. They had two children - Sandra and Joseph.

When World War II erupted, Larry enlisted in the U.S. Army on April 3, 1945 serving his adopted country for a full year. He was discharged as a Corporal on May 14, 1946.

Born July 21, 1913 in Supino, Lorenzo Tolfa died at home in St. Johnsville on June 15, 1994.

Olga Mary Sackett was born April 28, 1914 in St. Johnsville and passed away June 14, 2003 in Cohoes. You will find more about Olga Sackett in *Le Sorella Giovampietro.*

CLARA MARTHA TOLFA had a huge zest for life, always with a smile for everyone, especially the teachers and students she mingled with for over 40 years, while working as the Secretary to the Supervising Principal at St. Johnsville High School. Clara even worked alongside her brother-in-law, Romeo Battisti during the many years he served as Principal.

Graduating with the Class of 1935, she went on to Mildred Elley Secretarial School in Albany, as so many before and after her. Before returning to her alma mater, she was employed as a stenographer with the Treasury Department.

On April 4, 1959 Clara Tolfa married Paul Edward Frezza from Little Falls. They shared 25 years together before his passing. They had no children.

Clara loved to entertain friends and travel, especially to Italy, where she had visited in 1926 as a young girl of 11 years. She also returned to Italy as a tourist, arriving back in New York City on September 21, 1955 onboard the Conte Buencamino. This may have been the time there was a small group, including Ralph Palombi, from St. Johnsville who traveled to Italy?

She was an active member of the St. Johnsville Business Girls and enjoyed being a Red Hatter in later years.

The first sibling born in America, Clara Martha Tolfa was born July 12, 1915 in St. Johnsville and passed away on January 22, 2012 at the St. Johnsville Nursing Home at the age of 97.

PETER PAUL TOLFA was born September 9, 1919 in St. Johnsville. Known in the village as "Mr. Baseball", Pete was a stellar athlete in high school. He enjoyed all sports and excelled at baseball, bowling and golf during his adult years. After graduation, Pete was employed at Luxor Mills, St. Johnsville.

After their engagement in January 1942, on April 11, 1942 Peter Paul Tolfa and Anna Bilobrowka, daughter of Onofre Bilobrowka and Tekla Neberezna, were joined in marriage at St. Patrick's Catholic Church. Attending them were Anna's sister-in-law, Elizabeth "Betty" Bilobrowka as maid of honor, Molly Tolfa and Julia Bilobrowka as bridesmaids, with Guido Tolfa serving his brother as best man. Peter Sackett and John Bilobrowka were ushers. Following the ceremony, a wedding breakfast was served at The Antlers, West St. Johnsville. The couple had three children - Laurie, Rebecca and Peter.

Peter Tolfa joined the Navy during World War II on April 25, 1944, being discharged on January 7, 1946 with the rank of Coxswain. First stationed at Sampson Naval Base, Seneca Falls, where most every Naval inductee first trained, he was then sent to California and on to New Guinea onboard an LST boat, finally landing in the Philippines.

With his father's retirement, Peter became co-owner of the Central Hotel with his brother, Larry. His wife, Anna worked her culinary skills in the kitchen serving some of her special dishes. With the sale of the business in May 1975 to James and Peggy Stever Blais, he went to work for the U.S. Postal Service as a mail carrier.

Peter Paul Tolfa passed away on July 23, 2004 at St. Elizabeth's Hospital in Utica. He was a member of the St. Johnsville Morris J. Edwards Post and the Little Falls Elks Lodge.

Anna Bilobrowka was born in St. Johnsville on February 13, 1919 and passed away at the St. Johnsville Nursing Home on December 20, 2010.

AMELIA A. "Molly" TOLFA was born - as a late family Christmas present - on December 26, 1920 at the family residence over the Central Hotel. She is the only sibling still surviving at this writing, residing in a Little Falls Nursing Home.

As a young girl of six years, Molly traveled to Supino, Italy, the natal home of her parents, along with her mother, sister Clara and two brothers, Peter and Guido. In 1926 they returned via the ship Duilio from Naples to New York City.

Molly was active in various activities such as cheerleading and participating in several stage plays in St. Johnsville High School, from where she graduated. In her adult years, she was a high scoring bowler in the Masonic Temple's Friday night Women's League and an avid golfer in a Women's League at Nick Stoner's Golf Course.

The day after Christmas, December 26, 1947, Romeo Battisti gifted Molly with an engagement ring on her birthday. On May 16, 1948 Amelia A. Tolfa married Romeo John Battisti at St. Patrick's Catholic Church. Molly's best friend, Laura Cochi served as maid of honor and Romeo's brother, James Battisti was best man. Lena Barca and Veronica Triumpho were bridesmaids with James Pietrocini and Constantino Terricola as ushers. A wedding dinner was held at the Creekside Restaurant, followed by a large reception at the Central Hotel. The couple had four children - Lorraine, Tina, Christa and Richard.

After living with Molly's parents a short time, the couple made their home on West Liberty Street for several years before moving to 10 John Street, where they lived out their lives. For many years, Molly provided Electrolysis services for hair removal from the John Street home.

Romeo John Battisti, the son of James Joseph Battisti and Secondini "Henrietta" Arduini, was born September 5, 1921 and passed away peacefully on Easter Sunday, April 8, 2007. He lived his entire life in St. Johnsville.

Romeo graduated from St. Johnsville High School, going on to St. Lawrence University, before enlisting in the Army Air Corps. After his discharge, he was hired by his alma mater to teach Junior High School Social Studies. He also coached the varsity basketball and baseball teams, later becoming High School Principal.

There is more of Romeo's extensive life story with his parents' history in *La Famiglia Battisti*.

After I graduated, I had the pleasure of socializing with Molly and Romeo on numerous occasions for many of my adult years.

GUIDO P. TOLFA aka "Skeets" moved to Utica with his marriage to Margaret Rich on September 20, 1947. They were the parents of four children - Debra, Virginia, Robert and Larry. Margaret passed away on December 7, 1995.

Like his brother Pete, Skeets also played baseball and basketball at St. Johnsville High School. In his adult years, as a member of the prestigious Yahnundasis Golf Club in New Hartford, he became an avid accomplished golfer, winning several tournaments, which made him the Club Champion. He was known as the Golf Master.

In 1940, after graduation, Guido worked as a janitor at the St. Johnsville School, before enlisting in the U.S. Navy. From 1942 to 1946 he was a bombardier fighter off the coast of South America.

Guido shared his father's musicality. As a St. Johnsville student, he was a member of bandleader Loren Cross, Jr's Collegians aka "Crossy's Collegians", which included two other young Italian musicians, Leondro Macci and Herman Scaccia. Guido was also a member of one of the two St. Johnsville Bands, mostly made up of Italian men, including his father, Joseph.

Guido also had a "gift of gab", which he employed with his business, the Utica Spray and Chemical Company in Utica. After his retirement, he worked for his son and now owner, Robert, until he was 90 years old.

Born April 15, 1922 in St. Johnsville, Guido P. Tolfa passed away in Utica on May 3, 2016 at age 94. He was buried with full military honors. He was a member of the Knights of Columbus and VFW. His lengthy obituary recognizes Attorney Carl Cochi as his great friend. Cochi is the son of Carlo and Lena Cochi.

JESSIE TOLFA was the youngest child of Giuseppe and Loretta Tolfa. Jessie was born March 3, 1924 in St. Johnsville. Her obituary states Italy. However, the 1925 Census shows her at two years of age residing with the rest of the Tolfa family, so I might dispute her birth in Italy.

The 1930 Census claims Jessie at six years old, living with the family. On December 20, 1937, I found Jessie Tolfa, age 14, coming from Italy alone to her home at 16 East Main. Apparently, as a young child she had gone to Italy for some reason. Sometimes, young Italian children were sent back to stay with relatives if they had a lingering illness. 1940 also shows her at age 16 residing with her family. I did also find a Jessie Tolfa later residing in Frankfort.

Jessie Tolfa passed away at St. Joseph's Nursing Home in Utica. It seems she had been in ill health most of her lengthy life. She died on May 11, 2014 at 90 years of age. Jessie never married.

ERMINIO TOLFA, age 29, arrived on December 30, 1921 headed to join his brother, Giuseppe at 16 East Main Street. He claimed his mother as Antonia, which isn't the same mother as Giuseppe's. Immigration records of April 27, 1926 show him at age 34 heading to Mechanic Street. He also claimed a sister, Maria.

I found further information that he may have lived and been employed at the Ford Automobile Factory in Detroit MI. His birth records state his birth on January 24, 1892 in Supino and death in March 1985, his last residence being the U.S. Consulate in Italy.

ANGELO TOLFA was born April 15, 1893 in Supino, son of Angelo Tolfa and Nazzarine "Lena" Martini. He arrived in America in 1914. He was a cousin of Joe Tolfa.

In the 1915 Census there is an Acilo Torfa boarding at 44 Hough Street with the Carmine Peruzzi family and others, working at a knitting mill. World War I records of June 5, 1917 show Angelo living on Ann Street, working on the railroad.

On June 4, 1918, Angelo married 17 year old Eva Miles at the home of her parents. In 1920 the couple was living at 28 Hough Street, both working in the knitting mill. Eva died three years later on January 19, 1923 of diphtheria at their home on Sanders Street. I don't find any children. However, I did locate a grave in Prospect View Cemetery for an infant Tolfa, buried July 1, 1919.

1925 finds Angelo, a widower, boarding with his cousin, Joe Tolfa and his family at 16 East Main Street. I lose track of him between 1925 and 1940. The Census of 1940 shows Angelo living with Joseph Benny, manager of a hotel, as a lodger, widowed and working as a carpenter's assistant. I checked Benny out. He was the owner of the Kyser Hotel for many years. He seemed to be a rather shady character.

Registering for the World War II draft in 1942, at 48 years of age, Angelo gave his address as 32 West Main Street, and claimed William J. Crangle employed him. I discovered a notice issued by Crangle, who seemed to be the administrator of Angelo's estate. The names of Mary Tolfa and Peter Tolfa were mentioned?

Angelo, aka Woodchuck, seemed to have lost his way after his young wife of four and a half years died. For a short while he had conducted a Café in St. Johnsville and violated the prohibition law. I don't find the name or location. He was arrested for disorderly conduct at 38 years of age in Little Falls. He had worked as a bartender for his cousin, Joe Tolfa at the Central Hotel and also the Kyser Hotel.

On January 20, 1944, at the age of 50, Angelo Tolfa's life ended tragically, when he was struck and killed by a hit and run driver while walking home from a tavern near his home in Yosts, outside of Fonda. At the time he was working as a section hand for the New York Central Railroad. He is buried in Prospect View Cemetery.

It seems Angelo had a brother, Antonio Tolfa, born in 1903 and died November 23, 1927. He was married to Lena Manuel and lived in Fredonia NY.

NEW YORK CENTRAL RAILROAD
Saint Johnsville, New York ~ Early 1900's

Built in 1901, the New York Central Railroad system was an important amenity in the lives of the Italian immigrants of St. Johnsville. Not only was it a source of income for so many, it was relied on for convenient transportation to surrounding towns, especially Little Falls, where many shopped for items not available locally. And, it served as transportation for the immigrants coming to the village from Ellis Island.

I made several trips with my grandmother, Edvige (Cacciotti) Sindici, who could use the pass my grandfather was awarded as an employee. I always looked forward to the lollipops the conductors would hand out.

When arriving at the port of New York City, those not settling in the city boarded the trains to shuttle them elsewhere. Coming to St. Johnsville was easy. They had an easy exit with the train station being right across the tracks from Sanders Street. Paul Salvagni always told his family the story of crossing the tracks to get to his Sanders Street home. One could also walk over the Mohawk River Bridge to arrive at their destination in the village.

Not only was the New York Central Railroad Company a major source of employment for many Italian men, it was also hard labor! The US Immigration Department sent immigrants to St. Johnsville to work on the railroad. Joseph (Zaccheo) Sackett was hired as a *Padrone* to oversee the increasing labor force. He spoke English and could relate to his Italian piasanos, whom he treated as friends. Many other areas of the country treated them like slaves.

I found an Ad dated August 15, 1946, which states as follows: "Trackman wanted. Experience not necessary. 18-45. Rate 84 ½ cents per hour. ½ time after 8 hours. Rate increase after one year."

Even though they did suffer discrimination, I would definitely say that St. Johnsville NY and the surrounding area was the best place for immigrants to settle. I have read some real horror stories about the treatment of Italian immigrants in America in other areas of the country.

Antonio Mancini, Peter Tucci, Thomas Triumpho and Saverio "Sam" Papa were among the original NYCRR foremen. Tragically, Gino Polidori, Anthony Vicciarelli, John Ponzi and John Pedro were also victims of what was the most significant form of employment for Italian immigrant men.

My grandfather, Giuseppe Sindici worked most of his life keeping the system in good shape by replacing railroad ties. It was a filthy job. Already having a Southern Italy dark complexion, he went home daily covered with the soot of the trains roaring by. He was nicknamed "Blackie"!

Speaking of trains roaring by, I loved staying overnight at my grandparents home, which was located at the end of Roth Street, wide open to the whistling sounds of midnight runs. I always insisted I sleep in their front bedroom where the noise and rumblings would lull me to sleep.

World War II caused a lack of railroad workers, so about 25 Mexican immigrants were sent to work locally on the rails. They were housed in the Klock Park's building, now the H.C. Smith Benefit Club and transported back and forth to work daily. I recall that Hilda and Arby Green oversaw their living quarters. Some of them did meander into the village, patronizing local bars and making a few friends. They had quite the eye for the ladies. It is said they caused the Bridge Street Grill to be called the "Bucket of Blood" through instigating altercations.

It's interesting that they were responsible for the creation of "Mexican Hots", which became so popular. The story is that Turpin's Restaurant, which supplied most of their food, ran short of ground beef for hamburgers, so they added peppers, onions, breadcrumbs and spices to extend the amount needed. Viola! Mexican Hots!!

The NYCRR not only brought Mexicans into the village, transient "hobos" were quite evident, knocking on doors, begging for food. Most were harmless, but we were always cautioned not to open the door. I know of an instance when one, apparently a pedophile, came up Bridge Street to the home where a grandson of Carmine Terranova's was riding his bicycle, grabbed the boy and headed back to the tracks. He was captured with the boy being unharmed.

As one of the major American railroads that connected the East Coast with the interior lands, the New York Central Railroad was founded in 1853. It was a consolidation of 10 small railroads that paralleled the Erie Canal between Albany and Buffalo; the earliest was the Mohawk and Hudson, New York State's first railway, which opened in 1831.

On April 19, 1940, one of the worst disasters in the Mohawk Valley involved the tragic derailment on the Gulf Curve of the New York Central Railroad system near Little Falls NY, killing 30 people and injuring 100. Joe Sindici and many other railroad workers were dispatched to the scene, where they worked 60 hours with minimal breaks, clearing the cluttered tracks of debris.

Although Joseph Sackett was responsible for hiring many of the railroad workers, it remains a mystery how many of the original Italian emigrants discovered this quaint little known village along the Mohawk River aka Barge Canal. My grandfather, Giuseppe Sindici, worked most of his life under Sackett, but he didn't come here specifically to work the railroad.

I could count on one hand the number of first generation Italians who owned a vehicle. The only one who comes to mind is Carmine Terranova, uncle of Carmela (Terranova) Palma, who owned a Roadster. It wasn't until the second generations were old enough to learn to drive, and could afford the purchase, that they had an easier means of transportation. I recall, as a child, making visits to Rome NY with my grandmother, where my mom Rose (Sindici) Perry's godparents lived. By this time, my mom or dad most likely drove us there. And now, I'm curious about her godparents being so far away, who they were?

ITALIAN COMMUNITY BAKE OVEN
1891 - 1893

Located on Route 167 from Little Falls to Dolgeville are the remnants of an old Italian Bake Oven, which was used daily in the years between 1891 and 1893 to make large quanitities of Italian bread for the Italian immigrants who worked on the Little Falls-Dolgeville Railroad and lived in a makeshift work camp nearby.

Built in 1891 the spacious rectangular oven was erected of brick and stone masonry. It featured a huge opening in the front where the bread would be placed.

In 2006 the Italian Community Bake Oven was listed on the National Register of Historical Places.

~ *Le Sorella GIOVAMPIETRO* ~

SACKETT ~ MACCI ~ TERRICOLA

In the early part of the 19th century, three young Italian sisters from Maenza, Italy began their journey to America. They didn't come together, but all settled in the village of St. Johnsville for the remainder of their lives. They had a cousin, Rocco Giovampietro, who had come over in 1903. Later, another cousin, Antonetta Giovampietro arrived and stayed with the sisters for a short time.

The sisters were the children of Felicissimi Giovampietro and Luisa Nolfi of Maenza, Italy. Clara was the first to arrive in 1912, followed by Romilda, who came with her friends, Delia Forcinelli Pietrocini and Leonina Forcinelli Cochi in 1913. Velina emigrated in 1914.

Sometime between 1915 and 1920, the three Giovampietro sisters - Clara, Velina and Romilda married, had children and were all living together in the 2 Roth Street home that had been occupied by the Guglielmo "William" Macci family in 1915.

The 1915 Census shows the 2 Roth Street residents included Guglielmo, his wife Attilio and their infant daughter, Elgisio. Another couple sharing the home was Procolo Milansi and his wife, Maddelene. Guglielmo and his family later moved to Troy NY, where many of the original Italian immigrants ended up due to better employment opportunities.

Guglielmo Macci was the oldest brother of Isaia Macci. Isaia "Joseph" Macci married the middle Giovampietro sister, Velina "Lena". Including two boarders – Isaia's brother's family, Cesare Macci and Velina's cousin, Antonetta Giovampietro, there were 16 residents in the home in 1920. I believe it was originally a two-family home. I knew it as a single family home when just Isaia and Lena owned it and lived there with their family.

The 1925 NYS Census shows only the three Giovampietro sisters and their families living at 2 Roth Street. These included the Sackett family – Joseph and Clara with their three children, Olga, Fulvia and Peter; the Macci family – Isaia and Velina and two of their children, Flora and Leandro and the Terricola family – Graziano and Romilda with two of their children, Constantino and Terenzio.

It seems that in 1930 Joseph Sackett and Isaia Macci shared ownership of the 2 Roth Street home and the Terricola family had moved elsewhere. By 1940 the Sackett family was residing at 5 West Liberty in a 2-family duplex shared with his sister-in-law, Romilda and her two sons, Constantino and Felice. Graziano Terricola and son, Terenzio, had both passed away in tragic accidents.

~ CLARA GIOVAMPIETRO et GIUSEPPE (ZACCHEO) SACKETT ~

CLARA GIOVAMPIETRO, born 1887 in Maenza, Italy, was the eldest of the three sisters. She was the first to venture out and emigrate in 1912. While living with the Guglielmo "William" Macci family, she met and married Giuseppe Zaccheo, better known as Joseph Sackett. He "Americanized" his name when immigrating to America from Sezze, Italy.

Arriving in 1907, Sackett was hired by the New York Central Railroad system as a foreman, overseeing the daily responsibilities of his crew to maintain the railroad tracks. This was a position he maintained his entire working life. As he was one of the few who could speak the English language, he was sent by the Immigration Department to oversee the construction of this famous rail line. He would reach out and contact men from Italy, encouraging them to relocate to the area. Every man – Italian or not – worked under his supervision with some of the duties shared with Assistant Foremen, such as Giuseppe "Pepe" Terricola, among others.

Three years after arriving, I found Sackett in the 1910 Census residing on Sanders Street in the Italian Quarters, with 26 residents, 16 of them boarders like him. At age 27, he was working as a Section Man on the New York Central Railroad before his promotion. Other railroad workers, John Ponzi, Verginia Colorito and Umberto Sanguine were also boarding with him at that time.

I didn't find him listed in the NYS 1915 Census, which doesn't surprise me, as I've found they missed so many of the Italians that year. World War I registration records of 1917 show he is married and living at the 2 Roth Street address. At this time he had been promoted to the foreman position.

On October 25, 1913, Clara Giovampietro married Joseph Sackett. They were the parents of four children - Pierro, who apparently died at an early age, Olga Mary, Fulvia, and Pierro (Peter).

In November of 1938, a group of 25 Italian men joined together to form the St. Johnsville Citizens Club. Joe Sackett was elected president. Other officers were vice-president Dominick Papa, treasurer Amy Castrucci, and secretary James Pietrocini, with trustees - Joseph Tolfa, Paul Salvagni, Frank Colorito and Sam Annunzio. It served as a social club with the purpose of stressing the education of Italians to assist them in becoming better American citizens.

Joseph Sackett was a 3rd degree member of the Knights of Columbus. In his retirement he served on the Village Board of Assessors.

GIUSEPPE ZACCHEO aka Joseph Sackett, born October 25, 1889 in Sezze, Italy, was the son of Luca Zaccheo and Gratzia Savarosa. He is the only person I have found coming from Sezze.

It seems Clara Giovampietro was what we today call "a stay at home mom". She passed away April 4, 1963. The family members were my neighbors during my childhood years.

After the death of his wife, Clara, Joe moved in with his daughter, Olga. Joseph Sackett passed away in Little Falls Hospital April 10, 1974, eleven years after his beloved Clara.

OLGA MARY SACKETT, the oldest sibling, was born April 28, 1914 in St. Johnsville.

After graduating from St. Johnsville High School in 1933, she attended Mildred Elley Secretarial School in Albany. Most of her working life Olga was employed with Central National Bank, being appointed manager of the St. Johnsville branch in September 1962. Her resume also included employment with several other financial companies and the Little Falls Felt Shoe in its accounting department.

Olga was very active in community activities through the years, serving as an organization's officer at times.

She was a good friend of my mom, Rose Sindici Perry. Just a couple of years ago, while perusing a 1930s St. Johnsville High School newsletter someone had given me, I discovered that Olga and my dad, Floyd Perry were an "item" in high school. Who knew?

Olga Sackett married Lorenzo Tolfa, son of Joseph Tolfa and Loretta Coggi of Supino, Italy. Olga and Larry had two children - Sandra and Joseph.

On May 26 1914, Larry came to St. Johnsville with his mother as an infant of nine months, to join his father living at 28 Bridge Street. There is more information about Larry in *La Famiglia Tolfa*.

Olga Sackett passed away June 14, 2003 in Cohoes NY at the home of her daughter, Sandra.

Larry Tolfa died on June 15, 1994 in St. Johnsville.

FULVIA SACKETT was born September 27, 1916 in St. Johnsville and died in Suffolk County, NY on January 31, 2010. I don't have much information about Fulvia, as she moved away shortly after graduation, living in the New York City area most of her life. She married Hubert P. Loustalot on February 2, 1950 in Manhattan. I don't know if they had any children.

DR. PIERRO SACKETT, better known as Peter, was born in St. Johnsville May 25, 1921. All of his records that I found state this birth date. However, the 1920 Census shows a Pierro living at 8 months old, which would make him born May 25, 1919. The only explanation would be that another son, Pierro had died and Peter was given the same name, as was very common?

Peter excelled in high school basketball like many of the other young Italian men his age. After graduation he went on to a Medical School in Philadelphia PA, then setting up his private practice as an Internist in Schoharie NY. Until his retirement, he served as the Schoharie County Coroner and in 1965 was appointed the Schoharie County Jail's physician. I don't find any details of his college attendance.

A Private in the Army, Peter was stationed in Philadelphia, PA, quite possibly where he met his wife, Kathleen Conway, a nurse. She worked in several hospitals, before assisting her husband in his medical practice.

They were married on June 18, 1949 in Pennsylvania. After celebrating 50 years of marriage, Peter passed away on Christmas Eve, December 24, 1999.

Kathleen Conway was born December 5, 1926 in Pine Grove PA and died at the age of 84 on March 21, 2011. They had five children.

~ VELINA GIOVAMPIETRO et ISAIA MACCI ~

Born in Maenza, Italy on June 25,1893, Velina "Lena" Giovampietro was the middle daughter of Felicissimi and Luisa Giovampietro. She was the last sister to come to America from Maenza on June 25, 1914 at 21 years old.

Also on board the ship was Antonia Coco, a sister of Rosa Coco, who was living in St. Johnsville at the time. You can read more of these sisters in *La Famiglia Coco*.

VELINA GIOVAMPIETRO was also the last sister to marry. While still living in Maenza she had been engaged to a soldier in the Italian Army, whom she hadn't seen for awhile. She made the decision to break off their relationship and go to America to join her two sisters. Here she met her husband, Isaia Macci.

On November 12, 1917, Velina Giovampietro joined in wedlock with Isaia Macci. They celebrated 50 years of marriage in December 1967. Isaia's brother, Guglielmo Macci and his wife, Attilia served as witnesses to the marriage. They had three children - Flora, Leondro and Angelo.

Living in the 2 Roth Street home their whole married life, they became the final owners, with the first being Isaia's brother, Guglielmo. With their passing, their daughter, Flora took over ownership and now her son, William "Bill" Austin resides there, most likely the only Italian left on Roth Street.

Lena worked at the Little Falls Felt Shoe on Hough Street, a short walk from her home, with many of her Italian lady neighbors. She and her two sisters established a very close-knit family with all of their children also being more like siblings throughout their lives.

When registering for World War I in June 1917, Isaia Macci was living and working in Herkimer at the Standard Furniture Company. Before his marriage he had moved to St. Johnsville, where he was working on the NYC Railroad and living with his brother, Guglielmo and others at the Roth Street home. He worked on the railroad much of his life, most likely recruited by his brother-in-law, Joseph Sackett. Isaia was a member of the Brotherhood of Maintenance of Way Employees.

ISAIA MACCI immigrated in 1912. He was born March 23, 1893 in Maenza, son of Angelo Macci and Costanza Terricola. He passed away on July 12, 1976 in Little Falls Hospital.

Velina Giovampietro passed away in August 1984.

FLORA MACCI AUSTIN resided almost 90 years at the 2 Roth Street address. Being born there on December 4, 1918, she was the oldest resident to ever live her entire life on Roth Street, quite possibly in the whole Italian community. At the age of 90 years, she passed away at the St. Johnsville Nursing Home on August 19, 2009.

Flora was another child of Italian immigrants who was also an exceptional student in school, always on the honor roll and active in school activities. She continued through the years serving the St. Johnsville community in many ways, working on fundraisers, as a Cub Scouts Den mother and other activities. For many years Flora was a high scoring bowler with the Friday Night Ladies League, winning numerous awards.

After her high school graduation, Flora also attended Mildred Elley Secretarial School. She was employed at Palatine Dye for a few years. In her later years, after raising her son, Bill, she was appointed by the Board of Education of the St. Johnsville Central School to serve as the Chief Financial Officer,

On Sunday December 26, 1954, Flora was united in marriage with Lawrence S. Austin.

Tragically, on Saturday evening March 10, 1956, while returning home from an evening out together, an accident on Route 5, Nelliston, caused Larry's immediate death and left their infant son, William, without a father. Flora survived some very serious injuries.

LEONDRO "Lee" MACCI was born August 28, 1921 at the family home. Lee also qualified for the list of exceptional Italian sportsmen at St. Johnsville High School. A graduate of the class of 1938, he was proficient in basketball and baseball. He played the trombone and helped organize the St. Johnsville Band, serving as president.

Lee was a World War II Veteran, serving as a Corporal with the Armed Forces from October 1942 with a discharge in 1946. He was sent to the Pilipino Island Camp in the Pacific Theatre. Upon his return home, he became a member of the Starr-Colorito Post VFW.

He was commencing a career as an Interior Decorator when he was taken seriously ill. There were many urgent requests for blood donations for him.

Leondro Macci died at Bassett Memorial Hospital, Cooperstown on August 17, 1947. He was buried with full military honors in Prospect View Cemetery, just before his 26th birthday, with some of his close friends serving as the bearers and color guard.

I recall Lee Macci as a really handsome guy. Although much older than me, I think I had a "crush" on him as a little girl, when I would see him while visiting my grandparents just two doors away.

ANGELO MACCI, born January 25, 1928, was also quite active in St. Johnsville High School activities and sports. In his sophomore year he was noted as an outstanding basketball team member, playing center on the undefeated 1944-1945 basketball team, which was coached by Ralph Anderson. As a baseball player and pitcher, he was a member of the winning St. Johnsville Saints.

Angelo served numerous times as an officer of his class and was selected as king of his senior prom with Elnora Fiacco as queen. He also was a member of the high school band.

Pvt. Angelo Macci also honored his country serving in the Army in World War II, stationed in Tokyo, Japan. After his discharge, he went on to further his education, graduating from Ithaca College with a Bachelor of Science degree in Physical Education. He taught at the Marlboro and Briarcliff Manor NY school systems.

On August 15, 1954 Angelo Macci married Diane Taylor in Madrid, St. Lawrence County. Diane was also a teacher, both at the Marlboro School at the time of their marriage. They had four children - Lee, John, Angela and Susan.

Angelo Macci passed away on November 29, 1986 at the age of 58 in Croton-on-Hudson, NY.

CESARE J. "Chester" MACCI immigrated in 1912. He lived in St. Johnsville for a short time around 1920, when he boarded with his brothers, Guglielmo "William" Macci and Isaia "Joseph" Macci. Cesare was also born in Maenza, Italy, son of Angelo Macci and Costanza Terricola on September 7, 1890.

Pvt. Cesare J. Macci volunteered for the Army in World War I in 1917. At the time he was living and working at the Standard Furniture Store in Herkimer.

He married his wife, Albertina. The couple later moved to Rensselaer, where he died December 22, 1978.

~ *La Famiglia TERRICOLA* ~

~ ROMILDA GIOVAMPIETRO et GRAZIANO TERRICOLA ~

ROMILDA GIOVAMPIETRO, known as Mildred, was the youngest of the close-knit sisters. I knew her as the sweetest little lady, strong and resilient. Like most Italian ladies, she could always be found in her aromatic kitchen preparing her special dishes. She was my neighbor for many years, first on West Liberty, then North Division Street.

When first arriving, Mildred worked at the Reaney Knitting Mills seven days a week, with payment of one-dollar per day. She was required to give one dollar back for Union dues. It seems Reaney may have taken advantage of the Italians?

Mildred was born in Maenza on February 1, 1898. She came to America as a young woman, settling into the little cul-de-sac of Roth Street, along with her two sisters, Clara and Velina. It was while living there that she met Graziano "James" Terricola, who was living and working in Utica at the time.

Romilda Giovampietro and Graziano Terricola were married on August 4, 1917 with her sister, Clara Giovampietro and husband, Giuseppe Sackett in attendance. They were the parents of three sons - Constantino, Terenzio, and Felice.

I find it interesting that Graziano's father, Contantino Terricola and Isaia Macci's mother, Costanza Terricola were cousins. I assume the two had a grandfather with a similar name so they were named after him, as was the custom. And, it usually carried down through the generations, thus making it really confusing to identify anyone.

GRAZIANO "James" TERRICOLA, arriving April 26, 1911 at 18 years of age, was born October 8, 1893 in Maenza, the son of Constantino Terricola and Vicinza Porta.

On August 26, 1918, he volunteered to serve in World War I. Private James Terricola served October 21, 1918 to April 28, 1919, being stationed overseas in the U.S. Army Infantry. While in the military, he became a U.S. citizen on September 18, 1918.

During his time in the Army, his wife, Mildred, was living at the 2 Roth Street address with their son, Constantino, among the other thirteen family members residing there.

On June 29, 1922, the couple applied for a passport to return to Italy, taking their three-year-old son, Constantino with them. They returned August 23, 1923 with another son, Terenzio, nine months old, who was born during the visit.

By the time he was 34 years old in 1930, the Prudential Life Insurance Company had employed James Terricola. The couple purchased half of a duplex home at 7 West Liberty Street, where the other side, 5 West Liberty was later shared with Clara and Joseph Sackett. By now they had their third son, Felice. Living with them was James' brother, Giuseppe, his wife, Auselia and infant son, Roland.

A tragic sledding accident took the life of their son, Terenzio in January 1934, while coasting down what has always been referred to as Fowler's hill on William Street. His cousin, Peter Sackett was on the back of the sled and suffered serious injuries. Terenzio was born in Maenza in December 1922, when the couple had returned to Maenza for a visit.

Having given up his Insurance Sales employment, on July 17, 1935 James applied for a restaurant liquor license for his business "Roman Garden", which he operated for two years. It was located at 36 Bridge Street. This address was very popular for various businesses, commencing with Carmine Terranova's Fruit Market and dissolving with John Francisco's Bridge Street Grill, when the building was torn down for the new Mohawk River Bridge.

Besides being a successful businessman, James was an active member of the American Legion, a Democratic County Committeeman and served as Town Assessor for a few years.

Sadly, on July 7, 1936 at the age of 43, James Terricola lost his life on a foggy night in a tragic automobile accident near the Beardslee Castle and old East Creek Bridge, Route 5 west of St. Johnsville, after colliding with a large fruit and vegetable delivery truck. Both drivers perished, dying instantly. Besides his immediate family, his brother, Joseph "Pepe" Terricola, four sisters and a half brother in Italy survived James.

Romilda remained at the 7 West Liberty home to raise their two sons. She worked at the Little Falls Felt Shoe Company most of her life. After her oldest son, Constantino "Cus" married, she lived with his family for the rest of her life, moving with them when they purchased the former William Lenz home on North Division Street.

Mildred passed away on September 17, 1997 at Little Falls Hospital, a resilient lady of 99 years.

CONSTANTINO "CJ/Cus" TERRICOLA and his wife, Lena Barca were well known members of not only the Italian community, but also St. Johnsville and surrounding areas. Terricola's Clothing Store was noted for quality merchandise and exceptional personal friendly service.

After returning from his service with World War II, C. J. Terricola purchased the business from Allen Samuels of Fort Plain. After serving the area for 38 years, the Terricola's retired, along with the business in February 1984. They spent their retirement years living part-time in Florida and traveling to Italy to become acquainted with other family members.

Being very familiar with Maenza, even though her parents were from Sicily, Lena has told me numerous stories about the comune. She mentioned meeting some sisters who were the daughters of my grandmother, Edvige Cacciotti Sindici's sister.

The Constantino Terricola and Lena Barca wedding took place on April 17, 1955 in St. Patrick's Catholic Church with the Rev. Joseph Reger, friend of the groom, officiating. Serving as Lena's only attendant was a close friend, Mary (Croce) Mastracco. Philip Terricola served his brother as best man, with ushers Carl Cochi and James Pietrocini. They had two children - Constance and Terence and two grandchildren.

Constantino Terricola was born in St. Johnsville May 4, 1919, to Graziano Terricola and Romilda Giovampietro, while they lived on Roth Street. He passed away just two months before his 91st birthday on February 6, 2010. Lena Barca Terricola is still living at this writing.

PHILIP J. TERRICOLA was the youngest son of Graziano Terricola and Romilda Giovampietro. He was born September 22, 1928 in St. Johnsville, where he lived his entire life of 86 years. He passed away on April 17, 2015 at St. Elizabeth Medical Center, Utica.

Phil graduated from St. Johnsville High School, class of 1947, where he also excelled in basketball and baseball. He, along with several other Italian young men, was a member of the 1944-1945 undefeated championship basketball team. Nicknamed "Flyin' Phil", he also played with the Mohawk Valley semi-pro basketball team.

Phil attended Hartwick College on a baseball scholarship and was later recruited by the St. Louis Brown's, Pine Bluff, Arkansas, along with his good friend, Dominick Fontana. He played with the St. Johnsville Saints winning baseball team. He was the first player to hit a homerun under the new lights of the Soldiers and Sailors Memorial Park in St. Johnsville. Phil was proficient in every sport he enjoyed - golf, bowling and the two aforementioned.

At one time Phil was a Metropolitan Insurance Agent. In October of 1959 he purchased Cap's Cigar Store from Arminio Caponera, selling it a year later to Maurice Everett. He worked part-time for his brother, CJ Terricola and later became a rural mail carrier with the St. Johnsville Post Office, retiring after 25 years of employment.

On June 4, 1950 Philip Terricola and Josephine Palma, high school sweethearts and king and queen of their senior prom, were united in marriage at St. Patrick's Catholic Church. They had two daughters - Phyllis and Linda and one granddaughter, Wendy Johnson. You can read more about Josephine Palma in *La Famiglia Palma*.

* Lena Barca Terricola, with the assistance of her daughter, Connie, has contributed a great deal to the Giovampietro articles. Grazie!

~ GIUSEPPE TERRICOLA et AUSILIA PALLADINE ~

Best known by many in the village as "Pepe", Giuseppe Terricola came to America at the age of 18 on September 16, 1920, to join his brother, Graziano. I also found a sister Alfresa, but could find no further information. They also had other siblings still living in Maenza.

Pepe was employed most of his life on the New York Central Railroad, serving as an Assistant Foreman under Joseph Sackett, in charge of the "right of way" gang. Before his employment there, it seems he had been living and working in Herkimer at the time he met and married Ausilia Palladine.

The daughter of Amadeo Palladine and Teresa Paccioni from Herkimer, Ausilia was born December 5, 1910 in Maenza and arrived in America on September 30, 1927. The couple was married the following year on September 19, 1928. They may have known each other in their hometown of Maenza, Italy.

In 1930 they had an infant son, Roland, and were living with his brother, Graziano and family at 7 West Liberty Street. They also had three other children - Vincenza, Carl, and Annunziata "Nancy".

The 1940 Census shows them living at 13 Bridge Street, with "Pepe" working on the railroad. A Gloversville City Census shows the couple living there from1941 to 1943, where Ausilia's parents and two sisters resided. They had originally lived in Herkimer, Ausilia's two sisters, Virginia and Floridia, being born there.

I remember all but Ausilia later living for many years at 10 Sanders Street, a duplex near the Mohawk River Bridge. Pepe's good friend, Enrico "Henry" Iacobucci and his family had been living there in 1940.

All the Terricola siblings graduated from St. Johnsville High School. Carl was in my class; we were good friends for many years.

AUSILIA PALLADINI took ill and spent the last years of her life hospitalized in Utica. I believe she had an inoperable brain tumor. She died April 29, 1954 at 43 years. Besides her immediate family, her mother, Teresa and three sisters survived her, one in Herkimer and two in Johnstown. At the time of her death, both of her sons were in the Military. Roland was serving in the Marines and Carl in the Army.

GIUSEPPE TERRICOLA was born July 25, 1902 in Maenza. He passed away on August 15, 1996 in Albany Medical Center at 94. Pepe survived a stabbing in his youth in a scuffle with another young Italian man from St. Johnsville and also a near fatal automobile accident in his later years.

ROLAND A. TERRICOLA graduated with the St. Johnsville High School Class of 1948, where he was on the basketball team. A month later, Staff Sergeant Roland A. Terricola joined the Marines on July 27, 1948. He was a 20-year Marine Corps Veteran, and honorably discharged July 31, 1968. He participated in both the Korean Conflict and Vietnam War, receiving many honorable medals. He was a lifelong member of the Marine Corps League and former member of the Mohawk American Legion in Mohawk NY.

After his retirement, Roland was employed at Griffis Air Force Base in Rome NY as a Radar Technician Supervisor. He later owned and operated the Riverside Motel in Fultonville.

1954 was a busy year for "Coke", as he was best known. He was promoted from Gunnery Sergeant to Staff Sergeant and commenced with a marriage on September 15, 1954 to Livia Iacobucci, daughter of Henry Iacobucci and Lena Jacobucci. She was able to reside with him through most of his tour of duty. They had two daughters - JoAnne and Paula.

"Coke" and Livia later divorced, but remained friends. He married a gal named Ginny. On October 1, 2004, he again remarried June Daniels from Ilion.

Born October 19, 1929, in St. Johnsville, Roland Terricola passed away on August 19, 2005 in Ilion after a long battle with cancer.

VINCENZA "Vinnie" TERRICOLA was born in 1932 in St. Johnsville. She was also a graduate of St. Johnsville, Class of 1950. Vinnie never married. As far as I know, she is still living and residing in Ilion. I have no further information of her.

CARL JOSEPH TERRICOLA entered the Army in April 1954, a year after leaving high school. Serving with the 11th Armored Cavalry, Spec. 3rd Class Carl Joseph Terricola was involved with "Exercise Sage Bush" in Louisiana, the largest Army-Air Force maneuver since World War II. He was discharged October 24, 1955.

Always being very involved with his class and extra-curricular activities in high school, Carl was selected to be a class representative on the Student Council for four years.

When Carl returned from service he met and married Darlene Frances Horning, daughter of Mr. and Mrs. Frank Horning on September 6, 1956 at St. Peter's and Paul's Catholic Church in Canajoharie. Carl's sister, Nancy, was the maid of honor; my husband, John Palma was best man. Another friend, Sam Papa served as an usher.

The couple lived with his father and two sisters in the 10 Sanders Street home for a few years before purchasing the William Wilsey home at 113 West Main Street sometime before 1960. Pepe resided with them for the remainder of his life. Nearing their retirement years they built a log home outside Lassellsville. Carl and Darlene had three daughters - Toni, Carla and Teresa.

Carl was employed with the Village of St. Johnsville for a few years as the Superintendent of the Department of Public Works. He spent most of his working life in the employ of the New York State Department of Transportation. He was also a member of the Volunteer Fire Department.

ANNUNZIATA "Nancy" TERRICOLA was born April 28, 1938 in St. Johnsville. She was named after her great-grandmother, Annunziata Olivieri, her mother, Ausilia's grandmother. I've found several Olivieri's living in St. Johnsville.

Like her siblings, Nancy graduated St. Johnsville High School and went on to Utica School of Commerce. Later, she became a certified nursing assistant, working with the Mohawk Valley Nursing Home in Ilion.

Nancy Terricola was united in marriage with Walter R. Raffle of Ilion on November 29, 1969. They had two children - Robert and Rae Marie.

Nancy passed away on February 18, 2004 at her home in Frankfort after battling cancer.

~ *La Famiglia BARCA* ~

~ ANDREA BARCA et GIACOMA BAUDONE ~

ANDREA BARCA was born in Gratteri, Sicily on January 28, 1882 to Pietro Barca and Antonia Baudone. He died in November 1966 at Albany Medical Center at the age of 84.

GIACOMA "Jennie" BAUDONE was also born in Sicily. On June 22, 1982 she died at the age of 93 at St. Elizabeth's Hospital, Utica NY.

While living in New York City, Andrea Barca married Giacoma "Jennie" Baudone, originally from his hometown in Sicily. It is said it was an arranged marriage. Married June 6, 1907 in New York City, they moved to St. Johnsville in 1908. After their move to St. Johnsville, Andrew and Jennie became the parents of six children - Anna, Lucy, Peter, Louis, Joseph and Lena.

At the time, Andrea was the only St. Johnsville Italian immigrant from Sicily and one of the first Italian businessmen in the village. He lived most of his life in the community and became well known for his bakery, the aromas of his trademark Italian bread permeating the entire village.

Andrea's cousin, Frank Barca, had arrived in St. Johnsville earlier and opened a bakery at 2 Bridge Street, which was the attached wooden structure to the building on the corner of Bridge and 1 West Main Street. The downstairs housed the bakery with family living quarters on the second floor.

Frank Barca convinced Andrea to join him in a partnership with the bakery he had established. The business flourished, but Frank decided to return to New York City, due to the cold winters.

Viewing a photo of 1912, I have discovered a Bakery sign on the 2-story building that takes up the entire space between the corner building and the 3-story brick building next door, which at one time was the I.O.O.F. – Odd Fellows Hall. The property appears much different now with a narrow driveway between the Main Street corner building and the former Odd Fellows Hall.

My father opened Perry's Luncheonette at the corner site in 1950, when Attorney Henry Lurie owned it. He utilized the attached wooden portion for storage. It later served as a Beauty Shop by Olivia Bommarito Davi.

In 1931 some robbers broke into the bakery, but were apprehended by Officer William Mac Mahon of the St. Johnsville Police Department. It seems they weren't successful with burglarizing four other businesses around the corner and realized they would definitely have a better chance of finding some "dough" at the bakery.

After 23 years at the 2 Bridge Street location, on August 1934, the Barca Bakery and it's owners moved to the East Liberty Street location next door to a lovely brick home on the corner of Bridge, which became the family home.

Andrea built a new shop with an enlarged brick oven, fully stocked with mainly Italian grocery items, with a rental apartment upstairs. It became a family affair with most of the children being employed at one time or another. It was the main source of income for siblings Anna, Peter and Louis most of their lives.

Giacoma "Jennie" was responsible for introducing pizzas and calzones to the area. Barca's pizza became the talk of the town and is instilled in the memories of so many that enjoyed the treat. The baked squares of homemade dough covered with fresh tomatoes, Parmesan cheese and sprinkled herbs was a popular item and sold as a fundraiser at basketball games during intermission. Francisco's Market couldn't keep the slices in stock for the students who hurried there after school for their special treat. It tasted as good at room temperature as fresh out of the hot brick oven.

The bakery also featured cheese calzones on Fridays, with Italian Sponge Cakes and Ciamelle "Easter Bread" available for special holidays. I doubt there wasn't a soul in St. Johnsville - Italian or not - who had never enjoyed one of Barca's homemade specialties.

I recall as a young girl, living on the corner of South Division and West Liberty across from Castrucci's Italian Market - later Papa's - sitting at the kitchen window salivating for Barca's delivery truck to come with the fresh-out-of-the-oven Italian bread, usually unsliced. We'd run to buy it along with some hand sliced salami. It was the best lunch, ever! Whenever I spent the night with my grandparents, my special breakfast treat was this same bread, hand-sliced, toasted in the oven, buttered and washed down with what I called "pla-pla" - warm milk with a beaten raw egg and a touch of sugar – a warm eggnog.

Barca's also had a special recipe for American bread. In the early years, the new bakery featured pastry made by a German baker, Fred Gehring, who was noted for his cream puffs. At one time he had his own bakery in the 18 Bridge Street building that he sold in 1930 to Gaetano "Guy" Corso for his residence and tailoring business.

One year there was a terrible snowstorm, which blocked the roads and limited deliveries to the village, causing a bread famine. With much forethought, Barca had baked extra bread and was ready to accommodate those who were able to brave the storm to get to his bakery.

Andrew Barca was a member of the Republican Club, along with Philip Caponera, Natalino Iacobucci, Arthur Palombi, John Palma and Giuseppe Sindici, my grandfather. I know there were also several others as I have a photo of them at a Republican clambake. I'm sure Andrew must have been a member of the General Pershing Italian Club, which was headquartered just down the street from his home at 36 Bridge Street.

As time went on, the sons took over the baking and delivery. When Joseph and Louis were drafted into World War II, Peter became head baker and Lena became the delivery person. After Andrea passed away in 1966, his wife and children continued the business until 1970, when Gino Amaroso became owner.

With the expansion of the Bridge Street Railroad Bridge the home was torn down in 1975 to make room for the new bridge structure. The bakery building on East Liberty Street also fell to the wrecking ball.

And so, the 62-year history of the Barca Bakery concluded in 1970 with mouth-watering memories of the famous hometown Italian Bakery. Its legacy continues even today, as later generations of the St. Johnsville village recall the flavors of the unique slice of pizza.

ANTONIA H. "Anna" BARCA, the eldest child, was born in New York City, March 30, 1910. She passed away in the St. Johnsville Nursing Home on April 16, 2008, two weeks after her 98th birthday.

Anna was a staple behind the counter of Barca's Bakery, where she spent her entire life working and living with her parents.

Anna served as a bridesmaid for both Pedro twin sisters - Julia and Bertha. She never married.

LUCY BARCA was born in 1911 in St. Johnsville and passed away in Little Falls Hospital at age 18 on May 16, 1930, following surgery.

PIETRO "Pete" BARCA, the oldest son, was born in St. Johnsville on September 13, 1913. Pete passed away in May 1979. He spent most of his life in the employ of his parents at the bakery, serving as the head baker.

Peter Barca married Luella Osterhout. She was born around 1916 and died 1968, a resident of St. Johnsville. They had two children - a daughter, Andrea and son, Peter, Jr.

LOUIS ROCCO BARCA was born March 4, 1916 in St. Johnsville and was a life long resident until his tragic death on November 1, 1970.

In June 1932 at the age of 15, Louis narrowly escaped what could have been another tragic train accident. He was a passenger in a car driven by Fred Lagerman, which crossed the train tracks on the Mindenville road. Lagerman apparently tried to beat the train. His auto was demolished and, fortunately, they both were thrown out and not seriously injured.

Louis graduated from St. Johnsville High School in the class of 1935. Until Louis and his brother, Joseph were drafted into World War II on February 7, 1942, he was actively employed in his parents' bakery. He served in the European Theatre. On November 27, 1945, at the age of 26, he was deployed back to the United States via the Queen Mary from Le Havre, France. He was honored with a Bronze Star and honorably discharged on December 3, 1945.

He returned to his employment with the family bakery. Louis suffered for years with mental health issues due to his time in service. He was an honored 25-year member of the American Legion and also participated in the Sportsman Club.

Louis Barca married Evadean Grainer, daughter of Nancy Grainer. She was born 1911 and died in 2001 in Little Falls, buried in Oak Hill Cemetery, Herkimer.

At the age of 54, on Sunday, November 1, 1970, Louis went missing. After a 41 day intensive search by local and county officials, his body was discovered at Lock 15, Fort Plain on December 11. He was buried with full military rites in Prospect View Cemetery.

GIUSEPPE CHARLES "Joseph" BARCA, the youngest of the Barca boys, better known by Joe, was born on October 22, 1919. He also worked in the family bakery until being called to the service of his country from February 7, 1942 to September 28, 1945. As a member of General Patton's Army, he was stationed in Luxembourg, Germany and awarded the Silver Star.

After returning from service, Joe married Anne J. Baudone on June 12, 1947 at a ceremony in Queens NY. She was the daughter of Giacomo and Josephine Baudone of Long Island. Joseph and Anne were the parents of an infant daughter who died at birth in 1948, and a son, Andre John, who passed away in 2002 in Florida at the age of 48. They had two grandchildren, Adriana and Joseph.

In 1940 Joseph was a member of the St. Johnsville Drum Corps, which was composed mainly of Italian young men. The 15 members worked with the Defense Unit of the American Legion participating in special events such as Armistice Day. There were 12 Italian members: Edwin Pistilli, Manager & drums; Carlo Polidori, Nick Carroll (Carelli), Fred Lagerman, Mario Iacabucci, drums; Joseph Barca, Genero Croce, bass drums; Jack Mac Gregor, symbols; and John Nirri, Joseph Croce, Richard Mancini, James Howe, bugles.

Joseph Charles Barca passed away on August 14, 1979 on Long Island, where he resided. His wife, Anne died from a heart attack almost four years later on January 14, 1983.

LENA BARCA was born on April 21, 1925 in St. Johnsville, the youngest sibling. At this writing she is the only living member of the original Barca family.

Lena was a graduate of Mildred Elley Secretarial School in Albany. She was employed at the Knolls Atomic Power Lab, part of the General Electric Company in Schenectady, until her marriage to Constantino "Cuss" Terricola. After the marriage, she assisted her husband in the operation of Terricola's Clothing Store until its closing 38 years later in February 1984.

The Lena Barca - ConstantinoTerricola wedding took place on April 17, 1955 in St. Patrick's Catholic Church with the Rev. Joseph Reger, friend of the groom, officiating. Lena's only attendant was her best friend, Mary (Croce) Mastracco. Philip Terricola served his brother as best man, with Carl Cochi and James Pietrocini as ushers. Their friend, Susan Salvagni, was organist with vocalist Janet Castellucci. A reception followed at Capece's Restaurant in West St. Johnsville. Lena and Cus had two children - Constance and Terence, and two grandchildren, Heather and Aria.

Constantino Terricola was born in St. Johnsville May 4, 1919, to Graziano Terricola and Romilda Giovampietro at 5 Roth Street. He passed away February 6, 2010 just two months before his 91st birthday.

Barca's Bakery

By Lena (Barca) Terricola

Andrea "Andrew" Barca, an Italian immigrant from Gratteri, Sicily (Palermo Province) arrived in New York City in 1903. He worked on the docks at New York Harbor unloading overseas cargo from large ships.

In 1907, he married Giacoma Baudone, who was originally from his hometown in Gratteri. Sicily. In 1908, they moved from New York City to St. Johnsville.

A large number of Italian immigrants from Maenza, Supino, Terracina, Sezze, Frosinone, and Calabria settled in St. Johnsville, but at the time Andrea was the only Sicilian to immigrate to the area. Many of the immigrants worked at local factories, but the Immigration Department was sending most of the Italian immigrants to St. Johnsville to work for the New York Central Railroad as laborers. Joseph (Zaccheo) Sacket, Antonio Mancini, Peter Tucci and Tom Triumpho were among the original New York Central foremen or employees.

Andrea's cousin Frank had arrived in St. Johnsville earlier and offered Andrea a partnership in a bakery he had purchased at 2 Bridge Street. Business flourished at the bakery, but Frank decided to return to New York City after a year because he was unhappy with the cold winters in upstate New York. Andrea then became the sole owner.

Andrea and Giacoma's children - Anna, Lucy, Peter, Louis, Joseph and Lena were born and raised in St. Johnsville.

In 1930, to accommodate his growing business, Andrea relocated to the corner of Bridge and East Liberty Streets and built and opened a bakery with an enlarged brick oven and a grocery store. The bakery and grocery store became a family operated business. Bread was delivered six days a week to businesses in Nelliston, Fort Plain, Palatine Bridge and Canajoharie and the bakery also made home deliveries.

Mrs. Barca introduced pizzas and calzones to the area. Pizzas were sold during intermission at St. Johnsville High School basketball games for 10 cents a slice, at the St. Johnsville cafeterias, at local restaurants and at the bakery. Cheese calzones were popular on Fridays. Italian Sponge Cakes and *Ciamelle* (Easter Bread) were popular on holidays. Turkeys were baked in the brick oven at Thanksgiving for a price of 75 cents. Pizzas and calzones were delivered to the local factories to be served during breaks.

To this day, there are generations of Italian-Americans and others brought up on Barca's fresh Italian bread. No one can duplicate the taste of the brick oven bread and pizza. Barca's Bakery also had a special recipe for American bread. In the early years, the new bakery even featured pastry. The head of that department was Fred Gehring, a German baker, popular for his cream puffs, which sold for 5 cents each.

In the early days, bread was delivered by horse and buggy and later by truck. Ben Terranova, a champion boxer during that era, was the delivery truck driver. Years later, Andrea's sons took over the bread making and delivery business. During World War II, Andrea's sons Joseph and Louis were drafted. Peter became head baker and daughter Lena took over the deliveries until a delivery person was hired.

Andrea died in 1966 and the family continued the business until 1970. The business was then sold to Gino Ambroso.

In 1975, the new Bridge St. Railroad Bridge was built. To accomplish the project, the State of New York tore down 13 homes and businesses. This included the family home on Bridge St and the bakery on E. Liberty St. Giacoma passed away in 1982.

Lena Terricola is Andrea and Giacoma's only living child. She lives in St. Johnsville and spends winters in Florida.

Barca Bakery original location
2 Bridge Street
Second building on right with wagon

Giacoma Barca in new location
Corner Bridge & East Liberty Street

BARCA'S BREAD RECIPE

1 pkg. Dry Yeast
2 Cups Warm Water
1 tsp. Salt
1 tsp. Olive Oil
4 Cups Flour

Cover, let rise until double, then punch down
and let rise again.
Place on floured board, make 2 balls.
Cover, let rise ½ hour. No Kneading.
Shape, place on baking sheets, rise again.
Bake 375 degrees – 30-35 minutes

Grazie! Mary Jane Polidori for sharing this bread recipe.

Christine Francisco's Recipes as featured in Enterprise & News

ARANCINI aka Rice Patties

1 lb. Rice
Small amount Liver, gizzards
or other chicken parts, chopped
1 cup Spaghetti Sauce
1 T. Grated Cheese
3 Eggs, beaten
Salt-Pepper to taste
Bit of Parsley
Cracker Meal or Dry Bread Crumbs
Boil rice, drain.
Add Sauce, 3 beaten Eggs, seasonings
Add rice & enough crumbs to hold shape
Fry in deep fat

SPAGHETTI SAUCE

1 can Tomato Paste
1 can Tomatoes
1 cup Water
Parsley
Small amount Garlic, very finely chopped
Salt-pepper to taste
Put can of Paste & cup of Water in oily pan
Add Tomatoes, garlic, parsley

Cook at least 1 hour
Add water as it thickens

The secret is slowly cooking for long time!

~ *La Famiglia MAROCCO* ~

~ ANTONIO MAROCCO et GIOVANNA ZUCCARO (SUGAR) ~

Originally from Supino, Italy, the Marocco family made their way to the little village of St. Johnsville via Ontario, Canada, with a short stopover in Little Falls. It's not clear why they first settled in Canada, as the manifest shows them arriving in New York.

Married in Italy, Antonio Marocco and Jenny Zuccaro arrived separately. I discovered a ship's manifest of arrival for Antonio Marocco on March 14, 1909, but nothing further. Antonio must have come here to check out the "land of promise" and obviously returned to Supino, as his oldest children were born there in 1911 and 1914. Giovanna came to America via Canada on October 24, 1916 with the two oldest children, Roger, age five and Paragina, age two. Antonio was already in New York.

Giovanna Zuccaro had two brothers - Rocco and Enrico "Henry" Sugar and a sister, Anna, living in St. Johnsville at the time. Anna was the wife of Pio Mancini.

The Marocco's had seven children - Ruggiero "Roger" and Paragina "Paris", born in Supino; James, Irene Louise, Ida J. and Louise, all born in Smith Falls, Ontario, Canada; and John James, born in St. Johnsville.

In 1925, while living in Little Falls, Antonio worked as a tanner finisher. They lived at 263 West Main St. with Rocco Sugar (Zuccaro), his wife, Lucia Triumpho and son Harold. It seems it was a multi-family home as there were also three other families with a total of 21 more residents in the same house. Sometime after the NYS Census had been taken in June, the couple apparently moved to St. Johnsville, where their son, John, was born in November 1925.

The Marocco's resided in the village – off and on - for the remainder of their lives at 36 East Main Street. After Antonio's death, the home was sold to Stacey and Viola Iacobucci Dunton, who also lived there until Viola's death.

By 1930 the Marocco's opened the St. Johnsville Restaurant, featuring home-cooked Italian cuisine in the downstairs area of their home. Antonio was the chief cook. Jennie served as a waitress and her father, Antonio Zuccaro, who lived with them, helped out where needed. In later years the daughters also helped out.

The St. Johnsville Restaurant was in existence for 17 years. They catered many special occasions at their venue for the Italian families – wedding receptions, bridal showers, anniversaries, birthdays, etc. I have an image of patronizing the restaurant with my parents as a young child.

On October 6, 1930 Antonio and Jennie returned from a trip to Canada with two of their children, Paris and John. In 1932 the couple returned to their hometown of Supino, Italy, sailing on the "Europa" steamship, for an extended nearly three months visit with family, stopping in England, France and Switzerland along the way.

Their daughter, Paris and Jennie's sister, Anna with her husband, Pio Mancini were left in charge of the restaurant. A passenger manifest of February 25, 1932 shows the couple returning. Antonio stated on the record he was a farmer and they were citizens of Canada, which seems odd.

Sometime in 1932 Antonio approached the village board for a permit to add on to the building. However, it was denied due to not being fireproof. Then there was the rumor that they tried to buy the Biaggio Pistilli property next door, which was a large home with a fruit and vegetable business in the front. This never transpired.

It seems the couple may have become discouraged with the St. Johnsville Restaurant. According to an Amsterdam Recorder article, the family packed up their family and returned to Ontario, Canada in October 19, 1933, giving up the proprietorship of the business to Jennie's brother, Henry Sugar and his wife, Rose Gargiulo. It had been decided to open a new restaurant in Montreal, Canada. Perhaps they weren't certain if they wanted to permanently settle in St. Johnsville?

Within 6 months, in April 1934, the Sugars had turned over the management to Angelo Lamanna. By May 1935 the Marocco family returned to their original St. Johnsville home and took over as proprietors once again. By 1930 Henry and his wife, Rose, were living in Little Falls, as was Angelo Lamanna. I don't believe Lamanna had any experience with restaurant management, as he worked on the railroad.

ANTONIO MAROCCO was born in St. Mauro Cilento, Italy on May 24, 1887 to James Marocco and Louisa Calvetti. He had two sisters, Mrs. Francisco Bracci and Mrs. Antonio Boni, both in Supino. Antonio Marocco died of a heart attack June 27, 1947, at 60 years of age, while visiting his son, Roger in Detroit. He was on vacation from his job with Palatine Dye.

GIOVANNA ZUCCARO was born in Supino to Antonio Zuccaro and Mary Ciampini on July 12, 1893. She had five siblings, Rocco and Enrico "Henry" Zuccaro (Sugar), Anna and two other sisters in Italy. She passed away at her St. Johnsville home of a heart attack at 49 years of age on December 7, 1942. Antonio may have given up the restaurant business after her passing, but still lived in the home until his passing.

RUGGIERO CARL "Roger" MAROCCO was the oldest child, born in Supino, Italy on October 5, 1911. He came to North America with his mother and sister, Paris, at the age of five, arriving in Smith Falls, Ontario, Canada.

While attending St. Johnsville High School, Roger took up the sport of boxing, earning the nickname "Rocky". Along with other local young men - George Matis, my uncle William "Bill" Perry, and Ken Watkins of Indian Castle, he was involved with raising funds for the Red Cross. In 1932, "Rocky" and George, both weighing in at 145 pounds, gave a three round exhibition, which netted $120.00 for the Red Cross. The bout was a draw! Roger only attended high school for two years; therefore, these bouts were most likely not connected with the school.

Roger was married twice. On March 28, 1940, he married Elvira Romeo from Amsterdam. They had a son and daughter and later divorced. Elvira lived on Eagle Street, just a few blocks from "Izzy Dempskey" better known as Hollywood actor, Kirk Douglas.

During his first marriage, Roger became naturalized as an American citizen in Nashville, TN and committed himself to serving his country with a career in the Army Air Force. He enlisted on April 24, 1943 in Amsterdam and was honorably discharged February 5, 1946. In April 1944 Roger was in the South Pacific and New Caldonia as a Squadron Ordinance and Bomb Disposal Officer for the 13th Jungle Air Force.

Roger had quite a military history. Commissioned as a 2nd Lieutenant after attending Officer Candidate School, he was the recipient of the Bronze Star for meritorious service during his almost three months in North Korea. I found he had enlisted twice for World War II and was also a member of the National Guard. August 19, 1950 found him re-enlisting, this time for the Korean War. He completed his military service on July 31, 1962, retiring in the state of Washington, where he met and married Maude B. Brewer on March 5, 1963 in Tacoma. She was originally from England.

Ruggierio "Roger" Marocco died a true patriot of the country he had come to love and serve on February 17, 1984 at the age of 72 in Tacoma WA. He is at peace in the Haven of Rest Cemetery in Gig Harbor WA.

PARAGINA "Paris" MAROCCO was also born in Supino, Italy and arrived on Ellis Island with her mother and brother, Riggiero in October 1916 at two years of age. Upon arrival at the port, she had been admitted to the hospital before the family was released to complete their journey to Smith Falls, Ontario, Canada to meet her father.

Most village residents know Paris as a member of the St. Johnsville Central School Cafeteria staff, where she served the students for numerous years. She obviously received her food preparation and management skills working and supervising her family's restaurant for the three months her parents visited Italy. A special lady, always with a big smile, Paris was very popular with the St. Johnsville students.

On June 27, 1937, Paris Marocco married John Papa, son of Savario "Sam" Papa and Madelina Giaquinto of Ann Street. They had three sons – John Jr, Joseph and James.

John "Jack" Papa, Jr. graduated in 1955 from St. Johnsville High School, where he was active in sports, the high school band and dramatic club. He was an active member of the Boy Scouts and also employed part-time by Palma's Esso Service Station in St. Johnsville during his high school years.

After graduation Jack joined the U.S. Navy. In November 1957, he was promoted from 3rd mate to 2nd mate. He saw two years of active duty overseas in Hawaii and Japan. While on furlough, walking down a street in Honolulu, Hawaii, he was pleasantly surprised to meet his neighbor and high school Social Studies teacher, Miss Mabel Newman. He enjoyed an afternoon's visit with her and then made plans to visit Rev. George Haggerty in Formosa, a former St. Patrick's Catholic Church priest and resident.

In her classes, Mabel Newman spoke often of her great love for Hawaii, spending many of the summer vacations there. She never married.

In 1966 Jack was living with his new family in Monterey Park, California, where he passed away at a young age. I don't have any dates of birth or death. I assume he was born in 1936. Jack was a handsome young Italian man, who reminded everyone of the movie star, Victor Mature. He was best of friends with my brother Joseph "JoJo" Perry, Jon "JJ" Cairns, Primo Iacobucci and Rush Emory - the 5 Amigos!

Paragina Marocco was born September 30, 1914 in Supino and died January 19, 1992 in St. Johnsville. John Papa was born April 7, 1914 in Fonda. He died June 7, 1997 in St. Johnsville. The couple had been separated for many years.

JAMES MAROCCO was the first-born in Smith Falls, Ontario in 1917 and passed away as an infant on April 15, 1918.

IRENE LOUISE MAROCCO was born September 17, 1918 in Ontario, five months after James died.

Celebrating 58 years of marriage, on May 5, 1940, Irene Marocco had married Cataldo Daniel Vespa, son of Gesualdo "Joseph" Vespasiano and Rosalinda Zuccaro. They were the parents of Joseph, Robert, Daniel and Rosalind. Irene passed away in Little Falls Hospital on April 7, 2003.

Cataldo Daniel Vespa was born in Pittsburgh PA on May 2, 1914 and died on April 19, 1999 in Herkimer.

Robert D. Vespi, an Air Force veteran from 1966 to 1970 and member of the American Legion passed away in Oceanside, California on March 16, 2014 at age 65. Born March 28, 1948 in Little Falls Hospital, he graduated from SUNY Utica with a bachelor's degree in business management and worked for 30 years for the United States Postal Service. I recall that he played basketball with my brother, Richard Perry, and most likely, baseball.

LOUISE M. MAROCCO was born in Smith Falls, Ontario on January 12, 1920. She married William L. Starna in St. Patrick's Church on August 25, 1940. They were the parents of four children - Norinne J., William A., David P., and Richard T.

After their marriage, Bill Starna served in the Navy from October 28, 1943 to December 24, 1945 during World War II. The son of Henry and Antoinette Starna of Little Falls, William L. Starna was born on September 26, 1916 and passed away on October 28, 1985 in St. Johnsville.

Louise was a registered nurse serving in the Emergency Room of Little Falls Hospital for many years. After Bill's death she sold their lovely home on Monroe Street Extension to Daniel and Maxine Matis and moved to Cooperstown, where she passed away at age 94 at the Focus Rehab Nursing Center.

IDA JENNIE. MAROCCO was born in Smith Falls on June 30, 1921. She graduated from Utica School of Business. Ida worked and lived most of her life in Johnstown after marrying Salvatore Pagano on September 15, 1946. They had a son, John and daughter, Sallie.

Ida J. Marocco passed away at the age of 87 in Bennington VT on July 16, 2007.

Ida's son, John Pagano, has shared some interesting information regarding the Pagano family.

"Antonio Pagano came to America in 1929 from Graniti, Sicily. He had four sons - Antonio, Salvatore, Carmelo and Giuseppe. They were all involved with Pagano Gloves, Inc. on Church Street, Johnstown, until the death of the youngest son, Joseph, when the factory closed.

On December 1966, Ida's husband, Salvatore "Sam" died at the young age of 46 in Johnstown. He had contracted tuberculosis on his 1929 trip to America at the age of eleven. Through the years he was plagued with other diseases related to the leather business. Salvatore was born on New Year's Day, January 1, 1919 in Graniti, Sicily.

The Pagano and Fioravanti families were instrumental in the expansion of the glove industry in Johnstown and Gloversville."

William Fioravanti, author of "A Sicilian's Journey", recently joined Italians of St. Johnsville. In his novel he tells personal stories of his family's struggles to fit into their new surroundings and make a decent living to support the family. Fioravanti tells many fascinating tales of his ancestors. I recommend reading the book, which will give you more insight into the lives of all of the Italian immigrants. As I have, you'll recognize many surnames from the "twin" Glove Cities.

John Pagano and William Fioravanti are the best of friends, as is William's brother, Tom, with whom Pagano has traveled to Europe.

It is not known with later generations that mostly Sicilians settled in Johnstown with Napoletano's from Southern Italy settling in Gloversville. At the time the two Italian factions did not get along.

* Grazie, John Pagano, for sharing this interesting information.

JOHN J. MAROCCO was the only child born in St. Johnsville on November 17, 1925.

He graduated from St. Johnsville High as president of the Class of 1943, being very active in school activities. Delaying his further education, John followed his brother, Roger's lead with serving in the military. He joined the Marine Corps on January 18, 1944 - serving 15 years - until March 17, 1959. He was stationed at Camp Le Jeune, NC and promoted from Corporal to Sergeant in 1951.

After his discharge, John went on to Hartwick College in Oneonta with a major in Business Administration. He was also active at college, attaining the Dean's List and serving as treasurer of the sophomore class. He worked as a Cost Accountant at the Utica General Electric. At this time he was living at 7 William Street, St. Johnsville.

John Marocco married Justine Marie Finneran on her 24th birthday, August 2, 1954, in her hometown of Ithaca at the Immaculate Conception Church. Justine was a faculty member with the St. Johnsville school system. Ushers were his nephew, James Papa and John's good friend, Joseph Mastracco, who had married another St. Johnsville faculty member, Rosalie Finch. John and Justine were the parents of four children - Andrea, Claire, Felice Justine and James.

The couple moved to San Diego at some point in time. John passed away June 26, 1982 at the young age of 56 and was buried with honors at the Fort Rosecrans National Cemetery in San Diego.

Born August 2, 1930 in Ithaca, Justine Finneran died April 17, 2015 in San Diego at age 84.

La Famiglia Marocco

Back: Ida, Paris, Ruggiero, Irene
Front: Antonio, Louise, Giovanna, John

~ *La Famiglia ZUCCARO aka SUGAR* ~

~ ANTONIO ZUCCARO et MARIA CIAMPINI ~

The Zuccaro aka Sugar family is better known in the adjoining city of Little Falls. However, two of the sons - Rocco and Enrico "Henry" were original immigrants to St. Johnsville. Two of their sisters, Giovanna "Jennie" Marocco and Anna Mancini lived in St. Johnsville most of their lives. They also had two other sisters still in Italy, Leona and America, wives of Francisco Bracci and Antonio Boni. Obituaries confirm these are the only six siblings.

The Zuccaros have surfaced numerous times in my research. I've discovered the name with both the St. Johnsville and Little Falls families. According to Census records, the St. Johnsville family seems to be related to the Joseph Tolfa and James Battisti families, amongst others. There may also be a relationship with the Giovanni "John" Francisco family through his wife, Mary Zuccaro. This would be the Bridge Street tavern owner.

I also found a Rosa Sugar, who was the grandmother of Harry Palombi. She was married to Lawrence Battisti. They were parents of Amelia Battisti, Harry's mother.

A manifest of a Massachusetts bound passenger ship dated April 15, 1903 shows an Antonio Zuccaro, age 35 with his son, Cataldo, age 15, going to Giuseppe Ciampini's in Canajoharie. These might possibly be cousins of this Zuccaro family?

However, I'm unable to find any connections to any of these families without a great deal of detailed research?

ANTONIO ZUCCARO seems to have come to America and lived in St. Johnsville, as I located a news item in the Amsterdam Recorder, dated August 6, 1912 with his name listed as a member of the Italian "Intangible Roman Society of Mutual Aid". Another article of June 1928 states he will be a bugle player in the newly formed Little Falls American Legion Drum and Bugle Band.

MARIA CIAMPINI I find no information for Maria Ciampini except that according to some other family trees, the couple had four childen – Cataldo, Guy, Giovanna and Rocco. Some of the information I have discovered is rather confusing.

GIOVANNA "Jennie" ZUCCARO was born July 12, 1893 and died at her home at age 49 of a heart attack on December 7, 1942. She seemed to be a very hard worker, raising six children while also tending to the family's "St. Johnsville Restaurant" with her husband, Antonio Marocco. You can read more of her family story in *La Famiglia Marocco*. Her brothers, Rocco and Henry, were instrumental in bringing her family to the village.

ROCCO ZUCCARO was born August 16, 1896 in Supino. He immigrated in 1912 with Guy Sugar, who is most likely Cataldo and his cousin. Rocco's brother, Enrico "Henry" came later with their sister, Anna.

During World War I, a group from the Home Defense Reserve got together and formed the "Home Guard Band", with Rocco as the Leader. The band was made up with all but one Italian. His future wife, Elizabeth "Lucia" Triumpho and her sister, Philomena Triumpho, sang with the band during 1917 and 1918. (You'll find the history of the Home Guard Band in another article.)

In 1920 Rocco and his cousin, Guy, were boarders with another cousin, Pieter Battisti (not farmer) and family on Averill Street. Pieter is the brother of James Battisti. Rocco was working at Union Mills knitting mill at the time.

On June 24, 1920 Rocco Sugar, son of Antonio Zuccaro and Mary Ciampini, and Elizabeth "Lucia" Triumpho, daughter of Giuseppe Triumpho and Carmine Salvia were married at St. Patrick's Church. They had a son, Harold born in 1922 in Little Falls, where they were living at the time.

1925 Census records show Rocco and Lucia were living in Little Falls with their son. Rocco was working as a carpenter.

Elizabeth "Lucia" Triumpho was born in 1902 on the family farm in Mindenville. She was the daughter of Giuseppe Triumpho and Carmine Salvio.

Elizabeth passed away at the young age of 33 in May 1935 in the Utica State Hospital, where she had resided for a few years. I am wondering if she had suffered from "postpartum depression", which they didn't recognize and know how to treat at the time?

By 1940 Rocco had married Nellie Massucci from Little Falls and had a daughter, Dolores. Rocco was working in the bicycle factory.

Rocco Zuccaro (Sugar) passed away on January 5, 1944 at Faxton Hospital, Utica. He is buried in Prospect View Cemetery, St. Johnsville with his first wife, Lucia Triumpho.

ENRICO "Henry" ZUCARRO, a shoemaker, arrived in America at the age of 22 on August 10, 1921 with his sister, Anna, 17. They were headed to 15 Sanders Street to locate their older brother, Rocco, who was now married to Lucia Triumpho, apparently living with her parents.

It seems the two brothers had a lot of musicality in their genes. Henry also formed his own orchestra, providing music for dancing at a Sons of Italy affair in Fonda, among many other affairs in the 1930s. Besides playing the clarinet, he was noted as one of the "Sax Kings", a trio with Ed Wood and Temple Stahler.

Sometime in the early 1930s, Henry (Sugar) Zuccaro met and married Rose Gargiulo, daughter of Alfredo Gargiulo and Concetta Remini of Little Falls.

In October 1933, Henry's sister Jennie and her husband, Antonio Marocco decided to leave their St. Johnsville Restaurant and return to Montreal, Canada with their family to open a restaurant business there. Henry with his wife, Rose, took over the proprietorship. Within 6 months, in April 1934, the Sugars had turned over the management to Angelo Lamanna of Little Falls. By this time the couple also had an infant son, Henry, Jr.

Enrico "Henry" Zuccaro was born June 26, 1899 in Supino and died August 13, 1979 in Little Falls.

Rose Gargiulo was born May 15, 1910 in the Bronx and passed away May 21, 2008 in Little Falls, a week after celebrating her 98th birthday.

Their son, Henry Zuccaro, Jr. taught 6th grade in the St. Johnsville Elementary School and later became Superintendent of the Little Falls schools system. His wife, Leslie, was also a teacher for many years. I believe they divorced and Henry remarried.

Henry Zuccaro, Sr. and Rose Gargiulo also had a daughter, Rosemarie A., who married Alvaro J. Peruzzi of Little Falls, September 16, 1956. They were the parents of twin girls. Rosemarie passed away in 2008. I believe Alvaro is a cousin to the Peruzzi family of St. Johnsville?

ANNA ZUCCARO was born in Supino on September 15, 1904. She died January 19, 1945 at Little Falls Hospital at 40 years of age. She had recently become a US citizen in 1940.

On September 30, 1922, Anna Zuccaro, daughter of Antonio Zuccaro and Mary Ciampini, married Pio Mancini at St. Mary's Catholic Church in Little Falls. They had one son, Richard. After their marriage they moved to 61A East Main in the adjoining duplex of Pio's brother, Frank Mancini and his wife, Louisa Fiorini.

Anna was an active member of the St. Johnsville Navy Mother's Club of America, serving as a color bearer. As a member of St. Patrick's Church, she was also active in the Altar Rosary Society.

Immigrating July 3, 1920, Pio Mancini came to join his brother Frank. He worked at the Little Falls Felt Shoe most of his life. Pio was born September 15, 1897 in Rome, Italy. He died June 3, 1982 in Milton FL where he had retired after Anna's death.

You will find more information on Anna Zuccaro and her family in *La Famiglia Mancini*.

My dear friend, Betty Bilobrowka, wrote this article many years ago.
It personifies everything that I feel and have been trying to convey through the Italian Immigrants of St. Johnsville.

Ethnic Italian Immigrants Enriched Community

Of all the ethnic groups that have come to the St. Johnsville area, surely none have enriched our community more than the Italians. Their love for the earth, their fruitful gardens, their belief in the values of education and of good hard work, their fabulous cooking, their devotion to the better things of life – music, song, dance, art – and their fervent religious beliefs have affected the lives of all of us in our town.

Let's look at one family that exemplifies the above. Joseph A. and James C. Triumpho (originally Trionfo) came to America in 1888, like so many of their fellow citizens to work on the railroads and to seek the better life America promised. At first they worked on the New York Central in the Amsterdam area, but in 1891 they were transferred to the West Shore Railroad and moved to St. Johnsville, the first Italians in the area. By 1894 they were able to send for their wives and children in Italy. Joe's son, Thomas, was just 5½ years old, just the right age for entering school in the old Mindenville one-room schoolhouse.

In 1896 Joseph moved his family from Mindenville to St. Johnsville, residing on Sanders Street. There, son Thomas grew up. At age 23, Thomas went back to the land of his birth, Italy, to seek a wife. He found one Louise Bovino and they returned to the United States where Thomas soon became foreman of a New York Central crew in Amsterdam at first and then in St. Johnsville. But Thomas had, like his forefathers, a love for the land and growing things. In 1918 Thomas purchased the old Vedder farm in the town of St. Johnsville, and there he and Louise raised a family of twelve children. The farm is still the Triumpho farm, owned and operated now by Thomas' youngest son, Richard. Richard would be the first to agree that farming today is hardly the same as it was when his father Thomas started out.

Farming was extremely hard work in those days, demanding of both time and labor. There was no such thing as spare time. Just clearing the land, for example, cutting back the brush or pulling weeds like hawthorns was an endless task that had to be done over and over.

Winters were cold and presented special problems. "One winter", Richard recalls, "was so cold that even the manure froze in the gutters of the barn and Ma and Pa had to wear sheepskin coats and felt boots to keep warm as they did the milking (by hand, of course.)"

The other seasons of the year brought their own problems – years of drought, violent winds and rain that could flatten a field of corn in minutes, thunderstorms that drenched the ungathered hay lying in the fields, untimely frosts, swarms of hungry insects, or pounding hail. Nature is so often cruel. But father Thomas always looked on the good side. Despite the drenched hay at his feet, he would look up at the sky and exclaim, "What a beautiful rain!"

In those days the farmhouse used chuck wood in its furnace and kitchen stove. Each fall the old woodshed had to be filled with wood enough to last the winter. This was wood that had been cut and gathered a year ago and allowed to dry. But, this year's new supply for next year must be gathered. It took many loads on the big flat-bottomed bobsled pulled by a team of horses.

The bobsled was used for pleasure, too. The boys would spread a layer of straw in the sled and fetch the big bearskin rug for warmth. Sleigh bells on the horse collar added music to their merriment. And off the family would go, sometimes to visit, sometimes just to ride. And, almost always singing as they went.

And so the years passed. Thomas and Louise were typical Italian immigrants. They worked hard, raised their children to be God-loving, saw to it that they were educated, and taught them to love America and to respect others.

There were, of course, other Italians who, each in his own way contributed to the development of St. Johnsville. Who can forget the gift of music that James Pietrocini gave to our town. Or Prosper Napoleon, the policeman who was killed in the line of duty. (Please refer to *La Famiglia Napoleone* for Prosper's story.) Or Carmen Terranova, whose fruit stand was so tempting and so attractive. Or Guy Corso, whose plant offered employment to so many. Or Christine Francisco, whose dedication to her church was so great. And there were so many others. Indeed, St. Johnsville would be a poorer place without the rich heritage of our Italian families. May they never lose their traditions.

Written by Elizabeth "Betty" Bilobrowka. Shared with permission of her daughters, Ann, Jean and Rhea.

La Famiglia Triumpho
Giuseppe Triumpho, Thomas, Lillian, Frank
Carmina holding Joseph, Jr., Marie, Philomena, Lucia

~ *La Famiglia TRIUMPHO* ~

Francescantorio Trionfo and Livia Pitta were married in 1850 in Italy and had five sons - Vincenzo, Giuseppe, Nicholas, Domenico and Rocco. The first son to immigrate was Nicholas, who came to the U.S. in 1887. Domenico came in 1889; both of them settled in the Bronx in New York City.

Giuseppe came in 1892 and brought his 4-year-old son Domenico with him. Vincenzo also came in 1892, but without his wife, Vincenza Teta and daughters. Giuseppe (Joseph) and Vincenzo (James) eventually settled on farms in St. Johnsville with their families for the remainder of their lives. Joseph had the distinction of being the very first Italian to settle in St. Johnsville, followed by his brother, James.

Giuseppe and Vincenzo both first worked on the New York Central Railroad in Amsterdam. They were later transferred to the West Shore Railroad and moved to St. Johnsville.

Giuseppe sent for his wife, Carmina, in 1894, who reunited with him and their now 5-year-old son, Domenico, in Amsterdam. Vincenzo was not able to send for his wife and daughters until 1898.

~ VINCENZO C. TRIUMPHO et VINCENZA MERI TETA ~

VINCENZO C. "James" TRIUMPHO arrived in America in 1892, residing first in Amsterdam, where he worked on the New York Central Railroad with his brother, Joseph. They were later transferred to the West Shore Railroad and sent to South St. Johnsville (Mindenville).

I discovered a Passenger Manifest for a Vincenzo Triumpo, age 28 leaving Vietri, Italy and arriving in New York on April 13, 1893. Perhaps this might be our Vincenzo, as his brothers were in the Bronx? The early passenger manifests did not have as much information as the later ones did.

Coming directly to the town of Minden, James chose a farm home to begin his new life. The 1900 NYS Census shows James and his wife, Meri, with their two daughters, living in Minden. He was working on the railroad until 1915, before he was able to buy the farm and become a full time farmer. By 1920 he was the owner of the farm, valued at $4000.

James C. Triumpho and Meri "Marie" Teta were married in Balvano in 1880. Meri followed James to America, thence Minden in 1897 with their two daughters - Mary and Lillian. They had six children, with only the two girls surviving. Meri was quite a bit older than James.

While living in Balvano, James was a great friend of Dominick Capece. Instrumental in bringing Capece over in 1905, James later made arrangements to meet Dominick's wife and children at Ellis Island, bringing them to St. Johnsville on the New York Central train to unite with their husband and father. You can read about *La Famiglia Capece* in another article.

By July of 1931, James and other family members were residing in the new home that James had built on the Mindenville land. A lightning strike had hit the original home, causing considerable damage. That home was now being used for storage.

Vincenzo C. Triumpho was born October 15, 1860 in Vietri and died on March 14, 1945 in the Amsterdam Hospital. He is buried in Prospect View Cemetery in St. Johnsville.

VINCENZA MERI "Marie" TETA was born in Balvano in December 1854. She suffered a stroke due to a heart ailment and died sometime between 1915 and 1916.

MARY TRIUMPHO, the oldest daughter, was born September 28, 1889 in Balvano.

Mary Triumpho married Pietro Tucci, who was much older. The Tucci family lived most of their lives on the James Triumpho family farm. They had four children - James L., Angelina Marie, Lillian and Anthony.

As did her mother, Mary died suddenly at the farm home on May 15, 1934, of a stroke brought on by heart disease. Peter continued to reside on the farm with their children, assisting his father-in-law in the maintenance of the farm. He later moved to Palatine Bridge, where he passed away.

James Tucci died tragically at the age of 17, as he was walking home on the railroad tracks in 1924, another victim of the New York Central railroad. His father, Peter worked for the railroad.

LILLIAN "Livia" TRIUMPHO was born in 1890 in Balvano. She passed away in 1990, living a long life of almost 100 years.

Lillian was married twice. On October 11, 1913 she joined in marriage with her first husband, Costantino Bovino from Amsterdam; they had two sons - Salvatore and Vincent Bovino. Costantino died in 1918 at the young age of 30 during the Influenza epidemic. Perhaps Lillian's marriage to Bovino was pre-arranged by her cousin, Thomas and his wife, Louisa Bovino?

On June 11, 1928, Lillian Triumpho Bovino married Pasquale Catena of Newark NJ at the Fort Plain Catholic Church. Both had been previously married. They moved to Newark, where she lived out her life. Lillian and Pasquale had a daughter, Josephine.

I discovered a gravestone in a Newark cemetery with both the Catena and Bovino surnames etched. Lillian was buried here with her second husband, Pasquale Catena, along with her two sons, Salvatore and Vincent Bovino and their wives.

~ GIUSEPPE A. TRIUMPHO et CARMINA SALVIA ~

GIUSEPPE A. "Joseph" TRIUMPHO was the second son of Francescantorio Trionfo and Livia Pitta of Balvano, born March 14, 1864 in Vietri, Italy. Before leaving for the new world from Balvano, he and Carmina "Millie" Salvia were married in 1887.

Giuseppi immigrated in 1891, almost a year before his brother, James, traveling together with his wife, Carmina, and son, Thomas Franklin Dominico, the most well known of the Triumpho families. It was quite unusual for a husband and wife to emigrate together. Usually the husband arrived first and the wife and children followed after the husband had raised enough money to pay for their passage. I also found that he might have arrived February 2, 1894? Perhaps he had returned to Italy?

It is quite evident that the Triumpho family was the very first to come to St. Johnsville to literally plant their roots, which are still deep with descendant Richard Triumpho carrying on the tradition of the family dairy farm.

The 1900 Census shows the family living in Minden, where they resided for nine years; Joseph is working on the railroad. The family now has four more children - Lillian, Frank, and twins Mary and Anthony, three months old. It seems Anthony passed away before 1905, as I do not find him listed in any census records after 1900. By now, Libbie and Emma have joined the family. They are living at 15 Sanders Street in the home they purchased from Thomas Kinney, with boarders, Tony Rose and Daniel Lamont.

Still living at 15 Sanders Street in 1910 and 1915, Joseph is working on the Barge Canal. Thomas has left the nest and started his own family. Joseph and Carmina have another son, Joseph, making their total number of children eight with seven living.

By 1920 Joseph has been able to purchase his own dairy farm, with his son, Thomas's family residing with him, along with his wife, Louisa and their four children - Joseph, Anthony, James and Carmen. At the time, Joseph's wife, Millie, was living at 15 Sanders Street with their children - Frank, Mary, Elizabeth and Emma.

In the 1925 NYS Census, Joseph and Millie are living on Mechanic Street with a daughter, Philomena "Emma", age 21. Joseph is working as a farmer.

1930 shows that he owns the 15 Sanders Street home, valued at $1000. He still works the farm. Carmina and Joseph have their grandson, Eugene Forte, living with them.

In the 1940 Census, at 76 years old, Joseph is still working the farm with their son, Frank and grandchildren, Jane Forte, age 23 and Eugene Forte, 19, who also works on the farm. The oldest son, Thomas and his growing family now live on a farm nearby.

Giuseppe Triumpho passed away shortly after the 1940 Census on July 19, 1940 at his farm home from a short illness. His obituary described him as an "industrious tiller of the soil." Situated on the Vedders Corner Road, he had purchased the farm from Jonathan Vedder.

CARMINA SALVIA passed away suddenly at home on February 19, 1943, stricken with a heart attack. She was born in Balvano on September 4, 1864.

The following eight children of Giuseppe and Carmina are listed by dates of birth. I shall concentrate on the story of Thomas and his family in a separate article. I have already written the story of Elizabeth in *La Familia Zuccaro aka Sugar*, but will repeat here.

THOMAS FRANKLIN (DOMINICO) was the oldest sibling. His family history follows.

LILLIAN R. TRIUMPHO was born November 13, 1894 in Minden. She passed away suddenly on November 3, 1966, while waiting for a bus at the Albany Bus Terminal, Albany NY, traveling back home after visiting friends. She was a registered nurse.

On December 30, 1915, Lillian married Antonio Forte of St. Johnsville, son of Carlo Forte and Giovanna DiNota. They had two children - Jane and Eugene.

Lillian and her children lived on the farm with her parents, Giuseppe and Carmina Triumpho, while the children were growing up. 1920 Census records state that Lillian is a widow, living with her father, James and her two children.

It seems the couple did live in Amsterdam in 1924, after the 1920 Census. I found articles about Antonio being in the Taxi business in Amsterdam. I find no dates of birth or death for Antonio Forte, although he was mentioned in Lillian's obituary as having died years ago.

Jane and Eugene Forte apparently lived most of their young years on the farm and attended St. Johnsville schools. Eugene served his country in World War II as a Sergeant in the Army Air Corps, stationed in New Orleans LA. He later became an Air Traffic Controller. He was buried with honors in the Chattanooga National Cemetery in Tennessee January 24, 2017.

FRANK JOHN TRIUMPHO was born February 9, 1897 on Sanders Street in St. Johnsville. He attended St. Johnsville High School. He learned the printing trade by working part-time after school and later in a regular job as a compositor, setting hot lead type for Lou MacWethy, editor and publisher of the *Enterprise & News*.

Frank served in World War I. Although his discharge papers do not express this, he came home with significant trauma, which caused him to be confined in various VA Hospitals. His brother, Thomas served as his surrogate during this time. After his honorable discharge, the Dolgeville Republican newspaper employed him. He later worked with his father on the family farm.

Frank died in 1952 at the Veteran's Hospital in Canandaigua, NY. He was given a veteran's burial in the family plot in the Prospect View Cemetery in St. Johnsville. Retired editor, Lou MacWethy wrote this eulogy: *"May I have a bit of space to offer tribute to a lifelong friend and a clean character. Frank Triumpho came to me as a boy to learn the printing trade. At first, he worked after school and later had a regular job as floor man and compositor. He learned quickly and rarely had to be told twice. He had a passion for neatness and in a printing office, where many materials are constantly in use, this trait is as indispensable as it is rare. Once he saved the plant from burning by his quick wit. He came in early to light the linotype melting pot. He was alone and it was dark. The pot had developed a leak and he found himself in a roaring blaze. He did not run; he grabbed the fire extinguisher and promptly put out the blaze. It was cool thinking and saved the plant.*

He left to join the Navy in World War I and immediately was assigned to the print shop aboard the ship. Near the close of the war he suffered a mental breakdown and was incapacitated more or less the rest of his life, but the government took care of him. Besides his yen for order and neatness, he possessed a fine sense of honor and righteousness. He would have risen high had he not suffered the handicap, which barred him from his chosen occupation. He was a casualty of war, one among thousands who should not be, but mostly are, forgotten."

MARIA E. and ANTHONY TRIUMPHO were twins, born on February 17, 1900 in Minden. Apparently, Anthony died at birth, as I don't find him in any further records.

In December 1933, Marie Triumpho married John William Price of Canada, a World War I veteran. I found a marriage certificate stating that her surname was Eisenberg? Not certain if this was them? John died in 1942-43, suddenly, at Little Falls Hospital. He had been a farm worker for two years in St. Johnsville, presumably on Marie's parents', Giuseppe and Carmina's farm?

Living in Utica, Marie also served as a registered nurse. She died March 4, 1987.

ELIZABETH "Lucia" TRIUMPHO was born in 1902 on the family farm. In 1918 she was employed as a switchboard operator at Glen Telephone Company on Bridge Street - the very first telephone company in St. Johnsville.

On June 4, 1920 Elizabeth "Lucia" Triumpho married Rocco Zuccaro (Sugar), son of Antonio Zuccaro and Mary Ciampini, in St. Patrick's Catholic Church. Her sister, Lillian Forte served as matron-of-honor with Anthony Sugar as best man. A wedding breakfast was served at the Triumpho home on Sanders Street. The couple made their first home on Monroe Street. They had a son, Harold, born in 1922, while living in Little Falls.

Rocco Zuccaro was the leader of the Home Guard Band, comprised of mostly Italian musicians. Elizabeth and her sister, Philomena, sang with the band during 1917-1918.

In May 1935, Elizabeth passed away at the young age of 33, while confined in the Utica State Hospital, where she had resided for a few years. She had been ill for many years, quite possibly with "postpartum depression"?

PHILOMENA "Emma" TRIUMPHO, aka Phyllis, was born in1903. She passed away at her home in New Rochelle NY on December 3, 1947 at the age of 43. She was married to Stephen Comstock. They had a daughter, Shirley.

JOSEPH TRIUMPHO was the youngest sibling, born 1906. From news articles I have discovered, it seems he may have been the rebel of the family in his youth? He did play on a St. Johnsville school baseball team as a catcher. I find no details of his birth or death.

After he graduated from St. Johnsville High School, he attended the Utica School of Commerce and studied business. He then moved to Homewood IL, a suburb of Chicago, and married Diana Sabia. Joseph and Diana had five sons - Joe Jr., Carmen, Robert, Frank, Thomas and one daughter, Mary Ann.

Joseph and Diana went into the retail grocery business as the "Triumph Supermarket." He dropped the "o" from the name when he moved west.

~ THOMAS FRANKLIN DOMINICO TRIUMPHO et LUIGIA BOVINO ~

Thomas Triumpho, his wife, Louise Bovino and their family were well-respected members of the St. Johnsville dairy farming community for many years. Thomas' father, Giuseppe, and uncle, Vincenzo were the very first farmers emigrating from Italy, not to mention the very first immigrant Italians to locate in St. Johnsville.

Thomas immigrated to St. Johnsville with his father and his uncle Vincenzo in 1892. They lived first in Amsterdam and in 1894 moved to South St. Johnsville (Mindenville) when the two brothers were transferred to the West Shore Railroad. Thomas was the right age of six to enter school in the old Mindenville one-room schoolhouse.

In February 1894, Giuseppe sent for his wife, Carmina, and they all lived in Mindenville, where Lillian was born. In 1896, Joseph moved his family to St. Johnsville, where son Frank was born. For the next seven years, Thomas grew up on Sanders Street with the rest of the family. In 1907, at age 18, Thomas Dominico began working on the railroad with his father, Giuseppe.

On October 26, 1912, while living and working in Amsterdam as a foreman of the New York Central Railroad, Thomas "Dominico" Triumpho applied for a passport. He returned to Italy to seek a wife and his father, Joseph went with him to witness his marriage to Luigia Bovino on January 23, 1913. On February 7, 1913, Domenico and Luigia embarked from Naples on the SS Princess June and arrived in New York 13 days later on February 20, 1913. The ship's manifest shows that his father, Giuseppe accompanied them and all were designated U.S. Citizens, Luigia Bovino through her husband.

After their marriage, the couple first settled in Amsterdam, where Thomas returned to his employment with the New York Central Railroad. Their first two sons were born in Amsterdam. By May 22, 1916, when he was transferred to South St. Johnsville, Thomas had worked on the railroad for nine years and they relocated to 15 Sanders, where they had another son, before buying and moving to the farmstead in 1917, where nine more of the twelve siblings were born. The farm home was the family's final move.

His father, Giuseppe "Joseph", was living with them while his mother, Carmina still resided at the home on Sanders Street. Giuseppe went back and forth to work the farm with Thomas. In 1925, Giuseppe and Thomas Domenico bought an adjoining farm and Giuseppe moved his wife and children to that farm.

November 19, 1931 brought a fire that destroyed the wagon house along with numerous tools and farm equipment. Fires were quite prevalent with farmers at this time, usually caused by lightning strikes or wood stoves, and intensified by high winds.

In 1950, Thomas and Louise returned to their hometown of Balvano for a two-month visit, returning to their farm home on August 23, 1950.

Thomas Triumpho and Peter C. Battisti, another noted St. Johnsville dairy farmer in the Kringsbush area north of Averill Street, became great friends and worked together as active spokesmen and representatives of the many other farmers in the area. Joining them in their dedication to the farmers were George Matis and Charles Failing, both long time farmers. During a milk strike between 1939-1940, fearing violence and major damages to businesses, Triumpho and Battisti approached the village board requesting that the Dairymen's League plant be shut down until the strike was over. Their plea was denied. I don't know if anything further came of this?

In 1942 Thomas semi-retired from farming, and turned the business over to his sons. He went back to work with the New York Central Railroad in Utica in their mail and baggage department, retiring in 1954.

THOMAS FRANKLIN DOMINICO TRIUMPHO was born April 22, 1888. He passed away at his farm homestead on Triumpho Road, after an illness of several years, on May 27, 1956.

LUIGIA "Louise" BOVINO was born March 10, 1892 in Balvano to Antonio Pietro Bovino and Anna Rocco. She was a senior member and founder of an orphanage and nursing home in Balvano. Along with her remaining family in Italy, she supported this project. At one time an earthquake damaged the homes and caused them to be relocated.

At the age of 75, Louise attained her Equivalency Diploma through attending the evening classes of St. Johnsville High School. On her 90th birthday, before her passing on December 11, 1982, she received a congratulatory letter from President Ronald and Nancy Reagan.

JOSEPH J. TRIUMPHO, the oldest child was born December 15, 1913 in Amsterdam. He died September 28, 1994 in Little Falls Hospital.

Joe was a well-known contributing member of the St. Johnsville community. He was active in local politics, once serving as a Town Justice and as a village businessman.

On June 18, 1943, Joseph J. Triumpho married Elizabeth "Betty" Atwood, music instructor at the Oppenheim-Ephratah Central School, where she was employed for eight years. After their marriage, they made their first home at 112 West Main Street in St. Johnsville. On December 3, 1945 Joe and Betty purchased the farm of his late grandfather, Joseph Triumpho, on Triumpho Road.

In February 1950, after Betty's retirement, the couple entered into a partnership with Willard and Marian Beard, when they purchased the combined businesses of Sutherland's Men's Store and the Rose Shoppe from

Ralph Schlup, who had purchased it from Roy Sutherland, the original owner for many years. The Rose Shoppe was next door to the Sutherland store at the time, but later moved to the east corner of Main and Bridge Streets when the name was changed to "The Betty-Jo Shoppe." Joe continued to work on the farm. Sometime after 1956, they sold the Betty-Jo Shoppe to Ann Kraft and Sutherland's to Walter "Buzz" Davis, who had been employed there with Schlup. In 1971-1972 Betty returned to teaching fourth grade at the D.H. Robbins Elementary School.

In a partnership with his brother Anthony, Joseph Triumpho later supervised for several years the Triumpho Insurance Agency branch in St. Johnsville, located in the little building on the corner of Main and Mechanic Streets, which formerly housed the Rapacz Agency. He attended an intensive insurance training course in Hartford CN with the Traveler's Insurance Company in October 1968, which allowed him to sell all phases of insurance.

I remember Betty Triumpho during my Brownie and Girl Scout years, as my troop leader. We would meet in an upstairs room at the Community House once a week after school. Along with learning all the aspects of being a good scout, we worked on many creative projects. I still recall the colorful woven baskets we designed out of a flimsy paper plate and colorful rolled crepe paper, reminiscent of the straw baskets made by the southern Gulla families. My membership was so interesting and fun. She was a very talented lady with her musicality, performing her songs and piano solos, along with encouraging students to pursue music.

Elizabeth "Betty" Atwood was born May 1, 1918 in Waverly. She passed away on April 4, 2007 in the Bassett Hospital, Cooperstown.

ANTHONY FRANKLIN TRIUMPHO was born March 8, 1915 in Amsterdam. He died December 11, 2002 at St. Mary's Hospital in Amsterdam. A. Franklin, or Tony as he was best known, was a remarkably active individual with his ties to the Mohawk District of the Sir William Johnson Council of Boy Scouts of America, where he was quite prominent for many years.

Like many other young men who grew up during the Great Depression, Tony "worked his way" through college, earning tuition by working at odd jobs crammed between classes. He graduated from Colgate University in 1937 with a degree in business economics. Tony stayed active as an alumnus in planning the class reunions and other affairs of the college. In his mature years he endowed a scholarship fund to aid needy students at Colgate.

He served as president of the Canajoharie Building Savings and Loan Association and was an officer in the Community Chest.

Tony enlisted in the U.S. Army in December 1941 soon after Pearl Harbor. The Army sent him, along with other young college graduates, to officer candidate training in Fort Bragg NC, where he was commissioned a 2nd Lieutenant. He went from Fort Bragg NC to Fort Sill OK for artillery training and was assigned to the 250th field artillery as a forward observer. Upon completion of his training, his unit was shipped overseas to England, where they waited for the D-Day invasion at Normandy in June 1944. A few days after the invasion his unit joined the battle in France, where, over a cup of coffee in a Red Cross canteen, he met Jean Kettler serving the coffee and learned that she was from Canajoharie. And the rest is history!

From France, his unit advanced into Germany, where Tony earned his Captain's bars. At this point in time, Tony's battalion was assigned to General Patton's 5th Army. After serving 22 months with four campaigns in the European Theater, Captain Anthony Triumpho was discharged in 1946 after serving in France. He had the distinct honor of receiving the French Croix de Guerre with Silver Stars, the Bronze Star and the French Distinguished Unit Citation of the Order de Brigade.

On the 40th Anniversary of D-Day, Anthony and his wife, Jean, traveled to France with a reunion group and were entertained with several magnificent ceremonies. It was the thrill of their lifetime. Tony attended many subsequent reunions of the 250th field artillery battalion.

Upon his military discharge, he studied insurance at The Traveler's Insurance School in Hartford CN and soon afterward opened the Triumpho Insurance Agency in Canajoharie, which later branched out into St. Johnsville and Fort Plain, where he joined forces with Harvey Smith to form the Harvey-Triumpho agency. During this time, the American College of Life Underwriters in Cincinnati OH awarded Tony the coveted "Chartered Life Underwriter" designation.

After his marriage to Jean Louise Kettler, daughter of Fred and Eunice Kettler of Canajoharie, he lived the rest of his life in Canajoharie. Jean traveled with him on all four of their "round-the-world" trips. Having been a salesman for Beech-Nut, Tony never forgot to bring lots of Beech-Nut lifesavers to hand out on those trips. He was always a Canajoharie booster.

They had a son, Timothy. Jean Kettler was born June 17, 1917 in Canajoharie and died July 8, 2005 in her birthplace.

JAMES VINCENT TRIUMPHO acquired quite a resume during his lifetime with his accomplishment of becoming a self-made, self-employed millionaire. His unique career began as salutatorian of the 1934 graduating class from St. Johnsville High School. My mother, Rose Sindici, was a classmate. He went on to Syracuse University, where he graduated in 1942 with a Bachelor of Arts degree in language.

Portions of the following are reprinted here from a January 1, 1986 article in the Courier-Standard-Enterprise. His brother, Richard Triumpho has added some further information.

With his brother, Tony, being called to serve his country, Jim took over his position as a salesman with Beech-Nut Packing Company in Canajoharie. In less than a year, James, too, was called to service in the U.S. Air Force, where he was assigned to the Counter Intelligence Corps, later with reassignment to seeking Nazi's through the Prisoner Interrogation and War Crimes group. He could speak the languages of standard German, French, Spanish and Italian and also was versed in the regional dialects.

With the end of World War II, James returned to the farm in 1946 with his wife, Ethelda. For the next seven years he worked the farm in partnership with his brother, Joe and their father, Thomas. Jim built a house on the farm. His son, James Jr. was born in 1951 in Little Falls Hospital. Jim also did some work in insurance with his brother, Tony.

Jim gave up farming in 1953 and turned his interest toward electricity. He learned the trade by working several years with Chandler Electric in St. Johnsville. Eventually, he was employed by an international electrical firm, which sent him along with his wife and son to Bermuda and then to St. Croix, Virgin Islands in the Caribbean. Here he discovered his "American Paradise."

In 1963 James formed his own company, Triumpho Electrical, Inc. in St. Croix, the Virgin Islands, where he served as the chief electrical contractor and distributor. Due to the difficulty of obtaining needed supplies in the Caribbean, in 1967 Jim created the Triumpho Electrical Caribbean Supply Company, based in Miami FL. By 1978 he had set up a branch of the business in St. Thomas with his son, James, Jr. as manager. He was featured in a cover story of the October 1985 issue of the Electrical Wholesaling magazine.

James Vincent Triumpho was born January 6, 1917 at 15 Sanders Street, St. Johnsville. He died June 25, 2007 in Florence SC and was buried there in the military cemetery. He lived an amazing life of adventure and prosperity, while residing in his "American Paradise." Just one more inspiring story of a child of an immigrant Italian family making his mark in the world.

CARMINE TRIUMPHO was born August 21, 1918, the first child to be born at the new family farm. She died April 26, 2007 in Utica NY, where she had made her home for many years after her marriage.

Carmine aka Carmen was married to William P. Collins of Utica on November 21, 1941. They had two daughters - Judith Ann, born June 14, 1945 and Deborah Ann, who died at birth in 1953.

Carmen and my mother were good friends through the years. I vividly recall Sunday visits with her at the farm home in my youth.

ANNA LILLIAN TRIUMPHO was born March 30, 1920. After graduating from St. Johnsville High, she attended Utica School of Commerce. She then was employed as a secretary for 12 years at GE in Schenectady, where she met her husband, electrical engineer Alexander Smuszkiewicz of Chester PA.

Anna passed away at the age of 54, a victim of breast cancer, on November 27, 1974 in Malvern PA, where she had lived with her husband, Alexander and their four children - Joan, Martha, Mark and Jean.

VERONICA TRIUMPHO was born July 15, 1921. After graduation she attended Blue Ridge College in New Windsor MD, where she studied design and became an Interior Decorator. Veronica was a noted artist. During her college years, she was involved with several art exhibits.

In 1953 Veronica Triumpho and Dr. Raymond E. Wytrwal were united in marriage. They had a daughter, Mamie, born in 1955. Dr. Wytrwal had a son, Jere from his previous marriage.

With Dr. Wytrwal's retirement from the medical profession after 56 years, the couple spent the winters in Palm Beach FL, where he passed away at the Jupiter Medical Center on February 18, 2006 at the age of 86.

Along with his regular practice, Dr. Wytrwal delivered hundreds of St. Johnsville residents, including my two brothers, my daughter and me.

After his death, Veronica moved to Nashua NH to be near their daughter, Mamie, who lives in Cambridge MA with her husband, David Caponera, son of Joseph Caponera and Joyce Carbery. Veronica passed away on December 29, 2009 in Nashua NH.

ESTHER TRIUMPHO was born May 17, 1923 and died at the young age of 49 on December 21, 1972 in her home in Utica. After graduating high school, in 1942 she attended the Utica School of Commerce, and later enrolled at Plattsburgh State Teachers College. She taught school in the Albany area for several years and also Whitesboro Central School.

On April 20, 1956 Esther Triumpho married Lawrence Joslin Griswold of Utica, the ceremony performed at St. John's Reformed Church in St. Johnsville. Esther and Larry had three sons - David, Douglas and Christopher.

GRACE TRIUMPHO was born July 2, 1925. She passed away the day after Christmas, December 26, 2011 in Las Vegas, where she had made her home for 60 years. She was 86 years old.

Graduating in 1945 from St. Johnsville High School, Grace attended Business College. For a few years she was the Social Editor of the St. Johnsville *Enterprise & News*.

On November 3, 1951 Grace Triumpho married John D. Shaw Cairns in Las Vegas NV, where the couple made their home for the remainder of their lives. They had three children - Raven, Colin and Polly. John Cairns had been married to Hilda Pietrocini.

Around 1940, when my parents rented the spacious downstairs flat of the Leo Fitzpatrick home at 59 North Division Street, Grace resided with us. She was hired as a babysitter for my brother, Joseph and me. She would see that we had our breakfast, got us off to school and was there to greet us upon our return. I recall her cheerful laugh. She must have been in high school at the time.

ROSE ANNE TRIUMPHO was born in 1928. She graduated from St. Johnsville in June 1945. Rose, like her sisters, sang vocal solos, leading groups in song. She was joined in marriage to George Sullivan with whom she had two children - Thomas and Patricia. At this writing, Rose is still living.

ELIZABETH TRIUMPHO was born in 1929. She died from complications of appendicitis in August 1931 at the age of two years old.

RICHARD THOMAS TRIUMPHO was born October 4, 1931 on the family farm.

As a graduate of St. Johnsville High School, he attained the high average of Salutatorian. From there he went on to pursue his studies at Utica College and later at Union College, Schenectady, where he earned a B.S. degree in biology. With the death of his father, Richard took over the operation of the 400-acre dairy farm.

Not only does he have an intensive love of the land, Richard is a gifted author, who scribes with a sense of humor and a flair for beautiful visual imagery, inviting his reader to join him in the scenes he describes. "No

Richer Gift", published in 1979 by the Hoard's Dairy magazine, is a compilation of articles, which vividly portray the life of a dairy farmer. He has been a contributing columnist to this worldwide dairy farmer's magazine since 1973.

"Wait 'Til the Cows Come Home" and "No Richer Gift" are humorous memoirs of his life in the rural areas of St. Johnsville. They both were such a pleasure to read. I recognized so many of the people and places he described and highly recommend their perusal. Richard invites you to walk along with him as he works his land and farm and tickles your senses. You hear the welcoming trill of the birds. You see the spring flowers popping up in full bloom. You taste the homemade berry pies from his patches. He even makes the manure smell sweet. His stories identify him as an "industrious tiller of the soil", so appropriate to him, as it was for his grandfather, Joseph.

On September 27, 1963, Richard Triumpho and Bernadette De Blois from Utica were united in marriage at St. Patrick's Catholic Church. They had a daughter, Ann. She became an important part of tending the farm and its animals, especially the horses. Ann accompanied her father on his enlightening journeys to several dairy farms in Russia, China, Switzerland and New Zealand.

FRANCES PATRICIA TRIUMPHO was born August 27, 1935, the youngest of the 12 siblings. After graduating as an honor student from St. Johnsville High School in the Class of 1954, she went on to Utica College, later attending St. Lawrence University.

During her school years, she was a Girl Scout and a Drum Majorette with the High School Band. Fran and I were friends and classmates for a few years. When we were young girls of five or six, I recall many visits to the farm, when we would walk down through the fields across from the farm and play by the stream that went through the densely wooded area, while all the ladies, including my mother, visited in the house.

In September 1955, Frances Triumpho married Michael D. Malone from New Hartford. They were married at St. Patrick's Church after a breakfast at the Creekside and followed by a wedding reception at the family farm. They had two children - Susan and Michael, Jr.

Frances Patricia Triumpho passed away on March 26, 2016 in Laurens SC, near the home of her daughter, Susan.

The year 2017 celebrated 100 years of the Triumpho dairy farm and homestead, which was purchased in 1917. The farm continues to thrive under the management and hard work of the couple's son, Richard.

As per daughter, Rose Triumpho Sullivan, *"The house pre-dates the Civil War years, built circa 1845. Formerly being the Flanders farm, it was purchased from Jonathan Vedder, the son of Christian Vedder, who built the farmhouse. The Vedder's used the wood from their lumber mill to build the house. When purchased by Rose's parents it had been abandoned for many years and fallen into severe disrepair. They brought it back to its present state of grandeur."*

In conclusion, I have determined that the Triumpho's were an extremely close-knit family with an enormous amount of enterprising intelligence and musicality in their ancestral Italian genes.

* Richard Triumpho has edited and added a great deal of information to this article. Grazie!

Balvano

Balvano is a small city and *comune* in the Provence of Potenza, Basilicata region in Southern Italy. In 1980 it was nearly destroyed by an earthquake. Bovino is the fifth most common family name. There are currently 18 famiglia Bovino's and 114 famiglia Capece's living there. Triumpho (Trionfo) does not seem to be a common name.

~ *La Famiglia BOVINO* ~

EMMA BOVINO, born on May 4, 1936 was a much younger half-sister of Louisa Bovino Triumpho. They shared the same father, Antonio Pietro Bovino.

When Anna Rocca, the first wife of Antonio died, he married a second time to Diana Turturillo, and fathered two more children, Antonio and Emma, who thus were much younger half-siblings to Louise. They were also uncle and aunt to all the Triumpho siblings. Family relationships are like a Chinese puzzle!

Emma arrived in America on May 18, 1955, leaving her mother, Diana Tuotorella in Balvano. Louise and Thomas sponsored her immigration. Emma lived with them at the Triumpho farm for the first two years following her arrival.

Half-brother Anthony Bovino arrived in December 1954. He and Emma had a sister, Maria and brother, Vincenzio, still in Italy.

Emma Bovino easily adjusted to her new home in America, coming to a place very different from her mountain village home, where her parents made their living growing olives and grapes. She came to call St. Johnsville her home, sharing her ethnic customs with other family and friends. When visiting Emma, it wasn't unusual to see her homemade strips of pasta noodles hanging over her kitchen chairs, drying. In the summer she cooked over an open fire built in a wheelbarrow.

With Miriam Feldstein, daughter of Dr. Bernard Feldstein, as her tutor, Emma was able to acquire a better command of the English language and obtain her U.S. Citizenship.

While learning the English language, Emma met and married Frank LaCoppola, a man who spoke no Italian. They had three children - Joseph, Maria and Peter. Frank was the son of Joseph LaCoppola, a local Italian businessman and contractor, who settled in St. Johnsville in later years.

Emma first worked at the Felt Shoe and later at Corso Dress for 22 years, until it's closing, pressing famous maker's dresses, readying them for shipment to New York City.

Frank Joseph LaCoppola was born March 27, 1933 in St. Johnsville and passed away on December 30, 1992 after a hard fought battle with ALS.

* I obtained some of Emma Bovino's information from an article she was featured in with The Daily Gazette of Schenectady NY.

ANTHONY BOVINO was born on March 15, 1931 and died on December 5, 2012. He first came to St. Johnsville, where he lived at 15 South Division Street with his wife and three children - Diana, Thomas and Anthony, Jr, for several years.

The family later moved to Scotia, where General Electric employed him. With his retirement, Anthony returned to St. Johnsville, alone, and resided with his sister, Emma.

Serving as the baptismal godfather for one of Anthony's sons was my husband, John Palma.

~ La Famiglia CAPECE ~

Our Capece story opens with an accounting of the young life of Giuseppe "Joseph" Capece, son of Dominick Capece and Filomena Basolone, as told to and transcribed by his daughter, Margaret Capece Sternisha, in February 1987. These are his exact words! It is truly a prime image of the lives and struggles of all of our Italian immigrants.

MY LIFE STORY
As told by Joseph Capece

"I was born in Balvano, Italy on April 19, 1903. My father worked on a farm as a shareholder. The family lived in Balvano in an old stone house, cooked in a fireplace, and the bunk beds were three high. We lived very poor. My sister, Rose, was younger. One day she caught her dress on fire and I put it out. I would go to the farm once in a while to watch the sheep, so they wouldn't go in the garden. I must have been four or five then.

Around February 16, 1909, we left for the USA – my mother, Mary, Donato, Pasquale, Antonio, Giuseppe and Rose. My father came to the USA in 1906 to work so he could raise transportation fare for the rest of us to come to the USA. It took us 21 days to cross the Atlantic Ocean. We landed on Ellis Island and a friend of the family, Mr. Triumpho, came to receive us after going through the medical tests. We finally boarded the train on the New York Central Railroad and landed in St. Johnsville, where we met our father at the railroad station.

My father rented a house on Sanders Street. We lived there a little over a year. Then, my father bought a house about a quarter of a mile south of the Mohawk River. A little at a time we had to build a chicken house, so we could have eggs and meat to live on. The older children all worked in the knitting mill. My father worked on the railroad.

As time went on, we started to raise hogs so we could have more meat for the family. We started a large garden for our vegetables. We also had a few fruit trees such as apple, pear and plum. For the winter, we had a plan to put away in the cellar, bins of potatoes, apples, cabbage, pickled pears and sliced green tomatoes. In can jars, we had different fruit, cucumber, cooked meat like chicken and beef and tomatoes. We made our own paste. There was no refrigeration.

We had to prepare for the cold winters. We used to cut around 300 railroad ties for firewood to keep warm. We all had to help with the chores around the house, such as bringing water from the well, firewood from outdoors. My first year, after school vacation started in the summer, I would go to different farms to pull weeds, such as mustard and thistle, out of the cornfields for 25 cents a day. We worked in the hot sun on our knees against stones. Sometimes, I would go and pick cherries for two cents a quart and pears for 25 cents a bushel. We would do anything to make a little money.

When I was 9 years old I worked on a farm next to our house nights after school. I did things such as throwing down hay from the hayloft on top of the barn. Then, I would drag it along the stanchion in front of the cows so they could eat. On Saturday, we would go to the woods to cut trees for firewood. All this was done for $3.00 a month. I did this until I was 11 years old. Then I got a job in the knitting mill. I had to lie about my age because those days you had to be 13 years old to work. I worked mornings before school and after school until 6pm and then all day Saturday. My pay was 10 cents an hour. When I was 12 years old, besides going to school and working in the mill, I worked at Joe Cleary's cigar and pool room for 50 cents a night, racking pool balls from 7pm until 12pm.

I quit school at 15 years old and worked 10 hours a day in the mill making $16.50 a week and still kept my job in the pool parlor. As time passed by, I was figuring on making more money, so I thought of going west to dig for gold. I talked to my brother, Tony, and a friend, Peter DeAngelis, about going. We traveled by railroad and got as far as Denver CO, but we could not find work. After a couple of days there, we left to go back to New York State. We stopped in Depew NY and Tony and Peter got a job there, but I came back to St. Johnsville with two cents in my pocket.

I then started getting jobs on construction work, railroad work, and started training for boxing. I had a hard time getting a job as a laborer with a pick and shovel in Canajoharie. The superintendent would chase me away saying I could not stand the work. I tried four times and the last time, he wasn't around. I got my number button and was putting it on my jacket when he saw me and said, "What are you going to do?" "I'm going to work", I told him. He said, "We can't pay you a man's wages. We'll start you at 39 cents an hour. If you last two weeks, we will pay you the same as others." I worked there for five months until all the work was *done. It was hard work and he never gave me a raise. They would fire 50 to 75 men a day because they were not working hard enough.*

With my boxing, I would pick up a fight now and then, but the most I was paid was $10 to $25 a fight. I loved the game because I kept in good condition all the time. The most I got was $60 for a semi-final fight. I had 21 bouts in all and won all but one.

Around 1919, the Little Falls Felt Shoe Company came to town. I got fair wages for those days and was still doing a little boxing. I worked in the stamping soles department run by Robert Haak. He bought the Little Falls Fonda Bus Corporation and asked me to work for him. At that time, I was only 17 years old, so I had to lie to get my chauffeur's license, because you had to be 18 years old. I made out my application for the license. When the day came for the appointment, I had to go to Utica to try out for my test. Had to be there by 8am, but my train didn't come until 2pm. On January 16, 1920, I started driving bus between Canajoharie and Little Falls. I made four round trips a day, leaving at 5:45am and ending 7:35pm. The buses were hard to drive in those days. Hard to shift, and it was very cold. I had to drive with a blanket over my lap because the wind and snow would come up through little cracks around the cowl. You had to turn the windshield wipers by hand. For heat, we would run the exhaust pipe through the inside and around the bus. As long as the engine was running hard you had some heat. When the motor was idle, there was no heat. We tried gas heaters running from the carburetor. It made the engine run pretty rough. Then, the water heaters were invented and they worked okay. I worked seven days a week, including holidays, and did this for several years. All I saw was the road signs and landscaping on Route 5 going through towns."

More of Joseph Capece's story will be continued further down in this article.

~ DOMINICK CAPECE et FILOMENA BASOLONE ~

DOMINICK CAPECE was born on January 19, 1871 in Balvano, Italy, the son of Domenico Capece and Gama Bellaneano. He had a sister in Italy, who died at age 15.

FILOMENA "Emma" BASOLONE, the daughter of Mr. & Mrs. Pasquale Basolone, also from Balvano, was born February 18, 1873. She was from a family of nine siblings with three sisters and five brothers.

Dominick Capece and Filomena Basolone were married in Italy in 1890 where they lived in an old stone house. As shareholders, they worked on a farm where their first six children were born. It is thought that there was another child that died at birth.

The younger children would stay home while the parents and older children worked the farm. Sometimes, even the younger children would go to the farm to tend the sheep. Because they were very poor, it required the whole family to help out. Not only used for warmth, their fireplace was also implemented for year round cooking, as so many of the Italian families in those times.

In 1906, Dominick Capece arrived in America, sponsored by his friend, Vincenzo "James" Triumpho, who had come here in 1892. Working on the New York Central Railroad, he saved enough money in three years to bring his entire family of seven to this country.

During March 1909, Filomena and their six children sailed to Ellis Island, where James Triumpho received them while Dominick waited anxiously at the railroad station in St. Johnsville to greet his family.

Over the years, six more children were born for a total of thirteen. Everyone helped with chores and always kept the home immaculate. They needed very little from the local grocery store, as the cellar housed storage of Filomena's canned vegetables and fruits, baked bread and also, meats.

The 1915 Census shows the Capece family living in the Mindenville home. Maria had married and left the family nest, and Donato is not listed. The following siblings are listed - James 21, and Patsy 19, working on the railroad, Tony 16, Joseph 12, Rosina 11, Jimmie 5, Angela 4, Lucia 3, and Victor, infant.

In 1920, again Maria and Donato are not listed, James is now 24, working in a knitting mill and the second "Jim" is 9 years of age. It seems Maria and Donato are living back home in 1925, and the last child, Albert is born. The Massari family lives next door.

1930 now shows them as the proud owners of the farm home, valued at $3,000. Dominick continued to work on the railroad his entire working life. Their son, Pasquale was now married and living with his growing family further down the road. The second James is living in the rural home with his new wife, Frances George. The first James does not show up now. I'm thinking he may have died, as I'm unable to find any further records of him. Or perhaps moved elsewhere? His presence is quite a mystery to current family members.

On July 11, 1936, Filomena Basolone Capece, a hard working woman and devoted mother, died in Little Falls Hospital from a ruptured appendix following a fall from a tree, while picking cherries. She was 63.

Dominick Capece passed away on June 19, 1963 at the family home at the age of 93.

In 1963, after Dominick's death, the family home was sold to Joseph and Sadie Palombi. They utilized the services of Bellinger and Updyke to move the home further up Mindenville Road from the corner location. This was the time the NYS Thruway Authority came into existence and obtained the land by eminent domain to build the New York State Thruway.

MARIA CAPECE was the oldest child born in Balvano, June 3, 1892. She died January 28, 1965 in St. Johnsville at age 73. Maria's obituary states she was born in Terracina. I believe this to be incorrect. Two of her daughters and first husband were born there.

April 23, 1911, at age 19, Maria was married to Domenico Pondozi of Terracina, son of Ondred Pondozi and Teresia Pariselle. Serving as witnesses to the union were Tony and Angela Massaro. They had two daughters - Viola Marie, born 1922, and Amelia, 1925.

It seems there were also three other children - Albert, also born in St. Johnsville in 1912-13 and died 1913-14 in Italy. Born in Terracina, Italy, were Theresa in 1914 and Pauline in 1920. I'm assuming the Pondozi couple may have returned to Italy for a few years after their marriage, then back to St. Johnsville.

Domenico Pondozi was born in 1885; he died in 1942. I find no further records of him. Maria later married Arturo O. Palombo, a brother of Luca Palombo. The brothers had both come to St. Johnsville from Roccogorga before 1918. I don't find a connection with the other Palombo family.

Arturo Palombo arrived in America in 1914, going to meet his brother, Luca. In 1918 he was living at 32 South Division Street, when he was inducted into World War I between October 27, 1918 and September 26, 1919. He was a boarder at 3 Hough Street in 1920.

My records show Arturo Palombo born April 26, 1896 in Roccogorga, Italy. He died September 9, 1970 in St. Johnsville.

Luca Palombo arrived April 27, 1912 at age 23. His World War I record of 1917 shows him living at 26 Hough Street, married and working on the railroad. I find no further records of him.

In 1947, Maria was living at the home of her daughter, Viola and son-in-law, Joseph Ottaviano at 6 East Liberty Street. This was later the Potenziani home, close to Bridge Street and the railroad. They had a break-in while everyone was at work and Maria's money was stolen. The thief hadn't touched the valuables. Perhaps it may have been a "hobo" coming off the railroad, which was so prevalent at that time? They would seek the homes closer to the railroad begging for food. I recall one coming to the door of my home at the corner of South Division and West Liberty during the war; we didn't open the door. There were some Italian residents who responded to them.

The 1930 Census shows Joseph Ottaviano living with his family in Little Falls, next door to the Morotti family. Ironically, Joseph Morotti, a member of that family, married Philomena Capece, Maria's niece.

DONATO CAPECE was born February 4, 1894 and died on his 91st birthday, February 4, 1985 in St. Johnsville. Living at home most of his life, he was employed by the New York Central Railroad.

Donato never married. He was involved in some serious trouble, causing his incarceration for several years as a young adult.

PASQUALE "Patsy" CAPECE was born July 7, 1895. After a long productive life, Patsy died March 3, 1993 at the age of 97.

When registering for the World War I draft June 5, 1917, he was single and employed at Reaney's Knitting Mill on New Street.

On September 17, 1917, Pasquale Capece had married Anna Gomulka, a 1916 immigrant from Czechoslovakia, Austria. Living a short distance from his family home in Mindenville, they were renting and starting their own family with Leroy "Louis" age 3, and one-month old twins, Albert and Dominick. The three children were close in age to Patsy's siblings.

By 1930 Patsy was the owner of the property valued at $5,000. The Census shows his children as Lloyd (Leroy) actually Louis; Dominick, Joseph, Philomena and Donald, all born in St. Johnsville. Albert is missing. I believe that Albert died as an infant. Current family members do not know of his existence.

By 1940 Patsy had moved his family to 7 Sanders Street. During World War II in 1942, he was working for Denbar Sullivan.

ANNA GOMULKA was born March 26, 1899 in Poland and died April 14, 1967 at Little Falls Hospital. She was buried in the West St. Johnsville Cemetery near her son, Louis Capece's home. After Anna's death, Patsy moved near his son, Louis on Route 5 West.

Around 1952, Montgomery County was auctioning off all the rural schoolhouses. Patsy was able to purchase the brick building on Route 5 West of St. Johnsville. He dug a cellar and refurbished it with the intention of opening a restaurant. Since he could not read or speak English well, he decided it would be a better idea for his daughter, Philomena and son, Joseph to become the proprietors. He worked daily preparing homemade noodles, gnocchi and other traditional Italian dishes to serve.

Eventually, Capece's Restaurant became the sole proprietary of his daughter, Philomena and her husband, Joseph Marotti. When Patsy was no longer able to work, the restaurant contracted with Katie Carroll for the homemade noodles and Mary Stagliano to make the gnocchi.

My mother, Rose Sindici Perry was employed as a waitress, almost from the very beginning, until Joe sold it to the Ripepi family of Amsterdam. Margaret "Peggy" Fiacco Putman, Fedora Fiacco Richard and Patsy's grandson, Louis "Rusty" Capece, Jr. worked in the kitchen for several years. My cousin, Daniel Matis, Lena Sindici's son, worked as a handyman and all around helper in the kitchen. His sister, Sharon babysat the children.

These are the children of PASQUALE CAPECE and ANNA GOMULKA.
They were all born in St. Johnsville.

LOUIS ROBERT CAPECE was born June 24, 1918. He passed away at the home of his namesake, Louis "Rusty" Capece, in Nelliston on October 29, 2003 and is buried in the West St. Johnsville Cemetery on the hillside near his home of many years.

On October 10, 1936, Louis Capece and Olga George, daughter of Joseph George and Marcella Cotelli of Little Falls, were married at St. Patrick's Church. Olga was the sister of Frances George Capece, who married Louis' uncle, James Capece. They were the parents of three sons - George, Louis, Jr. and Ronald. In 1937 they were living on East Liberty Street, perhaps with James and Frances?

Louis Capece was quite the enterprising man, continuously coming up with unique ideas for income. He sold Amway products. He grew his special garlic, referred to as the "Lily of the Mohawk Valley" from the extensive garden he tended, and offered storage space rental in the hut near his home on Route 5 West, among other moneymaking deals. Louis and his son, "Rusty" had purchased the building from Case Agway. In 1979 he designed and built a unique chimney for wood stoves. He also proposed a large shopping center on Route 5 near Nelliston, which didn't come to fruition.

In their retirement years, Louis and his wife, Olga could be found at their son, George's Italian restaurant ~ Capece's Deli ~ in Fort Plain. Louis loved to cook. When employed at Manny's in Utica, George learned the recipe for their famous cheesecakes and served them as a specialty of the house.

Louis and Olga's son, "Rusty" was also quite enterprising. After attending embalming school, he purchased the Ottman home on North Division Street and opened the Capece Funeral Home, which he operated for several years. He also purchased the Gray Funeral Home in Fort Plain. He was instrumental in forming a county ambulance service and airline medical transport service, utilizing his own plane.

OLGA GEORGE was born August 11, 1917. She passed away at the St. Johnsville Nursing Home on October 28, 2011. It is said she became very ill after the passing of their son, George, just two weeks previous on October 16, 2011. Olga worked most of her life at the Little Falls Felt Shoe in St. Johnsville.

DOMINICK J. "Nicky" CAPECE was born January 16, 1920, and died October 6, 1971 at the Albany Veteran's Hospital.

Loomis Burrell of Little Falls had employed Dominick as his personal chauffeur for several years. He later worked at Remington Rand in Ilion.

Dominick married Anne Tomei on June 22, 1940. They had three children - Jean, Dominick and Alan.

He served in the Marines during World War II, fighting in the battle of Iwo Jima. It caused him to return home with shell shock, which he suffered for many years. He was listed as a casualty in 1945.

JOSEPH CAPECE was born October 6, 1921. He died January 22, 2013 at Folts Home, Herkimer, where he was residing. He was 91.

In December of 1937 at age 16, Joe and his brother Nick were installing a windshield at the garage owned by his Uncle Joe Capece and Warren Smith. A screwdriver flew from the hand of young Joe piercing his eye, causing loss of eyesight. Fortunately, they were able to save the eye.

Joseph Capece married Christina Compolo of Little Falls, the daughter of Rocco Compolo and Carmella Perry, on January 30, 1942 in Little Falls, where they continued to live throughout their married life. She was born May 30, 1922, and died November 8, 2008 in Little Falls Hospital. They had no children.

Joe and Christina first worked in a partnership with his sister, Philomena, with the opening of the popular Capece's Restaurant on Route 5 West of the village of St. Johnsville. The partnership later dissolved.

PHILOMENA CAPECE born June 28, 1924, was the only girl in the family. She died at home at the young age of 45 in February 1970, after a two-year bout with cancer.

During World War II, Phil served in the WACS, stationed at Brooks General Hospital, San Antonio TX.

Philomena Capece was married to Joseph Morotti, son of Lorenzo Morotti and Frances Montoni of Little Falls, on July 9, 1943 in Los Angeles, California. They had three children - Frances, Kirsten and James.

Joseph Morotti was born January 1, 1917 in Little Falls. He passed away at the Syracuse VA Hospital in 1983 at the age of 66. He had served in World War II.

As stated above with her father, Patsy's story, Philomena Capece and Joseph Marotti were the proprietors of Capece's Restaurant with the aid of Patsy, until Joe's retirement in 1976.

DONALD CAPECE was born September 21, 1929 and died February 19, 2007 in Fort Plain. He was married to Shirley Monk of Lassellsville, born September 17, 1933. She died August 20, 2010.

This concludes the history of the Pasquale "Patsy" Capece family.

JAMES CAPECE, as the third child of Dominick Capece and Filomena Bassolone was born 1896 in Balvano. He does not show up in any records after 1920. He may have died or moved away between 1920 and 1925. Current family members are not aware of him, but he is listed as a son in the two Census records.

ANTONIO CARL "Tony" CAPECE was born January 7, 1899 in Balvano and died September 13, 1973 in Little Falls Hospital. When he signed for the World War I draft in 1918, he was a boarder on Center Street and working for the Royal Gem Knitting Mill.

Antonio Capece was first married to Catherine Lawrence, daughter of Frank and Lillian Lawrence of Little Falls, on May 19, 1926. By 1930 they rented a home near his parents, Patsy and Anna, in Mindenville. They had three children - Beverly, Dorene and Harold.

Tony later married Maria D'Orio Calleri of Utica on April 26, 1952. His niece, Pauline Pondozi served as maid of honor.

Catherine Lawrence, was born September 21, 1909; she died July 29, 1987.

GIUSEPPE "Joseph" CAPECE, Sr. was born April 19, 1903. He lived a long active enterprising life of 90 years. Joe began his career as a Bus Chauffeur with the Darling Bus Lines. You've read a great deal about Joe's youth at the beginning of *La Famiglia Capece*.

On June 5, 1930, Joseph Capece married Rose George (Ciacci), daughter of Ralph George and Mary Wansho of Little Falls, in Fort Plain. They had four children - Joseph "Sonny" Jr., Margaret, Kenneth and Pamela.

Following is his version of how he met his beautiful Rose. He had been working as a bus driver for Little Falls Fonda Bus Corporation, owned by Robert Haak since 1922.

"In the early part of 1929, I met some girls at the corner of Second and Main Streets in Little Falls. That was the bus stop to layover one-half hour before starting the return trip back. I talked with Alice Graudens and Ruth Snyder, friends of Rose George. They asked me if I could take the following Sunday off to go out with their girl friend, Rose. When I got to the St. Johnsville Bus Terminal, I asked Mr. Haak, the owner, if I could take next Sunday off. He said, "Joe, how many years have you worked without taking a day off?" I said, "eight years." he said, "take next Sunday off."

I had a 1923 Oakland Touring car in which we went out for a ride toward Caroga Lake, Gloversville and Johnstown. I froze my feet. I guess there wasn't a heater in the car. Alice and Ruth, with their friends, had blankets to cover themselves, but my feet had to be out for the clutch and brake pedal. We kept company around a year or so because we both worked every day. She worked in the knitting mill in Little Falls and I was still driving bus.

Sometime in February 1930, we decided to get married. We got married by the Justice of Peace, Mr. Barton, in Fort Plain. Esther Tallman and Robert Mallet stood up with us. I didn't take any time off from working. This was done in the evening after work. Several months later, we got married again by Father Cunningham of St. Patrick Church in St. Johnsville."

In May of 1934, the family was living in the former St. Paul's Lutheran Church parsonage on East Liberty Street at the southeast corner of Mechanic Street. They're still there in 1935.

During these years, Joseph Capece and Warren Smith were the lessees/operators of the Canajoharie Little Falls Bus Line. I'm wondering if this is the building that sat next to the Palmer Grill where Dario Corso later had his businesses? By 1938, Smith had given full control to Capece. Located at the corner of West Main and Center Street for many years, they eventually purchased and moved to the property that once housed the Pyramid on Route 5 West.

Joe later expanded his bus line to transporting school children, contracting with not only St. Johnsville Central School, but surrounding school systems. His brother, Jim drove the school buses for him. With his retirement, he turned the prosperous expanding business of the Little Falls-Fonda Bus Company over to his sons, Joseph "Sonny" and Kenneth. It was eventually sold to the Brown Transportation in Fonda.

Along with the bus transportation business, Joe also owned a Studebaker Car dealership and auto repair garage, located at the corner of West Main and Center Streets. My parents purchased a stick shift Studebaker from him, which I learned to drive.

By 1940, Joseph and Rose Capece were proud owners of a lovely Federalist styled home on Route 5 at the eastern end of the township of St. Johnsville. Rose assisted her husband in his business ventures, besides her full time employment at Gilbert's Knitting Mill in Fort Plain.

Joe continues, *"In 1951, Rose and I decided to take a trip across the Untied States. We had a good trip and saw things we never saw before. In California we took the Southern end along the Gulf States to Florida and spent a little time with Henry Sanders and Chris Satler. We spent a couple of weeks there and had a good time. Then, we left for home and took our time seeing sights as we went along."*

Joe lost his beautiful wife, Rose, in an auto accident on November 9, 1952 in Warsaw NY. Following is his version of the tragic incident: "In 1952, Rose and I, Margaret and Pam took a weekend trip to Gowanda NY to see the Sternisha family, as Margaret was engaged to marry their son, Charles "Bud". He was in the Army serving in Korea and they had plans to marry as soon as he returned home. This was the first time we met his family. On Sunday afternoon we left to return home. We were traveling on Route 39, when we saw a car straddling the white line in the middle of the road. I said to my family, "I wonder what that guy is going to do, so I pulled off on the shoulder of the road. As I did, he struck me on the front left side, crashing into the car pretty good. Rose went against the dashboard, injured all ribs, as she dropped out of the door. Pam went forward under the front seat and fractured her skull. Margaret didn't get hurt. I was all broken up with my left knee and left leg broken in nine places. My heart was bruised badly and I was told later in the hospital that it would only beat at times. I was put in traction with pulleys holding my leg up for three months until all the broken bones were mended, before they could put the cast on. Rose was killed at the site of the accident. Pam was in the same hospital for two weeks before she could go home. This happened in Warsaw NY, which was 200 miles away, on November 9."

ROSE GEORGE (CIACCI) was born December 8, 1909 in Ithaca.

In 1953, after her death, Joe married Virginia Dockerty.

Joseph Capece died May 11, 1993 in St. Petersburg FL, where the couple had retired.

Their daughter, Marge Capece Sternisha and I have been best friends for over 65 years. She and my husband, John grew up as close friends and graduated together in 1950. They were crowned King and Queen of their Senior Prom; they were dating at the time. She lives on St. Simons Island, one of the Golden Isles of Georgia, being responsible for introducing other family members to the serenity of the peaceful spiritual sea island.

ROSINA "Rose" CAPECE was the last child born in Balvano on March 7, 1907, before the family came to America. She was two years old upon arrival.

Rosina Capece married Ettore "Harry" Palombi on October 2, 1922 at St. Patrick's Church with Harry's siblings, Joseph Palombi and Maria Palombi Caponera as witnesses to the union. They had three children - Dora Amelia, Lawrence and Richard.

The couple moved to a large home on Route 5 East of the village, where they lived out their lives. Rose was instrumental in the success of her husband, Harry and his business enterprises. Not only did she assist with his one-stop service station and appliance store, she opened a restaurant business with a license to serve beer and cider, which existed from July 1935 through at least 1946.

After Harry's death, with the assistance of her two sons, Lawrence and Richard, still at home, Rosina carried on with the gas station and restaurant businesses. She was also left to care for Harry's aging father, who died at the home four years later.

In May 1954, Rosina Capece passed away at the Mary Imogene Hospital in Cooperstown after ten weeks as a patient. You can read more about Rose in *La Famiglia Palombi*.

JAMES G. "Jimmy" CAPECE, Sr., born on September 3, 1910 in St. Johnsville, was the first child born in America at the home in Mindenville.

Jimmy was also a hard worker his entire life, almost up to the time of his passing. After many years of service, he retired as the Custodian of the St. Johnsville High School, along with being a school bus driver for his brother, Joe's Little Falls Fonda Bus service. He was also employed for a short term at the Snyder Bicycle Factory in Little Falls.

James G. Capece, age 19, married Frances George, age 17, daughter of Joseph George and Marcella Cotelli of Little Falls, on November 30, 1929 in St. Johnsville. They had one son, James, born New Year's Eve, December 31, 1931.

At the beginning of their marriage, they lived with Jim's parents in Minden. I believe they lived in the former St. Paul's Lutheran Church parsonage on East Liberty Street for a short while before purchasing their lovely secluded home, nestled on a dead-end street off Averill, overlooking the lush valley and the D.H. Robbins Elementary School.

When their son, Jim, Jr. retired from his educational position in Amsterdam and moved to St. Simons Island GA, Jim and Frances followed. They purchased another lovely home, where they both lived out their extended lives and kept a spacious garden.

Jim and Frances were the most remarkable and sweetest couple. Their devotion and respect for each other over the 83 years of their marriage was exemplary. I just loved them and their gracious hospitality. Frances was always a wealth of information. She loved to read and share any knowledge she acquired. They were extremely self sufficient into their late 90s. Even though plagued with arthritis, Jim mowed his own lawn and assisted Fran with the gardening. My husband, John and I spent many hours with them during our numerous visits to St. Simons Island.

James G. Capece died September 17, 2011 at his home on St. Simons Island at the age of 101. His beloved, Frances, followed him five months later on February 13, 2012 at age 99. Frances was born in Troy on October 13, 1912. She was the sister of Olga Capece.

ANGELA "Angie" CAPECE was born February 20, 1912. She died at Little Falls Hospital on July 14, 1987. Angie married Thomas Lawrence of Little Falls on July 19, 1929; they later divorced. They had two children - Marie and Thomas, Jr. I wonder if her husband, Thomas was related to her brother, Tony's wife, Catherine Lawrence?

CARMETA CAPECE was born May 25, 1913. She died January 31, 2003 in St. Johnsville.

On March 20, 1953, Carmeta was married to Martin Walrath, son of Mildred Walrath of St. Johnsville. Her sister Angie's family lived with them in the home they built next to Leo and Dora Mancini. I do seem to recall a mobile home on the property behind the house.

VICTOR B. CAPECE was born January 20, 1915. He died July 27, 1975 in St. Johnsville.

On August 15, 1937, Victor Capece was married to Ethel Bala of South Columbia NY. They had two sons - Victor, Jr. and Richard.

LUCIA OLIVIA "Libby" CAPECE was born October 3, 1916. Libby died on May 4, 2016 at the Palatine Nursing Home, shy of her 100th birthday.

Lucia Capece married Angelo "Yio" D'Arcangelis on January 31, 1937 at St. Patrick's Church. They had three children - Robert, Sheila and Desiree.

Yio D'Arcangelis was the owner/operator of Otsquago Construction Company in Fort Plain for many years. Upon his retirement in 1972 due to illness, his son, Robert, took over the business. Yio died at the St. Johnsville Nursing Home with Alzheimers.

The D'Arcangelis family was apparently quite gifted intellectually. In 1983 at a huge family reunion, they presented a plaque of appreciation to the Business Manager of Fort Plain High School, which honored 11 of the family members who had graduated as mostly Valedictorians, some Salutatorians. Included were Libby and Yio's children - Desiree, Valedictorian of her class and Robert, Salutatorian of his graduating class.

ALBERT THOMAS CAPECE was born December 16, 1919.

Enlisting on February 7, 1942 at Fort Niagara, Youngstown, Albert was a Corporal in the Army of World War II. He was stationed at Camp Gordon GA.

On September 14, 1942 Albert Capece married Lydia Terenzetti, daughter of Guido Terenzetti and Regina Marocco from Little Falls. The ceremony was performed by an Episcopal minister in Fredericksburg VA. They had a daughter, Carol.

Married three times, his second wife was Erline Moody, who died in January 1985. After her death, he met and married a woman named Dorothy from South Carolina, who unfortunately depleted his accounts during the two to three months of their marriage.

Albert later spent several months on St. Simons Island GA, where he met a widow, Viola Jones. With Viola not wanting to lose her insurance benefits from her late husband, a judge, they lived together many years near Atlanta GA. They later resided together in a nursing home in Suwanee GA. Viola passed away first with Albert following a few months later on May 17, 2009. He is buried with his wife, Erline in Columbia SC.

Margaret Capece Sternisha contributed a great deal to this article, including her father's life story. Grazie!

Glenna Johnson Capece, wife of Victor Capece, Jr., shared the detailed Family Tree of the Capece family, which Vinnie Capece, son of Kenneth Capece, composed and shared with all the living family members. Grazie!

Filomena Basolone et Dominick Capece

~ *La Famiglia PALOMBI* ~

~ LUIGI PALOMBI et AMELIA BATTISTI ~

The Palombi family is one of the oldest generations I have discovered with the Italian immigrants of St. Johnsville. The Triumpho brothers Giuseppe and Vincenzo have the distinction of being the first aliens locating in St. Johnsville.

LUIGI PALOMBI was born in Supino about 1872 and immigrated to this country on October 30, 1899, first settling in New York City with his companions, Edwardo Battisti and Cataldo Zuccaro (Sugar). By 1911 he had moved to Little Falls. Luigi became an American citizen in 1947 at the Fonda Court House.

AMELIA BATTISTI was the daughter of Lawrence Battisti and Rosa Sugar (Zuccaro). She was born January 4, 1864 in Supino. Edwardo Battisti was her brother. I find no link to any of the other Battisti's in St. Johnsville.

In 1912 Luigi's wife, Amelia followed him to America with two of their children born in Supino, Joseph and Maria. They came to St. Johnsville, where Luigi was now living. The oldest son, Ettore "Harry" had come over alone in 1910. There was also a daughter, Rosina, who remained in Italy. The siblings were all older when immigrating.

The 1915 Census shows them residing at 29 Ann Street with Amelia's brother, Edward Battisti aka Harry and his infant son, Albert also living with them. Ettore "Harry" and Joseph were both working at Engelhardt's Piano Factory. Luigi worked on the railroad. Edward Battisti was working on the Barge Canal. It appears that Edward's wife, Josephine Giamaria may have passed away and Amelia was involved with raising his son, Albert, who was only two at the time.

1920 shows the Palombi family now lives at 25 Ann Street with their daughter, Maria, now married to Philip Caponera and their two children, Geraldine and Victor. Edward and Albert Battisti still reside with them. It is quite evident that Edward's wife had passed away and he was raising his son, Albert alone. Italians rarely divorced in those days.

Luigi Palombi lived a long, somewhat contentious, life of 79 years. It seems he was always having a family member arrested. Born February 2, 1872 in Supino, he died suddenly July 26, 1951 at the home of his daughter-in-law, Rose Capece Palombi in East St. Johnsville.

His wife, Amelia Battisti, who was eight years older, passed away December 18, 1932 at the same home in East St. Johnsville at age 68.

ETTORE PALOMBI, well known as Harry, was born in Supino on February 21, 1894. At 23-years-old he immigrated to America on December 21, 1910, headed to Little Falls to meet his father, Luigi.

Residing at 29 Ann Street with his family, Ettore "Harry" was inducted into World War I at Fonda on October 5, 1917 to serve in the US Army Infantry. He was stationed overseas from May 1, 1918 until February 4, 1919, when he was discharged due to a wound he had received in action. He arrived in Hoboken NJ from Brest, France as a Private in the "C" Company 116th Ammunition Train. Before enlisting, he was working at Allter's Knitting Mill on upper North Division Street.

ROSINA CAPECE, daughter of Dominick Capece and Philomena Basolone, married Ettore Palombi on October 2, 1922 at St. Patrick's Church with Ettore's siblings, Joseph Palombi and Maria Palombi Caponera as witnesses to the union. They had three children - Dora Amelia, Lawrence and Richard.

By 1925 the couple was residing with Harry's parents on State Highway 5, east of the village, their home for the remainder of their lives. Their first child, Dora was born. Harry became the owner/operator of the beginning of a one-stop full service gas station, with his father, Luigi as an assistant. By 1930, their two sons, Lawrence and Richard, had joined the family.

Harry was quite the enterprising entrepreneur, later expanding his business ventures into the sales of radios and large appliances. By July 1935 through at least 1946, he and Rose had also opened a restaurant business obtaining a license to serve beer and cider. Guess it was the homebrewed cider that fermented into an alcoholic drink, so a license was needed to serve? My grandfather made it for many years. It had to be just right before imbibing.

Ettore Palombi died in Little Falls Hospital on July 6, 1947, one day after presenting his daughter, Dora in marriage to Leo T. Mancini. The funeral was delayed while police, NYS Troopers and Canadian officials tried to track down the honeymooners on their way to Niagara Falls, Canada, much to no avail. Cellphones and the Internet hadn't been invented yet.

The newspapers claimed it was the most largely attended funeral ever. There was such a profusion of flowers sent to the home, they had to ask for a delay in deliveries, as there was no more room. He was waked at home, as was the tradition at the time. All of the village of St. Johnsville businesses were closed during the church service out of respect for this esteemed gentleman. This was also a tradition for years after when a businessman passed away.

As a World War I Veteran and member of the Morris J. Edwards American Legion Post, Harry was honored with a full military funeral. The color guard and pallbearers marched with the body from the Palombi home at the eastern edge of the village on Route 5 to St. Patrick's Catholic Church on Center Street, then up the hill to the Prospect View Cemetery, where they placed him in the vault until his daughter and son-in-law arrived back home for the burial.

With the assistance of her two sons still at home, Rosina carried on with the gas station and restaurant businesses. She was also left to care for Harry's aging father, who passed away at the home four years later.

In May 1954, Rosina Capece passed away at the Mary Imogene Hospital in Cooperstown after ten weeks as a patient.

After their father's death, Lawrence and Richard took over the business, naming it Palombi Bros. Auto Service. They conducted a used car dealership, adding a Fiat franchise in 1965. As siblings, they got along very well. They loved to converse with their customers, which accounted for their salesmanship success.

During October of 1964 the village of St. Johnsville experienced a severe water shortage. The Palombi brothers graciously offered water from the artesian well on their property.

DORA AMELIA PALOMBI, the first child of Harry and Rosina, was born August 18, 1923 at the family home. She passed away May 25, 2003 in St. Johnsville.

Before the advent of World War II, Dora was engaged to James Colorito, son of Gino Colorito and Teresa Mastracco. James died in battle and was honored with the naming of the local VFW Post as Starr-Colorito. They lived across from each other on Route 5.

On July 5, 1947, Dora Amelia was joined in marriage with Leo T. Mancini, son of Francesco "Frank" Mancini and Louisa Fiorini. They had two sons - Leo Gregory and Michael H. I believe Dora was pretty much a stay at home mom most of her life. I find no source of employment for her.

Dora and Leo were quite the dancers, especially the jitterbug. Dora sure had some great moves.

Leo T. Mancini was born February 19, 1920. At the age of 97, Leo died September 27, 2017 at the home he had worked to develop – St. Johnsville Nursing and Rehabilitation Facility.

He was an honorable member of the American Legion for 72 years. You will read more about Leo Mancini in *La Famiglia Mancini*.

LAWRENCE J. PALOMBI aka Larry was born April 25, 1926 at the family home. He worked with his father for many years, learning the ropes of successful business. He was a World War II Veteran.

On September 21, 1955, Larry was married to Shirley Shaver of Cobleskill, and then later divorced. His obituary states that Ivana De Cresce was his companion for 45 years. I remember him as quite the ladies man.

Lawrence J. Palombi passed away at the St. Johnsville Nursing Home on November 13, 2014.

RICHARD C. PALOMBI was also born at the family home, which he never left, on January 22, 1928. He passed away at Basset Hospital, Cooperstown, on July 17, 2012.

A life devoted to the business and maintaining the family home, Richard never married. I believe he never got over a breakup with his first love.

Like his sister, Dora, "Richie" also loved to dance. After the close of business on the weekend, he would head to Shermans Dance Hall at Caroga Lake. There were several times when he would offer my girl friends and me to hitch a ride with him. My mom would be there at the close of the dances to bring us home. He was always very respectful of us.

JOSEPH PALOMBI lived most of his life in St. Johnsville, brought here by his mother, Amelia Battisti in 1912. Throughout his life he conducted various businesses along with his wife, Sadie Caselle.

In 1917, Joe was living with his parents and siblings at 29 Ann Street, working on the railroad. In the January 1920 Census he's still at home at 25 Ann Street.

On December 5, 1920 Joseph Palombi married Sadie Casselle of Fonda, daughter of Ralph Casselle and Elizabeth Luciano. Sadie had four sisters and two brothers living in Fonda at the time. Her mother may have remarried, as one of the brothers has the last name of Mancini. I do know the family was related to the Mancini's in Fonda.

By 1925 the couple had moved to 39 Bridge Street on the corner of New Street and became proprietors of a grocery store. They also became parents with the birth of two sons - Louis and Anthony. By 1930 they were now the proud owners of the large corner building housing their grocery store, valued at $6000. Siblings, Amelia and Ralph had now joined the family. It seems Sadie had given up the grocery store and later opened a restaurant, The American Grill at this site. They were still living there in 1942.

Classified ads of April 12, 1939 in the *Enterprise & News* newspaper advertise the Bridge Street property for sale; also a 2-story brick building and restaurant at 8 Main Street, where Sadie had moved her restaurant. I'm inclined to think this was 8 East Main, the building where Barbara Salvagni Stagliano has her beauty salon.

I recall them living on Bridge Street, so they were there for several years into the late 40s. By 1953-1954 they were in business with Sadie's Tavern at the eastern end of the village on Route 5, next to Joe's brother, Harry's business and home.

Joe and Sadie were in the restaurant business for 22 years, including the American Grill on Bridge Street, the restaurant on Main and thence to the final location, where they raised their family and lived out their lives. By this time the last of their children, Carmela was born.

In 1944 Joe was a bus driver for Central New York Coach Lines out of Utica. He also conducted his own Taxi Service in the area for a short while. During this time he was involved in an encounter with one of his passengers, who was obviously inebriated when he picked him up. Long story, short, Joe received injuries during the altercation with the man who was not from the St. Johnsville area. This occurred on Bridge Street near the railroad bridge. His nephew Lawrence Palombi and his friend, Lawrence Francisco happened to be nearby, most likely at the Bridge Street Grill where Francisco resided, and were able to come to his rescue.

When the NYS Thruway was readying the properties in Mindenville for demolition to build the Thruway, Joe purchased the former Anthony Capece home and had it transported further down the road, where it still sits today. He most likely had intentions of renting the property as the Capece family had moved into St. Johnsville.

Ogden Bellinger and his brother-in-law Updyke were hired to complete the job during a heavy rainstorm. Traffic was suspended from 6pm on Thursday night until early Saturday morning. The home still exists at the site today.

I recall Joe with his roadside stand near the Soldiers and Sailors Memorial Park, selling hot dogs, soda and ice cream. When he gave up the business, his son Ralph, a hairdresser set up his shop in the building. The site now houses the popular Park Side Restaurant with the proprietary of his grandson, Anthony Joseph Manikas and sons.

A World War I Veteran, Joe was active with the St. Johnsville Democratic Club and a member of the Columbus Fraternal Organization of Little Falls.

Joseph Palombi was born November 21, 1896 in Supino and passed away in November 1965 at Little Falls Hospital, close to his 69th birthday. He had been residing with his daughter, Carmella.

SADIE CASSELLE was born in Fonda on March 18, 1900. She succumbed to a heart attack at the age of 54 in 1954 at Little Falls Hospital. Sadie was a member of the American Legion Auxiliary.

LOUIS J. PALOMBI was named after his grandfather, being the first-born son on October 21, 1922. After graduating from St. Johnsville High School, he returned for a year to complete some courses before going on to Oswego State Teachers College. After his commencement at Oswego, he was hired as the 7th grade Science teacher at Little Falls High School.

Louis later married another teacher, Dolores, and moved to the hamlet of West Islip NY, where he participated in politics and served as a Town Councilman for several years. He retired to Stuart FL, where he passed away on January 4, 2004.

ANTONIO ROCCO PALOMBI lived a short life, being born October 23, 1926. After high school, it seems he was stricken with Incipient Pulmonary Tuberculosis. He was a resident of Ray Brook Sanitarium in the Adirondacks for two years. After his return home, his recuperation did not last long as he once again was confined for 15 months at the Homer Folks Hospital in Oneonta. He died in April 1948 at 23 years of age.

AMELIA ROSE PALOMBI was born February 18, 1926. She passed away on March 31, 2009 in Little Falls, where she lived after her marriage.

A member of the 1944 graduation class of St. Johnsville, she was very active in school activities. After graduation she went on to become a hairdresser, for a short time being in a partnership with her brother, Ralph.

On November 12, 1949, Amelia married Thomas Logan from Little Falls, moving her residence there. Also active in politics, she had the distinguished honor of being the first woman elected to the Little Falls City Council.

RALPH THOMAS PALOMBI was well known in the community, not only as a hair stylist, but also for his kindness, generosity and the recipient of numerous friends surrounding him. Known best as "Ralphie", he had a great sense of humor that some of his friends took advantage of with their teasing. However, he was always a good sport.

Ralphie was a good friend of my husband, John and me. I was pleased to have him transporting us from my home to the church, thence to the Community House family dinner and Klock's Park reception on our wedding day. We socialized quite often through the years.

Dancing must have been in the Palombi genes. Though a little on the stout side, Ralphie was a terrific dancer, light on his feet, and often asked to give demonstrations of his jitterbugging skills. He was a popular dance partner at Shermans. I loved to dance with him. He performed with the Little Theater Group, playing humorous parts, written by my uncle, William Perry.

A noted hairdresser, Ralphie employed his creative trade most of his life. He fussed over Mrs. Fowler and other ladies of the village who loved him. At one time he partnered in business with his sister, Amelia.

In December 1956, Ralph became engaged to Genevieve Angelicchio of Herkimer. I don't recall the breakup, but he later met and married Giovanna "Joanne" Piroli in November 1958. They had a son, Louis J. Palombi, born a year later.

The daughter of Luigi Piroli and Ines Mastrofrancesco, Joanne was the niece of Rose Mastrofancesco Iacobucci D'Arcangelis, who lived on Hough Street, a customer of Ralph's. I believe Rose introduced them. Joanne would also be connected to John Francisco (Bridge Street Grill), as he was her mother's brother. As a member of a large family, Joanne had several siblings, as her mother before her.

Ralphie and Joanne loved to exhibit their Italian culinary skills with their lavish dinners. Both loved to cook and bake, making up traditional Italian cookie trays for friends and family on holidays.

Giovanna "Joanne" Piroli was born October 15, 1930 in Supino, flying into Baltimore MD in August 1951 to come to America. She passed away May 3, 1995.

Ralph Thomas Palombi was born March 23, 1929. He passed away July 10, 2003. He served as a Private in the U.S. Army during the Korean War.

CARMELLA PALOMBI was born July 13, 1930. She passed away December 20, 2013 at Bassett Hospital, Cooperstown.

A graduate of the Class of 1950 at St. Johnsville High School, she was active in several clubs, including four years as a cheerleader. In later years she was a participant in the Friday Night Women's Bowling League. Known as "KiKi", she was a classmate and best friend to my husband, John Palma for many years.

Upon the death of her mother, Carmella took over the management of Sadie's Tavern into the 1960s. After selling the property, Life Savers in Canajoharie employed her.

On August 6, 1957, Carmella Palombi became the bride of Peter Manikas of Herkimer NY. Playing matchmaker, KiKi's good friend, Gloria Corso Laraway sent Pete to her home with the intent of selling her sewing machine needles. It was love at first sight! They had two sons - Anthony Joseph and Allan.

Pete fit right in with KiKi's friends and the community, becoming very active with the American Legion, Little League and church activities, among others. The U.S. Postal Service employed him for many years, serving as postmaster. Upon retirement he sold real estate.

This concludes the story of the Joseph Palombi family.

MARIA PALOMBI, the youngest child of Luigi Palombi and Amelia Battisti, was born November 23, 1898 in Supino. She came to St. Johnsville in 1912 with her mother. Her father had emigrated on October 30, 1899, working as a night watchman on the railroad.

On November 26, 1916, Maria Palombi, age 18, and Filiberto "Phil" Caponera, age 27, were married in St. Patrick's Church. In witness to the union were Rame and Maria Rovozzi of Little Falls. Rame was originally from Patrica, Italy. Maria Palombi served as the matron-of-honor in Bertha Pedro's wedding.

Mary and Phil were the parents of six children - Gilda, Victor, Anthony, twins Joseph and Arminio, and Rena, all born in St. Johnsville.

Filiberto Caponera was born February 2, 1889 in Furmone, Italy, son of Erminio Caponera and Mary Arduini. He had a sister, Giselda Uspesi in Rome, Italy.

Phil opened a Liquor Store on West Main Street that prospered for many years with their son, Joseph, inheriting the management and ownership after Phil's sudden death.

Filiberto "Philip" Caponera passed away suddenly on July 16, 1953 at their home at 29 Ann Street after a long illness. You will read more about Filiberto Caponera in *La Famiglia Caponera*.

Maria Palombi died at the family home on November 24, 1982, at the age of 91, many years after her spouse, Philip.

EDWARD L. BATTISTI was the brother of Amelia Battisti Palombi. He was born 1883 in Supino, the son of Lawrence Battisti and Rose Zuccaro (Sugar). We have another Zuccaro connection here.

Edward died March 27, 1936 in St. Johnsville, where he was buried in Prospect View Cemetery. His employment consisted of local factory work.

Immigrating on October 30, 1899 with Luigi Palombi and Cataldo Zuccaro, Edward originally went to New York City to meet his brother Rocco. By June 5, 1912, he lived in Barnesboro PA, where he married Josephine Giamaria, daughter of Lawrence and Clementiana Giamaria. They had a son, Albert. It seems Josephine had passed away so he moved to St. Johnsville to be with his sister.

ALBERT EDWARD BATTISTI was born December 4, 1912 in Barnesboro PA. Albert, only two years old, and his father, Edward were living in St. Johnsville with his sister, Amelia in 1915. They later moved out and were boarders with the Adeline Grattet family at 26 Lion Place.

Albert moved to Little Falls after his marriage to Lena Staffo, daughter of Mr. and Mrs. James Staffo, on November 4, 1939. He passed away on November 15, 1996. 1942 City records show him living in Little Falls.

Albert Battisti had served as best man for my uncle Robert Perry and aunt Anne Root at their wedding in November 1934. I recall my parents mentioning his name. I think they called him "Mag"? They may have all been friends.

I found a newspaper clipping of my father's from the Evening Times. It features the St. Johnsville High School football team of 1930 taken on a day they defeated Johnstown 7 to 6. Albert "Mag" Battisti is standing next to my Dad, Floyd Perry. Mag is rather short compared to the other players. His friend, Bob Perry is also shown. Another Italian, Perminio Laurora was also on the team.

~ *La Famiglia CAPONERA* ~

~ FILIBERTO CAPONERA et MARIA PALOMBI ~

Filiberto "Phil" Caponera, age 27, and Maria Palombi, age 18, were married in St. Patrick's Church on November 26, 1916. In witness to the union were Rame and Maria Rovozzi of Little Falls. Rame Rovozzi was originally from Patrica, Italy.

The couple was the parents of six children - Gilda, Victor, Anthony, twins Joseph and Arminio, and Rena, all born in St. Johnsville.

FILIBERTO CAPONERA was born February 23, 1889 in Furmone, Italy, son of Erminio Caponera and Mary Arduini. He had a sister, Giselda Uspesi in Rome, Italy.

Phil arrived in America on September 10, 1905 at the age of 16.

The 1917 World War I registration form shows him living at 29 Ann Street, St. Johnsville and working at Henry P. Burgard Company in Waddington NY.

MARIA PALOMBI was born November 23, 1898 in Supino, daughter of Luigi Palombi and Amelia Battisti. She came to St. Johnsville in 1912 with her mother. Her father had emigrated on October 30, 1899, working as a night watchman on the railroad.

Luigi Palombi and Amelia Battisti are also the parents of Harry Palombi and Joseph Palombi, well-known St. Johnsville Italian businessmen. There was also another daughter, Rosina Palombi Blene in Supino.

Amelia Battisti was born in Supino on January 4, 1864, daughter of Lawrence Battisti and Rosa Sugar. She had a brother Edward L. Battisti also living in St. Johnsville. Amelia died at home following an operation in an Amsterdam hospital on December 19, 1932. Luigi Palombi was born in 1872, Supino, Italy. He came to America at age 16 and died July 26, 1951 in St. Johnsville. You can read more about this family in *La Famiglia Palombi*.

The 1920 Census shows Luigi and Amelia, along with their two sons, Harry and Joseph and daughter Maria Palombi and her husband, Phil Caponera, their children, Gilda and Victor; Amelia's brother, Edward aka Harry and his son, Albert all living together at 25 Ann Street.

Returning to Filiberto, I have found him working on the railroad in 1920, and as a contractor in 1925. In 1930 Phil is a highway laborer, owning his own home at 29 Ann Street, where he originally lived with his in-laws after marriage. His obituary states that he was a commissary operator at one time, providing canteen service to the logging folks in the Adirondacks.

In 1934, Phil decided to open his own business providing alcoholic libations to the community of St. Johnsville. I'm certain he carried Anisette and Italian wines. Many old world Italians drank home-brewed wine from their grape vines, but loved their Anisette at the end of their Sunday and holiday meals. They weren't familiar with all of today's well-known Italian aperitifs and vast assortments of wines.

Caponera's Liquor Store prospered for many years, even after Phil's retirement and death. After his service in the Army, his son, Joseph and wife, Joyce took over as proprietors. They later sold the business to Frederick Smith of Smith's Market. After almost 70 years of serving the St. Johnsville community, it is no longer in existence.

In October of 1935, the Caponera's hosted a wedding reception at their home for Yolanda "Viola" Narducci and her husband, Alessandro Potenziani. Their daughter, Gilda served as a bridesmaid and son, Victor was an usher.

Filiberto "Philip" Caponera passed away suddenly at his home at 29 Ann Street after a long illness on July 16, 1953. Maria Palombi died at the family home on November 24, 1982.

GILDA CAPONERA was born September 24, 1917. She passed away in 1984.

In September 1940, Gilda married Gilbert J. Smith of N. Division Street. She was honored with a bridal shower at the St. Johnsville Dress Corporation, where she worked. She may have been married a second time, as she was also known as Gilda Swaty.

In 1935, serving as a bridesmaid, Gilda hosted a bridal shower for her friend, Viola Narducci who married Alesandro Potenziani on October 20, 1935. Her brother, Victor was the best man, Perina Nobile from Utica was maid of honor and Oscar Cochi served as an usher. A reception followed at the Caponera home. Perina Nobile was Viola Peruzzi's aunt.

Gilda was also a miniature bridesmaid in the wedding of Bertha Pedro and Lawrence Caponera aka Mastromoro.

VICTOR ALBERT CAPONERA was born on November 15, 1918 and passed away March 11, 1997 in Albany.

He worked for Green Island Construction, Glens Falls, where he resided after his marriage to Ida Rose Tarantelli in October 1940. Ida was the daughter of Mr. and Mrs. Salvatore Tarantelli of Saratoga Springs. The wedding took place at St. Peter's Church with a wedding dinner following at the Caponera home, followed by a reception at the I.O.O.F. Hall on Bridge Street. Victor's sister Rena served as maid of honor, Ida's brother was best man. The couple had two childen - Philip and Carol Ann.

T/4 Victor Caponera, age 26, was inducted to serve his country on August 17, 1944 at Camp Claiborne, Louisiana as an engineer. During 1945 he served overseas in the Philipines and at the Mariannes Base in Guam. It seems he owned his own construction business after the war.

ANTHONY ROCCO CAPONERA was born January 15, 1920 and died May 27, 1990 in Sharon Springs. He apparently served in the military, but I find no documents.

On May 20, 1950, Anthony Caponera married Winifred E. Mac Intyre from Buel in St. Patrick's Church. Anthony's cousins, Carmela Palombi and Louis Palombi were the attendants. At the time, Tony worked for Joseph Capece.

Identical twins Joseph Louis Caponera and Arminio Frank Caponera were born on January 24, 1921. They graduated from St. Johnsville High School in 1939.

Along with their brothers, Victor and Anthony, they served their country in World War II. In September 1942 at age 23, the twins enlisted together as Privates in the US Army; they were discharged in 1946.

Sgt. JOSEPH CAPONERA served in Panama as a Radar Technician, working to destroy enemy aircraft. His uncle, Harry Palombi, had employed him at his East End Filling Station before joining the Army. He returned to that employ after his discharge, until taking over his father's liquor store.

Shortly after returning from service, Joe met Joyce Carbary from Detroit, MI. They were married on December 21, 1950 in the parish house of St. Patrick's Church. Attendants were their good friends, Louis Salvagni and Barbara Van Slyke, the wife of Raymond Van Slyke of St. Johnsville. I met Joyce when she first moved to St. Johnsville. The story I recall hearing is that Joyce was visiting her close childhood friend, Barbara, also from Detroit. Barbara's mother owned the Stone Lodge in Palatine Bridge at the time. I think Ray Van Slyke was good friends with Joe and introduced the two of them.

Joe and Joyce had six children - Robert, who passed away May 10, 2009, Albert, David, Thomas, Donna and Linda.

When Joe took over the liquor store, Joyce was always there to assist him up until the time he sold it in the mid-1970s. Before color photography was available, Joyce would sit at her desk in her home for hours, plying her skilled Colorization art with the unique delicate process of coloring black and white photos for customers. You may have some old family photos from the late 1800s to the early 1900s that are either black and white or sepia and were enhanced? This art is coming back into vogue with people resurrecting old family photos.

Included with the purchase of their East Main Street home was St. Johnsville's famous watering hole aka the "springs". Many residents and their children quenched their thirst on their walk home after leaving the village ball park and playground.

Barney Allen, who lived on the corner of East Main and Ann, where the garage/body shop is now, sold them the brick home. David Caponera shared this story, *"Barney used to say the spring was part of the farm, where they kept their milk barrels cold in the summer.*" In the summertime, the Caponera's stored watermelons in the little building. To flush the spring once or twice a year, Joe would use an old bowling pin to plug the hole from the creek. Italians always knew how to improvise.

Joe served as the chairman of the Cancer Crusade for several years. He was an avid bowler in the Monday Night Men's Bowling League. After selling the liquor store, Joe worked for the village of St. Johnsville DPW for a few years.

On June 2, 1990, Joyce Carbary was stricken at home and died while being transported to Little Falls Hospital. She was born in Detroit on February 5, 1926 to Clark and Hilda Carbary.

Joseph Louis Caponera passed away March 3, 2001. Within five months, St. Johnsville lost three of its finest second-generation Italian men - Carmen Giaquinto, Joseph Caponera and John Palma, Jr., all friends. Another friend, Joseph Colorito passed away 10 years before them. They had all worked for the Village of St. Johnsville.

Tech/Sgt. ARMINIO CAPONERA was stationed at Fort Brady, Michigan in the mechanical division, serving in France and Germany. Before being called to serve his country, "Army" had been employed by a Dolgeville Shoe Factory, the New York Central Railroad and Helmont Textile Mill on Lyon Avenue.

I discovered a February 1943 news article in the Enterprise and News with the twins in uniform side-by-side, honoring their service. During World War II, the newspaper ran a weekly column featuring those who were in the service. The paper was always headlined with current news of the young men serving in the military from St. Johnsville and surrounding towns.

After returning home from World War II, Army conducted a Taxi Service in the village.

On June 16, 1951, he married Wilhelmina "Minnie" Fields Heiser from Fort Plain. They had no children.

Arminio aka Army was best known as the proprietor of Cap's Cigar and Billiards, which he owned on and off for many years. He originally purchased the business from Stacey "Jerry" Dunton on October 4, 1951 and sold it eight years later to Phil Terricola in October 1959, who sold it a year later to Maurice Everett. Army later purchased it again, I believe from Everett. Army and his wife, Minnie, conducted the cigar store and poolroom for 37 years. They resided upstairs over the business most of their lives.

Arminio Frank Caponera passed away on May 13, 1992. Army was a member of the American Legion, Starr-Colorito VFW and St. Johnsville Rod and Gun Club.

Minnie Heiser, born January 21, 1920 in Fort Plain, followed her husband three years later on June 19, 1995. Minnie was also very active in community affairs.

RENA CAPONERA was born July 20, 1922 and died on June 19, 2005 at Valley Health Services in Herkimer at 82 years.

She was first married to Henry Gerdin of Little Falls on December 3, 1944. Dora Palombi served her cousin as maid of honor. They had a daughter, Donna Gerdin Macrina who passed away in 2002. On April 16, 1950 Rena was united in marriage with James Buccaferno of Little Falls in St. Patrick's Catholic Church. He passed away on November 13, 1997. They had three daughters - Rose, Mary and Phillipa.

While her sister, Gilda was a mini-bridesmaid, Rena was the flower girl in the Pedro-Caponera aka Mastromorro wedding. Many of the Caponera and Palombi family members were in the wedding. Rena's mother, Mary was the matron-of-honor; Mary's brother, Joseph Palombi was best man and Joe's son, Louis was ring bearer. The maiden name of Larry Mastromoro's mother was Caponera.

Living most of her life in Little Falls, Rena was a member of the Holy Family Parish and the DeCarlo-Staffo Ladies Auxiliary.

~ *La Famiglia CAPRARA* ~

PETER A. CAPRARA aka Pete was born in Little Falls on June 17, 1910 to Albert Caprara and Anna Crissa. Apparently, his father died at a young age as his obituary states a stepfather, Sam Valiente of East Herkimer. Pete died February 21, 1964 at Little Falls Hospital after a long illness. He was a communicant of St. Patrick's Church.

For 18 years, long before recycling goods became a commodity, Pete made his living literally picking up and getting rid of "waste" – paper, metal, etc. An August 15, 1946 advertisement I found in the *Enterprise & News* promotes his local trucking and selling of coal.

On July 4, 1935 Peter Caprara married Anna Mae Heiser of Fort Plain, a sister of Minnie Caponera. They had three children - Gloria Beaulieu, Carol Ann and Albert.

Anna Mae's sister, Mickey Heiser married John Warn, another well-known St. Johnsville young man, not of Italian heritage, but he lived among them.

~ NAPOLEON ~ CAPONERA ~
20 East Main ~ Early 1900s

Many of the old buildings located on Main Street, St. Johnsville have quite a history - one of them being the property at 20 East Main Street aka Cap's Cigar and Billiards. Dating back to the early 1900s, I shall attempt to bring its interesting history up to date.

As far back as I am able to research, Prospero J. Napoleone, who opened Napoleon's Café, purchased the 20 East Main Street building in St. Johnsville in August 1910. His father, Louis Napoleone served as bartender.

According to Census and City address records I've found, Napoleone moved to St. Johnsville after he married Victoria Terranova on September 17, 1908. Utilizing the whole building, the downstairs served as a bar and poolroom with a fine Italian-French restaurant, Roma Café and their living quarters upstairs. After his tragic death on May 31, 1915, his brother-in-law, Carmine Terranova handled the estate for Prosper's wife, Victoria, who was the recipient of the contents of his estate. You can read more about Prosper Napoleon in *La Famiglia Prospero J. Napoleone.*

From other information I have discovered, it seems Pietro Battisti, who boarded with the Joseph Tolfa family in 1915, may have taken over the bar/café for a couple years after Napoleone's death. The 1915 census claims his employment as "working in saloon". This was before Napoleone's death in May, so Pietro may have been working for Joe Tolfa, who had purchased his hotel/grill right next door on March 20, 1915. (Pietro was the brother of James Battisti, father of Romeo.)

Since we find no record of Pietro paying rent, I'm assuming he may have kept the business open for the Napoleone family, perhaps with a purchase option. However, a newspaper article I found states that on February 21, 1916 a fire completely destroyed the building, burning it to the ground, with a $6,000 loss. There were three fire companies in attendance, as it was threatening the business section. The article stated Peter Baptiste currently owned it.

The 1920 Census shows Battisti as a bartender and operator of a Liquor Store. By 1925, he was the proprietor of a Lunch Room at 24 East Main Street in the building right next door to 20 Main Street. Apparently, he had moved next door, where he either purchased or rented the property.

Now, it gets confusing! Sometime between the February 1916 fire and March 1918, the building must have been rebuilt, as per the previous photo.

Mat Rapacz located an old account book of "store rents". The first entry of March 1918 showed Roy Snell in account with P.J. Napoleone Estate. Roy Snell and Frank Glenar had opened a barbershop across the street in a hotel, where the post office stands today, then moved across the street to the Napoleone site. The barbers paid a monthly rent of $11.00 to C. Terranova until January of 1924.

In February 1924 the barbers began paying rent to Charlie Linter, who had a cigar store at that location. Linter apparently purchased the property from Carmine Terranova, who had moved to New York City. They continued paying rent to Charlie Linter, a current Town Supervisor, until May 1942, then to Maud Linter after Charlie's death. Entries in the book end July 29, 1946.

By 1930 the Census shows an Adelbert Smith living upstairs at this address.

After returning home from the Army in 1946, Stacey "Jerry" Dunton purchased the building and business from Mrs. Linter and opened a Cigar Store with a Pool Room. Jerry lived upstairs with his wife Viola Iacobucci and daughter, Cheryl. He also rented the other side to Snell and Glenar, barbers.

October 4, 1951 Stacey Dunton sold the building and business to Arminio Caponera and his wife, Minnie. Eight years later in October 1959 "Army" Caponera sold the business to Phil Terricola, who sold it a year later to Maurice Everett, who was the proprietor until May 1962. At some point, Caponera again became the owner and conducted the business for a total of 37 years.

Now, you know the history of the famous building at 20 East Main Street.

Napoleon Café on left before 1915 next to
Charles LaRosa bar before it became
Central Hotel with Tolfa purchase

Pietro Battisti Italian Restaurant
site of former Napoleon Café

Roma Italian Society

Due to Italy entering World War I on May 24, 1915, President Woodrow Wilson designated Friday, May 24, 1918 as "Italy Day." A huge celebration was held in St. Johnsville with Carmine Terranova, the patriarch of the Italian community, in charge of preparations.

The event saw a huge parade in celebration of the ending of World War I, led by the Home Guard Band, which had been organized by this time. Made up mostly of Italians, there was one wanna-be-Italian member. The Engelhardt Peerless Band also performed in other parades and celebrations in honor of Italian traditions.

Sometime during the 1900s, St. Johnsville Italians formed their own organization - Roma Italian Society - and were quite active in promoting their proud Italian heritage. I'm thinking Carmine Terranova was instrumental in organizing this society and most likely was president. Serving as its honorable secretary was his brother-in-law, Prospero Napoleone, also a respected member of the Italian community.

On Wednesday, May 15, 1912, the Roma Italian Society held services at St. Patrick's Roman Catholic Church honoring the christening of two new flags, the American and Italian, belonging to the Society. A parade preceded the service.

On the sad occasion of Prospero Napoleone's tragic death on May 31, 1915, the Home Guard Band preceded the funeral procession, passing by his place of business and home at 20 East Main Street on the way to the funeral service at St. Patrick's Church, followed by the march to Prospect View Cemetery, where he was laid to rest.

For several years, the Roma Italian Society celebrated traditional events such as Columbus Day. There were yearly tributes to their beloved patron, Saint Anthony of Padua.

On August 16, 1924 Saint Rocco's Day was celebrated. The storefronts along Main Street were draped with the stars and stripes and flags of Italy. Most of the homes in the village participated with decorations and flags. St. Johnsville literally came alive with respect for the Italian immigrants, who had become a prominent factor in increasing the economy of the growing village.

In June of 1926 (1928), Professor Pietro Cianfrocca, musician and well-known musical conductor from Rome NY and Italy, directed a band concert in honor of that date's St. Anthony's celebration. Throughout the years, Cianfrocca made several trips to and from his hometown of Alatri, Italy. Spending his final days there, he died January 12, 1964 at the age of 77 from complications of stomach cancer.

In November of 1938 twenty-five Italian Americans formed another Italian Club – the St. Johnsville Citizens Club. Officers of this group were President, Joseph Sackett; Vice-President, Dominick Papa; Treasurer, Amy Castrucci; and Secretary, James Pietrocini. Serving as Trustees were Joseph Tolfa, Paul Salvagni, Frank Colorito and Sam Annunzio.

~ *La Famiglia STAGLIANO* ~

The Stagliano families were early immigrants to America from Chiaravalle Centrale, Italy.

On August 22, 1905, Vincenzo Stagliano, a priest from Italy, immigrated and came directly to St. Johnsville. He soon settled in Troy NY, where he served as the pastor of Our Lady of Mount Carmel Catholic Church in Watervliet, which he developed. Vincenzo had purchased an old house and transformed it into an Italian Catholic Church. In March of 1911 the church suffered fire damage amounting to $5,000.

Rev. Vincenzo Stagliano retired in November 1911 and returned to Rome, Italy, where he was called to take charge of an Italian Mission.

DOMENICO STAGLIANO followed his brother, Rev. Vincenzo Stagliano to St. Johnsville, where he worked on the New York Central Railroad and also some construction projects. I found Domenico living at 15 Sanders Street in the 1912-1914 St. Johnsville Directory.

On August 29, 1909, Domenico Stagliano was united with Michelina Guarnacci Penna, daughter of Maria Catricala in Watervliet. I'm assuming his brother Vincent may have married them. They had a son Frank, born January 27, 1911 in St. Johnsville, where the family lived until 1915.

MICHELINA GUARNACCI PENNA had been married to another man before coming to America. They had two children - Michelina and Nicola. Penna apparently died in Italy and she came here to join her parents, Caesar Guarnacci and Maria Catricala.

Frank Stagliano was four years old when his parents, along with his two half-siblings, returned to their hometown, Chiaravalle Centrale, Italy. Frank returned to America and Nicola moved to Toronto, Canada.

~ FRANK STAGLIANO et MARIA IOZZO ~

On September 6, 1927, at the age of 16, Frank came back to the United States. It seems he made several voyages back and forth between Italy and St. Johnsville, including the time he returned to Chiaravalle, married his wife, Maria Iozzo and brought her back to St. Johnsville.

1930 Census records show Frank as a lodger in North Bergen NJ, where he may have worked in a drug store? Most of his life, he was employed with the Little Falls Felt Shoe Company, St. Johnsville.

Tech/4 FRANK STAGLIANO was drafted June 12, 1942, while living in New Jersey and served in World War II. He was sent to Algiers, North Africa, where he ironically happened upon his brother, Nicholas, who was serving in the Italian army. Nicholas was captured by the Americans and taken prisoner. They hadn't seen each other since Frank was sixteen. Another brother, Vincent, also a member of the Italian army, had been taken prisoner by the British and was imprisoned in England.

After leaving Algiers, Frank stopped in his hometown of Chiaravalle, Italy for a reunion with his parents, whose home had been damaged by the war. He was discharged November 29, 1945.

Once again, Frank returned to Italy. This time to bring back his new bride, Maria Iozzo to America. They arrived on September 16, 1947, heading to his home at 31 Mechanic Street. They had two sons - Dominick and Frank, Jr., both born in St. Johnsville.

Frank Stagliano passed away September 5, 2000 at the Little Falls Hospital at age 89.

MARIA IOZZO was born March 14, 1924 in Chiaravalle. She passed away on May 3, 2007, almost seven years after Frank's death in 2000.

After coming to America, records show Mary and Frank lived at 28 Center Street in their early marriage? This may not be accurate. In May 1951, they purchased the 26 Sanders Street home from Kain Fontana, where they lived the remainder of their lives.

Previously, the Salvagni family had owned the 26 Sanders Street home. It has stayed in the Salvagni-Stagliano family since with their son, Dominick marrying Barbara Salvagni. It is still occupied by a Stagliano descendant.

As a seamstress, Mary used her skills to tailor and repair clothing for many residents including Terricola's Family Clothing Store. She worked at the Corso Dress Company until they closed.

A fabulous cook and baker, Mary provided gnocchios to Capece's Restaurant for several years, after Pasquale Capece, Philomena's father was no longer able to make them. Philomena Capece and Joseph Marotti were the proprietors of the popular family friendly restaurant, located outside the village.

Mary had four brothers, Vincent in Canada, Paul, Nick and Tony. Also a sister, Josephine Iozzo Ponteduro, who predeceased her in St. Johnsville, and a step-sister, Isabella Lasadonte.

DOMENICK STAGLIANO served in the Vietnam War, where he was assigned to the 937th Engineer's Group in Vietnam as a combat engineer. While in the service he married Barbara Salvagni, daughter of Floyd and Esther Salvagni, on November 17, 1968.

Upon his discharge, he worked for the Rush Furniture Company in Herkimer, as a salesman. He had attended both Cobleskill Agricultural and Technical School and Fulton-Montgomery Community College.

Donnie, as he was better known, has always been very active in St. Johnsville and Montgomery County politics, serving both as Town Supervisor and Village Mayor.

Barbara Salvagni graduated from Harper School of Beauty and opened her own Beauty Salon on East Main Street.

The couple resides in the home previously occupied by the Guarnacci and Stagliano families at 31 Mechanic Street. All in the family!

FRANK STAGLIANO, Jr. was born around 1950. After graduating, he established his own photography business, Stagliano Photography. He later worked for Rich Plan in Utica, a company who provided home freezer plans. I was a customer for several years.

Frank was a member of the St. Johnsville Volunteer Fire Department and served as a Commissioner on the St. Johnsville Housing Authority.

I find no record, but Frank also served his country. He was a member of the St. Johnsville Morris J. Edwards American Legion Post.

In September of 1977, Frank married Cindy Wiers, daughter of Mr. and Mrs. Ray Wiers of Herkimer, formerly of Canajoharie.

~ *La Famiglia GUARNACCI* ~

~ CESARE GUARNACCI et MARIA GRAZIA CATRICOLA ~

As head of the Guarnacci household for many years until his death, Cesare "Charlie" Guarnacci was born in Normo (Rome), Italy on July 22, 1892 to Antonio Guarnacci and Felicia Gaetano.

At 16 years of age, Cesare arrived in America on April 14, 1909 with many other immigrant passengers from Normo. The passenger manifest states he went to Allentown PA.

World War I records of June 5, 1917 show he was now living at 28 Mechanic Street, single, and working on the New York Central Railroad at the age of 24.

By 1920 Cesare Guarnacci and Maria Grazie Catricola were married and living at 24 Ann Street with Maria's sister, Clara Catricola. In 1930 they have purchased the home at 31 Mechanic Street, where they both lived out their lives. I find no records of Clara Catricola.

The 1930 Census shows that Cesare and Maria had a daughter, Gretana, an 8-month-old baby. I find no further records of Gretana.

Also sharing the Mechanic Street home is Cesare's brother, Paolo "Paul" with his wife, Giovanna "Jennie" Gagliardi and her sister, Mary Gagliardi, age 18. The census states they were nieces of Cesare. Mary Gagliardi later married Dominick Papa.

By 1942, World War II records show that Cesare is 49 years old. He and Maria are still living at the 31 Mechanic Street address; he is working at Palatine Dyeing Company.

CESARE GUARNACCI died of a second heart attack in Little Falls Hospital on March 12, 1956. He suffered a heart attack at home and was being transported to the hospital, when the vehicle he was riding in was rear-ended. He received a fractured shoulder, followed by the fatal heart attack at the hospital.

MARIA GRAZIE CATRICOLA, several years older than Caesar, was born in Chiaravalle, Centrale, Italy on September 8, 1880. She immigrated to New York City on April 14, 1909, living there until her move to St. Johnsville. She was the daughter of Francisco Grazia Catricola. She died May 16, 1950 in St. Johnsville.

Maria had a son, Nicola, and daughter, Michelina Penna, from a previous marriage. Her daughter, Michelena Penna, was the mother of Frank Stagliano. Maria Catricola Guarnacci was Frank's grandmother.

In the early years of Italian immigration, 31 Mechanic Street was also one of the popular boarding places. I believe my grandfather, Giuseppe Sindici boarded there upon his arrival. The home has stayed in the Stagliano family to this time.

~ PAOLO GUARNACCI et GIOVANNA GAGLIARDI ~

As a young man, Paolo served in the Italian Army during World War I. After the war, he immigrated to St. Johnsville on May 13, 1921, joining his brother Cesare at 9 Bridge Street.

1925 Census records show Paul residing at 31 Mechanic Street with his brother, Cesare Guarnacci and his wife, Maria Catricola.

After becoming naturalized in Washington DC on September 12, 1928, Paul returned to Italy, where he married Giovanna "Jennie" Gagliardi. They returned together on February 4, 1929 and lived with his brother Caesar's family at 31 Mechanic Street.

PAOLO "Paul" GUARNACCI was born on May 14, 1898 in Chiaravalle. He died of a heart attack at home on February 20, 1967 at age 68. He was employed most of his life by Palatine Dyeing Company.

GIOVANNA "Jennie" GAGLIARDI was born on May 8, 1907. She died in January 1976 in Little Falls Hospital, also at age 68.

Jennie worked most of her life at the Corso Dress Company. She lived in Troy NY at one time where her sister, Mary Gagliardi was born.

In 1940 Paul, Jennie and their daughter, Susan were still living with Caesar and Maria. They later purchased their home at 23 South Division Street, where they lived out their lives.

23 South Division Street was also a popular boarding house in the early part of the 1900s.

SUSAN GRETANA GUARNACCI was born on the 14th of August 1929, to Paolo and Giovanna Gagliardi Guarnacci. She died October 10, 1998.

On August 29, 1954, Susan Guarnacci was joined in marriage with Louis Salvagni, son of Paul Salvagni and Adelgesia Pasquale. Serving as maid-of-honor was Nancy Battisti with Carl Cochi as best man. Bridesmaids included Elnora Fiacco, Josephine Terricola and Rita Papa. Ushers were cousin of the bride, Sam Papa and James Pietrocini, cousin of the groom and Rudy Salvagni, brother of the groom. Niece of the groom, Barbara Salvagni was flower girl and Dominick Stagliano, cousin of the bride, was the ring bearer. A wedding breakfast was served at the bride's home with a dinner at Capece's Restaurant, followed by the reception at Klock's Park. They had two sons - David and Daniel.

Susie was most noted for her dedication to St. Patrick's Catholic Church for many years as the musical director, which included - organist, soloist and choir director. She provided the music for numerous weddings and funerals throughout her lifetime. This included my wedding in 1955 and my daughter's in 1982.

La Famiglia Guarnacci – Stagliano – Papa
Family wedding in Toronto, Canada

Back: Jennie, Susie and Paul Guarnacci; Frank and Mary Stagliano; Josephine Iozzo,
Enza Stagliano; parents of bride, Angela and Nichola Stagliano; Mary, Diane and Sam Papa
Front: Frank, Jr. and Dominick Stagliano; Bride Lina Stagliano; Groom Vito Sgotto
Bride's brother Domenic Stagliano from Toronto Canada

~ *La Famiglia PAPA* ~

~ SAVERIO PAPA et MADELINA GIAQUINTO ~

On March 18, 1907, at 17 years of age, Saverio "Sam" Papa immigrated to America first going to his aunt Bonrea Pasquaniello's home in Newark NY, located on the Erie Canal near Rochester NY.

Within the next four years, Saverio Papa met his wife, Madelina "Mary" Giaquinto while working for the New York Central Railroad as a foreman in New York City. They were married at St. Mary's Church on November 6, 1911 in New York City. Both had been residents of Briano, Italy near Naples.

Sam's World War I records of June 1917 show they had moved to Fonda NY. Seven of their children, Dominick, John, Christine, Rose, Mary, Theresa, and Anna were born here. The 1920 Census shows them residing in Fonda. Their last child, Rita was born in St. Johnsville.

By 1930 the entire family had moved to the 32 Ann Street home, where the couple resided for 55 years of their lives. At this date, it is still the family homestead, now occupied by grandchildren.

After devoting 47 years to the New York Central Railroad as a foreman, Sam retired in 1956. In his retirement he worked as a night watchman at Helmont Mills, then caretaker of the Soldiers and Sailors Memorial Park.

SAVERIO PAPA passed away May 1970 at 79. There is a discrepancy with Sam's birth. World War I records state June 6, 1889. According to World War II records, he was born February 22, 1892 in Briano, Italy, son of Dominick Papa and Christine Laperupo. The latter is the birth date shown on his Social Security documents of death. Sam had a brother, Frank.

MADELINA GIAQUINTO was born May 2, 1893 in Naples, Italy. She was the daughter of Giovanni Giaquinto and Therese Christene. Mary followed Sam in death two years later in September 1972. She had a brother Cosmo Giaquinto still in Italy.

DOMINICK J. PAPA, being the eldest son, was named after his grandfather, which was the usual custom. Dominick was born February 21, 1913 in Fonda NY on his father's birthday.

Dominick J. Papa married Maria Gagliardi, sister of Giovanna "Jennie" Guarnacci, on September 3, 1933 in St. Patrick's Catholic Church. Dominick's sister Christine was maid-of-honor, with Frank Stagliano, Mary's cousin from Union City NJ at the time, serving as best man. Bridesmaids included Mary Giaquinto and Theresa Cerillo. Ushers were Dominick Peruzzi and John Papa, brother of the groom. Mary's niece, Susan Guarnacci and Dominick's sister, Rita Papa were flower girls with Carmen Giaquinto as ring bearer. A reception was held at the Democratic Club rooms in the Palombi building on Bridge Street. They celebrated 65 years of marriage before Dominick's passing.

While first living with his parents on Ann Street, sometime after 1940, Dom and Mary purchased their home at 27 East Liberty, where they lived the remainder of their lives. They had two children - Sam, also named after his grandfather and Diane.

At one time, Dominick was employed as an inspector in the Little Falls Felt Shoe factory, and also worked on the railroad. He spent most of his work life as a butcher.

In 1945 Dom and Mary purchased the Castrucci Italian Market at 14 South Division Street, across the street from their home, from the Amy Castrucci family, who lived in the apartment over the store. Castrucci's had closed the store after 20 years of service to the Italian community, with Amy and his son, Joseph opening Amy's Texaco Station in West St. Johnsville.

Dom was a lifesaver when I was married in 1955, storing my awesome *Zuppa Inglise* rum wedding cake in his cooler overnight, until it could be delivered to the afternoon reception. It had traveled in the back of my Aunt Viola Sindici and Uncle Torquato Perry's station wagon from Utica with all the windows closed, and no air conditioning. I think they were both feeling a little "woozy" by the time they arrived. Dom also came to my rescue with my daughter, Lisa's wedding with some food preparation assistance.

As I recall, after closing the South Division Street business, Dom took over Frank Don's Meat Market on West Main Street, renaming it Papa's Meat Market. He later worked as a meat cutter for Smith's Market for several years and lastly at Francisco's Market.

Dom belonged to the Knights of Columbus, St. Patrick's Church Holy Name Society, Auxiliary Police and St. Johnsville Retail Merchants Association. In his later years, he served as a Village of St. Johnsville Trustee and was very active in the Benefit Club. As a hobby, he enjoyed carpentry.

Dominick J. Papa died February 11, 1999 at 85 years on the day of his wife, Mary's birthday.

MARY GAGLIARDI passed away on Tuesday, April 5, 2005, at the age of 94, at Basset Hospital, Cooperstown NY. She was born in Troy NY on February 11, 1911 to Giovanni Gagliardi and Mary Fiaggo.

After her birth, Mary's parents traveled back to Italy, where she received her education. Immigration records show her arriving back in America July 20, 1927 at age 16, living at first with the Caesar Guarnacci family on Mechanic Street, where Mary's sister Jennie and Paolo Guarnacci resided.

An excellent seamstress, Mary first worked as a floor lady at the Cozzolino St. Johnsville Dress Company on New Street in the textile building, and for many years at the Corso Dress Company. She also took in alterations and dressmaking at home.

Sam Papa ~ What can I tell you about Sam Papa? I've known him since a young girl, when his parents Dominick Papa and Mary Gagliardi moved across the street from my family on South Division Street. Named after his grandfather, he was born in 1934, most likely at the home of his grandparents, Saverio Papa and Madelina Giaquinto, as his parents were residing there at the time.

My friend, Sam was a very popular, extremely well liked young man. He excelled at entertaining others, especially with his imitations of Red Skelton. While in college he vied with three other young fraternity men for the title of "The Wheel", representing the Alfa Delta Omega Fraternity. Sam could play emcee or auctioneer. Just give him a microphone.

Sam was another of the stellar Italian athletes of St. Johnsville during the early 1950s. He led the St. Johnsville High School to victories in both basketball and baseball. Graduating in 1952, he was recognized by Hartwick College, Oneonta for his proficiency in sports and awarded a full 4-year scholarship. During these four years, he captained the baseball and basketball teams. He was also voted President of his sophomore year in a class of almost 100 college students, one of the positions he usually held in his high school years.

After graduating from Hartwick College in Oneonta in June 1956 with a Bachelor of Science degree in business administration, Sam taught business for 17 years in Tully NY, served as a coach for 15 years and then became a guidance counselor at Lafayette High School.

On April 28, 1962, Sam Papa married Mary Barnhart from Salamanca NY. His childhood friends, John "Buttsy" Palma and Carl Terricola served as ushers. Sam and Mary had four children.

In 1974, after his retirement, Sam and Mary opened Papa's Sport Shop in Lafayette.

From childhood, when he was my neighbor, Sam was always one of my best friends. He served as best man in my wedding and remained friends with my husband, John "Buttsy" Palma until the date of John's passing, serving as pallbearer. He was there to support us during a very traumatic time in our lives.

The outpouring of love, friendship and respect for Sam Papa was most evident at the retirement party his peers planned in Lafayette. Sam and his wife, Mary are still living.

Diane M. Papa was born September 24, 1945, the daughter of Domenick Papa and Mary Gagliardi, in Little Falls Hospital. She lived a short life passing away at the age of 35 years in January 1980 at the home of her parents, where her mother lovingly cared for her.

Most of Diane's adult life was marred by the discovery of a brain tumor in her early thirties. Surviving the delicate surgery, she became paralyzed on one side. After her recovery, this did not deter her from being active in life. She edited a weekly social news column for the St. Johnsville *Enterprise & News* newspaper – "On Line With Diane."

Diane also became a wife and mother. On August 13, 1974 she married J. Quentin Moore from Fort Plain with a grand reception to follow at the General Herkimer Hotel in Herkimer NY. They soon had a daughter, Jennifer.

The H.C. Smith Benefit Club sponsored a huge chicken barbeque attended by at least 350 people, raising funds to alleviate some of the expenses incurred with her illness and surgery.

A graduate of Mohawk Valley Community College, Diane served on the board of the St. Johnsville Youth Commission.

JOHN PAPA was born in Fonda on April 7, 1914. He died June 7, 1997 in St. Johnsville.
On June 27, 1937 John Papa married Paragina "Paris" Marocco. They had three sons - John, Jr, Joseph and James. They later separated. John, Jr. aka Jack passed away in California at a young age.

In 1939 John leased a Socony Station right next door to their home, which he conducted for many years, on the corner of East Main and Ann. In 1944 a fire caused considerable damage.

PARIS MAROCCO passed away January 19, 1992. Born September 29, 1914 in Supino, Italy, Paris was the daughter of Antonio Marocco and Giovanna Zuccaro, who ran the St. Johnsville Restaurant on East Main Street, serving home-cooked Italian food. Most recently, it was the home of Viola Iacobucci and Stacey "Jerry" Dunton. You can read more about Paris and her family in *La Famiglia Marocco*.

At one time, Paris' parents made a visit to their hometown of Supino and left her in charge of the restaurant. Growing up with food preparation, Paris certainly had excellent qualifications to manage the St. Johnsville School's cafeteria program. She was very popular with the students.

CHRISTINE CECELIA PAPA, like the rest of her siblings, was born in Fonda NY on October 22, 1915. Chris died in Little Falls Hospital in March 1983 at 67 years of age.

Christine was an exceptional student, winning numerous scholastic awards. She worked for many years at Corso Dress Company.

Christine Papa joined in marriage with Astinio Denofrio on September 12, 1937. Serving as best man and maid of honor were her brother, John Papa and his wife, Paris Marocco. Other attendants were Irene Marocco, Louise Marocco, Christine's sisters Mary and Rose, and Mary Denofrio, Astinio's sister, as bridesmaids. Ushers included Aldo Palombo, Astinio's brother, Nello Denofrio, A. Montegiorgio, James Giaquinto and Angelo Giaquinto, cousins of the bride. Her youngest sister, Rita Papa was the flower girl; Ralph Colorito was the ring bearer. Following the ceremony, a dinner was served at the Papa home to about 100 guests. A reception for 300 guests was held at the Palombi American Restaurant on Bridge Street. They were the parents of three daughters - Maria, Ann and Jeanne.

ASTINIO DENOFRIO, the son of Romano and Elena Denofrio of Spring Street, was born April 16, 1915. He died July 13, 1989. He served in the Army as a Private, enlisting December 23, 1942. You can read more about him in *La Famiglia Denofrio*.

ROSE M. PAPA was also born in Fonda on February 16, 1918. She later moved to St. Johnsville with her parents and siblings. She worked for 50 years at Luxuray Mills in Fort Plain before retiring at age 71. Very active physically, Rose bowled in the Friday night Women's League. She could be seen walking all over the village in her later years.

On November 23, 1950, Rose Papa married Burton Dolan in St. Patrick's Catholic Church. They had one son, Peter and one grandson, Christopher, who was the "apple of Rosie's eye". A tragic accident on November 25, 2014 took his life too soon.

With her loving son, Peter and his wife, Valerie at her side, Rose passed away peacefully in her home on Church Street at 98 years of age on May 28, 2016. It is said she died of a broken heart due to the tragic death of her beloved grandson. The home had been purchased from James Sanguine.

Burton Dolan passed away on March 13, 1997. He served in the military in World War II.

MARY PAPA was also born in Fonda on February 21, 1920. She died at the St. Johnsville Nursing Home on June 17, 2016 at the age of 96.

Mary was well known for the creative ceramics she produced at her Ceramic's Shop on Main Street, which she had purchased from Mildred Chandler. She was a dedicated employee of Helmont Mills most of her life.

On August 8, 1943 Mary Papa joined in matrimony with Sigmund "Ziggy" Stankewich. They shared 67 blessed years together before his death on June 23, 2011 at the St. Johnsville Nursing Home at 90 years. They had no children.

Sigmund Stankewich was born March 24, 1921 in St. Johnsville, the son of Polish immigrants. His sister, Sophia was married to Anthony Circhirillo, who served as best man at the wedding.

Mary Papa served as Maid of Honor for the wedding of my Aunt Susan Sindici to Guido Corso.

THERESA PAPA married Anthony C. Dolan of Boonville, brother of Burton, on May 2, 1949. Serving as maid of honor was her sister, Rose Papa, with another sister, Ann and best friend, Clara Palitti as bridesmaids. Burton Dolan was best man with two other brothers as ushers. A breakfast was served at the Ann Street home of the bride's parents followed by a reception at the Century Tavern. The couple had two sons - Anthony, Jr. and David.

Anthony C. Dolan was born October 29, 1917 in Lowville NY. He passed away on December 6, 1994 at 77 years. He also served in the military in World War II.

Theresa Papa was born in Fonda in 1922. At this writing, she still resides in the family homestead.

ANN PAPA was born in Fonda on February 26, 1925. February seems to be a significant month for the Papa family births, as four of the seven children were born during that month.

Ann Papa married Frank Piaggio October 1, 1950, making their home in Albany NY. They had a daughter, Kathleen. Records show she had been engaged in September 1944 to Albert Battisti, son of Peter Battisti and Anna Piniaha.

Tragically, Ann was killed in a fatal auto accident in February 1953 as the automobile she was a passenger in was hit head-on, while turning into a wedding reception hall. She died of a cerebral hemorrhage at the age of 27. Their daughter, Kathleen was 18 months old.

RITA MADELINE PAPA, being the last of the children, was the only one born in St. Johnsville on November 17, 1926. The 1925 Census shows the family living at 20 East Liberty Street with the Leopoldo Iacobucci family.

Rita Papa married Walter H. Vincent from Albany on November 30, 1952. She was his second wife. Walter was born August 22, 1920 in Albany and died October 20, 1996 while the couple lived in St. Johnsville. Rita passed away on May 23, 2005. They had no children together.

~ *La Famiglia GIAQUINTO* ~

~ FRANCESCO GIAQUINTO et GIOVANNINA CAMPAGNANO ~

Francesco "Frank" Giaquinto followed his cousin, Madelina "Mary" Giaquinto Papa to America in 1913, joining her family in Fonda, town of Mohawk. He came to work on the New York Central Railroad, probably through the urging of Madelina's husband, Saverio "Sam" Papa, who was a foreman. There he met his wife, Giovannina "Jennie" Campagnano who had arrived in 1912. Campagnano, aka Compani, is a well-known name in the Fonda area.

FRANCESCO GIAQUINTO was born in Briano di Caserta, Italy, on November 25, 1892, son of Angelo Giaquinto and Maddalena Cristillo. He passed away on June 10, 1977 in St. Johnsville.

After coming to the United States, Frank sent for his sister, Annunziata Giaquinto Arcesi. They left three siblings in Italy – Giovanni, Vincenzo and Giuseppa. Four other siblings, Francesco, Maria Giuseppa, Giuseppe and Antonio all died at the very young ages of one to two years old.

GIOVANNINA CAMPAGNANO was born August 8, 1893 in Squille, Italy and died a few years after her husband, Frank in July 1983 at the Palatine Nursing Home at the age of 89. She was the daughter of Giuseppe Compagnano and Maria Aldi.

It's interesting that Lavena Loccia married Ralph Campagnano from Fonda, whose parents were Frank and Jennie Aldi. I'm wondering if, perhaps the two families are related? I did find Frank Giaquinto's family lived right next door to the Frank Campagnano family in the 1930 Census.

From records I find, Jennie had two sisters, Balbina Pellegrino of Gloversville, and Theresa Riccio of Amsterdam, and a brother, Biaggio Campagnano in Canada. There may have been one or two brothers left in Italy, also one or two in Canada.

Francesco Giaquinto and Giovannina Campagnano were married July 25, 1915 at St. Cecilia's Catholic Church in Fonda. They had four children - one daughter, Mary Madeline, and three sons, Angelo A., Dominick A., and Carmen Frank, all born in Fonda.

The family lived on Switzer Hill outside of Fonda in 1920. They owned the home and Frank worked on the railroad. The 1930 Census shows the family living at 81 State Highway in the Mohawk Township of Fonda. It also claims they own the home worth $1500. This could be the same home as 1920. Frank was a truck driver for New York State.

Again, following his cousin and her husband, Madelina and Saverio Papa, Frank moved his family to St. Johnsville in 1930, settling in at the 12 Spring Street home they had purchased from Angelo Battisti. Valued at $4000 and already established as a grocery store, Jennie continued as the proprietor for at least ten years. The store was most likely in the front porch area of their large two-story home. Frank continued to work on the railroad. They resided here for the rest of their lives.

In the early years of immigration to St. Johnsville, 12 Spring Street apparently was on the list of places to rent or board when arriving in St. Johnsville. I have discovered so many of the young Italians beginning their new lives at this location. By the 1930s, migration had subsided and new immigrants weren't coming to St. Johnsville.

Frank also had a little sideline business in the mid-1930s during the Great Depression. For several years, he contracted with the village of St. Johnsville for garbage and coal ashes pickup. Many residents relied on burning coal during these times. By 1936 he earned all of $1000 for the year from the village.

MARY MADELINE GIAQUINTO, named after her paternal grandmother, was born May 2, 1916 in Fonda. Mary was joined in wedlock with John R. Vesp, Sr. from Fort Plain, where they both lived and worked at the Luxuray Factory – most likely where they met.

John R. Vesp was born July 21, 1912 in Fort Plain. He died New Year's Eve, December 31, 1985. Mary passed away on November 8, 2007 in the St. Johnsville Nursing Home at age 91.

Mary and John Vesp had three children - William Frank, John Jr, and Joan.

William "Bill" Vesp was born March 1, 1938 and passed away on December 9, 2006. He had been married to Christa Kraft of St. Johnsville and had two daughters.

Bill was noted for the career he established from his love of sports. After graduating Fort Plain Central School, lettering in basketball as an all time scorer and also excelling in baseball and soccer, he went on to Ithaca College, where he received a Masters of Science Degree. He served as the head coach of basketball at Utica College and both basketball and golf at Colgate University. Bill was appointed Assistant Executive Secretary of the New York State Public High School Athletic Association.

All three of the Giaquinto brothers served their country in the military during World War II.

ANGELO A. GIAQUINTO enlisted in World War II on June 25, 1941 as a Private in the U.S. Army. He returned home with his "war bride", Audrey Carter, daughter of Mr. and Mrs. Harry T. Carter of England. Upon their arrival in the U.S., they were married in New York City on November 13, 1946. On January 16, 1947, they re-affirmed their vows in the Fort Plain Catholic Church parish home with Angelo's sister, Mary and husband, John as witnesses. Angelo and Audrey were the parents of three children - Susan, Thomas and Michael.

As with so many of the second generations of Italian immigrants, Angelo was very active in community affairs. He served as Village Mayor and a trustee for many years. He was employed in Fonda as the Montgomery County Civil Defense Director. As a member of the St. Johnsville American Legion, he served as Commander.

Angelo Giaquinto was born in Fonda on December 8, 1917. He passed away in Florida at the age of 88 on November 1, 2006.

Audrey Carter was born November 19, 1923 in England and died five months after Angelo on April 3, 2007.

DOMINICK A. GIAQUINTO, at age 22, served in the U.S. Army during World War II from April 12, 1942 and was honorably discharged December 27, 1942.

Dominick Giaquinto married Lucia Fortucci of Little Falls on September 25, 1943. The ceremony was followed by a dinner at Marocco's St. Johnsville Restaurant in St. Johnsville, then a wedding reception in Little Falls. The couple made their home with Dominick's parents in the 12 Spring Street two-family home their entire married life, raising their three children - Marie, Frank and Dominick.

Dominick worked over twenty years as an electrician with Casatelli Electric of Utica. He was a member of the International Brotherhood of Electrical Workers, as well as the Auxiliary Police of St. Johnsville.

Dominick was born on March 4, 1920 and passed away on August 14, 2008 at the age of 88. He was buried with military honors.

Lucy Fortucci worked for many years at the Corso Dress Company, until their closing. Born in Little Falls on May 15, 1921, she passed away on March 23, 2014 at the St. Johnsville Nursing Home.

Both Dom and Lucy were very proud of their Italian heritage and passed these wonderful traditions down to their children and grandchildren.

CARMEN FRANK GIAQUINTO served in the U.S. Navy in World War II from April 1944 to May 1946. Before being assigned to active duty, he completed his training with his friend and neighbor, Henry Mastracco. He was honorably discharged as a Gunner's Mate 3rd Class. Years later, they lived next door to each other in newly built homes.

Carmen also was very much involved in community affairs. He was a member of the American Legion Post, served as President of the Auxiliary Police, member of the St. Johnsville Housing Authority Board and was on the Executive Committee of the St. Johnsville Volunteer Ambulance Corps.

Carmen had studied at the Troy Vocational School and utilized his education in various jobs throughout his life. It seems his first employment may have been on the maintenance crew at Palatine Dye Company and as a carpenter for Burgess Fuel Company. From April 1959 to May 1964, the St. Johnsville Village Board appointed him yearly as the Superintendent of the Department of Public Works. Several years after his retirement from the DPW, he returned to work under the supervision of John "Buttsy" Palma. He was also the St. Johnsville Post Office custodian for many years.

Carmen Giaquinto married Dorothy Perih, a neighbor and daughter of Steve and Anna Perih, on April 10, 1948 in New York City. I'm assuming she was working in the city after her graduation from Mount Sinai Hospital School of Nursing in September 23, 1944 at age 19.

Dorothy was a member of the U.S. Cadet Nurse's Corps during World War II. She later worked as an Industrial Nurse with Beech-Nut Corporation and at Little Falls Hospital. Dorothy was selected as the director of the Montgomery County Heart Association.

As a member of many social groups, she had a talent for art and crafts. Dorothy participated and taught Ceramic classes in her home. She became a dedicated student of mine in later years with China Painting.

Carmen and Dorothy were both active members of the St. Johnsville Senior Saints and loved to travel. Besides the various tours they took on their own, they were frequent travelers with my Motorcoach Tour business, Cora Lee Tours, always being the first to sign up.

Sadly, I vividly recall Carmen's last trip with me; he passed away within a week after. He was always such a pleasure and the life of the party, entertaining other passengers with his great humor. Dorothy continued her love of travel, accompanying me to travel shows.

The youngest child, Carmen Frank Giaquinto was born on September 4, 1926 and died suddenly at home on December 14, 2000. The couple had two daughters - JoAnn and Janet.

Dorothy Perih was born in St. Johnsville on December 30, 1924. She passed away at St. Luke's Hospital, Utica on March 10, 2008.

~ *La Famiglia* DENOFRIO ~

~ ROMANO DENOFRIO et ANNILUCCI FRANCESCONI ~

ROMANO DENOFRIO made two attempts to come to America. On April 30, 1909 he was rejected for some reason and most likely sent back to Maenza. One year later, almost to the same date, on April 25, 1910, he arrived with Angelo Pietrocini, who was joining his brother Augustino in Nelliston. Romano spent his entire life in St. Johnsville, working for 45 years on the New York Central Railroad.

ANNILUCCI "Elena" FRANCESCONI followed her husband to the new world on June 2, 1914. Also on board the passenger ship were Anista Cortese, coming to meet her husband, V. Polidoro, Amadeo Polidoro and Liberatore Montegiorgio, coming to meet his son, Alessandro. Alessandro married Felicia Loccia on May 7, 1916.

In 1915, Romano and Elena first resided at 32 Mechanic Street, where their son, Astinio was born just before the census was taken. Also sharing the home were Dominic Romano, his wife Vittoria and son, Frank.

1920 shows the Denofrio's living at 28 Hough Street, the eventual home of James and Henrietta Battisti. By this date, their three oldest sons, Astinio, Argivio and Nello had been born. Sharing this residence were Angelo Tolfa, his wife, Eva and two boarders, Anthony Orticello and Lewis Coco.

By 1925 their daughter, Mary was born and the entire family was living at 5 Spring Street, the family homestead for the remainder of Romano and Elena's lives. Their son, Boblo and daughter, Mary and her husband resided there in later years.

The 1930 Census shows Romano and Elena were now owners of the 5 Spring Street home, which was valued at $2500. All of the children were still living at home.

Romano Denofrio was born October 12, 1890 in Maenza, the son of Luigi Denofrio and Alexandria Francesconi. It's interesting that his wife's maiden name is the same as his mother's. This occurred often; sometimes cousins married cousins. He passed away April 3, 1959 at Little Falls Hospital after being stricken with a stroke. He was 68 years old.

Annilucci "Elena" Francesconi was also born in Maenza on September 15, 1891. I find no parents. She died on November 22, 1969 at the Palatine Nursing Home at 78 years old.

All four of the Denofrio brothers served in World War II. They were all employed by the St. Johnsville location of Little Falls Felt Shoe at the time. A St. Johnsville *Enterprise & News* article, dated July 8, 1943 features photos of Bobalo, Nello and Astinio in their respective uniforms.

During World War II the *Enterprise & News* ran a weekly column featuring local servicemen. Another article about local boy Ralph Hill, tells how he met up with Nello Denofrio, Anthony Montegero, Fred Sanguine and Ralph Grisel in North Africa.

ASTINIO EDWARD DENOFRIO was born April 16, 1915 at 32 Mechanic Street. He passed away on July 13, 1989.

On September 12, 1937, Astinio Denofrio married Christine Papa, daughter of Saverio Papa and Madeline Giaquinto. They had a beautiful St. Patrick's Catholic Church wedding and became the parents of three daughters - Maria, Ann and Jeanne.

Two days before Christmas, December 23, 1942, Astinio enlisted in the Army serving in the Coast Artillery as a Private with the warrant officers.

Christine Papa was born in Fonda on October 22, 1915 and died in March 1983 at Little Falls Hospital. Corso Dress Company employed her for many years.

ARGIVIO DENOFRIO aka Gibbeo, born on August 2, 1916, lived a rather sad dejected life, somewhat like a "black sheep" of the family. He was a kind gentle soul, who never married. I knew him well as he spent several years of his daily adult life hanging out at my husband, John "Buttsy" Palma's Esso Station, enjoying the camaraderie of the many guys who came in and took time to kibitz with him.

Although he possessed very little, he had a heart of gold. Daily, you could see him walk up West Main Street to John's parents' Palmer Grill to pick up and bring back the lunch that Carmela prepared for her son. She would always make a little extra for Gibbeo. He also kept an eye on the front office.

Gibbeo would take his afternoon siestas at Cap's Cigar Room, dozing on a back room couch. He was always willing to run errands for Army and Minnie Caponera. One day they had given him a handful of coins to take across the street to another business to perhaps exchange for dollar bills. Main Street was well traveled, as the NYS Thruway had not been built yet. As he crossed the street, he started flipping the coins in his hand until they dropped and scattered all over the road, stopping traffic. Drivers were tooting and yelling as he was on his hands and knees gathering up the coins.

Argivio served his country in the Army from June 25, 1942 until December 17, 1942, when he was given a medical discharge due to a brain injury. He was a member of the American Legion and had worked at Palatine Dye. He passed away June 15, 1973 at the Albany Veteran's Hospital.

NELLO ORLANDO DENOFRIO was born February 5, 1918.

Enlisting in the U.S. Army Medical Corps, Nello had quite a resume with his active service from January 16, 1942 to September 27, 1945. Stationed at Camp Lee, VA before being shipped overseas, he was the first soldier from St. Johnsville to receive the Soldiers Medal for Heroism.

Nello risked his life by saving five other enlisted men when their tank struck an enemy mine and sank 12 miles off the NE Coast of Corsica on New Years Eve 1943. The five men were trapped in the sinking ship. Nello and six comrades descended into the water below deck to retrieve the trapped men. The ship sank shortly after their rescue.

He was later stationed in North Africa when he wrote home, "I get to town once in a while for a shave and ice cream." Staff Sergeant Nello Denofrio was listed on the Puerto Rico Crew List as returning from Trinidad and arriving at Bennington Airfield on June 11, 1945. He received an honorable discharge.

On May 29, 1949 Nello Denofrio married Margaret Mamrosch from Herkimer at St. Patrick's Church. They were the parents of two children - Daniel and Deborah Ann.

Nello Orlando Denofrio died on November 11, 1999.

I'm not able to find any information about Nello's wife, Margaret.

BOBLO P. DENOFRIO, the youngest of the four sons, was born August 12, 1920 and died at age 63 on October 3, 1983 in St. Elizabeth Hospital, Utica. Living his whole life in St. Johnsville, he remained in the family home that his sister, Mary had taken over after the death of their parents. He never married. Boblo also entered the U.S. Army as a Private, serving his country from October 8, 1942 to October 29, 1945 in the Coast Artillery. He was honorably discharged with the rank of Corporal.

MARY DENOFRIO, the youngest child and only daughter, was born August 12, 1922. As far as I know, Mary is still living. After residing in Little Falls for a few years after her marriage, she returned to St. Johnsville to live in the family homestead at 5 Spring Street, most likely to care for her aging widowed mother.

On April 26, 1947, Mary Denofrio married William Paluzzi from Little Falls. He was the son of Alberto Paluzzi and Amelia Augustine. Attendants at the wedding were her friend, Lucy Riscica as maid-of-honor; her brother Nello as best man and bridesmaids Mary Papa and William's sister, Ida Bisconte. The couple had one son, Terry.

I find no links with the following five families to any other St. Johnsville Italian immigrants.

~ *La Famiglia POLIDORI* ~

~ GINO POLIDORI et THERESA CARESTIA ~

As one of the hundreds of passengers on the ship Napoli, arriving from Napoli, Italy, on July 19, 1913 Gino Polidori was listed as #692. He was registered as a 16-year-old farm laborer, which was quite a common occupation for the majority of Italian young men coming to America. The young women were usually registered as housewives, married or not.

GINO POLIDORI was part of the group of eleven, who came directly to St. Johnsville, including my grandmother Edvige Cacciotti, quite possibly a cousin. Gino's mother's maiden name was Cacciotti. He was able to read and write, which was quite important when going through Ellis Island. With $30.00 in his pocket, he headed out to meet his Uncle Vincenzo Polidori in St. Johnsville. He left behind a brother, Ferdinand and sister, Olinda.

Although I couldn't find Vincenzo in the census records, I did find Iagnacco Polidoro as a boarder, with the occupation of shoemaker, at the popular 21 Sanders Street address, which I believe was the designated Box 88 final destination immigrants used when registering for their voyage.

I find Gino registered for the U.S. World War I draft in 1917, single, working on the railroad and living at 32 South Division Street. In 1942 he also registered for the World War II draft.

Shortly after his arrival, Gino became a U.S. Citizen at Fonda. By 1925, he had married Theresa Carestia on July 22, 1923 and they had moved to 22 Sanders Street with their one-year-old son, Carlo. At the time of their marriage, Gino was living and working in Herkimer. Serving as witnesses at the Catholic ceremony were John Pedro and Ida Salvagni, now owners of the 21 Sanders Street property.

The son of Thomas Polidori and Angelina Cacciotti, Gino Polidori was born in Maenza on June 9, 1896 and died tragically on March 9, 1944 in St. Johnsville.

TERESA CARESTIA was born in Maenza on April 17, 1899 and died in St. Johnsvile on March 14, 1952.

Gino and Theresa also had two daughters - Geralda Rose "Geri" and Maria J. "Mary Jane".

Also from the commune of Maenza, Theresa Carestia, daughter of Enrico Carestia and Domitellia Santerelli, arrived on October 21, 1922 as a single 22-year-old housewife. She could read and write Italian. She was headed for Springfield MA to join her father.

The 1930 Census shows the Polidori family still renting at 22 Sanders Street, sharing the home with the Pasquale Montoni and Elena Vecciarelli family. Elena also came from Maenza and may have previously known Gino or Theresa. I was told Gino and Theresa didn't know each other in Maenza before coming to America.

By 1940 the couple had moved to 21 East Liberty Street, where they lived out their lives. Theresa's widowed father, Enrico, was residing with them at this time. Both Gino and Enrico worked on the New York Central Railroad.

Enrico Carestia was born in Fermo, Italy on December 3, 1870. He died at the home of his daughter, Theresa on December 1, 1940, two days before his 70th birthday. He was buried in Prospect View Cemetery on his birthday.

Enrico came to America August 9, 1902 and lived in Springfield MA before moving to St. Johnsville. Doing an extensive search of the Santerelli's in Springfield, I was not able to find any information about his wife, Domitellia Santerelli.

Sadly, Gino Polidori was another unfortunate victim of employment with the New York Central Railroad. After working more than 20 years as a track worker, on March 9, 1944 he was struck by a passing train near the old St. Johnsville baseball park bleachers, as he was pushing a wheelbarrow full of cinders. It seems the cinders were used to melt the winter ice on sidewalks. He had taken over the job of Charles J. Tilton, who was killed in the same manner just two and a half weeks previous. His wife and three children survived him. At the time of his death, his son, Carlo was serving in the U.S. Navy.

Having also lost her father, Enrico in 1940, Theresa was now left alone as a widow to raise her two daughters, Geri and infant Mary Jane. To make ends meet, she worked in the Little Falls Felt Shoe factory, also working at home preparing homemade noodles for the Century Tavern in Mindenville, along with providing alteration services.

It is recalled by Mary Jane that her mother would send huge boxes of much needed goods back to Italy several times a year. I also recall my grandmother bundling up items in old sheets, binding them with heavy string, to send to her family. From what I know of Maenza, these Italians were very poor.

When Carlo returned from his service in World War II, he returned to the East Liberty family home. After his mother's death, he raised his youngest sister, Mary Jane, as was his mother's wish. Geri had graduated in 1951 and was on her own.

CARLO JOSEPH POLIDORI was born on May 14, 1924 at 22 Sanders Street during the Prohibition era, son of Gino Polidori and Theresa Carestia. Carlo was an exceptionally active member of the St. Johnsville community, the epitome of a good community citizen.

Most of us remember Carlo as a police officer, where he served the community for most of his life, beginning his career in 1952. In 1963, a 25-year veteran as a patrolman, he was recognized by the Canajoharie Moose organization as the "Outstanding Law Enforcement Officer of the Year". His resume was then submitted to the NYS Moose organization for consideration. He had many citations including the St. Johnsville Police Department and Village Board, and the Penn Central Railroad police. Then Police Chief Ben Walrath and the FBI commended him with halting a train derailment in 1959. No matter what the situation, Carlo had a handle on it, often going above the call of duty to settle disagreements. He certainly had a nose for detective work. He retired in 1985 as Chief of Police.

Whenever anyone was in need, it was Carlo to the rescue. I need to share my scary, humorous story with you. One hot summer night, I awoke to a noise downstairs. I thought it was my husband, John knocking something over in the downstairs living room, where he would sometimes retire to sleep near the open front door. We had no air conditioning. I called down the stairs to him; he answered me from the front bedroom. With me close behind, on went the lights as we cautiously stepped down the stairs to check things out in the living room. As I looked around I noticed a little glass vase had fallen out of its spot on the windowsill. As I began to pick it up to place it back, an ugly bat that had been perched on the sill came flying at me. I ran screaming up the stairs, where I remained. In the meantime, my husband got a broom, opened the back door and tried to shoo the rodent out. Not budging, it decided to cling to the kitchen curtains. John told me to call Carlo who would be going on police duty shortly. He apparently was very adept at catching these horrible critters. Within minutes it was Carlo to the rescue, swooping up the creature and disposing of it in the back yard. With the doors wide open before Carlo's arrival, one of the neighborhood felines came strolling into my kitchen to see what was happening. The whole scenario was hilarious!

When the village of St. Johnsville decided to develop the Marina area, Director Carlo was the man in charge. Dignitaries from all over NY State attended the grand opening on May 29, 1960. He served in many capacities with numerous community development projects through the years - organizing the many fabulous drum corps parades in the village and serving as the Bicentennial Commission Chairman in 1972, when I had the pleasure of working with him. He was impressively organized, knowing how to make things come together.

Carlo was an active member of the St. Johnsville Volunteer Fire Department and the Volunteer Ambulance Corps, also the Fort Plain VFW and American Legion. Unfortunately, he ran an unsuccessful political campaign for Montgomery County Sheriff, a huge disappointment to so many in our community. At the time, it was difficult to beat the down-county politicians.

For many years Carlo conducted a Hunter's Safety Course, dating back to the late 1940s when he taught several of my schoolmates how to handle a rifle. I recall walking up to Main Street with my rifle over my shoulder, on my way to the site located under the building on West Main, where Terricola's Clothing and the Frank Christiance Appliance store were located. Always dedicated and very involved with the youth of St. Johnsville and with his compassionate understanding, Carlo was responsible for keeping them out of trouble. They respected and looked up to him as a guiding light. I refer to him as the "mediator."

On April 1, 1967, the Morris J. Edwards Post 168 American Legion announced three recipients of community service awards. Recipient of the first time ever award given for Police Achievement was Police Officer Carlo Polidori for his outstanding work in the local police department. National Legion Commander John E. Davis endorsed the new Certificate of Achievement.

My Dad, Floyd Perry was named for the individual Legion award for his work with the village youth. The Group Award was accepted by Mrs. Seward Walrath, president of the King's Daughter's Society.

As a hobby, Carlo set up a small studio in his home to develop professional style photos including my engagement picture. While researching this amazing man, I also discovered that he was quite the Italian vocalist, performing several times through the years, once with another musically talented young Italian man, Terry Terricola. I never heard the pleasure of his voice. I could go on and on with his many, many accomplishments. It would definitely fill its own book.

While working on the railroad, on September 29, 1942 at 19 years of age, Carlo was inducted into the U.S. Navy and deployed to the South Pacific for a year and a half. Serving until January 14, 1946, he was discharged as a Yeoman 2nd Class. Carlo was the recipient of the American Theater Ribbon, Victory Ribbon, Good Conduct Medal and the Asiatic Pacific Ribbon with one star.

After his honorable discharge, he returned to St. Johnsville to assist his mother and sisters after the tragic early death of his father.

On February 1, 1952 Carlo Joseph Polidori married Margaret Eileen Cunningham, daughter of Charles Cunningham and Mary Bannon. They had three sons - Lawrence, Nino and Joseph.

Margaret was born June 23, 1929 and died June 25, 2000 both in St. Johnsville.

Carlo Joseph Polidori passed away October 28, 1996 in Faxton Hospital, Utica. A life truly well lived!

GERALDA ROSE POLIDORI, better known to all as Geri, was born to Gino Polidori and Theresa Carestia on September 20, 1932 in St. Johnsville.

She graduated from St. Johnsville High School, Class of 1951. After graduation, Geri worked as a receptionist at Palatine Dye Company, St. Johnsville. With her marriage, she moved to Little Falls and later began her employment with the Little Falls Hospital.

On June 22, 1952, Geralda Rose Polidori joined in marriage with Raymond T. George of Little Falls, son of Joseph George and Marcella Cotelli, at St. Patrick's Catholic Church. Her brother, Carlo, gave her in marriage. Rose Marie LaCoppola served her friend as maid of honor, with her sister Mary Jane as junior bridesmaid. Raymond's brother, John George, a NYS trooper was best man. The couple had two daughters - Marcella and Gina.

Raymond and John George are brothers of Frances (James) Capece and Olga (Louis) Capece.

Geralda Rose Polidori passed away April 17, 2001 in a hospital in Utica.

MARIA J. "Mary Jane" POLIDORI was born August 3, 1942, most likely at Little Falls Hospital.

Graduating St. Johnsville High School in 1960, she went on to attend Utica School of Commerce. She was employed as a secretary at Palatine Dye Company.

On February 17, 1962, Mary Jane became the bride of John D. Manore of Frankfort. They later divorced in 1982 and she married Ralph Lamb from Dolgeville.

* *Mary Jane Polidori has been most helpful in filling in some of the blanks with this article. Grazie!*

St. Johnsville Mafioso
Louis Chiodo, Anthony Carroll, Carlo Polidori, James Campione

~ *La Famiglia CARELLI* ~

~ VINCENZO CARELLI et MARY CONSELO ~

The Carelli family was one of the very first to immigrate to St. Johnsville, quite possibly in 1894. Not a familiar name to many, those of the younger generations would be more familiar with the name Carroll. Obviously, it was Americanized, as many others were.

VINCENZO "James" CARELLI was married twice. His first wife was Mary Conselo. He later married a much younger woman, Maria Gulla. James worked for the New York Central Railroad most of his life.

I first discovered Vincenzo "James" Carrelli in 1905, living on Ann Street with his wife, Mary, and three children - Nicholas, Lillian and Mary. The 1910 Census shows them living on Sanders Street. Vincenzo and his son, Nicholas aren't mentioned, but that's not unusual. By this time Nicholas may have left the family home or quite possibly passed away at an early age. I'm assuming the latter, as you will see as I progress with the story.

In 1915 the family had moved to 28 Mechanic Street. They had two more daughters, Virginia (Vincenza) and Rosana, but Lillian was not listed. She, too, may have passed away. The mortality rate was very high in the early 1900s, especially during the Influenza Epidemic during World War I.

It's rather confusing trying to identify all the children. 1920 finds that the family has moved again to Bridge Street. The children listed are Vincent as a 10 year old daughter, most likely Virginia (Vincenza), Rose, 8, Tony, 5 and Nick, 1½. They had also taken in boarders, Frank Pendenza and Antonio Ficiliano.

The 1925 Census records state the name as Vincenzo Carella with his wife Elizabeth "Marie", along with Vincenza, Rose, Nick and Tony. The reason I believe the first Nicholas had passed away is they gave this younger son the same name. This was quite common with the death of a previous child.

By 1930 James and his second wife, Maria had moved back to 28 Mechanic Street with only the three youngest children. In 1940 they were living at 21 Mechanic Street with only Nick and Tony. Rose had married and was living at 6 West Liberty Street with her husband, James La Lone and daughter, Jean.

I find no information regarding either wife of Vincenzo Carelli.

VINCENZA "Virginia" CARROLL was born in 1910 and died in 1990 in Herkimer. She was married to Antonio Rei, born 1898 and died 1975 in Herkimer, where Antonio was most likely from.

ROSE CARROLL married James La Lone from Herkimer at Christmas time on December 22, 1935 at St. Patrick's Church. They had a daughter, Jean born in 1936. I wonder if Rose met James through her sister Virginia?

Rose La Lone's family first lived at 6 West Liberty Street, a duplex. My uncle William Perry and his family lived next door for a few years. The La Lone family later moved further down the street, where they became the owners of two identical homes, living in one, renting the other. Romeo and Molly Tolfa Battisti were occupants of the rental for several years before purchasing their John Street home.

Living just two doors east of the La Lone family in the early 1940s, Jean and I became playmates. She was a member of my brother, Joseph Perry's graduating class of 1955.

NICHOLAS "Nick" CARROLL served his country in France, Africa and the Mid-East during World War II. He was born around 1918 and died in 1969, at the age of 51, at the Veteran's Hospital in Albany. His wife, Margaret, two sisters, Rose La Lone and Vincenza Rei and brother, Tony, survived him.

Nick married Margaret Fuhs in 1949 in Sharon Springs and adopted her two sons - Owen and Arthur. Arthur Fuhs was married to Carol Dockerty of St. Johnsville.

ANTHONY JOHN CARROLL aka Tony, born in 1919 was the youngest child of James Carelli and Mary Conselo. After Tony's death, his son, Jim found two birth certificates – the original with his given name of Tony Carelli and another with his name listed as Anthony John Carroll. His sister, Rose also had two birth certificates.

They both had "Americanized" their names from Carelli to Carroll. There was an application process, which was brought before a court to authorize this procedure. This was done with Tony's enlistment in World War II.

We of the younger generation knew Tony best as an active contributing presence in the community. He was a member of the SAVAC Ambulance Corps, the St. Johnsville Firemen and American Legion, where he served as designated bugler for sounding taps. He served in the U.S. Navy during World War II.

Tony was a consistently high bowler participating in the Masonic Temple league bowling. While attending St. Johnsville Central School, he was active in school activities.

On May 11, 1946, after returning from the war, Anthony Carroll married Katherine "Katie" Leve, daughter of Joseph Leve and Anna Majicka of Little Falls, at St. Joseph's Catholic Church, Little Falls. They were the parents of three children - Patricia, Joan and James. He and Katie took over the family home at 28 Mechanic Street, where they lived out their lives.

Anthony John Carroll aka Anthony Carelli died on June 29, 1997 in St. Johnsville.

Katherine Leve or Katie, as she was best known, was born July 27, 1923 in Little Falls and passed away August 14, 2003 at St. Elizabeth's Hospital, Utica.

Employed for 35 years at Corso Dress Company, she was most noted for her love of baking and making the "best" homemade noodles. She also provided the noodles for Capece's Restaurant. I was the recipient of the latter many times, which she always claimed she made for her boyfriend, my husband, John "Buttsy" Palma.

~ *La Famiglia CASTELLUCCI* ~

~ GINO CASTELLUCCI et EUFRASIA DI PEPPI ~

GINO CASTELLUCCI arrived in Boston MA from Maenza on September 2, 1913 bound for St. Johnsville to join his mother, Giovanna "Jennie" Ceci, who had preceded him to America with his brother, Umberto, age 14, on September 13, 1911.

Umberto apparently returned to Italy, as he arrived a second time at age 23 on October 24, 1920, going to his mother's home. I find nothing further with Umberto.

I do not locate any documents regarding Gino's father, Giovanni. A June 11, 1901 passenger manifest does show a Giovanni Castellucci, age 47, arriving from Maenza. It seems he passed away before 1920. In 1920 only Gino and his mother were living at 9 New Street.

On January 23, 1921, Gino Castellucci and Eufrasia "Frances" Di Peppi were united in marriage at St. Patrick's Catholic Church with Lillian Mancini and Domenico Yacobucci as witnesses.

EUFRASIA Di PEPPI aka Frances had arrived October 30, 1920 from Civile, Italy. She was living at 32 South Division Street. This is the address of what was later the Rapacz Market, but before that James Pietrocini and Carlo Cochi occupied the property. They apparently took in boarders as I've found this address listed several times as a new arrival's home.

By 1925 Gino, his wife and first two children, Amelia and Gino, were living at 10 Mechanic Street, where they resided for many years. Also living with them were his mother, Giovanna and brother, Vincenzo. Gino worked in a knitting mill.

Vincenzo Castellucci arrived in America July 8, 1923 and came to St. Johnsville to join his mother and brother, Gino. He was a tailor by trade. His wife was Silvina Lattanzi, who was still in Italy. He had traveled back to Italy, only to return October 13, 1928 to Mechanic Street. He may have gone elsewhere after that.

In 1930 the Castellucci family is still residing at 10 Mechanic Street, which they own and is valued at $2500. Another son, Alfred has been added to the family. Giovanna and Vincenzo still reside with them. By 1940 the couple's daughter, Janet has joined the family. Giovanna has passed away and her son, Vincenzo has moved on. Gino and Frances are both working in a dress factory.

Born about 1855 in Maenza, Giovanna Castellucci died in St. Johnsville February 21, 1931.

Sometime after 1940 the Castellucci family moved to 30 Bridge Street, the large Colonial home between the Masonic Temple and Barca residence.

Frances was stricken with a debilitating illness, which left her confined to a wheel chair. She passed away at home on May 18, 1954. A brother, Frank, in Italy survived her.

Gino Castellucci was born June 4, 1898 in Maenza and passed away on November 5, 1986 in Seminole FL, where he had been living with his daughter, Janet and her husband, Sandy.

AMELIA ROSE CASTELLUCCI was born June 21, 1922 in St. Johnsville. She died February 5, 2013 after retiring as an Accounting Clerk with the Syracuse Fire Department. Her husband, Walter Miller preceded her in death in 2001.

Amelia was valedictorian of her graduating class of 1939. She married Walter C. Miller from Canajoharie. The couple had two daughters - Judy and Nancy.

GENE JOSEPH CASTELLUCCI was born in 1924. He died on March 18, 1950 when he was caught in a wintry blizzard on Route 5 near Nelliston, while driving home from his employment with the Fort Plain Creamery. He was killed in a horrific auto accident, being struck by a tractor-trailer after pulling off to the side of the road due to the blinding storm.

Gene was 26 years old. He had been married only the year before to Ruth Spence and had an infant daughter, Carol Jean. His mother was confined to Little Falls Hospital at the time.

Paul Battisti had served as best man for Gene's wedding.

On January 23, 1943, Gene Castellucci enlisted in the Army to serve in World War II.

ALFRED CASTELLUCCI married a Fulton County girl, Patricia Fisher in 1955. He worked at Palatine Dye. I find no further information regarding Alfred.

JANET CASTELLUCCI graduated in the Class of 1950 with my husband, John "Buttsy" Palma. For four years she was active in various clubs and cheerleading. Janet particularly excelled in the Glee Club with her beautiful singing voice. She was a soloist for many years at St. Patrick's Catholic Church, where she married Alexander "Sandy" Lastarza of Amsterdam on September 13, 1953. They had three children - Larry, Mary Jo and Amy.

Janet grew up in the same neighborhood with Buttsy. There was a whole gang of mostly Italian youngsters that hung together on Mechanic Street. I have a picture of them.

Janet became a great friend of mine during high school. Her husband, Sandy served as an usher in our wedding. Janet blessed us with her beautiful vocal renderings during the ceremony.

When General Electric transferred Sandy to Syracuse, Janet's father, Gino went with them. He sold the home in December 1956 to Victor and Lucille Paluzzi, who later sold the property to Frank LaCoppola and his wife, Emma Bovino. This would be the stately pillared home that was transported to the opposite side of Bridge Street when the new bridge spanning the Mohawk River and New York Central Railroad was built in 1975.

At this time, Janet Castellucci and Sandy LaStarza are still living in Florida, where they had retired.

~ *La Famiglia PERFETTA* ~

~ JOHN PERFETTA et LENA OLIVERI ~

For most of their lives, the Perfetta family lived a rather quiet existence at their 16 Spring Street home. Though not well known, John Perfetta was one of the earliest Italian immigrants living in the village.

JOHN PERFETTA arrived in 1900. He was born in Naples, Italy, December 20, 1888 and died June 16, 1967 at the age of 78 years.

In 1910 John Perfetta was a boarder at a home on Bridge Street and worked on the railroad.

LENA OLIVERI arrived in 1912 to join her brother, Umberto Oliveri, already a resident of St. Johnsville. She had left two other brothers and two sisters in Maenza, where she was born in 1888. Lena passed away at Little Falls Hospital on July 9, 1962.

By 1915, John and Lena had married and had their first daughter, Concetta, while living at 13 Bridge Street. Between 1920 and 1925 they had moved to their final residence at 16 Spring Street, with the birth of their second daughter, Marfina. 1930 Census records show they now had ownership of the property.

While John had initially worked on construction, the couple both worked most of their lives in the textile mills, such as the Luxuray in Fort Plain. After John's retirement, he shared the fruits of his garden labor with a truck garden business. I recall the large garden he had next to his home.

After retiring, John and Lena Perfetta would take evening walks from their Spring Street home by way of Ann Street, then New Street to the Bridge Street Grill with their Springer Spaniel, Ginger, which they had purchased from owner, John Francisco's, daughter-in-law, Betty, wife of Larry.

While Lena would enjoy female conversations and wine with John's wife, Mary in the comfort of their home, John would sit at the bar with Ginger at his side and order two beers from the tap. The first he would guzzle down, the second he sipped slowly, while visiting with John Francisco and other patrons.

CONCETTA PERFETTA married a man from Arizona and moved there. I have no further information.

MARFINA PERFETTA was born March 1, 1921 and died at the young age of 42 on May 5, 1968 after a lingering illness. The H.C. Smith Benefit Club had a chicken BBQ fundraiser to assist with her tremendous medical expenses.

Marfina was a member of St. Patrick's Altar Rosary Society, an avid bowler and a very active member of the Starr-Colorito VFW Post Auxiliary, serving as an officer at various times.

On September 7, 1941 Marfina Perfetta married Ferris Charles Gabriele, son of Anthony and Rose Gabriele of Little Falls. They had two children - Cheryl and Anthony. The Gabriel's first owned the home at 3 Roth Street, later moving to 28 Sanders Street.

Enlisting in the US Army in World War II, Tec/3 Ferris Gabriele was also active in the VFW Post and several other community organizations. He was installed as commander of the Old Tryon County Council VFW in Gloversville. Ferris was a director on the board of the St. Johnsville Little League with my father, Floyd Perry.

Ferris Charles Gabriele was born June 25, 1921 in Little Falls. He died June 5, 1998 in Herkimer, where he may have moved after Marfina's death.

Cheryl Gabriel married Ronald DiCamillo, son of Dominick and Perina Fontana DiCamillo, on November 19, 1966. They had a son, Michael and were later divorced. Like her mother, she passed away at an early age. Her son, Michael died unexpectedly in 2006 at 38 years of age.

Anthony J. Gabriele, named after his grandfather, was born June 12, 1942 and passed away November 7, 2012 at the age of 70 at Faxton-St. Luke's Healthcare.

A proud member of the US Army, he served during the Vietnam War. Anthony was Captain of the St. Johnsville Fire Department, a certified EMT Specialist and member of the Morris J. Edwards American Legion Post 168. He was employed as Lock Chief of the Erie Canal with the NYS Department of Transportation for over 20 years.

The Anthony J. Gabrielle family members of Herkimer were dedicated military members. Anthony Sr. served in World War I. His oldest son, Ferris served in World War II and the youngest son, Colonel Anthony, Jr. was a career professional serving in the US Army Infantry Division in both the Korean and Vietnam wars. The latter has quite a history of service. He is honored in the NYS Military Museum. You can listen to his interesting oral history of his military experiences on youtube.com. The resemblance to his older brother, Ferris is amazing.

~ *La Famiglia FIOGGIA* ~

~ LUCIANO FIOGGIA et ELIZABETH LOMAN ~

LUCIANO "John" FIOGGIA was born in Supino, Italy in 1893. He came to America, thence St. Johnsville via Pittsburgh PA, on April 25, 1910. He died July 2, 1978.

John first worked at one of the knitting mills and later for the NYC Railroad. After his retirement, being a good friend of Phil, he worked part-time for the Francisco Market.

John Fioggia, son of James Foggia and Mary Marocco, married Elizabeth Loman, daughter of John Loman and Christina Baffam, at St. Patrick's parish home on November 27, 1916. John Baffam and Lucina Folcinelli witnessed the marriage.

ELIZABETH "Lizzie" LOMAN was from Austria, arriving in 1913. She was born September 1, 1897. She died on March 1, 1979, eight months after her husband, John. I recall her as a very sweet friendly lady.

The 1920 Census shows they are living at 26 Sanders Street and have a daughter, Leona, almost three years old. I believe the child may have died, as she does not show up in the 1925 Census when the couple is living at 32 Mechanic Street. I don't recall them every having a child in their home.

By 1930 the couple has purchased the 7 Hough Street home next door to the Montoni family, where they lived out their lives. Lizzie first worked at a knitting mill, then later just a short walk down to the Little Falls Felt Shoe.

On September 9, 1960 John returned from Rome, Italy, where he had visited relatives in Supino.

In Conclusion

Web of Italian Intrigue ~ A Legacy of St. Johnsville Immigrants is a Genealogical Memoir containing a wealth of detailed information about the immigrant Italian families who settled in the village of St. Johnsville, New York in the early 1900s.

There may be some discrepancies, but it is an excellent resource for those current families researching their immigrant Italian ancestors. Nothing is written in stone. My specific research of dates, events, etc. was mostly acquired through Ancestry.com.

There is much more to uncover and be known about these remarkable immigrant families, but I leave it to their descendants to make more discoveries.

It is such a satisfying feeling for me that I have connected so many St. Johnsville Italian immigrant families to each other, tying knots as the Web continued to increase. My sincerest wish is that my efforts will inspire others to persue their roots.

Through the *Italians of St. Johnsville* Facebook page, I have also had the enormous satisfaction of reuniting numerous cousins ~ some who have first discovered each other. I urge you to check out the page, join our ever-growing group and share your Italian immigrant stories.

My greatest pleasure and pure satisfaction is that so many have graciously spurred me on in my quest with this massive genealogy project.

To all, I say Grazie! Grazie!

Cora Lee Perry Palma

About the Author

Cora Lee Palma (Hayden) was born and raised in the village of St. Johnsville, New York. The daughter of Floyd B. Perry and Rose M. Sindici, she is a third generation descendant of immigrant Italians, who settled there. In a determined quest to discover her familial Italian roots, she became involved with genealogical research, constructing her own family tree and numerous others for this publication. With visits to Prospect View Cemetery in St. Johnsville, she photographed and documented information of the Italian family gravestones.

While living in Florida she joined a Jewish Genealogical Group and is now a current member of the Grand Strand Genealogy Club in Myrtle Beach SC.

Cora Lee traveled three times to Italy including Sicily, experiencing the incomparable Old World customs, viewing its ancient art and architecture and tasting the ethnic foods of her heritage. She walked the path of St. Francis of Assisi and personally visited the village of her grandmother's birthplace, Maenza, Italy, in search of her roots.

Among the numerous hats she has worn, Cora Lee has been a writer, poet, author and artist for the greater part of her long life. She was a founding member of the Margaret Reaney Memorial Library writers' group, Poets of Palm Beach County as treasurer, International Women's Writers and National League of American Pen Women as secretary, vice-president and president. She was a founding member of the Ponte Vecchio West Italian Club, serving as secretary and president.

Other publications by the author are A Touch of Venus ~ Wedding Planning with the Bridal Zodiac, an astrological guide to planning dream weddings; two poetry chapbooks - bella Italia and Saint Simons Island and other Spiritual Sojourns, both filled with personal short stories and poetry. She has been featured in several poetry anthologies. Also included are several self-published family photo memory albums, which share adventurous stories of her travels. Currently waiting in the wings are two other manuscripts – "Crossroads ~ Journey of My Soul", a personal memoir, and "Desiree", a novelette inspired by a recent journey to Florence, Italy.

As a Porcelain artist, Cora Lee Palma is noted for her China Painting skills, selling her vintage heirlooms all over the United States and Canada. Many of her creations have won awards and appeared in magazines with one being featured at the China Painting Museum in Oklahoma City OK. She held memberships in various organizations including the World Organization of China Painters, the New York State China Painters and the Adirondack China Painters. In later years, she dabbled as a Watercolorist.

While residing in her birthplace of St. Johnsville NY, she was the owner-operator of The Red Palette Bridal Center and Cora Lee Tours. Cora Lee was always active in community functions.

NOTES

NOTES

NOTES